JUVENILE JUSTICE

POLICIES, PROGRAMS, AND SERVICES

D1638164

Juvenile Justice

POLICIES, PROGRAMS, AND SERVICES

Albert R. Roberts

School of Social Work
Rutgers, The State University of New Jersey
New Brunswick, New Jersey

THE DORSEY PRESS
Chicago, Illinois 60604

© RICHARD D. IRWIN, INC., 1989

Acquisitions editor: Leo A. W. Wiegman
Project editor: Paula M. Buschman
Production manager: Bette Ittersagen
Cover design: Diana Yost
Compositor: Weimer Typesetting Co., Inc.
Typeface: 10/12 Palatino
Printer: The Maple-Vail Book Manufacturing Group

Library of Congress Cataloging-in-Publication Data

Roberts, Albert R.
    Juvenile justice : policies, programs, and services / Albert R. Roberts.
        p. cm.
    Includes index.
    ISBN 0-256-06019-3 : $35.00. ISBN 0-256-06996-4 (pbk.) : $25.00
    1. Juvenile justice, Administration of—United States.   I. Title.
HV9104.R6 1989
364.3'6'0973—dc19   88–14787

Printed in the United States of America
    2 3 4 5 6 7 8 9 0 MP 5 4 3 2 1 0 9

*This book is dedicated to my wife, Beverly,
and son, Herbie, whose love and understanding
have served as a source of strength,
invigoration, and growth.*

*To the memory of my parents, Harry and Evelyn, whose
love, faith, and encouragement during
my turbulent adolescent years still serve as
an inspiration to me.*

List of Contributors

ARNOLD BINDER, Ph.D.
Professor
Program in Social Ecology
University of California at Irvine
Irvine, California

ROBERT B. COATES, Ph.D.
Professor
Graduate School of Social Work
University of Utah
Salt Lake City, Utah

CHARLES E. FRAZIER, Ph.D.
Professor of Sociology and
    Associate Director
Center for Studies in Criminology
    and Law
University of Florida
Gainesville, Florida

ROSLYN MURASKIN, Ph.D.
Assistant Dean and Professor
    of Criminal Justice
School of Business and Public
    Administration
Long Island University—
    C. W. Post Campus
Brookville, New York

H. TED RUBIN, M.S.W., J.D.
Senior Associate for Juvenile and
    Criminal Justice
Institute for Court Management
    of the National Center for
    State Courts
Denver, Colorado

Foreword

It is a difficult, demanding, and almost impossible task to delineate the parameters of *juvenile justice*. The subject is massive in nature and it approaches amorphousness in definition. More than 34 years of direct experience in this field have led me to this inescapable conclusion.

For the uninitiated, the *system* frequently presents a mystery. Even the advanced observer or practitioner will often be lost in the sea of concepts, philosophies, approaches, and doctrines addressing the subject.

Very few single works adequately describe this compelling umbrella of interlaced disciplines which address troubled young people in our society. Thus, it is with pleasure that I invite the reader's attention to this extraordinarily inclusive effort of Dr. Albert R. Roberts. His very title, *Juvenile Justice: Policies, Programs, and Services,* is most descriptive of the broad and comprehensive coverage he intended for the serious student of a societal dilemma.

As one quickly discovers, the children confronting the *system* are not merely the concern of judges and policemen. A large number of disciplines and activities are involved. These include law, medicine, mental health, sociology, social work, criminology, law enforcement, education, recreation, religion, public health, corrections, nutrition, psychology, and geography. There are others.

What Dr. Roberts does is place these in rational perspective so as to provide the reader with an orderly means of exposing a challenging milieu of fact and concept. He focuses on the evolution, development, and implementation of organization, structure, policies, and services in a very effective strategy. For example, research issues became more cogent because they appear in each chapter directly related to chapter subject material rather than in a stand-alone segment at the end of the text, as is often regrettably the case.

Appropriately organized into four sections, Roberts very accurately portrays the overview and historical background of the juvenile justice system. In Section III, entitled "Contemporary Approaches," he employs widely known and respected contributing authors for key chapters addressing police, courts, corrections, and dispositional alternatives. Particularly impressive are the chapters on Advocacy and the

Epilogue by Robert B. Coates. In short and in essence, Coates makes sense of advocacy and he clearly defines the dilemma of polarity in conflicting and demanding ideologies. There is vast emotion when considering the problems of children and this frequently clouds arguments made for and against proposed remedial concepts.

I am enthusiastic about this work and I strongly believe it has applicability in a number of areas. While Dr. Roberts meant it for the advanced social work and criminal justice student, my own experience in conducting numerous workshops, conferences, seminars, and continuing education programs, is that it would serve as a valuable resource for judges, attorneys, prosecutors, probation officers, corrections personnel, school teachers, policemen, and others. It has value also for policy makers at the executive and legislative level.

Louis W. McHardy
Executive Director, National Council of
 Juvenile and Family Court Judges, and
Dean, National College of Juvenile and Family Law
University of Nevada
Reno, Nevada

Preface

This textbook provides a comprehensive overview of the field of juvenile justice. The decision to write this textbook was based on the author's belief that an up-to-date text was needed by upper-division undergraduate and graduate students (in both social work and criminal justice) that addressed juvenile justice trends, policies, and programs. This volume should also prove useful to practitioners and supervisors both as a basic reference and as a resource for updating their knowledge about contemporary practices and interventions with juvenile offenders.

Juvenile Justice: Policies, Programs and Services examines and analyzes the history of and contemporary trends in the control, care, and treatment of juvenile offenders. The book's four sections focus on the following:

- Definitions, types of offenders, and official and unofficial statistics.
- Historical developments in the handling of juvenile offenders.
- The current state of the art in objectives, legal responsibilities, and functions of the juvenile justice agencies that intervene on behalf of juvenile delinquents.
- An exploration of future directions for the effective processing and treatment of troubled juveniles.

The field of juvenile justice is too complex in its subsystems—police, juvenile court and probation, detention, and corrections—for any one person to be an expert in all facets of it. Therefore, to supplement my seven chapters, I invited five prominent juvenile justice specialists, each with extensive knowledge and expertise in a specific area of juvenile justice, to prepare original chapters for this book. These chapters summarize current developments and emerging trends in the handling of juvenile offenders.

Throughout this book the reader is exposed to alternative types of treatment strategies used in both institutional and community-based settings, as well as research on their effectiveness. Several chapters underscore the importance of conducting methodologically sound research to determine the effectiveness of different methods of intervention.

Professionals in the field of juvenile justice often have conflicting ideologies on how best to intervene with juvenile offenders. Three basic philosophies have emerged: one group advocates for punitive measures (particularly with serious or sex offenders); those in the second group advocate for an array of treatment and rehabilitation services for all juvenile offenders; and a third group supports differential treatment based on the individual needs of the offender, often suggesting a combination of punitive sanctions and rehabilitation programs. Carolyn Needleman has documented the ideologically based dissatisfaction and struggle among social workers employed by juvenile courts and probation departments that have a punitive orientation.[1] In such settings there is a considerable amount of disagreement on the most appropriate methods for handling juvenile offenders.

Despite conflicting ideologies and perspectives there is much which is encouraging. During the past two decades several promising rehabilitation strategies and treatment programs have been implemented: alternative sentencing projects and juvenile restitution programs (see Chapter 8 and the Epilogue), police social worker programs (see Chapter 6), juvenile diversion programs (Chapters 5 and 9), wilderness challenge programs (Chapter 10), and family counseling programs (Chapter 11). This book provides a detailed examination of salient program developments.

It is my earnest expectation that in the next ten years legislators, correctional policymakers and administrators, juvenile court judges, and researchers will focus greater attention on remedying the problems of juvenile delinquents and status offenders. A concerted effort focused on increasing the development of humanistic treatment and prevention programs can accomplish this.

A SYNOPSIS OF CONTENT AREAS

This book is for practitioners and students who want to increase their knowledge base and understanding of juvenile justice policies and practices. In order to comprehend the complexities and issues inherent in the juvenile justice system we must study it in its organizational context. Therefore, the first major part of the book focuses on historical themes and issues, and the second section focuses on the

---

[1]C. Needleman (1983). Social work and probation in the juvenile court. In A. R. Roberts (Ed.), *Social work in juvenile and criminal justice settings*. Springfield, IL: Charles C Thomas, 165–79.

current policies and practices with which juvenile justice practitioners and grappling. The book's twelve chapters and epilogue represent the spectrum of issues, programs, and services within the system.

Section I, Chapter 1, provides an overview of juvenile delinquency and the juvenile justice system. It answers these basic questions: What is a juvenile delinquent? What can official statistics teach us about the extent of the problem? Which agencies and programs have been developed to process and intervene with juvenile offenders?

Section II provides a historical perspective of the institutional and community methods for handling juveniles. Chapter 2 summarizes the historical roots of various treatment approaches used with youthful offenders from the 1500s to the 1800s. Then, beginning with the 1900s and continuing through to the 1970s, it comprehensively reviews rehabilitative services provided to juvenile offenders in institutional settings as well as in open settings.

Chapter 3 explores community strategies for the control and prevention of juvenile delinquency. The focus is on the best-known model community organization and detached worker projects of the past 80 years: California's Community Coordinating Councils, the Chicago Area Project, New York's Mobilization for Youth (MFY), Boston's Midcity Project, and the youth service bureaus of the late 1960s and 1970s.

The state and local judicial systems have had a profound impact on the treatment received by juvenile offenders. Chapter 4 describes the development and growth of the juvenile court system, beginning with the establishment of the first juvenile court in Cook County, Illinois, in 1899. This chapter also includes a discussion of volunteers to the court, child guidance clinics, and probation as they relate to juvenile court dispositions.

In Chapter 5 the emergence and early development of juvenile diversion programs is presented. The chapter provides students with an understanding of the key influences on the development of diversion, the definitions of diversion, its goals and objectives, the types of services provided by these programs, and their effectiveness.

The third section of the book describes contemporary approaches to the field of juvenile justice. Youthful offenders generally have their first contact with the juvenile justice system through an encounter with a police officer. This entry point is examined in Chapter 6. Emphasis is placed on police discretion and routine decisions in police work with juveniles—the warning or reprimand, referral to a community agency, and filing a petition to the local family or juvenile court. The impact of the *Gault* decision is examined as well as different police procedures, including unofficial, informal, and formal adjustments. The chapter also provides examples of the organization of established juvenile aid bureaus and police youth service units.

Chapter 7 reviews contemporary juvenile laws and juvenile court practices. This chapter begins with a review of the organizational structure of the juvenile court and its jurisdiction over delinquent offenses. Also examined are constitutional and legal constraints on the court's exercise of its powers, the functions of the probation departments, sentencing policies, and intervention with serious and violent juvenile offenders. The chapter points out that because juvenile courts are governed by their state statutes and appellate court decisions, there is great diversity in juvenile court practices from state to state; Supreme Court decisions on children's rights and revisions in state juvenile codes have required a redefinition of the role of the juvenile court. This chapter also includes a detailed discussion of the emergence and current policies and practices of court-ordered restitution.

Chapter 8, which focuses on juvenile detention policies and practices, begins with a discussion of the national trends and detention rates of juveniles. It also reviews the three main aims of detention of youths prior to their adjudication: protecting the community, protecting the child, and/or assuring the child's appearance in subsequent scheduled court hearings. Finally, this chapter considers (1) the consequences of the broad legal grounds that allow officials wide discretion in making detention decisions and (2) the harmful effects on juvenile detainees when detention practices are standardless. The juvenile's first encounter with incarceration often comes through temporary placement in a juvenile detention center; a youth living in a rural area that typically does not have a juvenile detention center may be placed in the county jail with adult offenders. Whether detention occurs in an urban or rural setting, it is often a degrading and frightening experience for the adolescent.

The topic of Chapter 9 is the policies, program components, and effectiveness of juvenile diversion programs. Many of these programs strive to provide the juvenile with comprehensive services, including behavioral contracting, group therapy, family counseling, tutoring, and job placement. The controversy regarding diversion is reviewed. The main issue in the debate is whether diversion results in "widening the net of social control"—creating new formal practices that produce a labeling effect similar to continued processing through the juvenile justice system. This chapter documents the usefulness of juvenile diversion in reducing negative labeling and recidivism while improving direct services to juvenile offenders and restitution to their victims.

Chapters 10 and 11 focus on two alternatives to incarceration: wilderness programs and family treatment, offering detailed descriptions of these two approaches. The goal of a wilderness experience is to provide an opportunity for youths to develop decision-making skills and to enhance their self-concept while working with others in a challenging, socially acceptable experience. Chapter 10 begins by outlining the similarities and differences between traditional training schools and wilderness programs. It then describes several wilderness programs in different parts of the United States, examining important programmatic factors such as goals of the program, ratio of juveniles to staff, program content, and evaluations of program effectiveness.

Chapter 11 concentrates on family-focused treatment, which views the youth's illegal behavior as one manifestation of a breakdown in the family system. This approach emphasizes treating the whole family system in an effort to restore the balance between juvenile and parents. The chapter begins by examining the retrospective research studies that indicate a strong association between child abuse and later delinquency. Also discussed are the other family influences (e.g., lack of parental discipline, neglect, and/or rejection) contributing to the emergence of delinquency patterns. Different types of family treatment approaches are described, including court-based family crisis intervention, in-home intensive family crisis intervention (e.g., Homebuilders), family therapy for probationers and their parents, and behavioral contracting approaches. This chapter concludes by examining the limited research on program effectiveness and calling for longitudinal experimental and quasi-experimental studies.

The growth of advocacy initiatives in the 1970s was part of federally funded efforts to deinstitutionalize, develop community-based alternatives, and make community agencies more responsive to the needs of youths. Chapter 12 examines the emergence and conceptual underpinnings of advocacy efforts during the 1970s as well as their general decline in the 1980s. Three types of advocacy are conceptualized: case advocacy, community advocacy, and class advocacy.

Section IV, the Epilogue, concentrates on the future of corrections. For the 1990s and beyond, it predicts the use of alternative sentencing plans for juveniles, determinate sentencing models, privately run corporations taking over the operation of juvenile facilities and contracting to develop juvenile treatment and education programs, and the increased development of victim–offender mediation and restitution programs.

ACKNOWLEDGMENTS

I am most appreciative of the support, and dedication to editorial excellence of Leo A. W. Wiegman, editor at the Dorsey Press. It was a pleasure to work with Leo, Publisher David C. Follmer, and the Dorsey Press staff in the production of this book. Special thanks go to Paula

Buschman, Project Editor, for her diligence and care for detail. I also wish to thank the following reviewers for their probing questions, suggestions, and sensitive comments: Dr. Vernon Fox, Florida State University; Dr. Sheldon Gelman, Pennsylvania State University; Dr. Joseph J. Grau, C. W. Post Center of Long Island University; Dr. Carolyn Needleman, Bryn Mawr College; and Professor Charles L. Schwartz, University of South Dakota.

I am grateful to the five contributors, leaders in the field of juvenile justice, for preparing outstanding original chapters for this book. I would also like to acknowledge the permission to reprint Appendixes A through E given by the California Youth Authority, the Massachusetts Department of Youth Services, and the editors of the *Juvenile and Family Court Journal*, *The Prison Journal*, and *Federal Probation*. I greatly appreciate the assistance of Mary Stanley, a reference librarian at Indiana University, who went far beyond the call of duty in locating and obtaining journal articles and books from distant libraries. Special thanks goes to my sister-in-law, Carole S. Roberts, for her creative and illuminating illustrations.

As with all of my previous books, my heartfelt appreciation goes to my wife, Beverly Schenkman Roberts, for her generous support, profound editorial suggestions, and self-taught typing skills on our newly acquired word processor. Bev has again managed to combine the demands of her own thriving career with her desire to be my sounding board in the development of this book, while also always being available to aid our son in his school and extracurricular activities. Anyone who has completed a doctoral dissertation or a book knows that writing a textbook is an immense undertaking. The sacrifices one makes are always significant. Thus I thank my son, Herbie, for his understanding of the numerous evenings and weekends when I was working in my den, deeply immersed in the rigors of this scholarly endeavor.

Albert R. Roberts

Contents

Overview

Overview

Chapter One

An Introduction and Overview of Juvenile Justice

Albert R. Roberts

ABSTRACT

This chapter provides an orientation to the issues, trends, policies, programs, and services of the juvenile justice system. The types, functions, and legal responsibilities of the various juvenile justice agencies and institutions are discussed. This overview chapter lays the groundwork for a study of juvenile delinquency and the juvenile justice process by delineating both the legal definitions of juvenile status offenses and juvenile delinquency and the scope of the problem in terms of official delinquency statistics.

A fifteen-year-old male runaway is brought before the juvenile court judge for possession of a concealed, unloaded .38-caliber handgun. The juvenile probation officer who conducted the predispositional investigation recommends detention for the youth on the handgun charge. The public defender states that the three days the youth has already spent in detention have had a profound effect on him and requests leniency. The judge rules that the youth and his parents must attend twelve sessions of family counseling provided through the Probation Department and that the stepfather, who works as a security guard, must keep his revolver in a lockbox so that the boy is not able to take it again.

A sixteen-year-old female named Suzie fought with another girl when it was learned that Suzie had become pregnant by the other girl's boyfriend. During the argument, Suzie cut the other girl with a broken bottle. The juvenile court judge suspends commitment to the girl's training school and places her in a group home for adolescent girls for one year.

A fifteen-year-old male breaks into the home of an elderly woman to search for cash and valuables. The woman returns home to find the youth ransacking her house; in a fit of rage he brutally assaults her. The judge rules that the boy, although only fifteen years of age, is to be tried as an adult. Found guilty by a jury, he is sentenced to two years of incarceration.

Candace, a fourteen-year-old female, stole a car and has repeatedly run away from the group home where she was placed because her mother could not handle her at home. Candace's mother has two jobs; the girl has never met her biological father. Candace was suspended from school three times in the past year for possession of marijuana. Her case record reflects that she was sexually abused by her mother's boyfriend. The judge adjudicates Candace to the girl's training school until she reaches age sixteen.

In actuality, youths can be charged with two types of wrongdoing: juvenile delinquency offenses, which are criminal acts (e.g., auto theft, breaking and entering) for which they would be held accountable if they were adults, and status offenses (e.g., truancy, incorrigibility, and running away from home), which are illegal only for juveniles. Violent juvenile crimes receive the most media attention and serve to intensify the fear and outrage of concerned citizens. This fear and outrage, in turn, frequently influence prosecutors, juvenile court judges, and correctional administrators to subject more juvenile offenders to harsher penalties. Far more prevalent than violent crimes are juveniles who commit status offenses or nonviolent property crimes, as in the following examples:

> A twelve-year-old boy was brought to the county juvenile detention center after his mother complained that he was on drugs and was uncontrollable. The social worker's investigation for the court revealed that the mother had been released from the state hospital three months earlier. She had a history of psychotic episodes. The judge ruled that the boy should live with the aunt and uncle with whom he had lived while his mother was confined in the state hospital.

> A sixteen-year-old male whose mother was an alcoholic had been reared in a home in which he was neglected and there was no discipline or limit setting. He had a history of twelve arrests for petty theft and shoplifting starting at the age of eleven. Following the most recent arrest, he was sent to a rehabilitation-oriented juvenile training school that provided group therapy three days a week, a behavior modification program, and vocational training. The youth was learning to be an auto mechanic and proudly demonstrated his knowledge of automobile repair.

Students and practitioners working in juvenile justice agencies, either on a volunteer or paid basis, encounter the discretionary, deficient, flawed, and often overwhelming system of juvenile justice. While the goal of justice-oriented agencies is to care for and rehabilitate our deviant children and youth, in actuality the juvenile justice system all too often labels, stigmatizes, and reinforces delinquent patterns of behavior. The controlling and punitive orientation of many juvenile justice officials has led to a revolving-door system in which we find an over-representation of children from neglectful and/or abusive homes.

This book examines the two divergent themes within the juvenile justice system: punishment-oriented policies and programs and rehabilitation-oriented policies and programs.

DEFINING JUVENILE JUSTICE

What is the juvenile justice system? It consists of the agencies and institutions whose primary responsibility is handling juvenile offenders. These agencies and their programs concern themselves with delinquent youths as well as those children and youths labeled incorrigible, truant, and/or runaway. Juvenile justice focuses on the needs of over 2 million youths who are: taken into custody; diverted into special programs; processed through the juvenile court and adjudicated; and placed on probation, referred to a community-based day treatment program, or placed in a group home or a secure facility.

The history of juvenile justice has involved the development of policies, programs, and agencies for dealing with youths involved in legal violations. As we examine the juvenile justice system we focus on the interrelated, yet different, functions of several agencies and programs: the police, pretrial diversion projects, the juvenile court, children's shelters and detention facilities, juvenile correctional facilities, group homes, wilderness programs, family counseling programs, restitution programs, and aftercare programs.

What has been done during the past 100 years to provide juvenile offenders with equal opportunities for justice? Which policies and program alternatives are currently prevalent within the juvenile justice subsystems (police, courts, and juvenile corrections)? What are the latest trends in processing and treating juvenile offenders? What does the future hold? This text will explore the answers to these questions.

DEFINING JUVENILE DELINQUENCY

Juvenile delinquency is a broad, generic term that includes many diverse forms of antisocial behavior by a minor. The specific acts on the part of the juvenile that constitute delinquent behavior vary from state to state. A definition that is broad in scope and commonly used was developed by the U. S. Children's Bureau (1967):

> Juvenile delinquency cases are those referred to courts for acts defined in the statutes of the State as the violation of a state law or municipal ordinance by children or youth of juvenile court age, or for conduct so seriously antisocial as to interfere with the rights of others or to menace the welfare of the delinquent himself or of the community.

Other agencies define as delinquent those juveniles who have been arrested or contacted by the police, even though many of these individuals are merely reprimanded or sent home when their parents pick them up. Less than half of the juveniles handled by the police are referred to the juvenile court. These are the children and youth whom the Children's Bureau would classify as delinquents.

There are two primary types of juvenile delinquency. First are the criminal offenses: those acts considered illegal whether committed by an adult or a juvenile. Such illegal acts include aggravated assault, arson, homicide, rape, burglary, larceny, auto theft, and drug-related crimes. These types of serious offenses are the primary concern of juvenile corrections officials. According to the national and local statutes on juvenile criminality, burglary and larceny are the most frequently committed offenses. The brutal crimes of homicide and forcible rape comprise only a small percentage of the total number of crimes committed by juveniles.

The second major type of juvenile delinquency is known as status offenses: misbehaviors that would not be considered a crime if engaged in by an adult. Examples of status offenses are truancy, incorrigibility, curfew violations, and running away from home. Approximately half of the states include status offenses in their definition of juvenile delinquency offenses. Other states have passed separate legislation that distinguishes juveniles who have committed criminal acts from those who have committed status offenses. In those states status offenders are viewed as individuals "in need of supervision" and are designated as CHINS, CINS, MINS, PINS, or JINS. The first letter of the acronyn varies, based on whether the initial word is *children, minors, persons,* or *juveniles,* but the rest of the phrase is always the same: in need of supervision.

All fifty states and the District of Columbia have legal statutes that define an upper age limit for juvenile court jurisdictions. But states differ on the age at which a juvenile's wrongdoing is handled as a criminal (adult) offense rather than a juvenile offense. The age at which an offender is no longer treated as a juvenile ranges from sixteen to nineteen. In thirty-seven states and the District of Columbia, an individual is under the jurisdiction of the juvenile court until the age of eighteen. Only in one state (Wyoming) is the upper age limit nineteen. However, youths in the states of Connecticut, New York, North Carolina, and Vermont who violate their state's criminal code when they are age sixteen (or older) are within the jurisdiction of the criminal court (Hamparian et al., 1982: 18–21).

In contrast to the above-mentioned practice of specifying maximum ages for juvenile court jurisdiction, only a few states designate a specific minimum age in their juvenile code. Most state juvenile and criminal codes implicitly follow the English common-law position that a child under the age of seven is incapable of criminal intent. Therefore, a child below the age of seven who commits a crime is not held morally or criminally responsible for that act.

An increasing number of state legislatures have determined that juvenile offenders accused of brutal crimes should be processed by the criminal court rather than the juvenile court. Many states have authorized a waiver of jurisdiction that automatically grants the adult criminal courts jurisdiction over certain violent juveniles. For example, in 1978, New York State passed legislation creating a classification of juvenile offenses called "designated felonies." Under this state law fourteen- and fifteen-year-olds charged with committing the crimes of murder, kidnapping, arson, manslaughter, rape, and/or assault were tried in Designated Felony Courts. If the accused offenders were found guilty of the charges, they could be imprisoned for up to five years (Prescott, 1981). This is an increase over the typical sentence for a juvenile offender, which averages twelve months. (Further information on the criminal courts' handling of and intervention with repeat violent juvenile offenders appears in Chapter 7.)

There has been considerable debate over the appropriate way to handle status offenders. The major issue is whether the juvenile court should retain authority over them. Those in favor of the court's continuing authority believe that youths' habitual misbehavior will eventually lead to more serious delinquent acts; therefore, it is wise for the court to retain its jurisdiction over status offenders. An opposing view (often advanced by deviance theorists with a societal reaction or labeling-theory perspective) holds that when one defines status offenders as delinquents, the youths may actually become delinquents as the result of a self-fulfilling prophecy, leading to secondary deviance (Becker, 1963; Lemert, 1971; Schur, 1973).

Another belief held by a number of social workers is that the needs of status offenders can be better met within the community social service and child welfare service systems (Boisvert & Wells, 1980; Roberts, 1987). For example, Roberts' research documented the need for the full range of social services, including 24-hour telephone hotlines, short-term runaway shelters, family treatment programs, education and treatment services for abusive parents, and vocational training and placement services.

At issue is the type of treatment status offenders should receive. Should they be sentenced to a secure juvenile facility or referred to a community social service agency for counseling? For many years it was common for juvenile status offenders to be sentenced to juvenile training schools, where they were confined in the same institution with youths convicted of serious crimes. The practice of sending status offenders to juvenile correctional institutions has become much less common in recent years due to the deinstitutionalization of status offenders. However, in certain circumstances a minor who has committed no crime can still be sent to a juvenile training school. For example, a youth with a history of chronic runaway behavior is placed in a group home by the court. If the juvenile then runs away from that facility, the court views that act as a delinquency offense, and the youth is usually sent to a secure juvenile institution.

Probation officers often believe that while most status offenders do not pose a danger to others, they do frequently exhibit destructive behavior patterns such as drug abuse, alcohol abuse, or suicide ideation. They often come from dysfunctional, conflict-ridden families where physical, sexual, and/or emotional abuse is prevalent. Thus the social work perspective urges that a continuum of services be provided for status offenders and their families through a social service agency, a family service agency, or a juvenile court–based program. Available services should include family counseling, individual and group counseling, addiction treatment, alternative education programs, and vocational evaluation, education, and training.

For an in-depth analysis of the nature and types of social service and counseling programs to which status offenders are referred, see Chapters 5 and 9 on the emergence, proliferation, and characteristics of contemporary juvenile diversion programs. The reader is also referred to Chapter 12 for a discussion of the federal and state initiatives begun in the 1970s to deinstitutionalize status offenders from the juvenile justice system and to develop community-based alternatives.

As defined in this chapter, delinquency refers to a juvenile who has been apprehended for any activity that is a violation of a state juvenile code. The juvenile justice system is concerned with caring for, punishing, and rehabilitating these juvenile law violators. Throughout this book, we will examine the policies, agencies, programs, and services that have been developed to control and rehabilitate juvenile offenders.

Juvenile delinquency trends and estimates of the scope of the delinquency problem come from both official and unofficial self-report studies. The three major sources of data on delinquency and victimization are:

1. Official police and juvenile court statistics, such as the FBI Uniform Crime Reports. This data is based on crimes reported to the police.
2. Self-report studies, such as the National Youth Survey, which involve asking youths whether they have engaged in one or more delinquent behaviors in the past year (e.g., damaging or destroying school property, making obscene phone calls, running away from home).
3. Victimization studies, such as the National Crime Survey (NCS), which involve asking a sample of individuals and household heads whether they have been victims of criminal acts.

OFFICIAL STATISTICS

Since 1927, the U.S. Children's Bureau has issued periodic estimates on the number of juvenile delinquents in the United States. Their figures, based on reports from a sampling of juvenile courts across the country, show a significant increase in the number of crimes committed by juveniles. In 1930, they estimated that there were

200,000 delinquents; in 1950, the figure climbed to 435,000 (Robison, 1960). In 1966, over 1 million individuals under the age of eighteen were arrested. Alfred Blumstein (1967) estimated that 27 percent of all male juveniles would probably be arrested before reaching their eighteenth birthday.

During the past two decades, the federal office of Youth Development has reported a significant increase in juvenile court cases. This surge has markedly exceeded the growth of the population of children in the ten to seventeen age group. Between 1960 and 1970 the number of delinquency cases more than doubled, climbing from 510,000 to 1,052,000, while the child population increased by only 29 percent, from 25.4 million to 32.6 million (Youth Development and Delinquency Prevention Administration, 1973).

By 1984, the total number of arrests for youths under eighteen years of age had exceeded 2 million (2,062,448). The juvenile most likely to be arrested (regardless of the type of offense) was over fifteen years of age, or between the ages of thirteen and eighteen, and had committed larceny/theft. In 1984, older juvenile offenders (between fifteen and eighteen years of age) outnumbered offenders under fifteen years of age by almost 3 to 1 (1,537,688 to 524,760). Table 1–1 lists the most frequent offense categories for older juveniles between the ages of fifteen and eighteen.

We now turn our attention to the eight major index crimes. As shown in Table 1–2 a vast majority of juvenile arrests were for property offenses rather than violent crimes. Property crimes include burglary, larceny, theft, motor vehicle theft, and arson. Violent crimes include murder, forcible rape, robbery, and aggravated assault.

TABLE 1–1   Most Frequent Offenses by Older Juveniles, 1984

Offense Charged	Number of Juveniles Arrested
Larceny/theft	338,785
Burglary	127,708
Runaway	114,275
Liquor law violations	101,904
Vandalism	87,135
Disorderly conduct	73,552
Curfew and loitering law violations	67,243
Drug abuse violations	67,211
Motor vehicle theft	33,838

Source: U.S. Department of Justice. (1985). *Crime in the United States: Uniform crime reports, 1984.* Washington, DC: U.S. Government Printing Office.

TABLE 1–2 Total Arrests of Juveniles for Property and Violent Crimes, 1984

Offense Charged	Number of Juveniles Arrested			Total, All Ages
	Under 15	15–17	18–20	
Property crimes	218,894	506,575	743,801	1,469,270
Violent crimes	18,791	64,344	122,543	205,678
Crime index total	237,685	570,919	866,344	1,674,948

SOURCE: U.S. Department of Justice. (1984). *Sourcebook of criminal justice statistics.* Washington, DC: U.S. Government Printing Office.

As documented in Table 1–2, juvenile crime increases dramatically with age. In comparing the crime rate for juveniles under fifteen with those aged fifteen to seventeen, arrests for property crimes more than doubled while arrests for violent crimes more than tripled.

Of the more than 1.6 million crimes committed by juveniles in 1984, 88 percent were property crimes, and 12 percent were violent crimes. Although most of the crimes were property-related, there is a noticeable trend toward violent crime as the juveniles become older. In the under-fifteen population, the rate of property crimes was 92 percent while the violent crime rate was 8 percent. Violent crime increased by 3 percentage points for the fifteen- to seventeen-year-olds, and another 3 points for the eighteen- to twenty-year-olds, who had a 14 percent rate of violent crime. These data on juvenile arrests represent only the tip of the iceberg. They do not include status offenses, nor do they reflect the number of juvenile lawbreakers who were not apprehended or who committed offenses that were never reported to the police.

While the official statistics may be appropriate in examining the extent of the labeling process, law enforcement and juvenile court statistics are of limited usefulness in measuring the full extent and volume of delinquent behavior. Since not all delinquent behavior is detected (and, therefore, cannot be officially recorded), the acts which are officially recorded do not represent a random sample of all delinquent acts. In other words, official statistics provide only a limited index of the total volume of delinquency.

Unofficial Methods of Measuring Delinquency

Researchers have been quite persistent in their attempts to identify juvenile delinquents and to measure juvenile delinquency. As mentioned previously, the primary sources of data have been self-reports, victimization surveys, and observational studies in gang hangouts and schools. The major limitation of these methods relates to the representativeness of the individuals reported as delinquent.

Self-Report Delinquency Studies.   Self-report questionnaires were first introduced as a method of measuring delinquency by Short and Nye (1957). Several other prominent sociologists and criminologists used the self-report approach: Empey and Erickson (1966); Gold (1966, 1970); Hindelang, Hirschi, & Weis (1981); and Hirschi (1969). Some self-report studies focus on measuring the proportion of youths who have engaged in delinquent acts, asking such questions as: "Have you ever stolen something?" or "Have you stolen something since you were nine years old?" These types of studies gather data on the extent of participation in specific delinquent behaviors. Other self-report delinquency studies make inquiries about the frequency of individual involvement in delinquent behaviors over a specific period, such as within the past year or two. Studies having time bounds of four or more years have only limited usefulness because of memory decay and filtering of recall.

Most self-report surveys indicate that the number of youths who break the law is much greater than official statistics report. These surveys reveal that the most common juvenile offenses are truancy, alcohol abuse, shoplifting, using a false I.D., fighting, using marijuana, and damaging the property of others (Farrington, 1973; Hindelang, 1973).

Some of the more striking findings of self-report studies relate to the extent of delinquency and status offenses. According to estimates of the President's Commission on Law Enforcement and the Administration of Justice (1967), self-report studies indicate that the overwhelming majority of all juveniles commit delinquent and criminal acts for which they could have been adjudicated.

Erickson and Empey (1963) studied self-reported delinquent behavior among high school boys aged fifteen to seventeen in Provo, Utah. Using a list of twenty-two criminal and delinquent offenses to question the youths about their illegal activities, the researchers found that in 90 percent of the cases, minor offenses (such as traffic violations, minor thefts, liquor law violations, and destroying property) went undetected. They compared the self-reported delinquency of boys who were officially nondelinquent with a group of official delinquents—those who had been processed by the court only once, those on probation, and those who were incarcerated. The results were surprising: the nondelinquents admitted to an average of almost 158 delinquent acts per youth. However, official delinquents' self-reports greatly exceeded the reports of nondelinquents: youths with a one-time court appearance had an average of 185 delinquent acts; repeat offenders who had been on probation had an average of 855 delinquent acts; and incarcerated delinquents had an average of 1,272 delinquent acts. Williams and Gold (1972) found that: "Eighty-eight percent of the teenagers in the sample confessed to committing at least one chargeable offense in the three years prior to their interview" (p. 213).

The "dark figure of crime"—the unreported delinquent acts—are difficult to determine. Self-report studies indicate that the dark or unknown figure may be more than nine times greater than the official estimate, since about nine of every ten juvenile law violations are either undetected or not officially acted upon. The overwhelming majority of juveniles have broken the law, even though their offenses are usually minor. Yet, a small group are chronic, violent offenders; these are the youths who habitually violate the law and, as a result, are more likely to be apprehended and formally adjudicated.

Empey (1982) offers an analogy comparing juvenile ofenders to fish being caught in a net in a large ocean:

> The chances are small that most fish will be caught. And even when some are caught, they manage to escape or are released because they are too small. But because a few fish are much more active than others, and because they are bigger, they are caught more than once. Each time this occurs, moreover, the chances that they will escape or be thrown back decrease. At the very end, therefore, they form a very select group whose behavior clearly separates them from most of the fish still in the ocean. (p. 113)

The most important and enlightening developments in research on hidden delinquency came from the national youth surveys. Beginning in 1967, the National Institute of Mental Health (NIMH) implemented the first national survey of a representative sample of adolescents, focusing on their attitudes and behaviors, including delinquent behavior. In 1972, the national youth survey (NYS) was repeated; in 1976, the National Institute of Juvenile Justice and Delinquency Prevention became the co-sponsor of what developed into an annual survey of self-reported delinquent behavior, based on a national probability panel of teenage youths from eleven to seventeen years of age (Weis, 1983).

These longitudinal national surveys were based on a carefully drawn sample ($N = 1,725$) of adolescents from throughout the United States who were asked to report on their delinquent behavior for five consecutive years.

The major survey findings indicate that the overwhelming majority of American youth (eleven to seventeen years old) in the sample admitted that they had committed one or more juvenile offenses. In agreement with other self-report studies, the NYS has found that the majority of youths had committed minor offenses, especially as they grew older. Less than 6 percent of the youths in the survey (Elliot,

1983) admitted having committed one of the more serious Index Offenses that are listed in the FBI Uniform Crime Reports. The trends in self-reported delinquency reveal that youths in the 1980s seem to be no more delinquent than youths in the early 1970s.

The survey found that those youths living with both natural parents reported lower delinquency rates than juveniles who came from single-parent or reconstituted families. It was also found that youths who stayed in school reported less involvement in delinquency than those who dropped out. In addition, school dropouts admitted they had participated in crimes such as felony assault and theft, hard drug use, disorderly conduct, and general delinquency to a much greater extent than the in-school youths. In contrast, the higher percentages of in-school youth indicated they had participated in minor assaults, vandalism, and school delinquency (Thornberry et al., 1985). Finally, the 1978–80 national youth surveys asked about attendance at religious services. Those youths who reported regular attendance at religious services also reported less involvement in virtually all types of delinquent behaviors.

Victimization Surveys.   Recently, victimization studies have been completed in a large number of cities throughout the United States. These studies have been conducted as joint efforts by the U.S. Bureau of Justice Statistics and the Bureau of the Census. The most well-known victimization survey is the National Crime Survey (NCS), a massive, annual, house-to-house survey of a random sample of 60,000 households and 136,000 individuals (Flanagan & McCloud, 1983). The NCS provides annual estimates of the total number of crimes committed by both adult and juvenile offenders. The six types of crime measured are rape, robbery, assault, household burglary, personal and household larceny, and motor vehicle theft. Based on the survey data, it has been estimated that *40 million serious crimes* occur each year in the United States. The NCS estimate is four times greater than that reported in the FBI Uniform Crime Reports. This data indicate that underreporting is far more pervasive than was generally recognized before the completion of the national victimization surveys.

This survey also provided estimates of the juvenile offense rates for a limited number of crimes: rape, robbery, assault, and personal larceny. The analysis by Laub and associates (1983) indicated that the rates of delinquency for the years 1973–1981 remained relatively stable. In addition, there has been very little change in the types of persons who are victimized by juveniles. For the most part, juvenile perpetrators victimized other youths, rather than adults; males were the victims twice as frequently as females.

The findings related to the extent of violence among juvenile offenders were: (1) There was very little change in the use of guns, knives, and other weapons during the nine-year period. (2) Only 27 percent of the juvenile crimes involved weapons use. This finding contradicts the view that most juvenile offenders use a deadly weapon. (3) The number of victims who required hospitalization in the aftermath of a delinquent act seemed to remain stable over the nine-year period.

Although juvenile delinquency rates have stabilized during the 1980s, millions of adolescents continue to become involved in juvenile delinquency each year, and it continues to be a complex and difficult social problem with no easy solutions.

SUMMARY

Every youth who violates the law is not labeled a juvenile delinquent. Many either escape detection entirely or, when apprehended by the local police, receive a strict lecture or warning and are then taken home. Most authorities do not consider law-breaking youths to be juvenile delinquents unless they are officially processed through the juvenile court and adjudicated a delinquent.

Youths can be referred to the juvenile court for two types of offenses:

- Delinquency offenses—illegal acts that are considered as crimes whether committed by an adult or a juvenile (e.g., aggravated assault, arson, burglary, drug-related offenses, theft, and rape).
- Status offenses—deviant acts or misbehaviors that, if engaged in by an adult, would not be considered crimes (e.g., truancy, incorrigibility, and running away from home.)

For status offenders many states have separate legislation that views these juveniles as individuals "in need of supervision." An array of crisis intervention services, runaway shelters, youth service bureaus, and family counseling programs have been developed to serve these youths.

This chapter laid the groundwork for an examination of the field of juvenile justice. This was done by presenting legalistic, sociological, and criminological information focusing on three areas: the nature of the juvenile justice system and its subsystems, the definition of the terms *juvenile delinquency* and *status offenses,* and official, as well as unofficial, trends and statistics on the extent of juvenile delinquency in the United States.

DISCUSSION QUESTIONS

1. Define juvenile delinquency.
2. Compare and contrast the terms *juvenile delinquency offenses* and *status offenses.*
3. Divide the class into two groups for a debate. Ask one group to adopt and defend a conservative perspective and the other group to adopt and defend a progressive perspective on the following issues:

   - Should state legislatures authorize a waiver of jurisdiction that automatically grants the adult criminal courts jurisdiction to process juvenile offenders who have been accused of brutal crimes and are over the age of fourteen?
   - Should the juvenile court retain jurisdiction over habitual status offenders or should they be diverted to a continuum of community social services?

4. Using official juvenile court statistics discuss the recent trends in juvenile delinquency.
5. List the agencies in your county or city that have primary responsibility for handling juvenile status offenders and juvenile delinquents.

REFERENCES

Becker, H. S. (1963). *Outsiders: Studies in the sociology of deviance.* New York: Free Press.

Binder, A. (1984). The juvenile court, the U.S. Constitution, and when the twain meet. *Journal of Criminal Justice, 12,* 355–366.

Blumstein, A. (1967). Systems analysis and the criminal justice system. *Annals of the American Academy of Political and Social Science* (Vol. 474).

Boisvert, M. J., & Wells, R. (1980). Toward a rational policy on status offenders. *Social Work, 25,* 230–234.

Elliot, D. S., Ageton, S. S., Huizinga, D., Knowles, B. A., & Canter, R. J. (1983). *The prevalence and incidence of delinquent behavior: 1976–1980.* Boulder, CO: Behavioral Research Institute.

Elliot, D. S., & Huizinga, D. (1983). Social class and delinquent behavior in a national youth panel: 1976–1980. *Criminology, 21* (May), 149–177.

Empey, L. T. (1982). *American delinquency: Its meaning and construction.* Chicago: Dorsey Press.

Empey, L. T. (1982). *American delinquency.* Chicago: Dorsey Press.

Empey, L. T., & Erickson, M. L. (1966). Hidden delinquency and social status. *Social Forces, 44* (June), 546–554.

Erickson, M. L., & Empey, L. T. (1963). Court records, undetected delinquency, and decision-making. *Journal of Criminal Law, Criminology, and Police Science, 54* (December), 456–469.

Farrington, D. P. (1973). Self-reports of deviant behavior: Predictive and stable? *Journal of Criminal Law and Criminology, 44* (March), 99–111.

Flanagan, T. J., & McCloud, M. (1983). *Sourcebook of criminal justice statistics, 1982.* Washington, DC: U.S. Department of Justice.

Gold, M. (1966). Undetected delinquent behavior. *Journal of Research in Crime and Delinquency, 3* (January), 27–46.

Gold, M. (1970). *Delinquent behavior in an American city.* Belmont, CA: Brooks/Cole Publishing Company.

Gold, M., & Reimer, D. J. (1974). Changing patterns of delinquent behavior among Americans 13–16 years old: 1967–1972. *National Survey of Youth*, Report No. 1. Ann Arbor: Institute for Social Research, University of Michigan.

Hamparian, D., et al. (1982). *Major issues in juvenile justice information and training, youth in adult courts: Between two worlds.* Washington, DC: U.S. Department of Justice.

Hindelang, M. J. (1973). Causes of delinquency: A partial replication and extension. *Social Problems, 20* (4), 471–487.

Hindelang, M. J., Hirschi, T., & Weis, J. (1981). *Measuring delinquency.* Beverly Hills, CA: Sage.

Hirschi, T. (1969). *Causes of delinquency.* Berkeley: University of California Press.

Huizinga, D., & Elliot, D. S. (1984). *Self-reported measures of delinquency and crime: Methodological issues and comparative findings.* Boulder, CO: Behavioral Research Institute.

Laub, J. H. (1983). *Juvenile criminal behavior in the United States: An analysis of offender and victim characteristics.* Albany, NY: The Michael J. Hindelang Criminal Justice Research Center, State University of New York at Albany.

Lemert, E. M. (1971). *Instead of court: Diversion in juvenile justice.* Chevy Chase, MD: National Institute of Mental Health, Center for the Studies of Crime and Delinquency.

Osgood, D. W., & Weichselbaum, H. F. (1984). Juvenile diversion: When practice matches theory. *Journal of Research in Crime and Delinquency, 21,* 33–35.

Prescott, P. S. (1981). *The child savers.* New York: Alfred A. Knopf.

President's Commission on Law Enforcement and Administration of Justice. (1967). *Task force report: Juvenile delinquency and youth crime.* Washington, DC: U.S. Government Printing Office.

Roberts, A. R. (1987). *Runaways and nonrunaways.* Chicago: Dorsey Press.

Robison, S. M. (1960). *Juvenile delinquency: Its nature and control.* New York: Holt, Rinehart & Winston.

Schur, E. (1973). *Radical nonintervention: Rethinking the delinquency problem.* Englewood Cliffs, NJ: Prentice-Hall.

Short, J. F., Jr., & Nye, F. I. (1958). Extent of unrecorded delinquency, tentative conclusions. *Journal of Criminal Law, 49* (November–December), 296–302.

Thornberry, T. P., Moore, M., & Christenson, R. L. (1985). The effect of dropping out of high school on subsequent criminal behavior. *Criminology, 23* (February), 3–18.

U.S. Children's Bureau. (1967). *Juvenile court statistics, 1966* Statistical Series 90. Washington, DC: U.S. Government Printing Office.

U.S. Children's Bureau. (1973). *Juvenile court statistics, 1972.* Washington, DC: U.S. Government Printing Office.

U.S. Department of Justice, Federal Bureau of Investigation. (1976). *Crime in the United States, 1975: Uniform crime reports.* Washington, DC: U.S. Government Printing Office.

U.S. Department of Justice, National Criminal Justice Information and Statistics Service. (1974). *Children in custody: A report on the juvenile detention and correctional facility census of 1971.* Washington, DC: U.S. Government Printing Office.

U.S. Department of Justice. (1983). *Crime in the United States, 1982: Uniform crime reports.* Washington, DC: U.S. Government Printing Office.

U.S. Department of Justice. (1985). *Crime in the United States, 1984: Uniform crime reports.* Washington, DC: U.S. Government Printing Office.

U.S. Department of Justice. (1984). *Sourcebook of criminal justice statistics.* Washington, DC: U.S. Government Printing Office.

Weis, J. G. (1983). Crime statistics: Reporting systems and methods. *Encyclopedia of Crime and Justice* (Vol. 1). New York: The Free Press.

Williams, J. R., & Gold, M. (1972). From delinquent behavior to official delinquency. *Social Problems, 20* (Fall), 209–229.

Youth Development and Delinquency Prevention Administration. (1973). *The challenge of youth service bureaus.* Washington, DC: U.S. Government Printing Office.

Historical Perspective

Chapter Two

Treating Juveniles in Institutional and Open Settings

Albert R. Roberts

ABSTRACT

This chapter reviews the history of institutional treatment for juveniles. It traces the point of departure to the early colonial practice of magistrates ordering parents to take their rowdy and out-of-control youths home for a whipping. The chapter then examines the American colonists' practice of incarcerating juveniles with adult offenders, as well as the completely separate facilities developed for juveniles in the 1800s. Also presented are the deplorable conditions in juvenile detention homes, with recommendations for change. The final section of this chapter focuses on the opening of forestry camps and junior probation camps during the 1930s, 1940s, and early 1950s.

HISTORICAL ROOTS OF INSTITUTIONAL TREATMENT

In England, the early institutions served as a catchall for all "needy" children, with no distinctions for background or behavior. For example, the purpose of Christ's Hospital, which opened in London in 1552, was to house orphaned, destitute, and delinquent children (Mennel, 1973). Later, differentiations as to who would receive which service were made on the basis of the degree of stigma involved. One such distinction was legitimacy at birth: "Different programs were organized for children born out of wedlock and for those born in wedlock but orphaned" (Kahn, 1953:3–4).

During Elizabethan times, public officials utilized a system of apprenticeships to exert social control over roguish juveniles. These apprenticeships, however, were vastly different from those that prepared youths to be master craftsmen. Destitute or delinquent boys were assigned to serve as laborers in generalized tasks such as farmers' helpers while girls were put to work as domestics. According to Dunlop and Denman (1912), the purpose of the Elizabethan apprenticeship laws "was not for the education of boys in arts but for charity to keep them and relieve them from turning to roguery and idleness so a man's house was, as it were, a hospital in that case, rather than a shop of trade."

It was common practice in both England and the American colonies for the head of the house to discipline all the young people who lived in his house. Punishment for juvenile delinquent acts was generally carried out in the home rather than in public institutions. For example, in Massachusetts, children brought before the magistrates because of delinquent acts were often sent to their own homes for a court-observed whipping. Another British method continued by the colonists was indenturing poor and delinquent children. It has been said that the most likely candidates to be transported to the colonies were the youths whose parents had encouraged them to pick pockets and commit other crimes.

However, by 1700, it was generally acknowledged that the system of apprenticeships often failed to teach or control the rowdy youths. It was not uncommon for apprentices to desert their apprenticeships (Mennel, 1973). When it became apparent that apprenticeships were not serving the intended purpose for delinquent youths, the American colonists turned to the alternative of incarcerating the youths in prisons that had been created for adult offenders. By the mid-1700s, it was common for juvenile and adult offenders to be locked up together.

During the 1700s, a change took place in the meaning society ascribed to the term *juvenile delinquency.* It ceased to mean "a form of misbehavior common to all children" and became instead a euphemism for the crimes and conditions of poor children. Rising distrust of the ability of poor families to raise their own children fused with dissatisfaction with the operation of the law as it affected delinquent children (Mennel, 1973:xxvi). Thus, when the 1800s began, the label of juvenile delinquent was already being applied mainly to children in the lower socioeconomic class. The children unfortunate enough to be apprehended were imprisoned with hardened adult offenders in dirty, rat-infested cells with very little in the way of recreation, education, or rehabilitative treatment.

The movement to establish separate institutions for juvenile offenders began in New York City in 1819, when the Society for the Prevention of Pauperism reported on the horrendous conditions at Bellevue Prison. They focused on the plight of young children confined there with adult offenders. This report and the subsequent study by the Society pointed to the correlation between crime and delinquency, and poverty and parental neglect. In 1823, the Society reorganized and became known as the Society for the Reformation of Juvenile Delinquents (New Jersey Juvenile Delinquency Commission, 1939).

The first prison for juveniles that was completely separate from an adult prison was called the House of Refuge. It opened in New York on January 21, 1825. Similar juvenile institutions opened in 1826 and 1828 in Boston and Philadelphia, respectively (Peirce, 1969). Between 1845 and 1854, several other large cities established houses of refuge for juvenile offenders (New Jersey Juvenile Delinquency Commission, 1939; Platt, 1969).

These first houses of refuge were built in order to counteract the poverty, vice, and neglectful families that were breeding grounds for delinquency. Based on a family model, these child-saving institutions were viewed as parent surrogates and as society's superparents. The houses of refuge were supposed to provide a home for unruly and troubled children, where they would be reformed, educated, and disciplined. Children were put in such places for protection from the temptations of immoral, unfit, and neglectful families and vice-ridden disorganized communities..

Houses of refuge were built as secure facilities. Some were surrounded by brick walls, and their interiors were designed to confine inmates securely while instilling order, respect for authority, and strict and steady discipline.

> The buildings were usually four stories high, with two long hallways running along either side of a row of cells. The rooms, following one after another, were all five by eight feet wide, seven feet high, windowless, with an iron-lattice slab for a door and flues for ventilation near the ceiling. Each group of eleven cells could be locked or unlocked simultaneously with one master key; every aperture within an inmate's reach was guarded by iron sashes; every exit door from the asylum was made of iron. . . . On the fourth floor were ten special punishment cells. In keeping with the external design, all inmates wore uniforms of coarse and solid-colored material. No sooner did they enter the institution then they were stripped, washed, their hair cut to a standard length, and put into common dress. (Rothman, 1971:226)

The basic schedule and daily routine at each institution were very similar; order, discipline, and moral teachings were emphasized. The youths were awakened by a bell at sunrise. Fifteen minutes later, the second bell sounded to signal the guards to unlock the cells. The youths marched in formation to the washroom, paraded outside for inspection, marched to chapel for prayer, attended school for one hour, and went to breakfast when the 7 o'clock bells rang. From 7:30 A.M. until 5 P.M. the boys worked in the shops, making brass nails or cane seats, while the girls mended clothes, did laundry, cooked, and cleaned. They did receive one hour from noon to 1 P.M. for lunch. After work at 5:00 P.M. they were allowed one-half hour for washing and eating. Following this was two and one-half hours of evening classes; then came evening prayers, a march back to their cells, and lock-in.

Silence was maintained at all times. Any youth that caused trouble or broke the rules was punished. The milder forms of punishment included either placing offenders on a bread and water diet or depriving them of meals altogether. More severe punishments included bread and water rations combined with solitary confinement, corporal punishment in the form of whippings with a cat-o'-nine-tails, or manacling with a ball and chain (Rothman, 1971).

The basic sentence for juveniles was indeterminate. In other words, the superintendents determined how long the youths would be confined. In the majority of cases confinement was under two years; only a few remained for over four years (Rothman, 1971). The average stay at the New York House of Refuge was sixteen months, at Philadelphia twelve months, and at Cincinnati fourteen months. The overwhelming majority of youths who had adhered to the institutions' rules were apprenticed to semiskilled artisans or placed in the homes of farmers. Juvenile offenders who did not show signs of improvement and were judged as untrustworthy were exiled out of the country on extended whaling voyages. The managers of the refuges were therefore able to get rid of the most recalcitrant inmates.

As a result of the depression of 1857, these institutions had become overcrowded by the beginning of the Civil War in 1861. Finding employment for the youths was also a common problem. These poor conditions did not change through the war years. The most serious criticism of the juvenile institutions came from reformers who felt that the refuges and reformatories were just like prisons for adults. Charles Loring Brace, the leading reformer and director of the New York Children's Aid Society, asserted that because of rigid punishments, strict schedules, and the military regimentation of the refuge, youths were not reformed. The longer the youth is in a refuge, "the less likely he is to do well in outside life" (Brace, 1872:224–225).

Brace contributed to the myth that institutions for children should be located in rural areas of the country. The child savers were against the evils of urban corruption—the dirty city with its taverns, gambling halls, and gangs. They asserted that placement in homes, farms, and institutions in rural areas would cleanse and reform children from the vice, evil associations, and bad habits of the city. Administrators and philanthropists at the National Conference of Charities and Correction supported and defended Brace's position. These prominent reformers included Enoch C. Wines, (secretary of the New York Prison Association and president of the First International Penal Congress, held in London in 1872), Theodore Dwight (the first dean of Columbia Law School), Zebulon Brockway (superintendent of Elmira Reformatory in upstate New York), and Frank Sanborn (secretary of the Massachusetts State Board of Charities) (Platt, 1969).

The late 1800s witnessed the flourishing of the reformatory movement. Enoch Wines is credited with being one of the nineteenth century's foremost American authorities on reformatories for children. In 1872 he became the first president of the International Penal Congress. The underlying philosophy behind the reformatory movement was that proper training in a residential environment could offset the early experiences of poverty, poor family life, and corruption. The goal was to prepare the youth for the future by removing him from his adverse living conditions and placing him "in the midst of wholesome material and moral surroundings"—the reformatory. Wines expressed great faith in the rehabilitative power of these institutions:

> The spirit of our reformatories is that of hope and effort, while listless indifference or despair too often reigns in our prisons. The sentences of young offenders are wisely regulated for their amendment; they are not absurdly shortened as if they signified only so much endurance of vindictive suffering. The whole machinery of the establishment is set in the reformatories for the good training of the child, while in prisons it is too often allowed to chafe and wear upon the moral nature and chill the best aspirations of the adult convict. America has little reason to be proud of her prisons; but she can justly take pride in her juvenile reformatories, from the very beginning of their work fifty years ago until now. (Wines, 1880:80–81)

The philosophy and goals of reformatories emphasized the values of sobriety, thrift, industry, prudence, and ambition. Juveniles were to receive only an elementary education so that they could direct the majority of their time and energy to industrial and agricultural training. Inmates were to be "protected" from idleness and laziness by means of military drill, physical exercise, and continual supervision. In addition to the aforementioned goals, which seem quite rigid and harsh, there were some philosophies that in theory sounded good. Juvenile offenders were to be segregated from the corrupting influences of adult offenders; the atmosphere in a reformatory was supposed to be one of love and guidance combined with firmness; indeterminate sentences were preferred over fixed determinate sentences to encourage youths to participate actively in their own reform (Elmore, 1884: 84–91). Although some of those goals appeared to be reasonable and workable, it was not long before theoretical and abstract philosophies were changed into a system very different from what had been hoped for.

The situation at Elmira Reformatory in New York illustrates the harsh reality of reformatories in the 1800s. Although thought to be a model reformatory, it suffered from serious overcrowding. In the late 1890s Elmira contained 500 cells, which were jammed with as many as 1,500 juveniles. Max Grunhut, an outspoken penal reformer, stated: "What had begun as a bold experiment lost the inspiring impulse of its first promotors and became routine work and mass treatment."

To make matters worse, influential Elmira physician Hamilton Wey (1888) held the view, popular in some circles in those days, that juvenile offenders as a group were physically different from nondelinquent youths. He insisted that the youthful criminal was usually "undersized, his weight being disproportionate to his height, with a tendency to flat-footedness. He is coarse in fiber and heavy in his movements, lacking anatomical symmetry and beauty. The head is markedly assymetrical, . . . characteristic of a degenerative physiognomy" (p. 191). As treatment for these deficiencies, Wey recommended strenuous physical training and military drills (1888:181–193; Platt, 1969:23–24).

Homer Folks, a consistent critic of the American reformatory system, stated in 1891 that in many cases a reformatory could not serve as a substitute for parental affection. He went on to suggest that reformatories could even have the effect of encouraging parents to evade moral and financial obligations to their children. Folks' theories were a forerunner of the sociological theories on the stigma of labeling. He spoke of the "inherent evil" of the reformatory system, and its effect of leaving an "enduring stigma" on its inmates. He criticized the system also because it did not prepare the youths for reintegration into society. He warned of the danger of confining youths in a reformatory environment and then, without adequate preparation, releasing them to resume their place on the outside. When the juvenile is released, said Folks, he is "thrown into the midst of temptation, doubly powerful because of novelty. Just at this moment the strict discipline must be withdrawn. The routine of life by which he has been carried along is removed" (p. 138).

Anthony Platt (1969) points to the fact that not only were juvenile offenders removed from their homes when they were placed in residential institutions, they were put into institutions in rural country settings, usually many miles from family and friends. The underlying philosophy was that the city was a "corrupting influence" on the youth. To help them become "reformed" it was necessary to remove them to the country, where they could be "reunited with nature and wholesomeness" (p. 65). Thus no effort was made to help the inmates adjust to the ways of life in the city—the environment from which they had come and in all probability the environment to which they would return.

It should be noted that Homer Folks was one of the more outspoken critics of the reformatory movement. While some others shared his beliefs, they comprised a small minority. The overwhelming majority of penologists during the late 1800s praised the reformatory for both its principles and its practices.

INSTITUTIONALIZED TREATMENT IN THE TWENTIETH CENTURY

In the 1930s, a new wave of concern for the treatment of juvenile offenders swept the country. Because of the serious financial plight wrought by the Great Depression, considerable numbers of juveniles truancy from school to find odd jobs, or to stealing to help families. Many of the youths who were arrested for various delinquent acts were unable to meet the stiff bail that was imposed.

Robert Bremner (1974) cited a 1934 report from Massachusetts which documents the fact that in that year 547 juveniles were sent to jail for temporary detention. In some instances, the detention resulted from the inability to furnish a high bail, ordinarily $2,500 and running as high as $6,000 (especially excessive by 1934 financial standards). To quote from the report: "The sole object of bail . . . being to insure the appearance of the child in court when wanted, these facts compel serious consideration of other means of securing that end. If the care of the child to his own home is not feasible, the provision of specially supervised foster homes is positively indicated" (p. 1008).

In addition to concerns about excessive bail, serious questions about the legal rights of juveniles were being raised. Three important issues evolved regarding treatment of juvenile offenders: (1) Were some juveniles (especially poor blacks) being given unusually stiff sentences? (2) Were some youths being denied basic legal rights that were granted to adult offenders? (3) Were juvenile offenders incarcerated in deplorable institutions? How could those conditions be ameliorated?

In July 1937, the *New York Times* contained a report that awakened many people to the realities of juvenile incarceration. It involved the case of the Scottsboro boys—four black youths convicted of rape in 1931 and sentenced to the electric chair. At the time of the rape, the accused juveniles (Eugene Williams, Roy Wright, Olen Montgomery, and Willie Roberson) were all under sixteen years of age. They were held in jail for six and one-half years before being set free. According to the *New York Times,* the day after the rape occurred a doctor had examined Willie Roberson, age twelve. The physician stated that Willie was "sick, suffering with a severe venereal disease, and that in his condition it would have been very painful for him to have committed that crime, and that he would not have had any inclination to commit it." With regard to another of the juveniles, Olen Montgomery (age thirteen), the paper reported: "He was practically blind and has also told a plausible story, which has been unshaken all through the litigation, which put him some distance from the commission of the crime. The State is without proof other than the prosecutrix as to his being in the gondola car, and we feel that it is a case of mistaken identity" (Bremner, 1974:1006). The newspaper report continued with the district attorney's decision to free the boys after more than six years in prison: "Counsel for the state think that in view of the fact they have been in jail for six-and-a-half years the ends of justice would be met at this time by releasing these . . . juveniles, on condition that they leave the state, never to return" (p. 1007).

In the 1930s and 1940s Roy Casey, an inspector for the Federal Bureau of Prisons, was concerned about the treatment children received while in jail awaiting a trial, hearing, or investigation. Based on visits that he made to most of the county jails in approximately half of the states, he made a number of observations and recommendations. He urged that "vindictiveness" on the part of police officers and prosecuting attorneys be abated. Casey (1943:175) estimated that there were "tens of thousands" of children in U.S. jails and lockups:

> The unfitness of the vast majority of city and county jails for the incarceration of adults should be well known. . . . If then these jails are unfit for adults from every standard held by modern penology, what can be said of them as places to confine first offenders, and girls and boys of the lower teen ages? Simply this, that society is committing a crime not only against these children but also against itself in permitting this deplorable situation to continue.

Casey (1943) provides vivid case examples from his inspections of the jails. On the day of his inspection at one institution (Casey declined to give its name) it held twenty children, all of them seventeen years old and younger.

> Among them was a sixteen-year-old boy who had been given two sentences of one year each to run consecutively for the offense of larceny. Another boy was in the same cell block awaiting transfer to the state penitentiary. He was only fifteen years of age and his commitment papers indicated that he had once been an inmate in the state institution for the feebleminded. His offense was burglary and larceny without deadly weapons, yet he was being sent to a penitentiary notoriously known . . . for the desperate and hardened criminals and perverts among its inmates, and the child's three sentences read one to ten years, one to twenty-five years, and one year to life. (p. 176)

In describing the lack of segregation between juveniles and adults, Casey (1943) called for the development of detention centers for juveniles completely separate from jails for adults. He described the conditions in a jail located in the capital city of a northern state:

> The jail held four children somewhere within the dark and filthy cells of its vermin-infested cell blocks, along with criminals, vags, sex perverts, and the insane. The officials spoke of how they were handicapped by not having segregation quarters for juveniles, but it did not appear that they were greatly concerned over the matter and had considered it only a minor thing to have to put fifteen, sixteen, and seventeen-year-old boys with hardened criminals. . . . They laughingly recited the details of how sodomy was practiced on one of the fat boys and the discomfort he experienced from lacerations. (pp. 178–179)

As further indication of the horrendous problem that existed in the 1930s and 1940s, Negley Teeters and John Reinemann cited statistics pointing to the magnitude of the problem of children in prison. The report of the Wickersham Commission in 1931 stated that 54.8 percent of the prisoner population at that time was under the age of twenty-one when committed. Teeters and Reinemann reported that in 1946 approximately 166 public facilities served juvenile offenders. Of these, 115 were state and national institutions and 51 were under county and municipal auspices. The authors estimated that more than 30,000 juveniles were imprisoned (Teeters and Reinemann, 1950:448 and 514).

Sherwood Norman reported to the 1946 National Conference of Social Work that the National Probation Association had undertaken a study of the best detention facilities in the United States for the purpose of developing principles and standards. The study covered sixty-eight facilities in twenty-two states throughout the country. In 1944 they studied twenty-nine communities and found a total of 2,382 children. However, since in many places no records were kept, that figure is actually just a low estimate. Norman (1947) commented on the routine practices that were uncovered in the study and needed to be changed.

> We found that some courts detained routinely every child on whom a petition was filed, and the petitions were filed recklessly. In most courts children who should never have been detained were thus penalized for the simple reason that the juvenile court offices were closed for the day or for the week-end and there was no court representative available to take the responsibility for releasing them to their homes. This practice is almost universal. . . . We found no uniformity in the administration of detention homes. Two thirds of the homes were overcrowded. Sometimes two and three times as many children were held as could be normally provided for by the quarters.
>
> . . . There was a tendency in almost every community to concentrate on one type of detention care to the detriment of the children who needed other types of care. For instance, detention homes geared to the care of dependent and neglected children failed to provide security for the older delinquent group who were relegated to the jail. Other homes were operated as though all the children detained therein were young criminals. Nowhere did we find really adequate provision for the sixteen and seventeen-year-old delinquent youngster, although juvenile court jurisdiction in over half of our states now includes this group. (pp. 399–400)

A key point made by Norman (1947) in his presentation at the conference was that some of the detention homes studied were characterized by the same conditions that had been recognized as contributing to delinquency in the community: the lack of concerned, warm relationships between the youths and adult workers; the presence of youths who had committed very serious crimes and from whom more sophisticated delinquent behavior could be learned; the scarcity of an adequate recreation program; the nonexistence of a meaningful educational program; and the lack of professional social work services. According to Norman's findings, institutionalization for juveniles was almost totally void of meaningful rehabilitation. In fact, the institutions were harmful to the youths because incarceration necessitated uprooting youths from family and community and taking away the rights of freedom of choice. Results of the study belied the claim that these institutions were in any way beneficial.

Norman (1947) also presented a composite picture of the atmosphere and standards at the majority of detention homes. To provide a vivid picture of the situation encountered by thousands of juveniles, he presented scenarios in which he is receiving a guided tour of a detention center. He is the narrator, and the "tour guide" is a composite of many administrators encountered on his visits:

> "And we are really proud of the food we serve these children. It costs the county only thirty-five cents a day for each child." You remember that this was the minimum standard set for children's institutions in 1941 and that there has been considerable increase in food costs since then. From the window you see a small courtyard where boys are milling about with a ball. "Can't they have baseball bats?" you ask. "Oh, no!" is the reply, "the space isn't large enough, and anyway a bat in the hands of these delinquent boys would be too dangerous for our staff.". . .
>
> Twenty-five girls are lounging about in a sparsely furnished recreation room, playing cards, looking at comic books, or just sitting or looking wistfully out of the window. "Couldn't this room have a shuffleboard game painted on the floor, a victrola, or perhaps a crafts corner?" Your guide is horrified at the danger of putting shuffleboard sticks in the hands of delinquents and tips you off that most of the matrons would quit if they had that sort of thing with which to contend. You hear from more than one of your own workers, "There's no point in giving them more things to do, they just break up anything you give them.". . .
>
> In returning to the office you pass the delinquent boys coming up from the yard in silence and marching in line with arms folded. "Why is this necessary?" you ask. "Because if they are allowed to talk they become too noisy, and if their arms are not folded they are always pushing each other. One person can handle twenty-five or thirty of these boys very smoothly by just sticking to these time-tested rules."
>
> To your growing list of frustrations you add the building, which is so ill adapted to any kind of meaningful life for children that regimentation is almost inevitable. Nothing can be done about the way the home is used by social agencies because of the loopholes in the juvenile court law and the difficulty of securing interagency cooperation. You cannot

secure psychological and casework services because the clinic has its hands full with routine diagnosis for the court. . . . You eat your heart out, seeing so many eager boys and girls with real potentialities thrust toward the prisons. (pp. 401–403)

Norman offered his opinion as to why these deplorable conditions existed. He believed that administrators in detention homes were unsure as to what components were needed in a rehabilitation-oriented detention facility. Norman said that blame should not necessarily be placed on the superintendents of the institutions. Many superintendents were sincerely trying to provide adequate detention facilities but were hindered by limited budgets, untrained staff, and, above all, narrow concepts.

However, the picture Norman presented was not totally bleak. At least five juvenile courts had devised satisfactory controls for detention intake. Professional casework services were provided at several facilities, and on a few occasions a child guidance clinic was used to provide in-service training. There were occasional facilities in which the adult–youth relationship seemed to be more a camper–counselor arrangement than a prisoner–guard one. In these facilities, children were helped to use the program as a creative outlet for their tensions and anxieties.

On the basis of his findings, Norman (1947:408) made recommendations for improving the system of detention for juveniles. He urged:

1. Revamping of the whole detention concept. If priorities were reorganized, safe physical care and custody (which had yet to be achieved in many places) would not be the only concerns. The goal of meeting the emotional needs of the populations served was vitally important.

2. Strengthening the court intake process so that children who did not need to be detained could be kept out of detention.

3. Strengthening community services, with the following goals: keep children out of court, shorten the length of stay by making available improved institutional and foster home placements, and upgrade the level of detention home administrators.

Finally, he urged that social workers and the courts work together to improve the availability and quality of services.

Norman (1958) estimated that approximately half of all the children and youths (aged seven to seventeen) who were brought before the court were held in some type of detention facility or jail. About 100,000 youths were detained in county jails and police lockups prior to adjudication, while another 100,000 were confined in juvenile detention centers, detention homes, or basement cells. Many of these facilities were substandard, with poor heating and ventilation, and void of any educational programs or medical care.

By the late 1960s, the conditions in short-term detention facilities had improved to some degree, although a number of jurisdictions continued to "warehouse" juvenile offenders throughout the decade. During the first half of the 1960s, in accord with the National Council on Crime and Delinquency's (NCCD) guidelines for detention home design, over 100 specially designed detention centers were built, primarily in urban areas, to replace old county jails and makeshift facilities. Many modern facilities included specialized group units for eight to fifteen juveniles. A number of the new facilities also had individual rooms for each detainee, with attractive, yet sturdy, metal furnishings. These new facilities were staffed increasingly by professionally trained employees and provided group work and group counseling, casework services, school programs, and recreational programs.

In the mid-1960s, the total number of juveniles confined to detention homes and jails was above 409,000. The length of detention ranged from one day to sixty-eight days, with the average being eighteen days (President's Commission on Law Enforcement and Administration of Justice, 1967).

An NCCD national survey of conditions in detention facilities documented the lack of constructive educational, therapeutic, and recreational programs, such as:

- 28 percent of the detention facilities did not have any provisions for regular medical care of detainees.

- 58 percent did not have any casework or counseling services.

- 53 percent did not have even one full-time or part-time visiting teacher to provide educational services.

- 52 percent had no recreational program (President's Commission, 1967:120–121).

For an in-depth analysis of detention trends, policies, and practices of the 1970s and 1980s, see Chapter 8.

Although treatment of juvenile offenders has improved considerably since the end of World War II, there have been numerous instances of atrocities perpetrated against juveniles being held in detention facilities and training schools. As an illustration, two reports from 1971 are cited here.

The first case is of Nathan Smith, Jr., a 15-year-old black youth. He was an inmate of the Mississippi County Penal Farm, where he drowned in the strong current of a deep drainage ditch. Before being sent to the penal farm, he had been convicted in his hometown of Osceola, Arkansas, of petty larceny for allegedly stealing several inexpensive items from a local store. At the trial, Nathan Smith, not represented by counsel, was sentenced to six months at the penal farm. An account of his death was provided by a prisoner who had been an eyewitness:

> "The captain dropped his can of tobacco into the water and told the kid to go down and get it." The witness said the youth was reluctant because the stream was swollen by recent heavy rain and the current was extremely swift. The guard drew his pistol, the prisoner's account contends, and forced the youngster into the water. After the can of tobacco was retrieved, the guard ordered the boy to stay in the water and shove large timbers away from the bank and into the current. "Somehow the kid got caught in the timber and that was the last we saw of him". . . (Bremner, 1974:1015–1016)

In the second case, eighty-five black high school students were arrested and put in the county jail in Warrenton, North Carolina, on December 2, 1970, following two days of disturbances at a local high school. Although the students were held in jail for only a short time, they reported receiving "harsh and brutal" treatment. With the rising number of student demonstrations in the late 1960s and early 1970s, mass arrests leading to brief periods in jail were not uncommon. The students' account of their treatment in jail was reported in a 1971 issue of *New South*:

> The thirty-eight girls arrested told of being herded together in cells and given no food or water. They were insulted by white guards, refused bathroom facilities. Those in need of sanitary supplies said they were not only denied such supplies but that their requests were responded to with suggestive and obscene language. They were denied the right to make a telephone call. (Tornquist, 1971:63)

However, these students were relatively lucky. They were allowed out on bail after only one day in jail.

Treating Juvenile Offenders in Open Settings

The deleterious effects of incarcerating a youthful offender in a prison atmosphere were discussed in the previous section. However, many policymakers, while recognizing the weaknesses of institutional treatment, were unaware of viable alternatives for dealing with juveniles who had committed delinquent acts. One extreme approach would be to send the youth back to his community without providing any treatment services whatsoever; at the other extreme would be putting the youth in a prison or reformatory where rehabilitative and educational services were sorely lacking. Rehabilitation-minded policymakers recognized that neither extreme was sound, and gradually there emerged the concept of forestry camps—a hoped-for middle ground between two unworkable alternatives that would be suitable for certain types of youths.

The first known camp of its type was established in 1932. The concept was developed by Judge Samuel R. Blake, Kenyon Scudder, and Karl Holton to meet the needs of transient boys; implementation was carried out by the Los Angeles County Probation Department. In 1935, the California legislature passed a bill providing for forestry camps to be set up for juvenile offenders, who would be sent there by the juvenile courts. These camps were to be run by the county (Kogon, 1958). According to Weber (1960), the early camps for juvenile delinquents were generally modeled after the Civilian Conservation Corps camps that were operating between 1933 and 1943. The goal of those camps was to provide a treatment program that included conservation of natural resources in addition to employment and vocational training.

Forestry camps were utilized because they were an open setting with no gates, bars, guns, or isolation facilities. In short, it was not a prison atmosphere. However, boys with a long history of delinquent behavior were not referred, nor were boys with "deep-seated emotional problems requiring psychotherapy." Boys had to be of average intelligence to benefit from the school program, which was an integral part of the forestry camp. Youths with physical handicaps had to be excluded. Boys were usually given an indeterminate stay but generally stayed an average of six to nine months (Kogon, 1958:36).

Two basic types of camps developed in the late 1940s and early 1950s: senior forestry camps and junior probation camps. A senior forestry camp was for youths between the ages of sixteen and eighteen. Emphasis was on work such as nursery, reforestation, various maintenance and construction activities, brush clearance, and fire suppression (Kamm, Hunt, & Flemming, 1968). Most camps had their own nursery where, under the guidance of a forestry horticulturist, youths were shown how to gather and bed seeds in the mountainous areas. These were taken care of until they could be planted in burned-out areas (Kogon, 1958). According to Kamm, et al., the senior forestry camps also focused on counseling and group activity programs. The night school classes consisted of regular public school subjects geared to the individuals' needs (remedial education was often needed). In the junior camps, for boys between the ages of thirteen and fifteen, the emphasis was mainly on education. The youths attended a minimum of four hours of classes each day. There was also an active athletic program and some counseling. Each day the youths participated in two-hour work sessions very similar to the work the senior boys were doing.

During World War II, the forestry camps added to their program training in the fundamentals of military life and drill (provided by the army). A number of boys who received this training went directly from the camp into military service, where they served their country well (Bremner, 1974).

Kogon (1958) states that by the 1950s probation camps in California had evolved into an integral part of the probation process. A youth was sent to the camp by the juvenile court and assigned to a probation officer. The relationship between youth and probation officer continued during the stay in the camp and then for approximately six months after the juvenile returned to his own home. In Kogon's opinion, delinquent youths who were sent to these camps learned how to relate constructively to peers and staff. As an example of the good work done by these boys, Kogon stated that in 1957 youths in California forestry camps responded to 848 fire calls, where they rendered invaluable assistance to the professional fire fighters.

Another type of camping experience for juvenile delinquents developed in Dallas, Texas. The impetus for the program came from a group of people who had formed the Salesmanship Club in Dallas in 1921. The emphasis on children in trouble began in 1946 under the leadership of Campbell Loughmiller. The core of this program has been a year-round rugged camp in northeastern Texas. Boys sleep outdoors winter and summer in canvas shelters that they have built. The camp is under the supervision of social workers, who deal mainly with the parents of these boys. There is also an eight-bed halfway house for youths whose home situations are so destructive that they cannot go home (James, 1969).

At the Texas camp the boys are divided by age into four groups of ten. Each group is guided by two sensitive, rugged college graduates. Activities include mountain climbing, canoeing, fishing, hiking, and learning to survive in the wilderness. A type of group therapy is practiced—dealing with individual or group problems whenever they develop. Boys can remain in the program up to two years. Juveniles are referred from a number of sources including the court, welfare department, schools, and mental health officials. This program claims a good rate of returning boys to public schools, though no follow-up has been provided.

Kogon (1958) and Kamm et al. (1968) have reported that the forestry camps are a valuable placement for youthful offenders, offering distinct advantages to the traditional prison environment. However, Weber (1960) has stated his concern that the camps did not provide consistent or complete treatment programs. He raised questions about the counseling, which is a stated component of the treatment approach:

> The counseling techniques . . . frequently fail to meet the basic problems at the root of the delinquency and are usually restricted to surface problems that arise in a boy's adjustment to the camp. . . . In practice, the camps are often characterized by diverse aims and methods. On the one hand, they emphasize conservation work and education; on the other hand, they try to be an institution of treatment. (p. 447)

While I agree with Weber that the counseling component at many of the camps was probably not highly developed, I take issue with his criticism of the camp model and believe the camp atmosphere was certainly preferable to the confining prison environment. It would seem that the potential for meaningful rehabilitation is present in a forestry camp with the addition of a more structured outdoor experience as well as a group work and aftercare component. (The promising and highly structured wilderness challenge and outdoor adventure programs of the 1970s and 1980s are examined in detail in Chapter 10.)

SUMMARY

Early apprenticeship systems and institutional facilities were developed in response to the perceived problem of having a large number of individuals identified as either neglected, abandoned, destitute, or idle or causing embarrassment or pain to community members through delinquent acts. Initially, public officials developed a system of apprenticeships to exert social control over needy and troubled youths. When it became apparent that the juveniles were being exploited and many were deserting their apprenticeships, the practice of incarcerating law-breaking youths in adult prisons became widely used.

Several leading reformers and societies became aware of the plight of young children incarcerated in horrendous, unsanitary, and corrupting facilities, such as New York's Bellevue Prison. Reformers (including Enoch C. Wines, Frank Sanborn, and Homer Folks) and advocacy groups such as the Society for the Reformation of Juvenile Delinquents studied the problem, prepared reports, and advocated with legislators to change the system. Norman's national study of the horrendous conditions in sixty-eight detention facilities provided a detailed description of the problems that existed in the 1930s and 1940s, the administrative reasons for the deplorable conditions, and recommendations for improving the detention system.

The final section of the chapter describes the emergence of forestry camps and junior probation camps during the 1940s and 1950s.

DISCUSSION QUESTIONS

1. Identify the purpose and nature of apprenticeships for roguish juveniles during Elizabethan times.
2. Discuss the major contribution of the Society for the Reformation of Juvenile Delinquents during the first half of the 1800s.
3. What was the purpose of the early houses of refuge?
4. Describe the schedule and daily routine at the houses of refuge.
5. Identify the philosophy and goals of Elmira and other reformatories.
6. What was Homer Folks' specific criticism about the American reformatory system?
7. Based on the survey of sixty-eight detention facilities throughout the United States, what were Sherwood Norman's (National Probation Association) three recommendations?
8. Discuss the major strength as well as the major weakness of the forestry camps and probation camps of the 1930s and 1940s.

REFERENCES

Brace, C. L. (1872). *The dangerous classes of New York and twenty years work among them.* New York: N.A.S.W. Classic Series, 1973.

Bremner, R. H. (Ed.) (1974). *Children and youth in America: A documentary history* (Vol. 3, pts. 5–7). Cambridge, MA: Harvard University Press.

Casey, R. (1943). Children in jail, In M. Bell (Ed.), *Delinquency and the community in wartime: Yearbook of the National Probation Association* (pp. 175–179). New York: National Probation Association.

Dunlop, J. O. & Denman, R. D. (1912). *English apprenticeship and child labour: A history.* New York: Macmillan.

Elmore, A. E. (1884). Report of the Committee on Reformatories and Houses of Refuge. *Proceedings of the National Conference of Charities and Correction* (pp. 84–91).

Folks, H. (1891). The care of delinquent children. *Proceedings of the National Conference of Charities and Correction.*

Grunhut, M. (1948). *Penal reform.* Oxford: Clarendon Press.

James, H. (1969). *Children in trouble, a national scandal.* New York: David McKay.

Kahn, A. J. (1953). *A court for children: A study of the New York City Children's Court.* New York: Columbia University Press.

Kamm, E. R., Hunt, D., & Fleming, J. A. (1968). *Juvenile law and procedure in California.* Beverly Hills, CA: Glencoe Press.

Kogon, B. (1958, September). Probation camps. *Federal probation,* 22(3), 35–36.

Mennel, R. M. (1973). *Thorns and thistles: Juvenile delinquents in the United States, 1825–1940*. Hanover, NH: University Press of New England.

New Jersey Juvenile Delinquency Commission. (1939, November). *Justice and the child in New Jersey*. Trenton, NJ: Author.

Norman, S. (1947). Detention facilities for children. *Proceedings of the National Conference of Social Work*, 1946 (pp. 399–400). New York: Columbia University Press.

Norman, S. (1958). *Standards and guides for the detention of children and youth*. New York: National Probation and Parole Association.

Peirce, B. K. (1969). *A half century with juvenile delinquents: The New York House of Refuge and its times*, Montclair, NJ: Patterson Smith.

Platt, M. (1969). *The child savers*. Chicago: University of Chicago Press.

President's Commission on Law Enforcement and Administration of Justice. (1967) (pp. 120–126). *Task force report: Corrections*. Washington, DC: U.S. Government Printing Office.

Rothman, D. J. (1971). *The discovery of the asylum*. Boston: Little, Brown.

Teeters, N. K. & Reinemann, J. O. (1950). *The challenge of delinquency*. New York: Prentice-Hall.

Tornquist, E. (1971, Summer). Juvenile corrections in North Carolina, *New South 26*, 63–68.

Weber, G. H. (1960), *Camps for delinquent boys: A guide to planning*, (Children's Bureau Publication No. 385). Washington, DC: U.S. Government Printing Office.

Wey, H. (1888). A plea for physical training of youthful criminals. *Proceedings of the Annual Conference of the National Prison Association*, (pp. 181–193). Boston.

Wines, E. C. (1880). *The state of prisons and of child saving institutions in the civilized world*. Cambridge, MA: Harvard University Press.

Chapter Three

Community Strategies with Juvenile Offenders

Albert R. Roberts

ABSTRACT

Chapter 3 shows how community organization approaches to delinquency prevention were developed out of an ecological model and Cloward and Ohlin's (1960) *opportunity theory*. Also presented are the objectives and accomplishments of several of the most widely known examples of a coordinated community program aimed at both reduction and prevention of juvenile delinquency: the Chicago Area Project, New York City's Mobilization for Youth (MFY), and Boston's Midcity Project. The last section of this chapter examines the modern-day version of a coordinating council—the youth service bureau. The reader will learn about the five basic goals, the sources of funding, the organizational structure and staffing patterns, and the youth development and delinquency prevention activities and services common to youth service bureaus.

The overriding purpose of the early community organizational strategies was to combine community groups and agencies in an umbrella type of community service approach to delinquency prevention. McMillen (1947), in outlining the role of community organization in social work, identified the following needs:

1. To strengthen intergroup cooperation for the full attainment of welfare objectives;
2. To make the public aware of community resources;
3. To assist in effective case-finding and referral practices.

Based on the writings of McMillen (1947) and Beam (1936), three levels of participation in early community organization can be delineated: At the first level, agencies concentrated their efforts primarily on community organization activities, generally in areas of social work specialization such as child labor, tuberculosis, or delinquency (e.g., the community coordinating council). In this type of community agency, any direct assistance to clients represents a secondary function of the agency. The second level of participation included agencies that concentrated their efforts primarily on organizational concerns, directing their efforts more globally to encompass many areas of social welfare. Councils of social agencies, welfare federations, community chests, and neighborhood youth councils are examples of this type of agency. The third level is comprised of agencies that provided direct service to clients as their primary function, with community organization activities being of secondary importance. Most voluntary and governmental social agencies were of this type.

The field of delinquency prevention has involved various community organization strategies ranging from neighborhood-run councils to social workers doing outreach with urban gangs. Five of the best-known projects and approaches of the past eighty years geared to delinquency prevention are:

- Community coordinating councils.
- Chicago Area Project.
- Boston's Midcity Project.
- New York's Mobilization for Youth project.
- Youth service bureaus.

COMMUNITY COORDINATING COUNCILS

The coordinating council movement was a significant step in the treatment and prevention of juvenile delinquency. Its roots can be traced to the founding of several national organizations in the early 1900s: the National Probation Association in 1907, the Family Welfare Association in 1911, the Big Brother and Big Sister Federation in 1917, and the Child Welfare League of America in 1920. The major focus of these organizations was on improvement of standards of community service and development of national policies.

The community coordinating council movement to combat juvenile delinquency began in Berkeley, California, in 1919. The original objectives of the Berkeley Coordinating Council were to conduct research and professional conferences as well as to work with problem children. This council contained three committees—"the adjustment committee, the character building committee, and the environment committee" (Pursuit, et al., 1972, p. 42). During the 1930s, coordinating councils proliferated rapidly with the expansion of the Los Angeles Coordinating Councils for the Prevention of Delinquency (Beam, 1937; Scudder, 1936). They continued to grow during the 1940s, when their efforts to combat delinquency were publicly acclaimed by men such as Kenyon Scudder (warden at the California Institution for Men, located in Chino). Speaking at the Attorney General's Conference on Crime in December 1944, Scudder made the following remarks:

> The conference recognizes that criminal careers usually originate in the early years of neglected childhood, and the most fundamental and hopeful measures of crime prevention are those directed toward discovering the underlying factors in the delinquency of children and strengthening and coordinating the resources of the home, the school, and the community. . . . It commends the progress that has been made in certain states and localities in drawing together through such agencies as coordinating councils all available local forces to combat unwholesome influences upon youth. It urges state and national lead-

ership through appropriate governmental and voluntary organizations, in fostering the development of these coordinating agencies, the provision of constructive educational, vocational, and recreational opportunities for youth, and provision of competent, skilled service to children in need of guidance and correction.

The success of these councils was based on their ability to enlist the cooperation and coordinated efforts of community facilities. Councils that functioned most effectively not only stimulated and utilized the skills of local residents but also had access to a planning board or a broader coordinated community organization that supplied personnel, funds, and planners.

Social historians have noted that the coordinating council movement played an active role in delinquency prevention efforts during the 1930s. Beam's (1937) survey (sponsored by the National Probation Association) indicated the widespread adoption of these community efforts. He reported that over 250 coordinating councils were operating in 163 cities and towns in 20 states during 1935 and 1936.

CHICAGO AREA PROJECT

One of the most widely known examples of a coordinated program aimed at the reduction of juvenile delinquency was the Chicago Area Project, initiated by the Institute for Juvenile Research and the Behavioral Research Fund in 1929. Clifford R. Shaw was the founder and director of the project, which consisted of a series of studies from 1929 to 1933 as well as a legendary experiment in delinquency prevention at the local level that lasted until 1962. The studies conducted by Shaw and McKay (1972) concentrated on two areas: (1) the epidemiology of delinquency in different areas of Chicago and (2) the acquisition of delinquent beliefs and behavior from delinquent subcultures. Shaw and McKay found that a disproportionately large number of juvenile delinquents came from certain areas of Chicago. The high rate sectors were termed *delinquency areas* (Kobrin, 1959).

Shaw and his associates found that people who lived in the delinquency areas were primarily immigrants who had lived a rural lifestyle before coming to the United States. "As a group they occupied the least desirable status in the economic, political and social hierarchies of the metropolitan society" (Kobrin, 1959: 21). The studies indicated that in Chicago and other cities, the areas located within the central business district and adjacent to industrial and manufacturing plants had had disproportionately high rates of delinquency for many decades.

This ecological phenomenon began at the beginning of the twentieth century. As urban areas grew and commercial and industrial facilities expanded, large numbers of people moved to the suburbs, out of the less desirable and overcrowded areas. Researchers concluded that those areas, which had high rates of delinquency, were lacking in social stability, normative consensus, and social cohesion. In the high-delinquency area various forms of lawlessness had been passed from one generation to the next. Such cultural transmission of delinquency was demonstrated through in-depth case histories of individual delinquents (Shaw, 1930, 1931).

The basic assumptions and objectives of the Chicago Area Project were summarized as follows:

> The Chicago Project operates on the assumption that much of the delinquency of slum areas is to be attributed to lack of neighborhood cohesiveness and to the consequent lack of concern on the part of many residents about the welfare of children. The project strives to counteract this situation through encouraging local self-help enterprises through which a sense of neighborliness and mutual responsibility will develop. It is expected that delinquency will decline as youngsters become better integrated into community life and thereby influenced by the values of conventional society rather than those of the underworld. (Witmer & Tufts, 1954: 11)

The major finding of the Chicago Area Project was that in most instances delinquent behavior was attributable to the simple process of social learning as a result of the breakdown of "the machinery of spontaneous social control." Kobrin described this breakdown:

> The breakdown is precipitated by the cataclysmic pace of social change to which migrants from a peasant or rural background are subjected when they enter the city. In its more specific aspects, delinquency was seen as adaptive behavior on the part of the male child of rural migrants acting as members of adolescent peer groups in their efforts to find their way to meaningful and respected adult roles essentially unaided by the older generation and under the influence of criminal models for whom the inner city areas furnish a haven. (Kobrin, 1959: 23)

Other findings of the project were:

1. Youth welfare organizations could be developed among residents of high delinquency areas, thus justifying Shaw's assumption that the high-delinquency sectors had the capacity to contribute to the solution of the problems.

2. Existing programs in the local recreation and character-building agencies were not adequate for modifying the behavior of the boys involved in delinquent acts. "In all probability, the Chicago Area Project was the first organized program in the United

States to use workers to establish direct and personal contact with the 'unreached' boys" (Kobrin, 1959: 28).

3. Disorganization was not so severe as to be devoid of individuals to serve as positive role models. A major effort of the project was directed toward finding an effective method whereby social workers, police, and teachers could work effectively with these juveniles.

4. The project was a pioneer in exploring the way in which an urban bureaucracy (schools, police officers, probation departments, training schools, etc.) attempted to control and correct delinquent youths.

After Shaw and McKay conducted their early research and documentation of ecological causations of delinquency in Chicago's slum neighborhoods, community committees were developed in six parts of the city: Hegewisch, Russell Square, South Side, Near North Side, Near West Side, and Near Northwest Side (Kobrin, 1959; Schlossman & Sedlak, 1983). Neighborhood centers were formed that reached over 7,500 children and youth in these areas.

The core of this self-help community crime prevention effort was the neighborhood center, a recreational facility or educational center staffed by community residents. Over twenty different projects were initiated, including discussion groups, counseling services, hobby groups, adult education programs, summer camps, and recreation activities (Schlossman & Sedlak, 1983; Shaw & McKay, 1972; Sorrentino, 1983).

Neighborhood committees were organized with the assistance of a staff member from the Chicago Area Project, who served primarily as an advisor (for example, to mobilize resources if the committee requested such assistance). Professional field-workers functioned as consultants and community organizers, offering guidance but avoiding the tendency to manipulate or control the local leaders. To a great extent these community organizational efforts used the natural leaders from within each neighborhood to plan, staff, and manage project activities. It was the responsibility of the neighborhood committee to make all policy decisions and to select the director, who was required to be a neighborhood resident.

Besides developing community resources and activities for youths, committees made efforts to prevent further delinquency by regular contact with local police youth officers, probation officers, and parole officers. In five of the area projects, community groups worked intensively with young parolees, local residents often assisting the parolees in obtaining jobs and returning to school. It was not uncommon for successful parolees to join the local community committees and eventually be elected as officers of the committees.

Efforts similar to those initiated in Chicago were developed in such other cities as Cleveland, Detroit, Philadelphia, and Richmond. In downstate Illinois approximately 100 self-governing citizens' groups were established.

BOSTON'S MIDCITY PROJECT (1954–1957)

In the 1950s, other delinquency control programs somewhat similar to the Chicago Area Project were initiated. One of the best known was the Midcity Project, which was developed in 1954 in one of Boston's lower-class districts. This social action demonstration project— utilizing a "total community" philosophy—focused on improving three of the societal units that seemed to be an important influence in the genesis and perpetuation of delinquency: the gang, the community, and the family (Miller, 1962).

The project's primary emphasis was its work with gangs. Professional social workers known as "detached street workers" reached out to approximately 400 youths who were members of 21 gangs. The staff met with the groups three to four times a week, visiting with the gang members for five to six hours at a time. Contact was maintained for a period ranging from ten to thirty-four months.

The approach used by project staff differed from earlier programs in three ways: first, all staff were professional social workers; second, each staff member (with one exception) worked primarily with one group over an extended period of time; third, workers were able to consult regularly with psychiatric specialists.

The community component of the project had two major goals: (1) helping to establish and strengthen area citizens' groups so that they could act on their own to combat problems such as juvenile delinquency and (2) forging a cooperative approach among local professional organizations having contact with juveniles (e.g., schools, courts, settlement houses, and psychiatric and medical clinics).

The family component of the Midcity Project was geared toward treating "chronic-problem" families. Project staff identified families having a long-term history of receiving public welfare services and provided them with intensive, psychiatrically oriented casework services (Miller, 1962; Miller, Baum, & McNeil, 1968).

As part of a thorough evaluation of the Midcity Project, researchers analyzed the following fourteen behavior categories: theft, assault, drinking, sex, mating, work, education, religion, and involvement with the courts, police, corrections, social welfare, family and other gangs. Of these fourteen areas, only one category—school-oriented be-

havior—showed a statistically significant decrease in inappropriate behavior. The researchers also concluded that there was no significant
reduction in the frequency of illegal activity as a result of the project.
A slight decrease was found in the total sample, but it was attributable
to minor offenses and reduced illegal activity by the girls in the sample. In contrast, major offenses by boys actually increased in frequency
during the project, while "major offenses by younger boys increased
most of all" (Miller, 1962; 180).

MOBILIZATION FOR YOUTH

In 1961, one of the most ambitious efforts to prevent and control
juvenile delinquency was developed. This demonstration project—New
York's Mobilization for Youth (MFY)—became the prototype for many
federally funded delinquency prevention programs developed in other
cities during the Kennedy and Johnson administrations. Originally
funded under a grant from the National Institute of Mental Health
(NIMH), in 1962 it received an action grant from President Kennedy's
Committee on Juvenile Delinquency and Youth Crime.

The target area chosen for the MFY demonstration project was
Manhattan's Lower East Side, the longtime port of entry into the
United States for new immigrant groups. This location was chosen by
the pioneering area settlement houses: the Grand Street, Henry Street,
and University Settlement Houses.

In the early 1960s, the Lower East Side was characterized by the
typical problems of overcrowded lower-class slum neighborhoods, with
high rates of unemployment, juvenile delinquency, school failure, drug
addiction, petty crime, and families receiving public assistance. In response to the alarmingly high incidence of juvenile delinquency and
gang welfare on the Lower East Side, Helen Hall (director of the Henry
Street Settlement House) and sociologist Richard Cloward (of Columbia University's School of Social Work) developed the plan for Mobilization for Youth, with Cloward becoming its first director.

Cloward and Ohlin's (1960) opportunity theory postulated that delinquent subcultures emerge because lower-class youths strive to
achieve legitimate goals—primarily the acquisition of money—and are
unsuccessful because legitimate avenues for success are blocked. They
stated: "It is our view that pressures toward the formation of delinquent subcultures originate in marked discrepancies between cultur-
ally induced aspirations among lower-class youth and the possibilities
of achieving them by legitimate means" (p. 105).

Opportunity theory asserts that there is a major disparity between
the aspirations of lower-class youth and the legitimate opportunities
available to them. Lower-class youths internalize a set of conventional

values and goals. Despite very limited access to legitimate avenues for achieving these goals, they are unable to lower their aspirations. Blaming others rather than themselves for their limited access to the opportunity structure, many of these alienated youths join delinquent subcultures.

Thus according to this theory the organization of a neighborhood resulted in the formation of both legitimate and illegitimate opportunity structures to which youths in the community were differentially exposed. To maximize the long-term impact of antidelinquency programs, it was therefore important to modify the opportunity structures as well as the delinquent subcultures they spawned.

Alfred Kahn (1967) acclaimed the MFY effort because it resulted in the development of "indigenous social organizations" and was more "attuned to complex urban political processes" (p. 495). The program sought to reduce delinquency by orienting the youths toward social change; it emphasized education, work, and social organization, including the use of social casework. MFY sought to convince youths that there were viable, law-abiding ways to participate in community life.

Mobilization for Youth included thirty separate "action" programs in the four major areas of work, education, community organization, and group service. As previously mentioned, one of the underlying themes of MFY was that urban lower-class adolescents must be given genuine opportunities to act in nondelinquent ways to prevent them from participating in delinquent acts.

An important aspect of the program was related to job training and placement. An Urban Youth Service Corps was developed that hired several hundred unemployed neighborhood youths to work in a variety of activities, including conservation. The Youth Service Corps focused on fostering the types of attitudes and behaviors (e.g., following orders, reporting to work on time) necessary to succeed in the world of work and on strengthening the participants' job skills. A Youth Jobs Center was created to locate permanent jobs for those who successfully completed the training program.

Many educational programs were initiated, such as the "Homework Helper" program, in which bright, low-income high school students were hired to tutor children in elementary school. By August 1964, over 1,000 Lower East Side children had been taught to read. MFY also established a laboratory school in which effective ways to teach lower-class children were demonstrated.

In the area of community involvement, much effort was devoted to strengthening an already established organization, the Lower East Side Neighborhood Association. MFY staff also sought to develop social organizations among neighborhood residents who had not been affiliated with any community group. "Problem" families living in the target area received social services from neighborhood service centers, which were developed in four locations.

The group service aspect of the project included services for delinquent youths who had joined a gang, as well as a delinquency prevention program aimed at children. For youths eight to twelve years of age MFY developed a character-building organization similar to the Boy Scouts and Girl Scouts. This organization, known as the Adventure Corps, was designed to reach delinquency-prone youths. It provided exciting recreational and educational activities for young people as an alternative to gang membership. Squad leaders and their assistants were neighborhood residents who were paid a stipend (Task Force on Juvenile Delinquency, 1967).

Cloward and Ohlin's writings had a significant impact on delinquency prevention policy. They urged that those interested in alleviating delinquency take action to reorganize slum neighborhoods:

> The major effort of those who wish to eliminate delinquency should be directed to the reorganization of slum communities. Slum neighborhoods appear . . . to be undergoing progressive disintegration. The old structures, which provided social control and avenues of social ascent, are breaking down. Legitimate but functional substitutes for these traditional structures must be developed if we are to stem the trend toward violence and retreatism among adolescents in urban slums. (1960: 211)

In the early 1960s this approach to delinquency prevention became the major strategy for the new federal delinquency initiatives endorsed by the President's Committee on Juvenile Delinquency and Youth Crime (Knapp, 1971; Maris & Rein, 1967; Moynihan, 1970; and Schlesinger, 1977). The work of President Kennedy's committees led to the funding of sixteen urban planning grants and five major delinquency prevention projects following the model developed by New York City's Mobilization for Youth project. It became the prototype project for many of the federally funded "war on poverty" programs developed during the 1960s.

YOUTH SERVICE BUREAUS

The modern-day version of a coordinating council is a youth service bureau (YSB). Developed to provide and coordinate programs and services for both delinquent and nondelinquent youths, these youth service bureaus have five basic goals:

1. Divert juveniles from the juvenile justice system.
2. Fill gaps in service by advocating for and developing services for youths and their families.

3. Provide case coordination and program coordinating.

4. Provide modification of systems of youth services.

5. Involve youth in the decision-making process.

In 1967, President Johnson's Commission on Law Enforcement and Administration of Justice provided a strong impetus for the establishment of youth service bureaus. Its major recommendation for preventing delinquency called for the development of such bureaus throughout the nation. It envisioned them as model coordinating units for the delivery of communitywide services to youth.

The commission urged communities to set up central coordinating units to serve status offenders, delinquents, and nondelinquents referred by the police, juvenile courts, probation departments, and schools. Many of these bureaus were federally funded through the Law Enforcement Assistance Administration (LEAA), the Youth Development and Delinquency Prevention Administration (YDDPA) of the Department of Health, Education, and Welfare, and the Model Cities Program of the Department of Housing and Urban Development (HUD). Only a small percentage of referrals came from the police; youths generally learned about the program from a parent, friend, or schoolmate.

The commission's recommendation appeared in its 1967 report entitled *The Challenge of Crime in a Free Society.* The report described the concept and focus for youth service bureaus:

> Communities should establish neighborhood youth service agencies—Youth Service Bureaus—located if possible in comprehensive neighborhood community centers and receiving juveniles (delinquent and nondelinquent) referred by the police, the juvenile court, parents, schools and other sources. These agencies would act as central coordinators of all community services for young people and would also provide services lacking in the community or neighborhood, especially ones designed for less seriously delinquent juveniles. (President's Commission, 1967; 83)

However, the commission did not identify the specific process for establishing and operating these bureaus. In recognition of the need to prepare program development guidelines, the Youth Development and Delinquency Prevention Administration (YDDPA) held a series of meetings which resulted in the 1971 publication of a booklet, *Youth Service Bureaus and Delinquency Prevention,* containing suggestions and guidelines for implementing and coordinating services in a youth service bureau.

The National Council on Crime and Delinquency also developed operational guidelines for youth service bureaus. It began by defining the YSB as a:

noncoercive independent public agency established to divert children and youth from the justice system by: 1) Mobilizing community resources to solve youth problems; 2) strengthening existing youth resources and developing new ones; and 3) promoting positive programs to remedy delinquency-breeding conditions. (Norman, 1972; 8)

By 1971, four years after the strong endorsement of the President's Commission on Law Enforcement and Administration of Justice and with the aid of federal funding, 262 youth service bureaus had been developed (Youth Development and Delinquency Prevention Administration, 1973).

Studies on YSBs were conducted by such researchers as John Martin, William Underwood, and Elaine Duxbury. In 1972, Martin and his associates conducted a national study of 195 youth service bureaus (Youth Development and Delinquency Prevention Administration, 1973). Their findings provide an overview of the organizational structure and function of youth service bureaus in the early 1970s.

The staffing patterns of these bureaus ranged from one full-time person assisted by a few volunteers to large staffs of ten or more employees. Typically, programs were staffed by five to six full-time workers and anywhere from one to fifty volunteers. The majority of program directors (63.8 percent) indicated that diverting youths from the juvenile justice system was their primary objective. Other directors described their primary activities as delinquency prevention or youth development projects such as recreation programs, tutoring, group counseling, drug treatment, family counseling, and/or job referral.

Two thirds of the 195 programs were located in urban or Model City neighborhoods. These areas were primarily lower socioeconomic class and were characterized by high rates of unemployment and crime and limited resources for youth.

The target population was youths in the fourteen to seventeen age group. The survey found that program participants were on average fifteen and one-half years old. Approximately 60 percent of the participants were male and the average project served 350 youths each year. Referrals came from several sources, including the police, school, parents, and self-referrals, but no single source appeared to be dominant.

Information on funding was provided by 188 of the programs. Eight-two percent of the programs indicated that their primary funding source was a federal grant. The most frequent source of federal funding was the LEAA, through the state criminal justice planning agencies; of the 155 programs receiving federal funds, 135 had an LEAA grant. The other federal agencies that provided funding were YDDPA, Model Cities, and the U.S. Department of Labor (Youth Development, 1973). The average annual budget of youth service bureaus ranged from $50,000 to $75,000. In order to obtain a federal grant, a program was required to have in-kind matching funds, which usually came from either a local or state agency (e.g., the state's Division of Youth Services).

In Underwood's (1972) nationwide study of 400 cases from twenty-eight youth service bureaus, he found that approximately 13 percent of the referrals were from law enforcement agencies, while the most frequent referral source (30 percent) was self-referrals, friends, or family. The second most frequent referral source was the schools (21 percent). Duxbury's (1972) study of California's nine pilot community youth service bureaus indicated a slightly higher percentage of referrals from law enforcement (21 percent). In that study only 13 percent of the referrals came from the schools, while an additional 11 percent came from county probation agencies. Duxbury indicated that 47.7 percent or 2,069 new cases, were individuals referred by themselves or by parents, friends, or neighbors. These studies reveal that youth service bureaus were underutilized by criminal justice agencies and the largest proportion of youth voluntarily sought the assistance of YSBs.

In contrast to the above-mentioned pattern of referrals, a number of communities established programs in neighborhood storefronts or in offices close to the local police department. In addition, in several communities police juvenile officers were assigned full-time (on a rotating basis) to counsel youths and their families at local youth service bureaus. Such efforts were matched by YSB social workers who participated in police ride-along programs. Predictably, youth service bureaus that made an effort to work closely with the police received a large percentage of their referrals from the police department.

The success of YSBs was often directly related to their location and accessibility to the population they were intended to serve. For example, many bureaus remained open at night and on weekends to serve juveniles in their community. Youth service bureaus located near a high school, near the police department, or in a downtown area frequented by youths were more likely to have a greater number of referrals.

By the late 1970s, LEAA had shifted its priority to funding law enforcement and rehabilitation programs rather than prevention projects. LEAA had intended its YSB grants to be limited to seed money (usually for two to three years), with the understanding that county or city government or private agencies would gradually assume full fiscal responsibility. In some cases, when the federal grant ended, the local agency did provide full funding for the youth service bureau under its auspices. However, by 1982, as a direct result of the demise of LEAA and other cutbacks in federal funding for juvenile justice, a number of these model youth service bureaus (those that were not supported by full funding from another source) were phased out due to a lack of funds.

CONCLUSION

Juvenile delinquency is a social problem that requires comprehensive care and service delivery to children and youths before they become serious and chronic offenders. Integral to the development of comprehensive services is the expansion of neighborhood-based delinquency prevention programs.

Delinquency prevention strategies should involve neighborhood residents and professional social workers (as was evident in the past). Prevention efforts should also provide individual and family counseling, job training and placement, substance abuse treatment, and school remediation programs. (See Chapter 9 for an examination of current community youth diversion programs, which focus on providing academic education, social skills, recreational activities, and family counseling to delinquent and predelinquent juveniles.)

DISCUSSION QUESTIONS

1. Discuss the basic assumptions and objectives of the Chicago Area Project.
2. List the three approaches used by the staff of Boston's Midcity Project that differed from earlier delinquency control and prevention programs.
3. New York's Mobilization for Youth (MFY) demonstration project was based on Cloward and Ohlin's opportunity theory. Discuss the postulates of opportunity theory.
4. List and describe the purpose of three specific MFY action programs.
5. List the five basic goals of youth service bureaus.
6. What three federal agencies provided major funding to local youth service bureaus?
7. The success of youth service bureaus was often attributed to their location and accessibility to the population they were intended to serve. Discuss two examples of ways in which the location and operating hours of a youth service bureau improved participation by local youths.

REFERENCES

Beam, S. (1937). Community coordination for prevention of delinquency. *National Probation Association Yearbook*, 89–90, 113–115.

Beam, S. (1937). Community organization. *National Probation Association Yearbook*.

Cloward, R., & Ohlin, L. (1960). *Delinquency and opportunity: A theory of delinquent gangs.* New York: Free Press.

Duxbury, E. (1972). *Youth service bureaus in California* (Progress Report No. 3, State of California). Sacramento, CA: Department of the Youth Authority.

Gibbons, D. C., & Krohn, M. D. (1986). *Delinquent behavior* (4th ed.). Englewood Cliffs, NJ: Prentice-Hall.

Grosser, C. R. (1968). *Helping youth: A study of six community organization programs.* Washington, DC: U.S. Department of Health, Education, and Welfare, Office of Juvenile Delinquency and Youth Development.

Kahn. A. J. (1967). From delinquency treatment to community development. In P. F. Lazarsfeld, W. H. Sewell, & H. L. Wilensky (Eds.), *The uses of sociology* (pp. 477–505). New York: Basic Books.

Knapp, J. (1971). *Scouting the war on poverty: Social reform politics in the Kennedy administration.* Lexington, MA: Lexington Books.

Kobrin, S. (1959, March). The Chicago Area Project—A 25-year assessment, *Annals of the American Academy of Political and Social Science, 322,* 20–29.

Lukas, E. J. (1945). Can crime preventive efforts by police be helpful? *Proceedings of the National Conference of Juvenile Agencies, 41*(4).

Maris, P., & Rein, M. (1967). *Dilemmas of social reform: Poverty and community action in the United States.* New York: Atherton Press.

McKay, H.D. (1967). A note on trends in rates of delinquency in certain areas in Chicago. In *Task force report: Juvenile delinquency and youth crime* (pp. 114–118). The President's Commission on Law Enforcement and Administration of Justice.

McMillen, W. (1947). Community organization in social work. *Social Work Yearbook,* 110–117.

Miller, W. B. (1962, Fall). The impact of a "total-community" delinquency control project. *Social Problems, 10,* 168–191.

Miller, W. B., Baum, R. C., & McNeil, R. (1968). Delinquency prevention and organizational relations. In Stanton Wheeler (Ed.), *Controlling delinquents (pp. 61–100).* New York: John Wiley & Sons.

Moynihan, D. P. (1970). *Maximum feasibile misunderstanding: Community action in the war on poverty.* New York: Free Press.

Norman, S. (1972). *The youth service bureau: A key to delinquency prevention.* Paramus, N.J.: National Council on Crime and Delinquency.

President's Commission on Law Enforcement and Administration of Justice. (1967). *The challenge of crime in a free society.* Washington, DC: U.S. Government Printing Office.

Pursuit, D. G., Gerletti, J. D., Brown, R. M., & Ward, S. M. (1972). *Police programs for preventing crime and delinquency.* Springfield, IL: Charles C. Thomas.

Report of the Advisory Committee. (1936). *National Probation Association Yearbook.*

Ryan, W. (1971). *Blaming the victim.* New York: Random House.

Schlesinger, A. M., Jr. (1977). *A thousand days.* Boston: Houghton Mifflin.

Schlossman, S. (1977). *Love and the American delinquent: The theory and practice of "progressive" juvenile justice, 1825–1920.* Chicago: University of Chicago Press.

Schlossman, S. & Sedlak, M. (1983). The Chicago Area Project revisited. *Crime and delinquency, 29,* 398–462.

Scudder, K. J. (1946). The coordinating council at work. *National Probation Association Yearbook,* 67–77.

Sexton, P. C. (1961). *Education and income.* New York: Viking Press.

Shaw, C. R. & McKay, H. D. (1972). *Juvenile delinquency and urban areas* (rev. ed.). Chicago: University of Chicago Press.

Shaw. C. R. (1931). *The natural history of a delinquent career.* Chicago: University of Chicago Press.

Shaw, C. R. (1930). *The jack-roller.* Chicago: University of Chicago Press.

Sorrentino, A. (1983). Community programs. In Sanford H. Kadish (Ed.). *Encyclopedia of crime and justice* (pp. 358–361). New York: Free Press.

Task Force on Juvenile Delinquency of the President's Commission on Law Enforcement and Administration of Justice. (1967). *Task force report: Juvenile delinquency and youth crime.* Washington, DC: U.S. Government Printing Office.

Underwood, W. (1972). *The national study of youth service bureaus.* Washington, DC: U.S. Department of Health, Education, and Welfare, Youth Development and Delinquency Prevention Administration.

U.S. House of Representatives, Committee on Education and Labor. (1974). *Juvenile justice and delinquency prevention and runaway youth.* Hearings before the Subcommittee on Equal Opportunities of the Committee on Education and Labor, 93rd Congress. Washington, DC: U.S. Government Printing Office.

Voss, H. L. & Peterson, D. (Eds.). (1971). *Ecology crime and delinquency.* New York: Appleton-Century-Crofts.

Witmer, H. L. & Tufts, E. (1954). *The effectiveness of delinquency prevention programs.* (U.S. Children's Bureau Publication No. 350). Washington, DC: U.S. Department of Health, Education, and Welfare.

Youth Development and Delinquency Prevention Administration. (1973). *The challenge of youth service bureaus* (Publication No. SRS 73–26024). Washington, DC: U.S. Government Printing Office.

Chapter Four

The Emergence of the Juvenile Court and Probation Services

Albert R. Roberts

CAROLE ROBERTS '98

ABSTRACT

Chapter 4, which highlights some of the developmental trends, problems, and accomplishments of the juvenile court, begins with a discussion of the impetus for the first juvenile court in America, established in 1899 in Cook County, Illinois. The chapter proceeds with a summary of the early surveys on the effectiveness of the juvenile court and documentation of several critical problems, such as lack of suitable facilities for placement of juveniles, lack of financial support for hiring and in-service training of caseworkers and probation officers, the heavy burden and numerous cases placed on juvenile court judges, and the lack of a uniform policy among juvenile courts. Also discussed are the use of volunteers to the court, the child guidance clinics' connection with the courts, and due process safeguards to protect the rights of juveniles. The chapter concludes by citing the progress made in the past decade toward more equitable and humane treatment of juveniles.

ESTABLISHMENT OF THE JUVENILE COURT

According to H. Warren Dunham, a precedent for the establishment of the juvenile court system in the United States came from the English courts, specifically from the 1772 case of *Eyre v. Shaftsbury.* From this case evolved the principle of *parens patriae,* enabling the court to act in lieu of the parents who were found to be unwilling or unable to give their child appropriate guidance. This paved the way for the juvenile court in the United States to assume jurisdiction for dependent and neglected children (Dunham, 1958).

There has been some confusion between the terms *parens patriae* and *in loco parentis.* The former refers to the responsibility of government to serve the welfare of the child, not (as the latter might suggest) to replace the parents. According to Schlossman (1983:962), "*parens patriae* had sanctioned the right of the Crown to interrupt or supplant natural family relations whenever a child's welfare was threatened." Although initially it was applied only in cases of property disputes regarding well-to-do juveniles, in later years the doctrine was interpreted more broadly. By the nineteenth century, all of the states had affirmed their right to serve as guardian for children in accordance with the states' "legal inheritance" from England.

The English common-law foundation for the juvenile court is from civil rather than criminal law. Great Britain's common-law doctrine is based on the idea of chancery or equity. "The essential idea of chancery is welfare or balancing of interest. It stands for flexibility, guardianship and protection rather than rigidity and punishment" (Lou, 1927:2). The founders of the first juvenile court in America had intended the juvenile court to be as much a place to educate errant children and negligent parents as an institution that handed down sanctions.

When the term *parens patriae* is used in modern times it generally refers to the state's legal obligation and right to protect the young, the dependent or neglected child, and the incompetent child. However, as stated by Supreme Court Justice Abe Fortas in the Court's decision on the *Gault* case: " . . . its meaning is murky and its historical credentials are of dubious relevance to juvenile delinquency proceedings" (*In re* Gault, 1967).

The doctrine of *parens patriae* was used in order to free the juvenile court judge to accept social and psychological evaluations and provide informal proceedings, thus departing from due process of law. It also justified the court's right to save children who had committed noncriminal offenses, such as disobeying parents, truancy, and associating with immoral and criminal persons.

Historically the state of Massachusetts has been an innovator of various movements to improve the type of treatment juvenile offenders receive. However, it was in New York City in 1825 that the first House of Refuge for children was opened (see Chapter 2). Boston established a similar project a year later. By 1860, sixteen similar institutions had been opened throughout the country. The impetus for building juvenile institutions came from the sound belief that youths who had violated a law should not be confined with adult criminals in prisons. Even though this belief had evolved in the early 1800s, a juvenile court for the purpose of separating and individualizing juveniles' cases was not established until 1899 (Dunham, 1958).

In Massachusetts in 1869, the first definite action was taken on behalf of a juvenile's rights in court. In that year a law was passed requiring the governor to assign a "visiting agent" to work for the best interest of the juvenile who was in trouble with the law. The visiting agent had to be informed before any youth under the age of sixteen could be committed to jail or any other type of institution. The visiting agent was present at the hearing and made recommendations to the judge with regard to the child's welfare (Sullenger, 1936). As of 1870, Massachusetts law required that juvenile offenders under the age of sixteen have their cases heard "separate from the general and ordinary criminal business" (Kamm, Hunt & Fleming, 1968:3). While this concept was a forerunner of the juvenile court, the law did not actually establish a separate juvenile court system.

The first juvenile court law in the United States was enacted by the Illinois state legislature on April 21, 1899.[1] It was a culmination of

---

[1] Not until June 1938 were federal courts given the legal authority to distinguish between juveniles and adults brought before them for violation of federal laws. The

a series of concerted efforts by a number of renowned social work professionals, lawyers and other humanitarians. At the time of the law's enactment, establishment of the juvenile court was seen as a milestone in the developmental process of American justice. Grace Abbott (1938) in her book, *The Child and the State,* described the efforts that paved the way for the first juvenile court:

> Lucy L. Flower, Julia C. Lathrop, and Jane Addams were the moving spirits in formulating the new and basically different conception of the treatment of juvenile delinquents which it represented. They first became interested in the more than 500 children in the Chicago House of Correction, and under their leadership the Chicago Woman's Club induced the Board of Education to establish a "school" for the boys in this institution. But this obviously did not meet the need, and they began a more fundamental attack on the problem. . . . A committee was appointed by the Illinois State Conference of Charities at its meeting in 1898. [They] urged that the conference undertake to get a law drafted. The problem was to find how to make a fundamental change in criminal law and criminal procedure which would be upheld by the courts as constitutional. In co-operation with a committee of the Chicago Bar Association, a bill was finally worked out and agreed upon by the interested groups. (Abbott, Abbott, & Breckinridge, 1938:330–331)

Julia Lathrop had been appointed by Illinois governor John Altgeld to the Board of State Commissioners of Public Charities. In this role she inspected all of the state's county jails and poorhouses; her attention was focused on the treatment of juveniles. She expressed her concern in an 1898 report:

> There are at the present moment in the State of Illinois, especially in the City of Chicago, thousands of children in need of active intervention for their preservation from physical, mental and moral destruction. Such intervention is demanded, not only by sympathetic consideration for their well-being, but also in the name of the commonwealth, for the preservation of the State. If the child is the material out of which men and women are made, the neglected child is the material out of which paupers and criminals are made. (Mennel, 1973:129)

In addition to Julia Lathrop, others helped to arouse public concern over the treatment of juveniles. For example, an encounter was reported between a Chicago police officer and a four-year-old child who was caught stealing cakes. The policeman, finally deciding to let the child go, yelled, "If you git into my hands again I'll cut your ears off close ter yer head, and I'll sew yer mouth up so's yer can't eat no cakes

---

Federal Juvenile Delinquency Act included provisions for hearing cases promptly, privately, and without a jury; detention apart from adult offenders; and greater flexibility in treatment of youths (Teeters & Reinemann, 1939:27).

. . . Now git. Yer little bastard, and ter hell wid you." (Mennel, 1973:129). Apparently such treatment of children was not uncommon in those days.

The law passed by the Illinois legislature (with widespread support from the Chicago Bar Association and philanthropic reformers) gave the juvenile court the power to send delinquent youths to appropriate institutions. But "the preference was . . . to place them on probation either in their own or foster homes." The court was also empowered to appoint as probation officers "one or more persons of good character" (Mennel, 1973:130). Thus, when the juvenile court system first developed, there was more emphasis on community-based treatment of juvenile offenders and less interest in sending youths to institutions.

The major features and components of the juvenile court were as follows:

1. An emphasis on informal procedures at every stage of court intake, adjudication, and disposition.

2. A separate, sanitary detention center where doctors, social workers, and other staff would systematically observe and study the child's personality and motivation. This evaluation would form part of the prehearing investigation.

3. Passage of enabling legislation that would have encouraged judges to fine and sentence adults to jail when they were negligent or had contributed to the delinquency of a minor.

4. Probation, the most important component of the new courts. The primary goal of the juvenile court was the rehabilitation of children and youth in their own homes.

Rothman's (1980) analysis of aggregate data from the 1920s and 1930s indicates that the most frequently pronounced disposition from the juvenile court was probation surveillance.

POSITIVE AND NEGATIVE REACTIONS TO THE JUVENILE COURT

In the early 1900s, widespread support for the new juvenile court system led to the establishment of many other juvenile courts modeled after the original one in Chicago. Progressive reformers, concerned with the treatment of juveniles, regarded the development of juvenile courts as a significant achievement. As stated in the previous section, Grace Abbott (who later served as chief of the U.S. Children's Bureau) and Jane Addams were among the many social work professionals who endorsed the juvenile court system. Addams (1935:137), talking about the climate soon after establishment of the first juvenile court, stated:

There was almost a change in mores when the juvenile court was established. The child was brought before the judge with no one to prosecute him and none to defend him—the judge and all concerned were merely trying to find out what could be done on his behalf. The element of conflict was absolutely eliminated and with it all notions of punishment as such.

Frederic Howe (1913:133) exclaimed that because of the juvenile court, "the budding crop of crime of the next decade will be largely diminished, at great savings to life and character, as well as to the purse of the community."

Judges too were supportive of the establishment of the juvenile courts. The willingness of many judges to utilize the new system can be seen in part from an endorsement made by Judge Edward Lindsey in 1914 after he and Judge Edward F. Waite had investigated the status of delinquent youth. He believed that every child had the right to a fair hearing of the type established by the juvenile court system: "No child should be restrained simply because he has been accused of crime, whether he is guilty or not" (Lindsey, 1914:145).

The broad-based support for the juvenile court in the early 1900s led some reformers to advocate the creation of a family court to treat the adult(s) responsible for the child's behavior. Flexner and Baldwin (1912:vii) urged that such a court could be more effective in reaching the family. They believed that the delinquent youth was just "a factor in the larger and more complicated problem." By 1923, all the states, with the exception of Connecticut and Wyoming,[2] had passed legislation defining a juvenile delinquent and establishing a special court for juveniles.[3] (Dunham, 1958:372).

Not all of the reactions to the juvenile court system were positive. Some, in the minority at first, questioned the thoroughness of the planning that preceded the establishment of the new system. In the opinion of Lemert (1971:5–6):

> The establishment of the first juvenile courts reveals them to have been less a carefully planned innovation than the climax of a nineteenth century reform movement to rescue children from the depravity and immorality of lower class urban environments. The envisioned ideal that delinquent children would thereafter be defined and treated as "neglected" proved false; in practice, the reverse often was true, that is,

---

[2]By the early 1940s Connecticut and Wyoming had gone along with the trend and set up special courts for juveniles.

[3]The age limit of juvenile court jurisdiction varies from state to state. As of 1939, the laws of nearly one half of the states in the Federal Juvenile Delinquency Act set an age limit of eighteen years or higher. The trend at the end of the 1930s was in the direction of raising the age limit rather than lowering it. (Teeters & Reinemann, 1939:29).

dependent and neglected children fell under the pall of delinquency and in many cases were subjected to the same kinds of sanctions.

A case study of the Milwaukee County juvenile court in the early 1900s reveals that while this court did attain the structure and components recommended by the founders, it failed to meet the progressive practices that the founders had expected. In 1901, the court opened with a makeshift detention center (acquired from a local charitable society), a contributory delinquency law, and a probation staff; unfortunately probation officers were assigned to an average of 200 cases at a time when 60 cases was viewed as a high caseload. Within a few years a new detention facility was built to provide a safe place for the confinement of juveniles, but the staff rarely provided the judge with individualized reports on the juvenile prior to adjudication. Finally, the contributory delinquency statute was rarely used against abusive parents or other community members who coaxed children into criminal conduct. The judge and probation officers in Milwaukee relied mainly on fear, threats, and short-term detention to coerce children into cooperating (Schlossman, 1977). In contrast to the situation in Milwaukee, other jurisdictions, such as Judge Lindsey's court in Denver, were known for being compassionate and having a highly efficient probation service.

During the early years of the twentieth century, at approximately the same time that juvenile courts were emerging throughout the country, the number of delinquent acts rose. Dunham (1958) attributes this to a combination of rapid industrialization and an influx of immigrants that led to rapid, unprecedented growth of the cities. European immigrants faced their own problems in trying to overcome cultural and language barriers and to support their families. Dunham suggested that the children of these families were caught in the upheaval of this new way of life, divided between European peasant values and the different values inherent in the American way of life, and responded to the confusion by committing acts which were labeled "delinquent." Many of their parents were unable to comprehend or cope with these situations. This situation fostered the need for the emerging family court to take on additional functions—for example, aiding immigrant families in the adjustment process, serving to acquaint families with American customs and values, and protecting the child from serious problems in the home (p.373).

One of the first surveys of the effectiveness of the juvenile court system was completed in 1927. Examining Pennsylvania's juvenile court system for the U.S. Children's Bureau, Judge Charles W. Hoffman was appalled to discover many youths languishing in detention homes and county jails despite state laws that specifically forbade imprisonment of juveniles. The judge raised two significant questions: "What has the advanced legal status accomplished? Is it not clear that the juvenile courts are not functioning?" (U.S. Children's Bureau, 1922:146). Hoffman's survey was the forerunner of numerous statements about the efficacy of the juvenile courts. Feelings were strong both for and against the competence and fairness of this system for treating the ever-rising numbers of juvenile offenders.

Over the years the factors that adversely affected the functioning of the juvenile courts have been examined. Criticism has centered on the lack of suitable facilities for placement of juveniles, the heavy burden placed on juvenile court judges, the lack of a uniform policy among juvenile courts, and the lack of financial support for hiring and in-service training of caseworkers and probation personnel.

Writing in the 1940s, Kahn (1953) pointed to the "perplexing and urgent problem" of finding suitable long-term placement for juvenile offenders. He was concerned because the juvenile courts faced the dilemma of effecting a suitable placement for adjudicated delinquents without having the direct power to remedy the severe problems that existed in the juvenile institutions. Kahn's study reviewed the case records of 152 juveniles on probation. The records showed that attempts at placement had been made for forty-five children. From the twenty-one institutions and agencies able to refuse admission to certain applicants, there had been forty-seven rejections and thirty-seven acceptances. Several of the forty-five children had been rejected by as many as four agencies and were finally placed on probation or sent to the New York State Training School, which could not refuse admission to youths referred by the court.

Kahn (1953) emphasized that he had reviewed only a small percentage of the case records. When the figures he obtained were multiplied ten or twenty times in the course of a year, the magnitude of the problem became obvious. He described the situation that developed when children had to wait for weeks or months until an appropriate placement could be arranged:

> Rejections often mean a series of court rehearings until an effective plan is made—or until the judge decides to try probation or the New York Training School instead. In the interim, delinquent children wait for weeks and neglected children for weeks, months, or even years in so-called "temporary" facilities, unable to settle down to a routine which permits a feeling of relative stability or to have the advantages of much needed services and programs prescribed for them. (p. 253)

Some of the major reasons for the difficulty in securing appropriate placements were, according to Kahn (1953), the shortage of facilities, restricted intake policies, and the inability of some facilities to assure that the child would receive casework help, psychotherapy, proper grade placement in the residential school, and remedial reading. He criticized the procedure in which it became the probation officer's responsibility to "shop" for an appropriate placement and try to convince the facility to take the juvenile. Probation officers set out to find placements without any coordination or effective communication with other probation officers. This resulted in the more experienced workers, who had developed personal contacts with agencies, making some successful placements while other workers were less successful in that endeavor.

Judge Paul Alexander, who served as president of the National Conference of Juvenile Agencies, attested to the continual pressure placed on juvenile court judges. He was deeply concerned that the unfair burden placed on the judges could have an adverse effect on equitable treatment of delinquent youths. Quoting Alexander's report in the 1944 *National Probation Association Yearbook:*

> I can bear personal witness to the fact that in almost every city of the country the juvenile court judge is the most overworked and harassed of all judges. . . . In only seventeen states can he look forward to a modest pension upon his retirement. . . . His court as well as his children are more often than not housed in dark, dingy, dilapidated, dirty and inadequate quarters. (p.38)

Alexander continued by talking about the immense pressure that juvenile court judges were under. "When he can give one hour to three cases, and ought to give three hours to one case somebody is going to suffer." He estimated the hours a juvenile court judge works were about double the hours worked by judges in other courts.

The September 1949 issue of *Federal Probation* was published in commemoration of the fiftieth anniversary of the founding of the first juvenile court. In that issue, Carr compiled a summary of problems facing a considerable number of juvenile courts. Recordkeeping, he felt, was inadequate. He criticized "sketchy documents called case records, compiled . . . without benefit of any trained caseworkers and sometimes not even compiled" (p. 29). Carr was especially concerned about the lack of qualified professional caseworkers and probation officers to provide needed services to juveniles in trouble.[4] The majority

---

[4]A 1963 study showed that a particular problem with the juvenile court system was the scarcity of qualified judges. Only 71 percent of the juvenile court judges studied had law degrees. Of those judges who were full-time appointees, 72 percent spent a quarter or less of their time on juvenile matters. Thus a juvenile delinquent's future sometimes rested on the decision of a judge who may not have had an appropriate legal background or devoted much time to the case (McCune & Skoler, 1965).

of juvenile courts did not have probation officers. Probation in those cases was merely a matter of "signing the book," assigning youths to their parents for probation (frequently the parents had caused the child's problems in the first place), or using untrained amateurs. Rural areas were particularly devoid of such services because they could not afford to hire professional social workers or probation officers, as could some of the big city juvenile court systems. In addition, the rural areas did not have enough work for full-time personnel (Carr, 1949:29–30).

Carr's article paid particular attention to the unique problems faced by courts in rural areas. He recognized that individual rural counties did not have the need or the budget to maintain fully staffed juvenile courts; the number of juvenile offenders appearing before a rural court was substantially less than the number appearing before city courts. However, when a juvenile from a rural area was brought into court, Carr believed that the juvenile was entitled to the same (though still too limited) rehabilitative services that would be available to a city youth. He suggested that rather than every rural county having its own juvenile court system, a few counties combine their resources to provide enough work for one well-equipped, technically competent court to replace the ten or twelve "imitations" then in existence. Carr (1949:30–31) described the situation as he saw it: "[The rural counties] do not produce enough delinquents to justify fully equipped modern courts; they could not possibly pay for such courts if the business were there; and yet one case mishandled by their well-meaning but untrained officials may cost their states many times the cost of efficient service."

Many of the problem areas delineated by Alexander (1944), Carr (1949), and Kahn (1953) in the 1940s were still apparent in the late 1950s. The organization and policies of juvenile courts continued to vary markedly throughout the United States. In general the large urban areas had a court devoted exclusively to hearing juvenile cases, while in the rural areas the probate judge served also as the juvenile court judge. According to Dunham (1958) the major differences in juvenile court policies in the late 1950s were: (1) the juvenile court judge was elected in some jurisdictions and appointed in others; (2) some judges took a human, personal interest in the youths, while others treated juveniles strictly within the framework of the law; (3) some juvenile courts had a staff of professional social workers, probation officers, and psychologists, while other courts had only minimal, untrained staff.

Dunham was expressly concerned that there were still a number of juvenile courts across the country that were not oriented toward social work policy. Nevertheless, he recognized that many juvenile courts did utilize social work principles, thereby upgrading the level of service available to juveniles. Dunham (1955:376) believed that five key factors had served to influence the progressive, social work–oriented juvenile court systems:

1) The aggressive social work orientation of the United States Children's Bureau; 2) the broadening jurisdiction of the juvenile court to include not only neglected and dependent children, but all matters of a legal nature involving children; 3) the gradual professionalization of social work; 4) various court decisions involving delinquency; 5) the growing prospects of treatment through the increased acceptance by social workers of psychoanalysis for getting at the roots of conflict which supposedly produce delinquency.

EARLY DEVELOPMENT OF JUVENILE PROBATION

Volunteers in Probation

The juvenile probation system originated as a volunteer rather than a paid program. John Augustus (1852), a successful bootmaker in Boston, is credited with being the first volunteer and the "father of probation." His voluntary probation work began in 1841, and during the next eighteen years, he dedicated himself to helping hundreds of juvenile and adult defendants. He worked primarily with delinquent children. Augustus completed extensive background investigations on most of his potential clients and kept a log of all the cases he worked with, showing their names, dates, addresses, case numbers, amount of bail, fines, and costs.

Lindner and Savarese (1984) have documented the importance of volunteers in the evolution of probation in Boston, Chicago, and New York City: "Volunteers continued to be important . . . in the evolution of probation with several of them playing very influential roles in having probation legislation enacted in their respective jurisdictions" (p. 7). For example, in Chicago, Julia Lathrop, Alzina Stevens, and Lucy Flower provided direct services to clients on probation and raised money to pay the salaries of probation officers. Dr. Samuel Barrows, David Willard, and Rebecca Salome Foster dedicated themselves to promoting passage of the first probation law in New York.

Emergence of the Professional Probation Worker

Evaluations of the quality of volunteers' work in the early 1900s uncovered several problems, including "inadequate training and supervision of volunteers" and an irregular work schedule (Lindner and Savarese, 1984:9). In 1905, the New York State Probation Commission criticized the work of volunteer probation officers throughout the state.

Even Maurice Parmelee (1918:403), himself a volunteer probation officer who later became a prominent criminologist, registered skepticism about the effectiveness of volunteers: "Much of this probation work has been done by volunteer workers who have been well-meaning, but many of whom, on account of lack of special training and experience and a sentimental point of view have not been very efficient."

One of the harshest critics of probation volunteers was Bernard Flexner (1918:610), who cautioned chief probation officers and other professionals against the "indiscriminate use of volunteers" and recommended that they be limited to working with only one to two probationers at any given time.

Only a few years after the passage of probation legislation (made possible by the noble and strenuous efforts of volunteers), most volunteer probation workers had been replaced by paid professionals. Lindner and Savarese (1984:10) summarized the volunteers' fate in the 1910s and 1920s: "With increased hiring of salaried probation officers, the fate of the volunteer in probation became apparent. Although they would continue to serve in smaller cities and rural areas for a considerable period of time, their overall influence in probation would rapidly diminish."

The use of juvenile probation had been sporadic until a few years after the juvenile court reform movement began. It then spread rapidly to all the states that had passed juvenile court legislation. By 1927, almost all the states had enacted juvenile court laws, and a juvenile probation system had been developed in every state except Wyoming. Probation was to be the alternative disposition that allowed judges to permit juveniles to be treated in their homes. Probation, an arm of the juvenile court, would supervise children in their own communities rather than by placing them in institutions.

According to Kahn (1953) volunteer services working with the juvenile court system (beginning in the 1940s) performed a valuable service to juveniles in trouble. In New York, two of the best-known organizations providing volunteer services were the Jewish Board of Guardians and the Catholic Charities (Guidance Institute of Catholic Charities, Youth Counseling Service). These agencies maintained a liaison at the juvenile court to coordinate referrals to appropriate treatment services. Protestant Big Brother and Big Sister movements also worked with the courts in an attempt to arrange a contact for a youth to have a Big Brother or Big Sister. However, Kahn stated that as of the early 1940s these services were generally not available where the need was the greatest—for Protestant Negro youths.

Representatives of the Jewish Board of Guardians and the Catholic Charities, in times of turnover among court personnel, contributed significantly to the orientation of new judges and probation officers. In Kahn's (1953:243) words: "All the voluntary agencies have been excellent friends of the court, interpreting court needs when it has been necessary to turn to authorities or to the public at large in connection with court problems."

By the mid-1960s, probation departments had been established in all fifty states and in hundreds of counties throughout the nation. However, there was a lack of uniformity in the way probation services were delivered in different states and counties. More specifically, a 1967 study by the National Council on Crime and Delinquency (NCCD) for the President's Commission on Law Enforcement and the Administration of Justice found that:

1. In thirty-one states all counties have probation staff service.
2. A total of 2,306 counties (74 percent of all counties in the United States) theoretically have such a service. In some of these, however, the service is only token.
3. In sixteen states that do not have probation staff coverage in every county, at least some services are available to courts in some counties from persons other than paid, full-time probation officers.
4. In 165 counties in four states, no juvenile probation services at all are available.

Generally, the country's most populous jurisdictions are included among the counties served by probation staff. However, in the smaller counties service may be expected to be spotty (p. 134).

For an examination of the organizational structure and functions of probation departments today, see Chapter 7.

CHILD GUIDANCE CLINICS AND THE JUVENILE COURTS

At the 1941 National Probation Association Conference, Homer expressed his concern about provision of treatment for juvenile delinquents. He became a strong advocate for a close working relationship between the juvenile courts and child guidance clinics. The first such connection had been established back in 1909 by Dr. William Healy, a psychiatrist. Healy's clinic worked in conjunction with the Juvenile Court of Cook County, Illinois, which had become the first juvenile court in the country only a decade earlier. Child guidance clinics received significant impetus for further growth in 1922, when the Commonwealth Fund undertook to sponsor eight demonstration clinics in various parts of the country. St. Louis was selected as the first site (Stevenson, 1934). By the 1930s and 1940s large numbers of psychiatric social workers had been hired to work in teams with psychiatrists to treat emotionally disturbed children, predelinquents, and delinquents.

Homer's complaint in 1941 was that working relationships between child guidance clinics and juvenile courts were not widespread; in too many areas such a relationship still needed to be formed. He urged prompt attention to the matter, believing that the future of both juvenile courts and child guidance clinics should consist of a close working relationship between the two.

> Any juvenile court which does not use or does not have available child-guidance services most certainly fails to make use of modern techniques for the diagnosis and treatment of behavior disorders in children. The clinic which is uninterested in delinquent children arbitrarily deprives a large proportion of children of a service which it is peculiarly suited to provide. Furthermore, it is undoubtedly true that small communities unable at present to finance a clinic, could do so with additional support from tax funds which the participation of court agencies would ensure. (Homer, 1949:180)

Although the clinics were usually directed by a psychiatrist, social workers formed the core of clinic operations as they worked with children, families, and school and court personnel. Levine and Levine (1970) found that social workers eventually came to dominate these diagnostic, treatment, and delinquency prevention clinics, if not in status then certainly in numbers and in their significant influence on practice with children exhibiting behavioral disorders. By the late 1950s, the number of child guidance clinics had grown to over 600, most of them located in large cities (Roberts & Kurtz, 1987; Robison, 1960).

PROBATION AND THE JUVENILE COURTS

The term *probation,* as defined by Shireman (1971;191) is "a legal status created by order of the sentencing court as an alternative to incarceration." According to Sullenger (1936), the term *probation* is derived from *probare,* meaning to prove; that is, it allows the juvenile offender the opportunity to prove himself.

In recent years probation for juveniles has been thought of in terms of professional probation officers providing juvenile offenders with supportive services and referrals that, depending upon the youth's individual needs, might include individual counseling, group counseling, referral to community mental health centers for outpatient treatment or inpatient psychiatric services, appropriate referrals to addiction treatment programs, family counseling, vocational training, assistance in finding employment, enrolling in alternative education programs, or preparing for the high school equivalency examination.

However, the availability of extensive probation services is a relatively recent development.

Massachusetts, in 1878, became the first state to enact legislation providing for probation for juvenile offenders (Teeters & Reinemann, 1950). In the years immediately following passage of this law, the courts did not set up any means of caring for children, initially relying upon existing agencies that volunteered their services. However, the resources provided by these sources were quite limited, necessitating the development of particular probation services to be linked with the court procedure.

Probation practices were greatly extended in the wake of the juvenile court movement twenty years later, but specific practices varied from one jurisdiction to another. By 1902, Rhode Island, Indiana, Minnesota, and New Jersey had followed Massachusetts' lead by passing legislation creating the position of paid state probation officers (Mennel, 1973). In the federal judiciary system it was not until 1925 that Congress authorized probation and not until 1930 that the federal courts made extensive use of probation as an alternative to incarceration (Teeters & Reinemann, 1950).

Considerable problems with probation practices developed during the early twentieth century. Because services provided by probation officers after adjudication can make the difference between whether or not a juvenile will participate in criminal activity in the future, it is appalling to realize the casual attitude and lack of professional standards that characterized probation practices for many years.

According to Mennel (1973:140), the rights of juveniles were not being fully supported because probation officers, "whatever their sympathies for delinquent children, considered themselves servants of the judge of the juvenile court, not defenders of the rights of children." Because the early probation officers did not receive professional training, a multiplicity of problems developed. Most juvenile courts utilized volunteer probation officers, which resulted in representatives from Protestant and Catholic child-saving societies taking on the responsibility of serving as probation officers. Mennel believed that the services these agencies provided should have been in addition to, rather than instead of, trained probation services.

In courts that did have probation officers, concerns were raised because of what Mennel (1973:142) termed an "authoritarian attitude" on the part of the probation personnel. Some workers were said to have exhibited threats in an effort to get the youth to straighten out. These actions probably occurred with some frequency because the workers had not received appropriate training for their jobs. The requirements for becoming a juvenile probation officer, entrusted with such heavy responsibility, were unbelievably lax, and they varied from state to state. Until 1913, in New York State (one of the more "progressive" of the states), the ranks of probation officers were made up of "kindly expolicemen or retired subway guards with political pull." Not until 1928 did the State issue the requirement that probation officers have a minimum of a high school diploma (Robison, 1960:285–286).

In the 1930s, the U.S. Children's Bureau (Sullenger, 1936:255), recognizing the need for professional standards for probation officers, devised educational and professional standards for minimal qualification as a probation officer working with juveniles:

1. Graduation from college or its equivalent, or from a school of social work.
2. At least one year of experience in casework under supervision.
3. A salary comparable to those paid to workers in other fields of social service.

The bureau also suggested policies for the handling of juveniles:

1. A child should only be required to report to the probation officer at regular intervals if it seemed clearly to be in the best interest of the juvenile. In any case, such reporting should never be regarded as a substitute for more constructive methods of casework.
2. Reconstructive work with the family should be carried out whenever necessary, either by the probation officer or in cooperation with other social agencies.

As with any other type of national guideline that is not enforceable, these standards and policies were adhered to in some jurisdictions and not in others, depending upon state and local civil service requirements.

In New York State between 1936 and 1948, children's court probation was not part of a civil service program. During those years, because there were no civil service job classifications for these workers, there was no job security, and salary increments were infrequent and inadequate. This resulted in a high turnover rate, with the most qualified workers leaving the system to seek jobs with more security elsewhere, and unqualified or partially qualified workers remaining in their jobs. Not until 1948 did New York State make requirements in line with the standards the U.S. Children's Bureau had set forth more than a decade earlier: a degree from an accredited four-year college plus thirty credits in social casework or allied courses, in addition to a minimum of one year of full-time paid experience in a child welfare or family service agency (Kahn, 1953:196–197).

Even as New York State was establishing more stringent requirements for becoming a juvenile probation officer, many counties still had no form of probation whatsoever. Teeters and Reinemann (1950) reported on a 1947 study conducted by the National Probation and Parole Association, which revealed that out of a total of 3,071 counties, 1,610 did not have probation services for juveniles. The reasons offered by Teeters and Reinemann (p. 393) were uninformed public, "penny-pinching" fiscal administrators, and judges who lacked social vision.

JUVENILE COURT POLICIES: A SUMMARY

When it was established in Cook County, Illinois, in 1899, the first juvenile court was viewed by the vast majority of social reformers as a milestone in the developmental process of American justice. The purpose and function of the court was to have been rehabilitation rather than punishment.

During the first quarter of the twentieth century, the juvenile court movement was warmly and enthusiastically hailed by both the general public and public officials as a panacea for the misbehavior, troubles, and social ills of children and youth. Whitlatch (1987:2), in the fiftieth anniversary issue of the *Juvenile and Family Court Journal*, summarized the high ideals and overly optimistic promise of the juvenile court legislation:

> It was naively believed that the legislation creating the juvenile court would, of itself, quickly reduce delinquency to an irreducible minimum. . . . Thus, while there was a positive dearth of knowledge, facilities and personnel, there was an over-supply of enthusiasm. The courts were expected to work miracles by judicial pronouncement and without necessary facilities and personnel, repair the damage that resulted from long continued neglect by the home, school and community. Hence, courts were often subject to unjust criticism because they were unable to accomplish the impossible.

It was fervently hoped that through provision of rehabilitation services, the juvenile court system would be successful in stemming the growing tide of juvenile delinquency. However, there have been many problems with this system. From the beginning, juvenile courts have been denied the necessary funds, staff, auxiliary services, and facilities to fulfill their rehabilitative ideal (President's Commission, 1967:23). By the late 1960s and early 1970s prominent criminologists and sociologists were advancing the belief that juvenile court processing may well damage the youth and lead to further delinquency through labeling and the stigma attached to institutional confinement. Since then, major issues affecting juveniles' rights have been argued— issues such as the juvenile being denied due process in court proceedings and the pervasive dearth of treatment resources.

In theory, youthful offenders were supposed to receive comprehensive rehabilitation services intended to replace due process. In actuality, juveniles were sent to institutions where living conditions were as bad as—or worse than—those in adult prisons. Until recently juveniles faced the risk of imprisonment without benefit of legal counsel and with abridged rights of due process. By the late 1960s and early 1970s, in the aftermath of the *Kent* (1966) and *Gault* (1967) decisions, many juveniles did finally receive the benefits of either a private attorney or, if the juvenile's family was indigent, a court-appointed public defender. However, because of unwieldy caseloads and the inexperience of some public defenders, juveniles still did not always receive adequate counsel.

Furthermore, the quality and scope of treatment services provided by this system has never equaled the need level of troubled youthful offenders. Only since the mid-1960s has the Supreme Court begun to address the important due process issues in juvenile justice. In the *Kent* (383 U.S. 541, 1966) and *Gault* (387 U.S. 1, 1967) decisions, the court held that children could not be denied the right to counsel and protection against self-incrimination—rights guaranteed to adults. In the *Winship* (397 U.S. 358, 1970) decision, the Supreme Court extended to juvenile court proceedings the "proof beyond a reasonable doubt" standard for conviction in adult proceedings.

We have come a long way in the past two decades, from the time when it was commonplace for juveniles to be ushered into a dimly lit, dingy, and dilapidated detention cell, with no idea about how long they would be detained. The next morning they would be brought into an old courtroom, where they were not told of their right to counsel, their right to remain silent, or their right to appeal. Although progress has been slow we have seen major achievements, and today the juvenile courts in many jurisdictions are efficient, equitable, and humanistic. Recent developments include continued strengthening of due process safeguards, accelerated case processing and reduced delays in scheduling trial dates, and a greater reliance on alternative sentencing options such as community service and victim restitution, addiction treatments, family counseling, juvenile diversion programs, and short-term secure detention.

Juvenile court judges have the greatest clout in improving the services, alternative programs, and placement options available to juvenile offenders. In recent years, judges and their chief probation officers have advocated for and developed restitution programs in the form of monetary and community work service assignments in order to hold juveniles accountable for their offenses. Juvenile offenders in property-related crimes are the most likely candidates for these restitution programs. In addition, during the current decade the threshold of public tolerance for violent juvenile offenders has decreased considerably. The result has been harsher handling by prosecutors and judges for violent and chronic juvenile offenders. To increase violent juveniles' accountability for their offenses, the strategy used with increasing frequency is the meting out of harsher and more severe penalties. (For a detailed examination of the current judicial policies, organizational structure, and functions of the juvenile court, as well as contemporary probation practices, see Chapter 7.)

DISCUSSION QUESTIONS

1. Discuss the concept of *parens patriae.*
2. Discuss the historical development of the juvenile court in the United States.
3. What was the basis for the endorsement given by Judge Edward Lindsey, and other judges, for the establishment of the juvenile court?
4. As of the 1940s, what were the major problems facing juvenile courts and probation?
5. What was the role of child guidance clinics with troubled juveniles?
6. What were the minimum educational and professional standards recommended for new juvenile probation officers by the U.S. Children's Bureau in the 1930s?
7. Which well-known voluntary organization provided volunteer services to New York City's juvenile court in the early 1950s?
8. According to a 1947 national survey, approximately how many counties had probation services for juveniles?

REFERENCES

Abbott, G., Abbott, E., & Breckinridge, S. P. (1938). *The child and the state.* Chicago: University of Chicago Press.

Addams, J. (1935). *My friend, Julia Lathrop.* New York: Macmillan.

Alexander, P. W. (1944), Speaking as one judge to another. In *National Probation Association Yearbook.* New York: National Probation Association, pp. 38–39.

Augustus, J. (1852; reprinted in 1939). *First probation officer.* (reprint of *A Report of the Labors of John Augustus,* Boston, 1852). New York: National Probation Association.

Carr, L. J. (1949, September). Most courts have to be substandard! *Federal Probation, 13,* 29–30.

Dunham, H. W. (1958, Summer). The juvenile court: Contradictory orientations in processing offenders. *Law and Contemporary Problems, 23,* 371–375.

Flexner, B. (February 5, 1910). The juvenile court as a social institution. *The Survey,* in Lindner, C. & Savarese, M. R. (1984). The evolution of probation. *Federal Probation, 48*(2), 3–10.

Flexner, B., & Baldwin, R. (1912). *Juvenile courts and probation.* New York: Century.

Homer, P. (1941). *National Probation Association Yearbook.*

Howe, F. (1913). *The city: The hope of democracy.* New York: Charles Scribner's Sons.

Illinois Board of State Commissioners of Public Charities. (1898). *Fifteenth Biennial Report,* p. 63.

In re Gault, 387 U.S. 1, 12–15 (1967).

In re Kent, 383 U.S. 541 (1966).

In re Winship, 397 U.S. 358 (1970).

Kahn, A. J. (1953). *A court for children: A study of the New York City children's court.* New York: Columbia University Press.

Kamm, E. R., Hunt, D. D., & Fleming, J. A. (1968). *Juvenile law and procedure in California.* Beverly Hills, CA: Glencoe Press.

Lemert, E. M. (1971). *Instead of court: Diversion in juvenile justice.* Rockville, MD: National Institute of Mental Health, Center for Studies of Crime and Delinquency.

Levine, M. & Levine, A. (1970). The more things change: A case history of child guidance clinics. *Journal of Social Issues, 26,* 19–34.

Lindner, C. & Savarese, M. R. (1984). The evolution of probation. *Federal Probation, 48*(2), 3–10.

Lindsey, E. L. (1914). The juvenile court from the lawyer's standpoint. *Annals of the American Academy of Political and Social Sciences, 52,* 145–147.

Lou, H. H. (1927). *Juvenile courts in the United States.* Chapel Hill: University of North Carolina Press.

McCune, S. & Skoler, D. S. (1965). Juvenile court judges in the United States: Part 1. *Crime and Delinquency, 11,* 121–131.

Mennel, R. M. (1973). *Thorns and thistles: Juvenile delinquents in the United States, 1825–1940.* Hanover, NH: University Press of New England.

National Council on Crime and Delinquency. (1967). "Data Summary from Corrections in the United States," in the President's Commission on Law Enforcement and the Administration of Justice. *Task Force Report: Corrections.* Washington, DC: U.S. Government Printing Office, 134–135.

Parmelee, M. (1918). *Criminology.* New York: Macmillan.

President's Commission on Law Enforcement and Administration of Justice. (1967). *Task Force Report: Corrections.* Washington. DC: U.S. Government Printing Office.

Roberts, A. R. & Kurtz, L. F. (1987, December). Historical perspectives on the care and treatment of the mentally ill. *Journal of Sociology and Social Welfare.* 4, 75–94.

Robison, S. M. (1960). *Juvenile delinquency: Its nature and control.* New York: Holt, Rinehart & Winston.

Rothman, D. (1980). *Conscience and convenience: The asylum and its alternatives in progressive America.* Boston: Little, Brown.

Schlossman, S. L. (1977). *Love and the American delinquent: The theory and practice of "progressive" juvenile justice, 1825–1920.* Chicago: University of Chicago Press.

Schlossman, S. L. (1983). Juvenile justice: History and philosophy. In S. H. Kadish (Ed.), *Encyclopedia of Crime and Justice.* New York: Free Press.

Shireman, C. H. (1971). Crime and delinquency: Probation and parole. *Encyclopedia of Social Work* (Vol. 1). New York: National Association of Social Workers, pp. 191–196.

Stevenson, G. S. (1934). *Child guidance clinics.* New York: Commonwealth Fund.

Sullenger, T. E. (1936). *Social determinants in juvenile delinquency.* New York: John Wiley & Sons.

Tappan, P. W. (1949). *Juvenile delinquency.* New York: McGraw-Hill.

Teeters, N. K. & Reinemann, J. O. (1950). *The challenge of delinquency.* New York: Prentice-Hall.

Teeters, N. K. & Reinemann, J. O. (1939, November). *Justice and the child in New Jersey.* Trenton: State of New Jersey Juvenile Delinquency Commission.

U.S. Children's Bureau. (1922). *Proceedings of the Conference on Juvenile Court Standards.* (Publication No. 97) Washington, DC: U.S. Government Printing Office.

Whitlatch, W. (1987). A brief history of the national council. *Juvenile and Family Court Journal.* 38(2):1–14.

Chapter Five

The Emergence and Proliferation of Juvenile Diversion Programs

Albert R. Roberts

ABSTRACT

Juvenile diversion projects emerged as a dominant movement from the late 1960s through the 1970s in cities and towns across the United States. Alternatives included police-based diversion programs, probation diversion, voluntary youth service bureau programs, and community outreach counseling services. The major objective of many of the early diversion programs was to provide a structured, community-based alternative to incarceration so that petty offenders and status offenders would not be exposed to the corrupting influences of the more hardened multiple offenders who populate juvenile institutions.

This chapter begins by defining the term *diversion* and discussing the theory, philosophy, and practicalities on which diversion programs were based. It also discusses the recommendations made by the President's Commission on Law Enforcement and Administration of Justice in 1967 and the influence of several agencies (Law Enforcement Assistance Administration, Office of Youth Development and Delinquency Prevention, and National Advisory Commission on Criminal Justice Standards and Goals) on the establishment of youth service bureaus and other diversion programs. The chapter concludes with a review of the diversion program evaluations that have been conducted.

DEFINING JUVENILE DIVERSION

Juvenile diversion is defined as any process that is used by components of the criminal justice system (police, prosecution, courts, corrections) whereby youths avoid formal juvenile court processing and adjudication. Diversion refers to "the channeling of cases to noncourt institutions, in instances where these cases would ordinarily have received an adjudicatory (or fact-finding) hearing by a court" (Nejelski, 1976:396).

In a sense, diversion is as old as the juvenile court itself: the major goal of the first juvenile courts, established at the turn of the century, was to provide an alternative to, and thereby divert youths from, the criminal court. The juvenile court was created to avoid the unfair and inhumane treatment to which juveniles were subjected when processed through the criminal court and incarcerated with adult felons.

In the 1930s, crime prevention bureaus were established in several of the larger cities. For example, the Crime Prevention Bureau of the New York City Police Department flourished between 1930 (when it began) and 1934 under the leadership of its first two directors, social workers Virginia Murray and Henrietta Additon. The bureau received police referrals of "wayward minors" and juveniles accused of committing a crime but not arrested. Most of these youths received some sort of social work intervention, usually in the form of diagnosis, counseling, and/or job placement. For treatment the bureau generally referred the juveniles to family and children's agencies, hospitals, clinics, and the Bureau of Child Guidance of the Board of Education (Glueck & Glueck, 1936; New York City Police Department, 1932b:220–222).

Diversion has also existed for a long time in the form of informal station adjustments and discretionary handling by police officers when they have given youths a warning and sent them back home. However, the development of formal programs for the purpose of diverting juveniles from adjudication in the juvenile justice system did not occur until the late 1960s.

THE LABELING PERSPECTIVE

A basic theme of the labeling perspective is that juveniles and adults who commit minor offenses become habitual offenders because they are singled out from their peers and differentially treated. In the making of a deviant or criminal, Tannenbaum (1938) contends, this official treatment plays a greater role than any other experience.

The labeling approach is not so much concerned with why juveniles commit delinquent acts as with what happens to such individuals when they are officially processed and labeled by the juvenile court. Labeling focuses on societal reactions, the individual's response to those reactions, consequences of the labeling for an individual, and why and how certain behaviors come to be defined as deviant. Societal reactions to what Lemert (1967) calls primary deviance (acts of deviance caused by a combination of etiological factors) often lead to secondary deviance. Secondary deviance involves the development of deviant self-concepts, deviant careers, and deviant acts as a result of the sanctions applied to, and stigmatization of, the individual through agents of social control.

According to the labeling perspective, there is no significant difference between the social-psychological characteristics of those youths labeled delinquent and those who engage in delinquency offenses but never get caught. Sociologists and social psychologists who have advanced the labeling explanation for delinquency have tended to focus on the negative consequences of being labeled.

Lemert (1967) points out that sociologists familiar with the workings and problems of the juvenile court concur that one major and unintended consequence of wardship or adjudication to a correctional institution is stigma. Stigma results in the juvenile being handicapped by the corrupting influences of the institution: "heightened police surveillance, neighborhood isolation, lowered receptivity and tolerance by school officials, and rejections of youth by prospective employers"

(p. 92). Thus, juvenile court wards often become stigmatized and labeled by probation officers, judges, and police as the type of youth "destined for failure" (p. 93).

In addition, data indicate that the more a youth is engulfed in the juvenile justice system, the greater are the chances of future arrests for serious delinquency acts (President's Commission on Law Enforcement and Administration of Justice, 1967). As aptly pointed out by Empey (1982:410), diversion programs were based upon the underlying belief that the "evils of children have been overly dramatized." Therefore, to avoid the inevitable effect of labeling and stigma, juveniles with the potential of being processed through the justice system "should be diverted away from the juvenile justice system into other less harmful agencies—youth service bureaus, welfare agencies, or special schools."

FEDERAL INITIATIVES

By the mid-1960s, the number of crimes committed by juveniles had escalated far beyond the increased number of youths in the ten to eighteen age group, the surge in juvenile crime obvious to correctional administrators, judicial officials, and criminologists. In 1966, over 1 million arrests were made of persons under the age of eighteen. Blumstein (1967) estimated that 27 percent of all male juveniles could expect to be arrested before they reached their eighteenth birthday. Approximately one half of all juveniles arrested were referred to the juvenile court.

With increased evidence of the criminal justice system's ineffectiveness in rehabilitating juvenile offenders during the 1950s and 1960s, President Johnson, in July 1965, established the Commission on Law Enforcement and Administration of Justice. Its mission was to conduct a comprehensive analysis of crime in America and the ways in which each component of the criminal justice system was handling the crime problem. The commission's objective was to develop recommendations and a national strategy for creating "a safer and more just society."

In the area of crimes committed by juveniles, the President's Commission (1967:81) recommended that the juvenile justice system and community agencies jointly develop alternative methods of treating juveniles: "In place of the formal system, dispositional alternatives to adjudication must be developed for dealing with juveniles, including agencies to provide and coordinate services and procedures to achieve necessary control without unnecessary stigma." The commission recommended development of a nationwide program that would divert thousands of youths each year from formal processing through the juvenile courts.

Aware that most existing community social service and youth-serving agencies would be unable to provide these large numbers of youths with the needed services, the commission proposed the establishment of a new type of agency—the youth service bureau—as an alternative to juvenile court. Through federal grants (primarily from the Law Enforcement Assistance Administration [LEAA] and the Office of Youth Development and Delinquency Prevention) and smaller matching grants from state and county governmental agencies, hundreds of youth service bureaus were developed nationwide. (See Chapter 3 for an extensive review of the development of youth service bureaus). LEAA funding also resulted in the development of alternative schools, job development and training programs, police social work programs, and family counseling programs for youths referred by the police, schools, and court intake personnel.

PROGRAM EXPANSION IN THE 1970S

During the 1970s, diversion programs continued to receive significant support from the federal government. In 1973, LEAA's National Advisory Commission on Criminal Justice Standards and Goals (1973b) was sufficiently convinced of the value of diversion programs that it recommended the following:

> Many of the problems considered as delinquency or predelinquency should be defined as family, educational or welfare problems, and diverted away from the juvenile court into other community agencies such as youth service bureaus. (p. 58)
>
> Each State should enact necessary legislation to fund partially and to encourage local establishment of youth service bureaus throughout the State. Legislation also should be enacted to permit the use of youth service bureaus as a voluntary diversion resource by agencies of the juvenile justice system. (Task Force on Community Crime Prevention, 1973:83)

In order to meet "the goal of minimizing the involvement of adolescents in the juvenile justice system," the National Advisory Commission (1973b:23–25) proposed that the 1973 rate of both delinquency and status offender cases processed by the juvenile court be cut in half by 1983. Furthermore, the commission indicated that since processing a youth through the court and confining him in a training school costs approximately $6,000 per year, diversion programs, being nonresidential, would probably also be much less costly than official processing.

The U.S. Juvenile Justice and Delinquency Prevention Act of 1974 provided another major boost to the development of social services for diverted youths, particularly status offenders (such as runaways). With the passage of Title III of this act, known as the Runaway Youth Act, millions of dollars in federal funds were allocated for the establishment of runaway shelters, youth telephone hotline services, and crisis counseling services (P.L. 93–415, 1974).

> As a direct result of the passage of the Runaway Youth Act, federal funds were used to develop runaway programs across the country. They provide emergency services such as food, shelter, and counseling services in a safe and wholesome environment which is separate from law enforcement and juvenile justice systems. Sixty-six grants were awarded in 1975 during the first funding cycle to support programs in thirty-two states, Puerto Rico, Guam, and the District of Columbia. (Roberts, 1987:8–9)

In 1976, the Office of Juvenile Justice and Delinquency Prevention (OJJDP) made $10 million available for the funding and development of eleven diversion programs in different parts of the United States and Puerto Rico (Dunford, Osgood, & Weichselbaum, 1982).

FOUR EARLY PROGRAMS

Four of the early diversion programs shared the common goals of (1) intervening with first offenders before court processing and commitment to an institution and (2) treating the youth in a community-based program. However, the underlying philosophy, methods, and services provided differ.

Project Crossroads

This diversion program (also known in those days as a pretrial intervention program) was located in Washington, D.C. It was highly structured and it provided multiple services and opportunities for youthful offenders. Funded by the U.S. Department of Labor, the project was guided by the philosophy that given adequate counseling, academic skills, and vocational training, youthful offenders can acquire a sense of self-pride and self-worth that will enable them to become productive and responsible members of society. It consisted of a 90-day, community-based program of manpower services, including counseling, remedial education, job training, and employment.

Project Crossroads' main objective was to provide vocational services to youthful first offenders between the ages of sixteen and twenty-six. The eligibility criteria were (1) agreeing to participate in the project, (2) having no prior convictions, (3) having been charged with a nonviolent crime, and (4) being "presently unemployed, underemployed, or in jeopardy of losing a current job" because of the arrest, only marginally enrolled in school, or a dropout (Trotter, 1970:5).

The average age of the participants was eighteen. The youths and their families often needed various social services but lacked the knowledge of how to obtain them. Project Crossroads established liaisons with several social service organizations, which provided the needed services. If the first attempt at job placement was not successful, repeated efforts were made until a suitable placement was found. Participants were informed that they would be terminated from the project if they neglected to attend job interviews or if they demonstrated a general lack of cooperation.

The St. Louis Diversion Program

The primary objective of this program (begun in 1971) was to provide home detention for juveniles who would otherwise have been confined to the overcrowded St. Louis Detention Center. A secondary objective was to increase the effectiveness of probationary services by assigning smaller caseloads to probation officers (Keve & Zamtek, 1972).

The staff person responsible for providing intensive supervision to the juveniles was a paraprofessional worker called a community youth leader (CYL). Each CYL had daily field contact with a caseload of five detainees who were given home detention during the period between their arrest and a court hearing. The CYL was responsible for working with the youth, his family, the school, and other involved organizations to help the youth "stay out of trouble." This included serving as a Big Brother by supervising and participating in a variety of sports activities designed to provide alternatives to delinquent activities.

A 1972 evaluation of the home detention program (Keve & Zamtek, 1972) showed that of the first 308 juveniles enrolled in the St. Louis program, only thirteen (5 percent) committed a new offense, and none of those offenses was of an assaultive nature. An additional fifty-three youths (21 percent) were returned to detention because they (and often their parents) were uncooperative. Cost-effectiveness data revealed a substantial savings from this program. The estimated average daily cost for home detention was $4.85 compared with a daily cost of $17.54 for secure detention (Hubbard, 1974).

Baltimore's Diversion Project

In 1971, a pretrial diversion project, financed by the U.S. Department of Labor, was initiated in Baltimore, Maryland. Eligibility was limited to multiple offenders between the ages of fifteen and seventeen who were not accused of capital offenses such as murder or rape. Because the program's emphasis was on job counseling and placement, program staff were particularly interested in working with juveniles who were school dropouts and unemployed.

The project operated under the belief that the people best equipped to steer youths straight were ex-inmates, who had been through the criminal justice process and knew why it must be avoided. Thus, in addition to providing employment and counseling services to selected youths at the pretrial stage, Baltimore's project also provided employment for ex-prison inmates. Director Eddie Harrison, himself an ex-inmate, described his views on the aim of counseling: "If a boy is sent off to a state training school the only thing he learns is how to become a better crook. He comes out and he's too old to return to school and statistics show that three out of four will commit another crime. Only this time he becomes a convicted felon" (Eddie Harrison, Personal Communication, March 1975).

The Sacramento County 601 Diversion Project

This experimental diversion project, based in Sacramento, California, began in October 1970. The project's objective was to show that a diversion program that focused on providing family crisis intervention and counseling early in the handling of a case would result in lower costs and less recidivism. Counseling services were provided by six deputy probation officers who had received special training in crisis intervention techniques and family counseling. In the first nine months of operation, the program treated 803 youths and their families (Baron, Feeney, & Thornton, 1973).

Many of the youths selected for the project were habitual runaways, were beyond the control of their parents, or were truant from school. They had all been designated as offenders under Section 601 of California's Welfare and Institution Code. In 1972, however, the project was expanded to include juveniles who had committed juvenile delinquency offenses (Section 602 offense category).

Juveniles were referred to the project by police, family members, or schools. Within one to two hours after the referral to the probation intake unit, the probation counselor arranged a family meeting. During this first session, the counselor focused on helping the family recognize that the problem needed to be worked on by the whole family. If the relationship between the youth and parents was too volatile for the young person to return home, an alternative placement was arranged with a volunteer family, a relative, or temporary foster care. The sessions were usually from one to two and one-half hours in length. The maximum number of sessions was five per family.

Seven months after the initial handling by the diversion project, follow-up data was collected: 35 percent of the project group had been

Case Example

It is March 1974 and George, age sixteen, is arrested for stealing a car. The juvenile court judge refers him to a local youth diversion program. During the intake interview, the social worker who coordinates the program learns that George has a troubled home life. His mother is presently institutionalized at a hospital for the mentally ill, and the father travels during the week and is rarely home. George is the youngest of three children, and both older siblings live out-of-town.

The initial action is to remove George from the neglectful home environment where he receives no adult love or guidance. Immediate shelter is needed, and the social worker refers George to an emergency youth shelter. She now has a few weeks to find George a stable living arrangement, probably in a local group home for adolescent boys. The social worker also arranges for George to be given achievement tests in math and English. Although the youth was getting Ds and Fs in public school, achievement test results show that his abilities are good enough for him to obtain a high school equivalency diploma.

George tells the social worker that he has been angry at the boys in his neighborhood because they repeatedly taunt him, saying his mother is "crazy" and "off her rocker" because she is in a mental hospital. He feels embarrassed and ashamed. The social worker provides short-term crisis counseling to help the boy cope with his feelings. She also helps him understand that the neighborhood boys' cruelty results from immaturity and callousness and that if a person had a broken ankle he would receive appropriate medical treatment; similarly, someone with heavy emotional problems has to go to a hospital to get well.

George expresses interest in being trained to work in the automobile repair field. Since the diversion project has access to a vocational evaluation program, George is able to participate in three weeks of evaluation to determine his vocational potential. During the vocational evaluation, the youth exhibits good ability for small engine repair as well as for carpentry and bench assembly. However, because of his expressed interest in car repair, the vocational evaluator recommends that George enter a six-month automobile repair program offered by the state rehabilitation center, where he can prepare for the high school equivalency exam in addition to receiving vocational training.

rearrested, compared to 45.5 percent of the control group (Baron et al., 1973). More significant was the difference in serious repeat offenses involving criminal conduct (Section 602). In this category, the recidivism rate for the diverted group was 15.3 percent compared to 23.4 percent for the control group. The evidence indicated that diversion to a family crisis counseling project can be effective in reducing recidivism, as well as costs. Since the project made use of existing probation staff, additional personnel resources were not needed. (For a detailed examination of the more recently developed family counseling diversion projects in California, Missouri, Texas, and Utah, see Chapter 11.)

The Sacramento diversion project was replicated in a number of other counties, including eleven in California (Palmer, Bohnstedt, & Lewis, 1978). For status offenders as well as juveniles with a history of criminal offenses, these programs provided family counseling, group counseling, behavioral contracting, and parent education. Follow-up studies indicated that the replicated programs also reduced recidivism, although to a lesser extent than the original project. (For an in-depth review of the services and methods of intervention in currently operating diversion programs, see Chapter 9.)

EFFECTIVENESS OF DIVERSION PROGRAMS

The main objectives of juvenile diversion were (1) avoid labeling; (2) reduce unnecessary detention and incarceration; (3) reduce repeat offenses; (4) provide counseling and other services; and (5) lower justice system costs (Palmer & Lewis, 1980). However, it was unrealistic to expect one type of intervention to be a panacea, to meet all five objectives for all troubled juveniles.

Viewed on a continuum, there are two groups of youths (those at the endpoints) for whom juvenile diversion did not seem to be appropriate. At one end were juveniles who committed an occasional childish prank or a deviant act, but as part of maturational development would likely outgrow their deviance without any involvement in a diversion program. These youths, were it not for the existence of a diversion program, would likely be released with no further action or involvement with the justice system. At the opposite end of the continuum were juveniles who committed violent offenses such as rape or aggravated assault and who required intensive treatment in a secure and highly structured facility. While almost all diversion programs recognized that the violent juvenile offender was not suited for diversion, a controversy arose over the practice of referring youths who committed status or minor offenses to such programs.

Over the years many evaluations of diversion programs have been conducted. Evidence shows that some programs succeeded in their aims while others fell far short of stated objectives.

Palmer and Lewis (1980), in reporting on the Evaluation of Juvenile Diversion Programs for the California Youth Authority, concluded that no single approach is appropriate for all youths. They recommended that several types of diversion alternatives be available so that juveniles could be matched to the alternative that most closely met their needs. In general, Palmer and Lewis found that individual counseling was beneficial to the juveniles, while family counseling was not helpful. They did note, however, that one program that relied on a family treatment approach was successful.

Bohnstedt (1978), discussing the same study on which Palmer and Lewis reported, elaborated on the one successful family counseling program—the Stockton project—which utilized the conjoint family therapy model originated by Virginia Satir. The follow-up study showed that of the eleven projects studied, the Stockton program had the largest difference in recidivism rates between the treatment group (26 percent) and the comparison group (61 percent).

Pogrebin, Poole, and Regoli (1984), in reporting on the Adams County Juvenile Diversion Project in Colorado (1977–1979), found a slightly lower rate of recidivism in the experimental project group (6 percent) compared to a recidivism rate of 11.5 percent for the control group. In this study of 560 juveniles, recidivism measures were calculated each month for an eighteen-month period. The target population was first- or second-time juvenile offenders referred by the intake counselor at the district attorney's office. Violent juveniles were not accepted for the project.

Collingwood and Wilson (1976) reviewed 107 community juvenile diversion projects throughout the United States. The project auspice varied from police diversion to probation diversion to youth service bureau. The focus of the programs varied as well, with different types of services provided. They included individual counseling, recreational programs, and/or parenting education. The results showed wide variance in recidivism between projects. Most of the studies, however, were based on subjective reports and lacked an experimental design based on true randomization.

Williams (1984) reported on the First Offender Program of the Dallas Police Department's Youth Section. This diversion project, utilizing a behavioral contracting program, focused on teaching youths interpersonal and decision-making skills and teaching their parents effective parenting, discipline, and home management skills. Williams found a significantly lower recidivism rate among the approximately 20,000 youths who completed the program (20.7 percent) than among the youths in the comparison group (64 percent).

Finally, Dunford et al. (1982) conducted a national evaluation of eleven federally funded diversion programs located throughout the United States. Four of the eleven projects were selected for an in-depth experimental analysis, primarily because those sites had formal agreements with their local juvenile justice agencies to (1) randomly select and assign youths to treatment and control groups and (2) ensure that an adequate number of juvenile cases were included in the sample pool for random assignment. The researchers concluded that three of the four projects studied had "reduced the penetration of youth through the justice system." However, it was also found that diversion programs were "no more successful in . . . improving social adjustment, or reducing delinquent behavior than normal justice processing or outright release" (p. 16).

It is important to note that all four of the diversion programs emphasized brokering and referral to community agencies. In addition, some of the programs also provided one month of case advocacy or recreation-oriented services. Even the one project that frequently provided individual or family counseling served as a brokering agency, referring youths to appropriate community counseling or recreation agencies and monitoring service delivery by the community agencies. Therefore, the reader should be cautioned that while the study findings may support the need to abandon diversion programs with a brokering or recreational role as their primary focus, these findings should not be generalized to all diversion programs. The successful programs already mentioned and those examined in Chapter 8 provide direct services including intensive family counseling, parenting education, and behavioral contracting, which differentiates them from the projects studied by Dunford et al. (For a detailed examination of more recent studies documenting the differential effectiveness of diversion, see Chapter 9.)

SUMMARY

The growth of diversion programs in the decade between 1967 and 1977 underscores the fact that this has been more than an experiment. These programs have become a viable alternative to official processing in the reform-oriented states in this country. The effectiveness of diversion as measured by program evaluations and follow-up studies varies widely from one program to the next. Although criminal justice officials may continue to recognize the fact that diversion programs were never fully operationalized as intended—as a total alternative for avoiding contact with the juvenile justice system—that no longer is the overriding concern. The issue is whether diversion will survive the federal and state budget cuts of the 1980s. Several states (e.g., California and Colorado) already have passed laws authorizing and appropriating funds for juvenile diversion programs, while other states have failed to support the continuation of diversion programs once the federal funding ended.

DISCUSSION QUESTIONS

1. Define the term *juvenile diversion.*
2. Why were the juvenile diversion programs developed?
3. What is the basic theme underlying the labeling perspective?
4. According to Lemert, what is one of the major and unintended consequences of wardship or adjudication to a correctional institution?
5. Summarize the major diversion recommendations made in 1967 by President Johnson's Commission on Law Enforcement and the Administration of Justice.
6. Discuss the objectives and content of one of the four diversion programs described in this chapter.
7. Researchers Palmer and Lewis reported on the Evaluation of Juvenile Diversion Programs for the California Youth Authority. What was their major conclusion regarding a differentiated approach to diversion?

REFERENCES

Baron, R., Feeney, F., & Thornton, W. (1973). Preventing delinquency through diversion: The Sacramento County 601 Diversion Project. *Federal Probation, 37*(1), 13–18.

Blumstein, A. (1967). Systems analysis and the criminal justice system. *Annals of the American Academy of Political and Social Sciences..*

Bohnstedt, M. (1978). Answers to three questions about juvenile diversion. *Journal of Research in Crime and Delinquency, 15*(1), 109–123.

Collingwood, T. R. & Wilson, R. D. (1976) National Survey of Diversion Projects, Dallas Police Department, Dallas, Texas.

Collingwood, T. R., Williams, H., & Douds, A. (1980). Juvenile diversion: The Dallas Police Department Youth Services Program. In R. R. Ross & P. Gendreau (Eds.), *Effective correctional treatment* (pp. 93–100). Toronto: Butterworths.

Dunford, F. W., Osgood, D. W., & Weichselbaum, H. F. (1982). *National evaluation of diversion projects.* Washington, DC: U.S. Department of Justice, Office of Juvenile Justice and Delinquency Prevention.

Empey, L. T. (1982). *American delinquency: Its meaning and construction.* Chicago: Dorsey Press.

Glueck, S., & Glueck, E. (1936). *Preventing crime: A symposium.* New York: McGraw-Hill.

Holahan, J. F. (1971). *A benefit-cost analysis of Project Crossroads.* Washington, DC: National Committee for Children and Youth. June 26.

Hubbard, J. (1974). ACSW projector, special probation services project. St. Louis, MO: *Personal Communication.*

Keve, P. W., & Zamtek, C. S. (1972). *Final report and evaluation of the home detention program, St. Louis, Missouri.* McLean, VA: Research Analysis.

Lemert E. M. (1951). *Social pathology.* New York: McGraw-Hill.

Lemert, E. M. (1967). The juvenile court: Quest and realities in the President's Commission on Law Enforcement and Administration of Justice. In *Task force report: Juvenile delinquency and youth crime.* (pp. 91–106). Washington, DC: U.S. Government Printing Office.

Lemert, E. M. (1971). *Instead of court: Diversion in juvenile justice.* Chevy Chase, MD: National Institute of Mental Health, Center for Studies of Crime and Delinquency.

National Advisory Commission on Criminal Justice Standards and Goals. (1973a). *A national strategy to reduce crime.* Washington, DC: U.S. Government Printing Office.

National Advisory Commission on Criminal Justice Standards and Goals. (1973b). *Task force on community crime prevention.* Washington, DC: U.S. Government Printing Office.

Nejelski, P. (1976). Diversion: The promise and the danger. *Crime and Delinquency. 22(4),* 393–410.

New York City Police Department. (1932a). *Annual report of the Crime Prevention Bureau.* New York: New York City Police Department.

New York City Police Department. (1932b). *Manual of procedure of the police department.* New York: Author.

Palmer, T., Bohnstedt, M., & Lewis, R. (1978). *The evaluation of juvenile diversion projects: Final report.* Sacramento: California Youth Authority, Division of Research.

Palmer T. B., & Lewis, R. V. (1980, July). A differential approach to juvenile diversion. *Journal of Research in Crime and Delinquency, 209–227.*

President's Commission on Law Enforcement and Administration of Justice. (1967). *Task force report: Juvenile delinquency and youth crime.* Washington, DC: U.S. Government Printing Office.

Roberts, A. R. (1987). *Runaways and nonrunaways.* Chicago: Dorsey Press.

Sarri, R. C. (1975). Diversion within or without the juvenile justice system. *Soundings on Youth, 2(2),* 11–12.

Tannenbaum, F. (1938). *Crime and the community.* New York: Columbia University Press.

Trotter, J. A., Jr. (1970). *Final report phase I, Project Crossroads: January 15, 1968–May 15, 1969.* Washington, DC: National Committee for Children and Youth.

Wilderman, E. (1984, Summer). Juvenile diversion: From politics to policy. *New England Journal of Human Services,* 19–23.

Williams, L. (1984). A police diversion alternative for juvenile offenders. *Police Chief, 51(2),* 54–57.

Contemporary Approaches

Chapter Six

Police Work and Juveniles

Roslyn Muraskin

CAROLE ROBERTS

ABSTRACT

When the juvenile justice system is considered, concern more often than not focuses on the official response of police to contacts with delinquent youth and on resolution in the juvenile court. Though such attention is warranted, most police encounters are concluded informally and do not wind up in juvenile court. This chapter, while not ignoring the adjudicatory process, deals with police–juvenile contacts that are resolved without a court referral. In particular, discussion will deal with the police decision to arrest, unofficial dispositions both formal and informal, and consideration of the structure and operation of specialized youth service units within a police department.

IMPACT OF GAULT

In the wake of the U. S. Supreme Court's *In re* Gault decision in 1967, juvenile courts throughout the country altered their practices to conform to new procedural requirements designed to safeguard the "due process" rights of juveniles (Davis, 1980). Despite language in the *Gault* case that indicated that the decision did not apply to preadjudicatory juvenile proceedings, it is thought to have set off a trend in the law of arrest that eliminates all differences between juveniles and adults (Davis, 1980:3–4). Prior to *Gault* the police generally believed that legal limitations in dealing with adults did not apply to juveniles (Remington, 1969:959). Since *Gault*, legal limitations placed upon the police vis-à-vis their relationship with juveniles have generally been imposed by courts in the same manner as the prohibitions on their relationships with adults.

Despite these restrictions, police response to juvenile crime has remained stable and is more in line with the Supreme Court's 1984 *Schall* v. *Martin* decision. In *Schall*, the Court upheld the preventive detention section of the New York Family Court Act, sec. 320.5(3)(b), which authorizes holding a juvenile if a judge finds "a serious risk that the [juvenile] may before the return date commit an act which if committed by an adult would constitute a crime." The court noted that a juvenile's interest in freedom must be qualified by the recognition that juveniles, as opposed to adults, are always in a form of custody. By definition they are assumed not to have the capacity to take care of themselves and are, therefore, subject to the control of their parents and, upon default thereof, the state in the interest of preserving and promoting the child's welfare. The determination, then to take a juvenile into custody remains as it always has been: a police decision.[1]

---

[1]But see Davis (1980:3–4), which suggests a toughening of the law of arrest by limiting police action vis-à-vis juveniles.

However far *Gault* may have extended into the pre-judicial state of juvenile proceedings, the police still exercise greater discretion in their handling of juveniles than they do with adults (Wilson, 1968:9–30).

JUVENILE PROCEDURES

Procedural reforms notwithstanding, the jurisdiction of the juvenile court remains expansive and includes conduct that if committed by an adult would be criminal (e.g., robbery), as well as a broad spectrum of activities that society disapproves of when committed by children, (e.g., truancy, runaway). Concommitant with the jurisdiction of the juvenile courts, a police officer may take a child into custody for acts for which he may arrest an adult (New York Family Court Act, sec. 721), as well as for acts in the broad area of noncriminal conduct within the juvenile court's jurisdiction. For example, even in New York, which requires the police to obtain a warrant to take a child into custody for noncriminal acts, exception is made where the officer has reason to believe the child is a runaway. And the officer may conclude the child is a runaway by a refusal of the juvenile to give his or her name and address (sec. 718).

In terms of practice, the exclusionary rules limiting police conduct apply to children and adults in the same fashion (Davis, 1980:3–14, 3–18). However, in relating decisional law such as *Mapp* v. *Ohio* (1961) (search and seizure) and *Miranda* v. *Arizona* 384 US 436 (1966) (interrogations) to children, care should be taken to recognize that these cases limit police action only in the sense that noncompliance renders evidence obtained inadmissible at the adjudicatory hearing. It therefore has far less impact on an officer's relationship with a child than would be expected. To the extent that these cases increase the formality of police conduct, they may make police officers more rigid in the exercise of their discretion.

POLICE ROLE

Usually the police are the child's first contact with the justice system. Their decision at this point is of prime importance because the legal machinery of the state goes into operation only if the juvenile is detained (Sutherland & Cressey, 1974:374). In actuality, the adjudicatory machinery is usually not set into motion, because an estimated 85 percent of police contacts with juveniles are resolved with some form of unofficial adjustment (Cox & Conrad, 1978:125, citing Black & Reiss, 1970).

While larger police departments may have specialized juvenile divisions, most police–juvenile contacts occur with uniformed or non-juvenile duty officers (Black & Reiss, 1970:65) because police response, whether initiated by the officers themselves or by a call from a layperson, is situation oriented without regard to the age of the person. As a consequence, juvenile aid divisions, where they exist, are often referral units accepting cases and clients from other departmental divisions, even where they investigate cases on their own.

Police responses to situations involving juveniles have usually been categorized as official or unofficial (Cox & Conrad, 1978:123). A closer look, however, suggests that unofficial responses should be further subdivided into informal and formal. An official response is taking the child into custody for the purpose of bringing him or her before the juvenile court. In an informal unofficial disposition the officer makes his own ad hoc adjustment, while in a formal unofficial resolution the matter is turned over to another part of the police bureaucracy, which resolves the matter according to a definite policy but without bringing the case to the courts. These options for handling juvenile contacts (Piliavin & Briar, 1964:206) are founded on the exercise of a considerable amount of discretion (Davis, 1971). Though the decision-making process is flawed by the nonobjectivity inherent in the exercise of individual judgment, a number of constant factors tend to influence police officers.

In general, the decision-making process for juveniles follows the grading of offenses found in the criminal law applied to adults (Black & Reiss, 1970:68). Officers have little difficulty deciding to arrest juveniles in cases of robbery, homicide, rape, arson, and felony levels of assault. As the perceived significance of the crime decreases, however, the number of dispositions other than arrest increases. And in cases of minor offenders (who comprise most of the police response) the specific violation of the law becomes less important in the officer's choice of action (Piliavin & Briar, 1964).

Black & Reiss (1970) suggest that the legal seriousness of the situation is more important in patrol officer contact with juveniles than in contacts between youth officers and juveniles. The reason given is that the patrol officer's sanction is the arrest, while a youth officer has access to more options and presumably more information. However, juvenile officers in the field but not on a specific investigation are at the same disadvantage as patrol officers and have only limited information vis-à-vis past records, school performance, and family problems. Even for them, the determination of what to do must be based on the information, if any, available at that time.

FACTORS DETERMINING WHETHER TO ARREST

There is some evidence that an officer may not arrest, even in a serious case, if the complainant does not wish to pursue the matter (Davis, 1971:3). Conversely, a complainant's attitude may very well trigger the arrest. A wronged citizen's demands for justice are not easily put aside by an officer, especially when the victim may file a complaint against the juvenile or even against the officer for failure to arrest. Preference, however, is only infrequently expressed. One major study, exploring preference in the context of black versus white arrests, noted that (1) a large proportion of complainants expressed no clear demand for police action and (2) when the preference was unclear the arrest rate fell somewhere between rates when complainants openly preferred arrest and when they sought a different type of disposition (Black & Reiss, 1970:71). The victim's preference for one type of action or another evidently is a factor in the officer's decision, but its weight is open to question because preference is not expressed in the majority of cases.

The race (Pope, 1984:75–94) and the sex (Cox & Conrad, 1978:123) of the offender are also factors that should not be ignored, although their influence on police decision making may not be as direct as anticipated (Sullivan & Siegel, 1972:253–262). Despite the increase in female juvenile arrests over the years (Cox & Conrad, 1978:123), gender is a criterion in deciding whether to take a child into custody. For example, police of the Port Authority of New York and New Jersey reported that of the ninety-seven criminal complaints/arrests made by their Youth Services Unit at the Port Authority bus terminal in Manhattan, thirty-four were female and sixty-three were male, though of their 2,515 total youth contacts for the calendar year 1985, 1,222 were female (Port Authority, 1986). Although systematic research on gender is limited, there seems to be a police bias in favor of girls who commit serious offenses and against them when the act is more trivial or not traditionally criminal (Cavan & Ferdinand, 1981:346–347).

A departmental policy or sanctioned pattern of racial prejudice will increase the arrest rate of the targeted group, for both adults and juveniles. But when individual prejudice is involved the tendency is to justify the arrest on certain supposed attributes of the group rather than on racial grounds. Thus Piliavin & Briar (1964) noted that eighteen of twenty-seven officers interviewed openly disliked blacks, indicated black youths were more likely than white to give them a hard time, and stopped them more often than whites because their color identified them as troublemakers. Race, then, is sublimated into some perceived objective criterion that allows the officer to manifest his bias while at the same time denying that, in fact, race caused him to act in the first place.

Race may negatively impact on an officer's perception of attitude and demeanor, but these latter two concerns are most significant in making the final decision to arrest, even in cases where skin color is not a factor. Indeed, for patrol officers, attitude is probably the most relevant factor next to offense. But this may be by default, not planning, because of the paucity of other available information at the time the officer has to make the judgment. For example, knowledge of the juvenile's prior involvement with police can influence an arrest decision. However, unless the officer is on a regular patrol that allows knowledge of the constituency (as opposed to a nonpatrol officer responding to a specific incident), he or she can rarely do more than check for warrants and a juvenile card or remember anecdotal information given by other officers. To the extent that information on prior contacts is available, it probably works to the disadvantage of the juvenile by increasing the likelihood of arrest.

Apart from a racial connection, attitude and demeanor are significant though the impact is usually limited to the extreme cases. According to Black & Reiss (1970), most children encountering a police officer act in a civil manner appropriate to the situation; only at the ends of the behavior continuum are juveniles either overly deferential or antagonistic. The reported arrest rate by Black & Reiss understandably was higher for antagonistic juveniles than for civil ones; but what was not anticipated was a similar high rate for very deferential youth. One answer suggested by the authors is that juveniles who commit acts that make them especially liable to arrest behave in an overly respectful manner in the vain hope of avoiding being taken into custody.

POLICE APPROACHES

Regardless of the influencing factors, only three approaches are available for resolving the encounter with the juvenile. First, the officer may release the youth. Second, the officer may officially take the child into custody in order to file a petition or otherwise bring him or her before the juvenile court. Third, the officer may unofficially resolve the encounter by his own informal adjustment or, if the department has the administrative capability, through a more formal bureaucratic procedure.

Unofficial adjustments, whether formal or informal, appear to be satisfactory especially where all the parties—complainant, police officer, juvenile, and parent or guardian—agree to the disposition. In the case of a group of juveniles congregating in front of a store or otherwise annoying a shopkeeper, for example, unofficial informal adjustments may mean as little as giving them a good talking to before dispersing them. Or the officer may take them to the station house, request a meeting with parents, and negotiate restitution or other "informal" punishment with the parents and complainant. A record of the disposition is kept, but it may be no more than the officer's normal report of any incident responded to. Sometimes a separate notation may be made at the precinct for use by other officers.

Unofficial formal adjustments are really along the same line but involve more bureaucracy and, hopefully, more expertise and objectivity. An example is the Diversion Alternative Program for first offenders set up by the Youth Section of the Dallas, Texas, Police Department. Following a child's arrest, an investigator from the Youth Section contacts the parents, completes information about the arrest, and establishes that the juvenile meets the program's eligibility requirements. These involve, in addition to attitude and seriousness of the offense, the agreement of the family to participate. After eligibility is established, an assigned intake counselor gathers more information from home, school, friends, relatives, and so on, and asks the parents for a plan to prevent further offenses. The counselor then determines whether the youth enters a two-night, short-term program of meetings or the longer, six-month program. When all meetings and assignments have been completed, the youth is discharged (Williams, 1984).

Both types of adjustment are subject to the criticism that guilt is assumed, with punishment being imposed without a hearing before an impartial tribunal. The agreed participation by the child and/or the parents, even when required by statute or program guideline, is also questionable; the alternative—official action in juvenile courts—impacts seriously on whether a consent to participate is truly voluntary.

The unofficial resolution suffers from other flaws. If the child is guilty and in need of help, the resources of the police program may be insufficient for the task, compared to those of the juvenile court. On the other hand, if a mistake was made with regard to the child's involvement, the entire proceeding is unfair because there is no chance

---

Case Example

In one major federal case (*Cuevas* v. *Leary*, 70 Civ. 2017, SDNY 6/23/72), parents of juveniles alleged that reports were being issued, maintained, and distributed by the New York City Police Department in violation of the children's rights to privacy and due process of law. The matter was disposed of in 1972 with significant limitations on access to the reports both inside and outside the department as well as a requirement that a report be destroyed when the child turns seventeen. Destruction is also required, regardless of age, whenever the report is established to be unfounded or withdrawn. To that end, when a report is issued, the parent or guardian must be notified of the right to a follow-up investigation to determine the validity of the allegations on forms that are prepared in both Spanish and English. The decision also required the setting up of a training program.

to assert a defense. The question also arises as to whether an unofficial program that is made a part of the police bureaucracy could withstand a subsequent challenge by an aggrieved parent and child claiming that participation in the project was not voluntary and the child was denied the rights and protections he or she would have been entitled to in the juvenile court. Training and objectivity can limit abuse (see Knodle, 1978), although some form of internal review of unofficial alternative dispositions better guarantees the fairness of the system.

Despite objections to the informal resolution, it is nevertheless a favored police practice. It is justified on the premise that informal resolutions avoid the stigma of a juvenile record and the possibility of detention.

POLICE TRAINING TO HANDLE JUVENILES

Because police contacts with children are numerous and often occur under stressful conditions, there is a need to train police in how to approach and deal with the problems encountered with juveniles. Official response to the need has been either by attempts at training individual officers[2] and/or by the creation of special youth divisions within the department.

In smaller localities, the regular police force handles juvenile matters without any division of tasks or specialized bureaus. While many jurisdictions now require departments to provide juvenile officers, financial constraints often prevent adequate training and/or specific assignment to juvenile matters. Indeed, many rural departments have no individuals specifically trained for juvenile cases, and where statutes require designation of special juvenile officers, the selection is made without prior training of the officer (Cox & Conrad, 1978:129–130; Jankovic et al, 1980:4–15). To overcome budget and manpower problems, juvenile officer appointments are sometimes based on a perceived ability to get along with kids. Such selection does not substitute for training and can readily reinforce an already held belief that juvenile work has less status than other police activities.

ESTABLISHED YOUTH PROGRAMS: EXAMPLES

In some locales, especially larger ones, the police force is augmented with special units, including youth squads or divisions that either supplement regular police officers in dealing with juvenile cases

---

[2]Such as the inclusion of a chapter on offenses related to juveniles in the 1978 curriculum revision at the New York City Police Academy.

or are organized into independent units. While duties of the units vary from city to city, they usually deal with particular problems (gangs, narcotics, etc.) and generally serve three functions: prevention, screening, and investigation.

Port Authority of New York and New Jersey

Perhaps typical of small units is the Youth Services Unit of the Port Authority of New York and New Jersey Police. The unit is stationed at Manhattan's Port Authority bus terminal, through which more than 200,000 people pass every day. The terminal, located near a high-crime and prostitution area, has long been a magnet to juveniles, who use it to come to or leave New York City.

The unit is headed by a sergeant who supervises three police officers, three social workers, and a secretary/statistician, who work in teams of one officer and one social worker. The teams operate seven days a week usually from 7 A.M. until 11 P.M., but sometimes later depending on such things as bus schedules or the arrival of a runaway's parents.

The unit was informally organized in 1972 by the assignment of a few officers to work full-time with runaways and other problem youths found in the terminal. It was expanded into a formal program with professional social workers in 1976. Though outside funding for the program ended the next year, the Port Authority institutionalized the unit. The stated goal of the service is to provide crisis intervention, referral services, short- and long-term counseling, and diversion.

In 1985 one third of the caseload involved runaways who came to the unit's attention through patrol or parent notification. Runaways are usually found during routine patrols by the unit, through other officers, or through parental notification. The unit also takes in truants, loiterers, and disorderly youth as well as victims of child abuse. Unless abuse is suspected, runaways are returned directly to their families, with counseling and support as well as referral to outside agencies made available to both parent and child.[3]

Nassau County

A larger, less specialized program would be the suburban example of the Nassau County, New York, Police Department's Youth Services Unit. According to available annual reports, the unit has two components: the Juvenile Aid Bureau and the Youth Projects Bureau. A third

---

[3]Information for this section comes from Port Authority (1985); Elique (1984).

service, long known as the Police Boys Club Unit but recently renamed the Police Activities League (PAL), maintains a close liaison with the Youth Services Unit.

The Juvenile Aid Bureau handles the more police-oriented work of the Youth Service Unit. This bureau has responsibility for processing all juveniles involved in illegal or antisocial activities or living in conditions detrimental to their welfare. Most police contacts are made by officers outside the bureau; but as soon as a child is taken into custody responsibility shifts to the juvenile officers. In addition to processing responsibilities, juvenile officers share the same but specialized police responsibility of all officers to locate and apprehend juveniles engaged in delinquent and criminal behavior.

The Missing Persons Bureau, a separate entity, immediately notifies the Juvenile Aid Bureau of all juveniles reported as missing.

A bureau officer also maintains a liaison with the family court, which has jurisdiction over juvenile cases, as well as with a community resource officer. The latter has responsibility for researching rehabilitative agencies in the community. Having such referrals permits bureau officers to exercise discretion in processing juvenile activity.

Activity reports of the bureau for 1984 and 1985 show a caseload of 7,195 and 8,301, respectively. While many of the matters handled are youth oriented (truancy, persons in need of supervision, fireworks violation, and minibike problems), the range also follows the hierarchy of the penal law and includes robbery, sodomy, drug abuse, and murder. Of the matters handled in those two years, only 1,032 and 1,056 were disposed of by arrest leading to a disposition in either the family (juvenile) court or, for the more heinous acts, the criminal courts.

New York City

Adjacent to Nassau County is New York City, which like its suburban counterpart maintains a Youth Services Division within its Police Department. Though one community is suburban and the other urban, their youth services divisions are similar in purpose, structure, and operation.

New York City's Youth Services Division is responsible for planning and coordinating procedures to divert juveniles from the justice system through the utilization of informal dispositions. The division supervises and aids station house youth officers who handle juvenile cases. It interfaces with community agencies and other departmental units in the prevention of youth crime, while outreach programs are aimed at the general juvenile population. Youth officers are trained in the implementation of departmental policies on youth matters (New York City Police Department, 1985:1–2).

Central to the division's work is the "juvenile report," which has been in use since the Crime Prevention Bureau in 1930 established the referral form as an alternative to arrest. The form is prepared for minor offenses when judicial disposition is not necessary but the juvenile's behavior requires follow-up investigation, especially where parental supervision is wanting (Youth Services Division, 1985, p. 4).

The report can be issued for cases of persons in need of supervision, runaways, juvenile delinquency, and penal law violations—except felonies, unlawful assembly, and certain serious misdemeanors where the taking of the child into custody for judicial disposition is required. In cases of less serious offenses, the precinct officer may use his discretion in preparing a juvenile report, considering such factors as age, nature of offense, prior record (formal or informal), recommendation of the youth officer, and other information as may be available.

If a juvenile report is issued, it is sent to the youth officer in the precinct where the child lives for a follow-up investigation which includes interviews with the complainant, school, and family members as well as social workers and others as necessary. An interview is conducted with the child and his parents to establish their attitude toward accepting treatment or services.

If the act is minor and isolated, the investigator sends a precautionary letter and/or counsels the parents and child who are also told of their right to a follow-up investigation to establish the validity of the allegations. If the facts warrant it, the child and parents are referred to appropriate public and/or private agencies for treatment and service. If a youth has previously been referred to an agency, referral may be made to the court. The stated objective of the division is to identify and separate children who exercise poor judgment from those whose police contacts indicate a pattern of delinquency.

The Youth Services Division also maintains runaway and truancy programs plus a gang intelligence unit that collects information on a city-wide basis (Youth Services Division, Annual Report 1986:15).

As part of community outreach, the division maintains a police–school liaison program in which uniformed officers team with regular teachers to teach in New York City high schools. The police athletic liaison unit runs an extensive sports, recreational, and cultural program with emphasis on teenagers in high-risk areas. A Youth Dialogue program promotes communication between youth and police and makes youngsters aware of the dangers of drug abuse (NYC Police Department, 9–10). A separate outreach program in cooperation with the Board of Education is also run by the division. In 1986 over 2,800 students participated in the program, which consisted of three-day workshops in homeroom classes conducted by the teacher and a police officer. The workshops are designed to motivate participants "to be productive and contributing members of society" (Annual Report,

New York City Police Department, 1986:17). The divisional command structure is charted in Figure 6–1.

While the stated goal of many youth services and juvenile aid bureaus is diversion, the past 15 years have seen an increase in the proportion of official action taken by the police against juveniles, though still far less than the number of unofficial dispositions (Krisberg, Schwartz, Litsky, & Austin, 1986:12). The general increase in the number of referrals to the juvenile court may simply be due to tougher law enforcement policies throughout the criminal justice system.[4] Krisberg et al. agree but add that as police increased the use of diversion the residual group of arrestees were charged with more serious matters and required greater restrictive disposition. However, an examination of national arrest statistics for 1970, 1975, 1980, and 1985 (see Table 6–1) shows a decrease in the last ten years in the percentage of arrests of children under eighteen, as compared to all ages.

More than the crime rate or even the post-*Gault* increase in concern for children's rights, the growth of police professionalism and the concomitant emphasis on investigation may have altered the way in which police deal with juveniles. Professional norms may make the police less discriminating; but in the exercise of discretion with juve-

TABLE 6–1   Total Arrests by Age: 1970, 1975, 1980, 1985 (with percentage and numerical breakdown)

	1970	1975	1980	1985
Number of agencies	5,270	8,051	12,042	11,249
Population	151,604,000	179,191,000	208,194,225	203,035,000 (est.)
Arrests				
Under age 15				
Number	607,133	716,206	603,927	585,745
Percent of total	9.2	8.9	6.2	5.7
Under age 18				
Number	1,660,643	2,078,459	2,025,713	1,762,539
Percent of total	25.3	25.9	20.9	17.1
All ages				
Number	6,570,473	8,013,645	9,703,181	10,289,609
Percent of total	100	100	100	100

SOURCE: U.S. Department of Justice, Federal Bureau of Investigation. (1970, 1975, 1980, 1985) *Uniform Crime Reports for the United States*: Washington, D.C., U.S. Government Printing Office.

[4]For example, see the introductions to annual reports of the Nassau County, New York, Legal Aid Society (1984, 1985).

FIGURE 6–1   Youth Services Division Organizational Chart

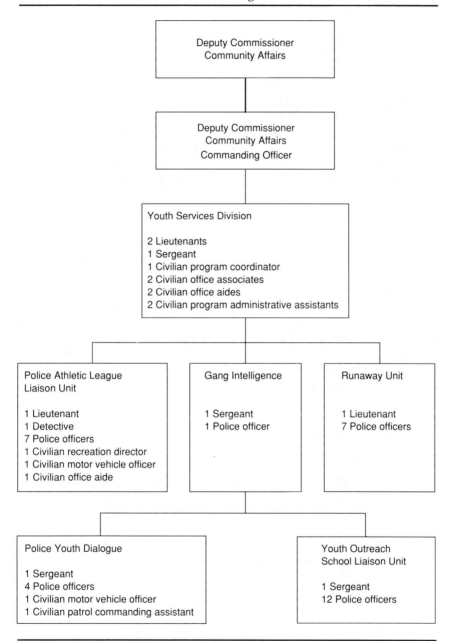

SOURCE: New York City Police Department, Youth Services Division.

niles, professionalism has tended to make police more formal and severe (Wilson, 1968).

CRIME PREVENTION PROGRAMS

Police work, in part, is preventive. To the extent that police, through regular or special divisions, check out youthful activity before the criminal act takes place, the work is very traditional. In many cities, however, the departmental programs that focus on prevention have expanded into recreational programs and other types of community service that have not been part of the traditional police role.

Recreational programs may be attractive to younger children and even to teenagers, but they are almost impossible to measure as a crime prevention tool. Cavan & Ferdinand (1981) note that recreational programs are subject to the charge that police are not trained to run them and that assigning officers to these projects weakens the force as a whole. One answer to the criticism is that the police are merely filling a gap in the community and providing a service that would otherwise be unfilled.

While the police should work closely with community organizations, a division of labor should be honored. To the extent that police basketball and baseball leagues coexist with organizations such as Little League, the police connection should be emphasized. If police sponsorship becomes so attenuated that neither parent nor child is aware of it, the department ends up providing a recreational service like any other community organization but without regard for the reason the project was put into place.

In addition to recreational projects, police juvenile aid bureaus and other units carry on a whole host of programs designed to prevent delinquency and perhaps to serve as public relations vehicles for the departments. Thus, in Nassau County in New York, the Youth Services Unit also has a Youth Projects Bureau, which as part of its crime prevention activities over the years has run such things as explorer programs and "show and tell." These programs, which usually include lectures and assemblies at schools and civic associations, deal with crime prevention, traffic safety, and the work of the police, as well as topics selected to meet special community needs.

The Juvenile Aid Bureau (Nassau County Police Department, interviews with headquarters staff, 1987) gives talks to church and parent-teacher groups, scouting programs, school assemblies, and classroom rap sessions on topics that include child molestation, bureau functions, babysitting tips, the law and you, and defensive tactics for women.

The obvious problem is that, constructive or not, the programs' effectiveness in preventing delinquency is unproven and, to the extent that they became public relations–oriented, they lessen the status of the officers in the bureau and reinforce already held beliefs that juvenile duty in not real police work. Further, programs that go beyond the sphere of the juvenile both dilute and demean the work of the youth unit.

SUMMARY

This chapter has dealt with the preadjudicatory discretionary phase of police work with juveniles. The importance of this phase in relation to the criminal justice system should not be underestimated: police handle many more cases than ever reach the court.

To a great measure it is the officer's exercise of discretion that really controls the disposition of juvenile cases. As has been noted, it is therefore important to consider (1) the factors that weigh upon an officer in making the decision (attitude, race, sex, or seriousness of the offense), (2) the several ways that police have been administratively organized to serve juveniles, and (3) some of the problems in the creation of specialized units and training in general.

DISCUSSION QUESTIONS

1. In the aftermath of the *Gault* (1967) decision requiring police officers and court personnel to safeguard due-process rights, has the predominant pattern of police dispositions remained relatively stable? Why? Please explain your answer.
2. Explain what is meant by "official" and "unofficial" police disposition.
3. Large urban police departments often have special youth divisions or juvenile aid bureaus within their department. Describe three components of a large police youth services unit, such as the one in New York City or in suburban Nassau County, New York.
4. Describe the role and services provided by police social workers at the Youth Services Unit of New York City's Port Authority Police.
5. What types of youth activities and programs are provided by police crime prevention units?

REFERENCES

Black, D., & Reiss, A., Jr. (1970). Police control of juveniles. *American Sociological Review, 35,* (1) 63–77.

Bittner, E., & Krantz, S. (1980). *Standards relating to police handling of juvenile problems.* Cambridge, MA: Ballinger.

Cavan, R., & Ferdinand, T. (1981). *Juvenile delinquency.* New York: Harper & Row.

Cox, S. M., & Conrad, J. J. (1978). *Juvenile justice.* Dubuque, IA: Wm. C. Brown.

Cuevas v. Leary (70 Civ. 2017, SDNY June 23, 1972).

Davis, S. (1971). Justice for the juvenile, the decision to arrest and due process. *Duke Law Journal (5), 913–937.*

Davis, S. M. (1980). *Rights of juveniles.* New York: Clark Boardman.

DeJames, J. (1980). Issues in rural juvenile justice. In J. Jankovic, J. L. Schultz, T. J. Fetter, C. L. Beale, L. G. Schultz, & G. H. Phillips, (Eds.), *Juvenile justice in rural America.* Washington, DC: Superintendent of Documents.

DeVito, E. (1975, April). Station house adjustments in juvenile cases. *Police Law Quarterly, 4,* 13–20.

Elique, J. (1984, February). The juvenile runaway phenomenon. *FBI Law Enforcement Bulletin, 53,* 1–6.

In re Gault, 387 U.S. 1 (1967).

Jankovic, J. (Eds.). (1980). *Juvenile justice in rural America.* Washington, DC: Superintendent of Documents.

Kenney, J. P., Pursuit, D., Fuller, D., & Barry, B. (1982). *Police work with juveniles and the administration of juvenile justice.* Springfield, IL: Charles C Thomas.

Knodle, K. (1978). *Discretion and dispositional alternatives in police handling of juvenile cases.* Carbondale, IL: Southern Illinois University, Center for the Study of Crime, Delinquency and Corrections.

Krisberg, B., Schwartz, A., Litsky, P., & Austin, J. (1986, January). The watershed of juvenile justice reform. *Crime and Delinquency, 32*(1), 5–38.

Mapp v. Ohio, 367 U.S. 643 (1961).

McKinney, (1983). Part 1: Family court act. In *McKinney's Consolidated Laws of New York* (Vol. 29A). St. Paul, MN: West Publishing.

Miranda v. Arizona, 384 US 436 (1966).

Nassau County Legal Aid Society (1984 and 1985) *Annual Reports,* Mineola, New York.

Nassau County Police Department, Youth Services Unit (1971, 1973, 1974). *Annual Reports,* Mineola, New York.

Nassau County Police Department, Youth Services Unit (1984, 1985). *Activity Reports,* Mineola, New York.

New York City Police Department (1985, June). *New York City Police Academy student officer training curriculum* (Rev.).

Phelps, T. R. (1976). *Juvenile delinquency.* Santa Monica, CA: Goodyear Publishing.

Piliavin, I., & Briar, S. (1964, September). Police encounters with juveniles. *American Journal of Sociology, 70,* 206–214.

Pope, C. E. (1984). Blacks and juvenile crime. In D. Georges-Abeyie (Ed.), *Criminal justice systems and blacks*. New York: Chandler Publishing.

Port Authority of New York and New Jersey, Youth Services Unit. (1986). *Annual Report, 1985*. New York.

Remington, F. J. (1969). *Criminal justice administration*. New York: Bobbs-Merrill.

Roche, M. (1979, Summer). Police disposition of juvenile cases. *South Dakota Law Review, 24*, 61–105.

Schall v. Martin, 81 L.2d 2d 207 (1984).

Shields, K., & Panciera, L. (1982). *Variations in juvenile law and police practice*. Washington, DC: National Institute of Justice.

Sullivan, D. C., & Siegel, L. J. (1972, July). How police use information to make decisions. *Crime and Delinquency, 18*, 253–262.

Sutherland, E., & Cressey, D. (1974). *Criminology*. New York: J. B. Lippincott.

Sutton, J. R., Rooney, T. L., & Pittman, P. E. (1981). *Police handling of juveniles*. Washington, DC: National Institute of Justice.

Swanson, C., & Bolland, J. (1983). Judgment policy and the exercise of police discretion. In S. Nagel, (Eds.), *Political science of criminal justice*. Springfield, IL: Charles C Thomas.

Thomas, C., & Fitch, W. (1981, February). Exercise of discretion in juvenile justice system. *Juvenile and Family Court Journal, 32*, 32–50.

Weiner, H., & Willie, C. (1971). Decisions by juvenile officers. *American Journal of Sociology, 77*, (2) 199–210.

Williams, L. (1984, February). A police diversion alternative for juvenile offenders. *Police Chief, 51*, 54–56.

Wilson, J. Q. (1968). The police and the delinquent in two cities. In S. Wheeler (Ed.), *Controlling delinquents* (pp. 9–30). New York: John Wiley & Sons.

Youth Services Division. (1985, August). *Introduction and history of police work with children and youth in New York City*. New York: New York City Police Department.

Youth Services Division. (1986). Annual Report.

Chapter Seven

The Juvenile Court Landscape

H. Ted Rubin

ABSTRACT

This chapter examines recent developments on the juvenile court vista and an array of issues critical to juvenile court policy and practice. Initially considered are the organizational structure of this court and its jurisdiction over delinquent offenses and other matters. Constitutional and legal constraints on the court's exercise of its powers are then reviewed. The probation department's function is described and the major processing events in the juvenile justice workload analyzed. Differential case management, in this setting used in reaching decisions and with sentencing policy and intervention, is examined with particular reference to more serious and repetitive juvenile offenders. A concluding section points to the need for improving juvenile justice and the roles different actors can play in this process.

Juvenile courts are governed by the statutes and appellate court decisions of their states; also they are bound by U.S.Supreme Court decisions and federal trial court and circuit court rulings in their state or region. The consequence is great diversity in juvenile court practices, with a certain commonality of procedures and provisions that have been held mandatory for the states by Supreme Court interpretations of the U.S. Constitution.

The juvenile court of today is a markedly different instrument than the juvenile court of two decades ago. Its intervention activities are more wedded with law and legal procedure. Its historic role to sanction status offenders who have violated no criminal laws but whose misbehaviors constitute conduct illegal for children has been sizably cut back. In a growing number of states, more serious or repetitive juvenile offenders now have their cases processed in a criminal court. Prosecutors have moved into this forum with considerable power, more than balancing the influence of earlier-arriving defense counsel. Probation departments, the primary service arms of the court, now pay increased attention to what a juvenile has done—rather than what a juvenile is like—in reaching screening decisions, in making recommendations for court dispositions, and in mobilizing intervention. Public policy and court practices have toughened. Punishment has gained legitimacy although rehabilitation remains a strong emphasis.

The requirement that a juvenile be held accountable for his offense—in the form of monetary and community work service restitution—has taken hold. A further component of accountability, "just deserts," is evident: sanctions are more severe when offenses and offense histories are more severe or chronic.

THE ORGANIZATIONAL STRUCTURE OF THE JUVENILE COURT

Form

This examination of contemporary juvenile justice begins with a discussion of the different approaches to juvenile court organization. Organizational structures vary from state to state and even within a state (Rubin, 1985b). A juvenile court may stand alone as a statutorily prescribed, separately organized entity. It may exist as part of a broader purpose family court. Most frequently, it is a unit of a general trial court, which is titled a circuit court, superior court, district court, or common pleas court, depending upon the state. Less often, it is a unit of a lower trial court, sometimes also known as a district court. A general trial court hears adult felony offenses, unlimited civil action claims, and usually divorce (dissolution) cases; a lower or limited jurisdiction trial court is usually concerned with adult misdemeanor charges, lesser civil action claims, and sometimes local ordinance violations. National standards consistently recommend that the juvenile court be structured as part of a family court division of the general trial court, which is the trial court of highest status in all communities (Institute of Judicial Administration, 1980a; National Advisory Commission, 1973; National Advisory Committee, 1980).

Utah has the best example of a separately organized juvenile court. There it is a separate, statewide entity with its own state administration. Its judges, probation officers, clerks, and other employees are paid with state funds. Its ten appointed judges hear juvenile matters exclusively in the different district juvenile courts.

Colorado is an example of a hybrid state. A separately organized juvenile court serves the city and county of Denver. Elsewhere in the state the juvenile court is a division of the district court, the general trial court. Georgia, Louisiana, Nebraska, and Tennessee are also hybrid states, maintaining separately organized juvenile courts in one or more jurisdictions but structuring the juvenile court as a part of a larger court entity elsewhere in the state.

At present, six states and the District of Columbia have authorized family courts on a statewide basis. Family courts are separately organized entities in Delaware, New York, Rhode Island, and South Carolina; they are a division of the general trial court in the District of Columbia, Hawaii, and New Jersey.

A family court's jurisdiction is very broad. Generally it has responsibility for the divorce or dissolution case, including child custody, support, and property settlement dimensions. Family courts also consider delinquency, status offense, and neglect and abuse concerns;

paternity and child support matters; the relinquishment of children; and the adoption of children. Some have authority over mental illness procedures related to children and over intrafamily criminal offenses. The family court in New York, however, lacks divorce jurisdiction. Virginia maintains a juvenile and domestic relations district court, similar to a family court except that it lacks jurisdiction over divorce.

It is well known that the first juvenile court began in Cook County (Chicago), Illinois, in 1899. But that juvenile court was not a separately organized court. Rather, it has always been a division of the circuit court. The first family court was instituted in Rhode Island in 1961. The prospect is for a growth in family courts, organized more commonly as a division of the general trial court. The most common juvenile court structure is as a division of a general trial court. California, Washington, and Pennsylvania are examples of this approach. Far less commonly the juvenile court is a division of a lower trial court, as in Maine and North Carolina. In Minnesota, the juvenile court is a division of the upper trial court in several of its largest counties but more generally is part of the lower trial court.

Historically, leading juvenile court advocates urged a separate juvenile court structure. They contended that specialist judges would have the necessary commitment and ability to understand the nature of adolescence, communicate effectively with juveniles, effect behavior change in concert with probation officer contributions, and mobilize communities to provide enriched services to court youths. This goal and the supporting rationales met only limited success. Separate juvenile courts became the exception rather than the rule.

There was a need to relate juvenile courts to an overall court structure. Although any number of trial court judges assigned to the juvenile division distinguished themselves, quite probably more of them lacked the desired motivation and skills. Further, the isolation of specialist judges and their preference for an absence of legal procedures and lawyers while they exercised their child-saving missions precipitated the abrupt reformulation required of this court by the *Gault* decision of 1967.

A major restructuring of American trial courts has been under way for the past fifteen or twenty years. The ultimate goal of this direction, known as the unified trial court movement, is a single trial court in each community (American Bar Association, 1974). This court and its divisions will be responsible for all matters requiring judicial intervention. Separately organized juvenile courts, family courts, traffic courts, lower trial courts, probate courts, and other courts would fit into the single court entity. Rationales for the unified trial court include singular rather than multiple administration, improved efficiency with court management, elimination of overlapping jurisdictions (where several trial courts have authority to hear a particular type of case), and more flexible utilization of judges and nonjudicial employees.

The District of Columbia and Illinois are outstanding examples of a single trial court structure. Other states, such as Florida, have reorganized their courts into two trial courts, an upper general trial court and a lower limited trial court. Previously existing separate juvenile courts in Connecticut have been terminated in recent years and their responsibilities merged with a unified trial court system. The direction toward one or two trial courts is certain to continue.

Judges and Hearing Officers

Juvenile court judges, like other jurists, take the bench by either election or appointment. A judge of a separately organized juvenile or family court serves this jurisdiction exclusively during his or her tenure. In multijudge general trial courts, one or more judges are normally assigned to the juvenile division function. The term of the assignment most often is one year; when a term ends, the judge is reassigned to the civil, criminal, probate, or other division of the court. This is a generalist judge rather than a specialist judge. But some general trial court judges assigned to the juvenile division maintain continuous assignment there for ten or more years, in effect becoming specialist judges. There also are multijudge courts where judges carry an unspecialized workload; each judge hears all types of cases that are filed, juvenile and otherwise, rather than undertaking a specialized assignment. In a one-judge trial court, the judge serves as the juvenile court judge if the court holds juvenile jurisdiction and as the judge of every other kind of matter that comes before the court.

In many states, judges are assisted by hearing officers known as referees, masters, or commissioners. With few exceptions, these are lawyers appointed by the court to serve on a full- or part-time basis to hear a range of juvenile court concerns. Traditionally these hearing officers enter findings and recommendations that require confirmation by the judge to become an order; also a party may appeal a referee decision to the judge. While many referees are careful and sensitive hearing officers, the overuse of these officials has been criticized. The better standard is that referees should be judicial supplements and not judicial substitutes (National Conference of Commissioners, 1968).

Juvenile courts in Baltimore, Maryland, and Wayne County (Detroit), Michigan, have had a ratio of one judge to eight masters and three judges to thirteen referees, respectively. In those communities, hearing officers are judicial substitutes rather than judicial supplements. Throughout Maryland and in Hennepin County (Minneapolis),

Minnesota, masters or referees hear 85 to 95 percent of juvenile matters. A referee-heavy court communicates a message that juvenile matters are not sufficiently important for judges to consider; it diminishes the status of the court.

There are other problems with referee use. A required judicial review of referee findings and recommendations often becomes a rubber-stamp process rather than a considered undertaking. A juvenile court judge may prefer multiple referees to sharing the bench with another judge. Referees as subordinate judicial officials generally serve at the pleasure of the judge and do not share the greater powers an additional judge would exercise. Funding bodies also may prefer to add a referee rather than a judge since the costs are substantially less (Rubin, 1981).

JURISDICTION OF THE JUVENILE COURT

Age of Offender

Juvenile delinquency is defined as a minor's commission of an offense that if committed by an adult would constitute a crime. The question of who is a minor is not simply answered. All states have statutes that provide the upper age limit for juvenile court jurisdiction, as shown by Table 7–1.

TABLE 7–1 Maximum Age of Initial Juvenile Court Delinquency Jurisdiction

State	Age
Wyoming	18
Alabama, Alaska, Arizona, Arkansas, California, Colorado, Delaware, District of Columbia, Florida, Hawaii, Idaho, Indiana, Iowa, Kansas, Kentucky, Maine, Maryland, Minnesota, Mississippi, Montana, Nebraska, Nevada, New Hampshire, New Jersey, New Mexico, North Dakota, Ohio, Oklahoma, Oregon, Pennsylvania, Rhode Island, South Dakota, Tennessee, Utah, Virginia, Washington, West Virginia, Wisconsin	17
Georgia, Illinois, Louisiana, Massachusetts, Michigan, Missouri, South Carolina, Texas	16
Connecticut, New York, North Carolina, Vermont	15

Adult courts are the processing center, then, for young people beginning with their nineteenth birthdays in Wyoming, eighteenth birthdays in Alabama, seventeenth birthdays in Georgia, and sixteenth birthdays in Connecticut. Wyoming prosecutors, however, can choose to process juveniles under nineteen years in either a juvenile court or an adult criminal court.

Despite public and legislative concern that at least certain juvenile offenders should be treated as adults and receive similar punishments, no state has lowered its maximum age of initial juvenile court delinquency jurisdiction. During the 1970s, Florida increased its maximum age from seventeen to eighteen years and Alabama increased its maximum age in two stages from sixteen years to eighteen years.

Formerly, Illinois, Texas, and Oklahoma had a lower maximum age for boys than for girls. These disparities were held unconstitutional as violative of the equal protection clause of the Constitution. In the case of Oklahoma, the sixteen-year maximum age for boys was then equalized with the eighteen-year maximum age for girls. Similarly, the Maryland provision for a lower maximum age for juveniles in Baltimore and a higher maximum age for juveniles elsewhere in the state was found unconstitutional.

National standards urge that all youths within juvenile court age be handled initially in a juvenile court (allowing for more serious or chronic offenders above a certain minimum age to be transferred to a criminal court following what is known as a transfer or waiver hearing). But a number of state legislatures have disagreed with this view (Institute of Judicial Administration, 1980b). More states now allow the initial handling of more juveniles to be held in a criminal court, totally bypassing the juvenile court. For example, since 1978, thirteen-, fourteen-, and fifteen-year-olds charged with certain more serious offenses in New York State must be processed initially in a criminal court; under mitigating circumstances and with district attorney concurrence, a juvenile may be "transferred downward" for juvenile justice processing. Florida prosecutors may go directly to a criminal court with sixteen- or seventeen-year-old youths when "the public interest requires that adult sanctions be considered or imposed" (Florida Statute Ann. sec. 39.04(e)4.).

Recent legislative changes have also made it significantly easier for juvenile courts to transfer certain juveniles to a criminal court. In those states where changes occurred, instead of the prosecution being required to show that the juvenile is not amenable to juvenile system rehabilitation, the burden is on the youth to provide sufficient evidence of his amenability. Another legislative approach that increases adult criminalization of juveniles is to drop the age for transfer eligibility (for example, from sixteen years to fourteen years of age).

At the other end of the spectrum is the minimum age, below which very young offenders cannot be brought for juvenile court sanction. Many statutes are silent on this subject. Several states provide minimum ages of seven years, others ten years, and at least one state twelve years. The legal rationale for minimum age relates to the old common-law precept that because of immaturity children under seven years could not be responsible for any offense and that offenses committed by youths seven through fourteen years of age carried a presumption that the youngster was unable to formulate the criminal intent necessary to be found guilty of a crime. The social rationale for a minimum age relates both to this immaturity and to a preference to avoid a coercive court forum and instead encourage noncoercive community agencies to work with such youngsters.

Other Dimensions of the Court's Workload

The jurisdiction of a juvenile court refers to the types of cases that can be heard in this setting. Statutes define these case types. Historically, the definition of juvenile delinquency was broader than that of adult criminal behavior. Delinquency also encompassed the status offenses. Truant, runaway, incorrigible, and curfew-violating juveniles, then, were delinquents.

In 1961, in California, began the movement to reclassify delinquency as a law violation only and to structure a new status offense classification known by such names as person in need of supervision (PINS), child in need of supervision (CHINS), or youth in need of supervision (YINS). Subsequent statutory changes, most notably in the 1970s, substantially curbed the court's authority to lock up status offenders prior to trial or commit them to state delinquency institutions (Murray, 1983). This reduced power to incarcerate has resulted in a significant reduction in the number of complaints requesting the court to exercise authority over such youngsters. As further consequence of this policy, public and private noncoercive, youth-serving agencies have accepted more of this workload, probation officers are no longer engaged or are much less engaged with these youths, schools and parents are left more to their own resources, many youngsters are left alone, and the juvenile court is concentrating more on its primary workloads of delinquent and neglected and abused children. Divestiture of the court's jurisdiction in status offenses was accomplished at least in Washington State and Maine. All juvenile courts have jurisdiction with neglected and abused children, a subject area that is not a part of this presentation.

THE JUVENILE COURT AND THE CONSTITUTION

Gault and the Growth of Law

The past two decades have witnessed the transformation of the juvenile court into one that adheres far more substantially to formal legal procedures. This direction was opposed by many judges, probation officials, community agency representatives, and, indeed, police officers. Instead of "we know best what children need and how they should be handled," the precept has become one that submerges well-intended interests to the governance of law. The law comes first.

Judges now start with the law instead of the child, but hopefully the child is not forgotten in this process. Rehabilitation efforts continue but are bounded by legal constraints. As prosecutors and defense attorneys have joined the cast of actors, probation officers and social agency workers have lost power; reports and testimony must now screen through attorneys and be subject to cross examination. But the result is an improved court. Instead of a juvenile court that functions as an authoritarian social agency, we now have a court that triggers the intervention of probation and social agency services.

May 15, 1967, can be isolated as the starting point of the legal reformation. On that day the U.S. Supreme Court announced its decision in the case of *In re* Gault. It shook the foundations of the juvenile court system. The decision, the formulations of the majority and the concurring and dissenting justices, offers clear insights into the deficiencies of the former informal courts. It constitutes an enlightened discourse on the nature of due process of law.

The basic facts are these: Fifteen-year-old Gerald Gault, on probation for a petty theft in Globe, Arizona, was taken into custody by the sheriff on the verbal complaint of a woman neighbor that Gerald and another boy had made lewd or indecent remarks. His parents were both at work. No efforts were made to inform the parents or leave a notice that Gerald had been taken to the detention facility. Later, the parents learned of Gerald's detention from the other boy's family. The probation officer, who was also the detention center administrator, prepared a petition alleging only that Gerald was a delinquent minor. The petition did not state the specific charge on which the petition was based and was not served on Gerald or his parents. At the court hearing, no record was made of the proceeding; no one was sworn; no summary of the proceeding was prepared. The complainant was not there; the probation officer relayed what the complainant had said. Gerald was not advised he could have a lawyer. Although the probation officer and the judge thought that Gerald had admitted making the lewd remarks, his mother's recall was that Gerald had said he had only dialed the telephone number and handed the telephone to his friend. Subsequently, Gerald was committed to the custody of the state industrial school until his twenty-first birthday unless sooner discharged.

The case made its way to the Supreme Court with the assistance of volunteer attorneys obtained by the family. In finding the proceedings unconstitutional, the court ruled on four of the issues raised:

1. Due process required that Gerald and his parents be provided written notice of the charge, set forth with particularity, sufficiently in advance of the hearing in order to prepare for the hearing and defend the charge.
2. Gerald and his parents should have been advised of the child's right to be represented by counsel, or free counsel if they were unable to afford a lawyer, since the proceeding could result in institutional commitment. Failure to notify was a due process violation.
3. The judge's failure to advise Gerald and his parents of Gerald's privilege against self-incrimination violated the language of the Fifth Amendment applicable to the states by operation of the Fourteenth Amendment.
4. The judge should not have accepted into evidence the hearsay statement of the complainant. Sworn testimony that can be subjected to cross-examination is required.

Certain choice phrases of the majority decision transmitted vigorous vibrations. "Under our Constitution, the condition of being a boy does not justify a kangaroo court"; "neither the Fourteenth Amendment nor the Bill of Rights is for adults alone"; "the history of American freedom is, in no small measure, the history of procedure"; "[the child] requires the guiding hand of counsel at every step in the proceedings against him." Many observers suggested that a due process revolution had been mandated for juvenile courts and that follow-up state and federal appellate decisions would extend the *Gault* direction. This happened but only in part.

For example, a federal court held that a mentally deficient youngster's confinement in a Wyoming institution was unconstitutional because at the local trial court commitment proceedings years earlier neither the child nor his mother had been advised of the right to counsel (*Heryford* v. *Parker*, 1968). However, another federal court refused to extend the right to counsel ruling to compel representation of a child at a school guidance conference where he was suspended for disciplinary reasons (*Madera* v. *Board of Education*, 1967).

One state supreme court interpreted the *Gault* decision to require a jury trial in that state (*Peyton* v. *Nord*, 1968), while another state appellate court did not go beyond the basic four holdings of *Gault* and rejected any constitutional right to a jury trial (*Commonwealth* v. *Johnson*, 1967). One court held that *Gault* must mean that a juvenile has a right to bail (*Marsden* v. *Commonwealth*, 1967), while another court found otherwise (*Cradle* v. *Payton*, 1967).

Eight Other U.S. Supreme Court Decisions

Many legislatures used the stimulant of *Gault* to overhaul and modernize their juvenile court acts or to tack on the express requirements of this decision. The year before the *Gault* decision, the Supreme Court in the *Kent* v. *United States* (1966) case set forth minimum constitutional procedures for transferring juveniles to criminal courts. The transfer requirements of *Kent* also were blended into statute after statute.

A third juvenile justice decision of the Court, *In re* Winship (1970), was also supportive of the defense viewpoint. It held that the Constitution required that the burden of proof in delinquency trials be set at the criminal standard: beyond a reasonable doubt. The juvenile court, traditionally, had been seen as a civil court since the issue was delinquent acts rather than crimes. Juvenile courts had used a proof standard of a preponderance of the evidence, or 50.1 percent. The hearing transcript of the *Winship* trial contained the following:

Counsel:
   Your honor is making a finding by the preponderance of the evidence.
Court:
   Well, it convinces me.
Counsel:
   It's not beyond a reasonable doubt, your honor.
Court:
   That is true. . . . Our statute says a preponderance and a preponderance it is.

The Supreme Court determined that the preponderance standard was insufficient in a juvenile proceeding, since a youth's loss of liberty is comparable in seriousness to an adult incarceration. The Court rejected the contention that a child's best interest is not promoted if he wins the trial. But it took pains to reassure juvenile courts that the higher proof standard will not compel the courts to abandon or displace any of the substantive benefits of the juvenile process.

The constitutionalization direction stopped short in 1971 in the *McKeiver* v. *Pennsylvania* case, when the Court held that the U.S. Constitution did not compel jury trials for delinquency matters in state courts. The Court added that the Constitution did not prohibit individual states from authorizing jury trials for juveniles by statute or by state constitutional interpretation. Jury trials are authorized in about a dozen states but are invoked only sparingly.

The final Supreme Court "pro-defense" ruling occurred in 1975 in *Breed* v. *Jones*. A California juvenile court judge had adjudicated a juvenile but at a subsequent hearing transferred him to a criminal court for a new adjudication. The Supreme Court held this was double jeopardy. Fundamental fairness was violated when the "respondent was subjected to the burden of two trials for the same offense; he was twice put to the task of marshalling his resources against those of the State, twice subjected to the 'heavy personal strain" which such an experience represents."

The four subsequent decisions by the Court rejected further expansion of juvenile rights. *Swisher* v. *Brady* (1978) ruled that the double jeopardy protection was not offended by a Maryland procedure that permitted a finding of a nondelinquency by a master or referee to be appealed to the juvenile court judge. A state court rule that the judge could accept, reject, or modify the proposed finding, but could hear additional evidence only with the consent of the parties, was held to constitute a single proceeding, unlike *Breed* v. *Jones* (1975).

In *Fare* v. *Michael C.* (1979) the Court held that a juvenile's request during police interrogation to talk with his probation officer did not have the same impact as a requested talk with an attorney. A request for an attorney would prohibit the use of any further statements made by the juvenile. But a probation officer is a peace officer as well as a rehabilitation agent, and statements made by a juvenile following an unsuccessful request to consult with his probation officer may be admitted into evidence.

In a challenge that positioned free press against the state's interest in maintaining the confidentiality of a juvenile offender, the Court ruled in *Smith* v. *Daily Mail Publishing Company* (1979) that a newspaper could not be criminally punished for publishing a juvenile's name when the identity was not illegally obtained.

Finally, in 1984, the Court upheld the constitutionality of the New York detention admission law and statutory procedures related to detained juveniles in *Schall* v. *Martin*. In this much criticized decision, the Court accepted a quite broad use of preventive detention, rejected the premise that secure pretrial detention is a form of punishment, was not excessively bothered by detainment based on the imperfect art of predicting whether a juvenile will reoffend, and was unimpressed by any liberty interest children may possess, since "juveniles, unlike adults, are always in some form of custody." New York does not grant juveniles a right to bail.

Neither the common assertion that juveniles have the same rights as adults nor the frequent plea that children should have more constitutional rights than adults is evidenced in the present state of the law. A clear majority of the states fail to grant juveniles four fundamental rights afforded adult offenders:

1. Right to bail.
2. Right to a public trial.
3. Right to a jury trial.
4. Right to protection against preventive pretrial detention.

State appellate courts and federal trial and appellate courts have also issued numerous rulings related to delinquency and status offense cases.

PROBATION SERVICES

Form

Juvenile probation grew up with the juvenile court. The first juvenile court judge in Chicago proclaimed that the probation function was "the cord upon which all the pearls of the juvenile court are strung" (Rothman, 1974:50). Probation gave judges an attractive middle course between release and incarceration. It implied a commitment by the state to treat children in their homes and to try to correct their delinquent tendencies without removing them from their families. Social studies (increasingly called predisposition reports) prepared by probation officers have enabled judges to individualize youngsters.

Juvenile probation takes four primary organizational forms:

1. Judicial branch, local administration.
2. Judicial branch, state administration.
3. Executive branch, local administration.
4. Executive branch, state administration.

The first format, probation services administered by the local judiciary, is believed to be the most common model. There are hybrid models in states such as Georgia and Louisiana, where in some jurisdictions local courts administer probation but elsewhere in the state the services are provided by the state executive. With the growth of state funding of local court systems, more judicial branch probation personnel are now paid from state funds; probation officers may be paid from a combination of local and state funds, as occurs in Illinois. Juvenile probation often is organized as a separate entity; alternatively, it may be a division of a combined juvenile and adult probation department.

There has been a modest trend to transfer judicially administered probation to executive administered probation. There is also some movement to transfer the administration of local pretrial detention centers to state executive administration. Florida and Maryland probation and detention services were transferred to state executive administration in the early 1970s. There, state agencies provide the entire gamut of juvenile services: intake and probation, detention, community correctional services, institutions, and aftercare.

Who should administer probation remains a contentious issue. Supporters of judicial control of probation argue that:

- Probation services the court.
- Due process safeguards can be more closely monitored.
- Judges will obtain better feedback information as to the effectiveness of their orders.
- Judicial influence can be activated more readily to obtain improved probation and rehabilitation resources.
- Judges will grant greater responsibilities to probation officers under their administration.
- Judicial probation takes a higher priority than executive probation, since the latter is part of a larger agency.
- Judicial administration is less bureaucratic than executive administration.

Those against judicial control of probation and in favor of executive administration argue that:

- A statewide executive agency can provide, across the state, more uniform levels of probation service together with better integrated service delivery.
- No constitutional questions arise with executive administration.
- The essential judicial function is to adjudicate cases and enter dispositions.
- The court can more objectively evaluate services provided by an executive agency than it can those of its own employees.
- Judges generally are poor administrators.
- Patronage considerations may affect judicial branch probation appointments.

- Professional probation standards are encouraged more by executive agencies.

What is clear is that, over time, more of the costs of probation services will be borne by state funds allocated to the state court system or to a state executive agency.

Qualifications and Training of Officers

The training that probation officers bring to their positions varies widely. The generally accepted minimum standard for probation officer entry is a bachelor's degree in the social sciences, social welfare, criminal justice, education, psychology, counseling and guidance, or related majors. A growing number of staff members now have graduate degrees in one of these disciplines. Although some departments are led by graduate-trained social workers, most chief probation officers (or directors of juvenile court services, as this top position is often now named) do not have this training.

The absence of a single training discipline for probation staff members is consistent with juvenile courts' multiple, conflicting philosophic stances: treatment, accountability, and punishment. Individual probation officers seek to integrate these several orientations. Some, by values or training, incline more one way than another. Further, courts may be more treatment oriented, more accountability oriented, or more punitively oriented, depending on the messages sent out by the judge, the court's leadership, community opinion, juvenile crime levels, statutory provisions, prosecutor tenacity, media opinions, and political considerations.

STAGES IN THE JUVENILE JUSTICE PROCESS

Let us now examine the critical processing stages of the juvenile justice process. They include detention screening, intake screening, adjudication, and dispositions and treatment.

Detention Screening

Separate Pretrial Holding Facilities.   A goal of early reformers was the creation of juvenile detention centers to replace adult jails for the holding of alleged juvenile offenders pending court hearing. The intent was to provide secure care with specially trained child care staff who could assist youngsters, help evaluate them, and prepare youths for return to their families or alternative placements as determined by the court. Medical evaluation, arrangements for medical treatment, and a school program were other features.

In American communities there are hundreds of detention centers, many of them constructed along with courtrooms and probation offices in a juvenile court center located some miles from a downtown area. The four organizational models of probation department administration set forth earlier apply as well to detention center administration. State-administered facilities often serve a geographical region rather than a single county. Locally administered centers may house juveniles from nearby counties where no facility exists; payment is made for this service.

Rural areas and less populous communities frequently lack a juvenile detention center. There, juveniles are often housed in jails, either in a separate juvenile cell unit or, still today, mixed with adult offenders. Although serious efforts have been mounted in a number of states in recent years to bar the placement of juveniles in adult jails, perhaps 300,000 youngsters annually are held in these settings. Although regulations seek to ensure that sight and sound separation from adult offenders is provided for juveniles, the requirement is often violated.

The Decision to Detain.   Historically, police or sheriff's officers held the key to the detention center door. If these officials wanted a youth admitted, that youngster was admitted. More recently, detention screening, most often conducted by probation officers, has been inserted in the process. They review whether a law enforcement request for detention should be accepted. Juvenile courts serving populations in excess of 500,000 persons often maintain twenty-four–hour, on-site detention screening. Other communities have this service on-site either eight or sixteen hours daily. In some communities, senior detention center staff perform this screening function. Elsewhere, probation officers perform screening part of the day, with detention center staff performing this function during night-shift hours. Another variation is the assignment of a probation officer to screen on an on-call rather than an on-site basis when the court is closed.

Typically, the law enforcement official hands in a police incident report when he delivers a youth to the center. The law enforcement agency is to notify the youth's parents to come to the detention facility to meet with their youngster and the screening officer. Sometimes a youth is releasable, but his parents either are not available or reject release.

The detention screener examines the police report and may talk to the police officer about the offense. Age and county of residence are checked out along with record information as to whether the youth is presently awaiting hearing on another offense or is on probation or parole status. The screener is aware of statutory criteria that allow detention, of court or departmental guidelines that help operationalize statutory criteria, of juvenile justice system norms as to who must, may, or shall not be detained, and of a preference for use of the least restrictive alternative when deprivation of freedom is considered.

The criterion on which most juveniles are detained is that the juvenile is dangerous to self or others if released. Less often used criteria are that detention is necessary to ensure the youth's attendance at court hearings or that no parent is available who can provide suitable care and supervision. Juveniles not released to their parents may, under certain circumstances, be placed in a nonsecure shelter facility. A well regarded detention alternative, home detention or home supervision, is in place in a number of communities, but youngsters more typically are placed into this close surveillance release program following a night or two in detention. With home detention, youngsters are on strict rules, leave home only for school or work or for other activities with parent or staff member approval, and are seen by staff four or more times weekly to maintain controls over the juveniles' activities. Detention screeners may decide that a drug- or alcohol-using youth should be taken to a health facility for special care. Youngsters presenting severe emotional disturbance may be taken to an emergency psychiatric facility.

Many youngsters, following police apprehension, are not taken to a detention facility. Further, police may or may not refer the youngster to the intake arm of the court for screening as to the need for formal court proceedings. National data show that 58 percent of police apprehensions of juvenile offenders are referred to the juvenile court for further processing consideration (*Sourcebook*, 1985:533).

The Pima County Juvenile Court in Tucson, Arizona, a court serving a population exceeding 500,000, received 3,124 physical referrals for detention admission in 1984. The twenty-four–hour, on-site screening program accepted 54 percent of these referrals for detention admission. In addition, the court's intake office received 3,279 paper referrals for further action consideration (Pima County Juvenile Court, 1985:50).

Increasingly, statutes provide that if a child is detained, a formal petition must be prepared within a very brief time period. Every state has now legislated that a detention hearing shall be held by a judge or other hearing officer within twenty-four to seventy-two hours of admission. The detention hearing reviews the need for further detention. As many as 50 percent of detained juveniles are released at the detention hearing. Probation officers who perform detention screening are often part of the department's intake division. Intake officers also play an important role in determining whether or not a referral shall be handled by formal court petition. (For a thorough review of the potential for abuse in detention decisions and the harmful effects of preadjudicatory detention, see the next chapter.)

Intake Screening

The Decision to Petition.   In making the filing decision, intake probation officers are often guided by very broad statutory criteria. A statute may provide only that a preliminary inquiry shall be conducted to determine whether the interests of the child or the community require further court action.

Intake is an office procedure, not a field procedure. The most frequently cited statement of the intake purpose is:

> It permits the court to screen its own intake not just on jurisdictional grounds, but, within some limits, upon social grounds as well. It can cull out cases which should not be dignified with further court processes. . . . It ferrets out the contested matters in the beginning and gives the opportunity for laying down guidelines for appointment of counsel and stopping all social investigation and reporting until the contested issues of fact have been adjudicated. It provides machinery for referral of cases to other agencies when appropriate and beneficial to the child. It gives the court an early opportunity to discover the attitudes of the child, the parents, the police, and any other referral sources. It is a real help in controlling the court's caseload. (Waalkes, 1964:117)

If the referral is not formally petitioned, the case is dismissed, redirected to another agency for service, or handled with an informal probation agreement that usually provides only limited supervision by probation staff. A variation is a consent decree procedure, where a petition is filed but a judge approves an agreement similar to an informal probation agreement. It allows dismissal of the petition following compliance with requirements over a three- or six-month interval.

In dismissing a case, an intake probation officer will warn a juvenile that a further violation of law will be handled formally and bring serious court sanction. Depending upon the seriousness of a subsequent offense and the amount of time lapse between offenses, the threat may or may not be exercised.

Knowledge of community agency resources is particularly important for intake probation officers. With lesser law violations and with status offenses, referrals can be made to different youth-serving, family, mental health, or other community agencies. Aided by federal funding, an extensive number of youth agency services were created during the 1970s to serve as alternatives to court processing. The term used, descriptive of the referral process, was *diversion.* Diversion could be either true diversion or diversion to minimize penetration into the juvenile justice system. True diversion meant that if a juvenile failed to follow through on the diversion referral, nothing would happen. Juveniles diverted to reduce penetration had a string attached: if they failed to fulfill the requirements of the diversion agency, the original charge could be resurrected and a formal petition filed. (For a comprehensive discussion of the content, scope, and growth of diversion programs see Chapters 5 and 9.)

In recent years, by statute or by practice, monetary and community work service restitution has been utilized in a growing number of juvenile courts as a strategy for nonformal case resolution. When a youth pays back a victim for losses sustained in the offense, a charge can be dismissed. Alternatively, as when no victim loss is sustained, performance of an agreed number of community work service hours can result in the dismissal of the charge. These restitution approaches are consistent with an accountability philosophy that holds a juvenile responsible to the victim, or to the community as the symbolic victim, for the injury that was done and sanctions a juvenile in proportion to the severity of the harm that was done. (For further information on the recent surge in the victim's movement, including restitution programs and victim–offender mediation programs, see Section IV, Epilogue.)

The Growing Prosecutor Role.   Rising juvenile crime rates in the early 1970s precipitated another development that has impacted intake screening substantially. By statute, by agreement with the court, or by assertion that their responsibilities include the intake decision-making role, prosecuting attorneys moved into influential position at this processing stage (Rubin, 1980). Prosecutor entry has taken different forms, among them:

1. Intake officers make the file, no-file decision. With cases filed, the prosecutor reviews all petitions for legal sufficiency and accuracy. This is the weakest of prosecutor approaches.
2. An intake probation officer cannot dismiss or divert a felony charge without prosecutor concurrence. The prosecutor approves the content of a petition.
3. Intake probation officers recommend for or against filing; prosecutors must approve all recommendations. A prosecutor can dismiss a charge for which a formal petition was recommended or file a charge that had been targeted for dismissal or diversion. The prosecutor approves the content of the petition.

4. More serious charges bypass the intake probation officer. They are reviewed by a prosecutor, with the expectation of a formal petition. The prosecutor may remand certain charges to intake for informal resolution. The prosecutor approves the content of any petition.

5. All police referrals bypass intake and go directly to a prosecutor. Decision making is performed by the prosecutor, who exclusively determines whether to prepare a petition for the court.

Prosecutors now dominate the intake processing stage in many jurisdictions. It should not be assumed that prosecutors, by definition, favor formal petitions more than intake probation officers do. Certainly there are courts where prosecutor entry has led to a substantial increase in formal petitions. But prosecutors generally restrict formal petitioning for status offenses more than do intake officers, and they are not very inclined to bring a first misdemeanor offense before a judge. They do want serious and chronic offenders brought formally before the court.

National data show that 43 percent of police referrals to the court result in formal petitions to the court (*Sourcebook*, 1984:480). The percentage varies, of course, between jurisdictions. Some file fewer than 20 percent of referrals; others petition as many as 70 percent of referrals.

Adjudication

Implementation of the Right to Defense Counsel.   Despite the legalization of the juvenile court, few trials occur. Probably fewer than 5 percent of petitioned juveniles undergo a trial with its requirement of legal proof. The absence of formal trials is common to other courts as well; only infrequently do adult felony courts record trials with more than 12 to 15 percent of their cases.

Following the filing of a formal juvenile court petition, an arraignment or initial appearance hearing is conducted. Here, advisement is made of the right to counsel and to free counsel, the right to trial, the right to have witnesses in support of the juvenile subpoenaed, and the opportunity for the juvenile or his attorney to cross-examine adverse witnesses. Vast numbers of juveniles admit to their offenses at this stage, waiving the right to counsel and to trial. Others request counsel, go outside the courtroom for five to ten minutes to talk with an attorney, then come back in to admit their offense or request a continuance of the case to enable more extended investigation by the lawyer.

Most urban juvenile courts are serviced by public defenders who establish reputations as strong advocates for the juveniles, although their heavy workloads place real constraints on case investigations and time available for the conduct of trials. When the evidence against a youth is weak, defenders will ask the prosecutor to dismiss the case, negotiate with the prosecutor for a favorable plea bargain, or go to trial. Trials are more commonly held when a juvenile faces institutionalization if found guilty, since for these cases prosecutors provide little plea-bargaining leeway.

Juvenile courts rely on the appointment of private attorneys to represent juveniles in the absence of a public defender system. Many of these attorneys provide good defense services, though the limited payment provided, together with the usual maximum payment lid, may discourage more comprehensive defense challenge. Some juveniles are represented by lawyers paid by their parents. This may slant lawyer performance toward negotiation and plea in order to lower the lawyer's bill.

Judges can reduce the number of trials they need to conduct by continuously appointing lawyers whose basic approach is to bargain with the prosecutor, avoid trial, and then argue for the least restrictive disposition. Other judges want rigorous defense advocacy and appoint lawyers who are not hesitant to go to trial or challenge the system.

The *Gault* (1967) decision required notification of the right to counsel and free counsel if institutionalization may occur. The decision did not require counsel, only notification of this right. Some states and any number of local jurisdictions have imposed a stronger requirement. New York law requires a defense attorney when there is a formal petition. Iowa will not permit a child to waive counsel from the detention hearing stage onward. A number of local juvenile courts, particularly those serviced by public defenders, mandate a lawyer for every juvenile. Almost universally, hearings concerning transfer of a juvenile to criminal court processing require a lawyer for the youth. Still, the extent of overall defense representation in many courts fails to exceed 15 percent.

The quality of defense representation is another issue. Though many defense attorneys perform extremely well in this forum, public defenders may be the newest recruits to that office, and private attorneys may have little knowledge of the complexities of the juvenile justice system that could be used advantageously in behalf of their youngsters. A study of the legal representation of children in New York State family courts entered discouraging findings: 45 percent of representation reflected either seriously inadequate or marginally adequate representation; 27 percent reflected acceptable representation, 4 percent effective representation; 24 percent of observations lacked sufficient information to be coded. Specific problems centered around lack of preparation and lack of contact with juveniles prior to and during a hearing. This research consisted of courtroom observations and transcript analysis of both trials and other courtroom proceedings (Knitzer & Sobie, 1984:8).

The Juvenile Court Trial.   The trial process is similar to criminal court proceedings except for the generalized absence of jury trials. Prosecutors present their evidence; defense attorneys cross-examine prosecution witnesses. The defense may impanel defense witnesses; the defendant may or may not testify. Prosecution may use rebuttal witnesses. The ruling is pronounced. Far more juveniles are found guilty than are found innocent.

Prior to the entry of the prosecutor into the juvenile court, probation officers sometimes performed this function—at a substantial disadvantage when there was defense counsel. Alternatively, judges awkwardly tried to elicit the evidence against a child and, when there was no defense attorney, also sought to help bring out a juvenile's defense. Today's lawyer-oriented system represents a significant improvement.

Probation officers tend to be present at initial appearance hearings, particularly in those courts that move into a dispositional hearing immediately following entry of a plea admitting the offense. In more adversarial juvenile courts, dispositional hearings take place from three to five weeks following the entry of the plea or finding of guilt.

A notable development is the growing requirement that juvenile cases be processed speedily. These requirements, imposed by statute or by state or local court rule, mandate swifter processing time for detained juveniles than for those who are not detained. Speedy processing is sought in order to reduce witness memory problems, lead to a faster delivery of intervention services, shorten pretrial deprivation of liberty, or, alternatively, secure the removal of a juvenile from the community to an institution so that new intervention efforts can be initiated.

Disposition and Treatment

The Dispositional Hearing.   Probation officers substantially impact judicial or referee decisions that sanction a juvenile and set in place a "treatment plan." The social study, or predisposition report, is prepared by a probation officer, who interviews the juvenile and his parents during a home study, obtains a school report, contacts other agencies that have worked with the youth, and chronicles a juvenile's prior history with the court; victim loss statements are secured for monetary restitution consideration. Copies of the predisposition report are distributed to the judicial hearing officer and to prosecution and defense counsel. The report may be shared with the youth and the parents, a practice that is troublesome for some probation departments as the report may include critical comments regarding the parents and the probation officer's recommendations may be challenged. But this is good practice.

The actual hearing usually begins with an oral summary of the report by the probation officer. The rules of evidence are relaxed for this hearing: hearsay statements are permitted, although, for example, when a psychological evaluation has been conducted, a defense attorney may require that the psychologist be present for cross-examination rather than rely on the written report. Psychological and even psychiatric evaluations are commonly conducted in larger juvenile courts with cases involving chronic delinquency, violence, sexual offenses, arson, or the appearance of significant emotional disturbance. Substantial weight is given to these reports although the predictability of their recommendations arouses skepticism. Frequently, they point to the need for greater structure in a youth's life and recommend residential care to provide that structure.

Different courts have different dispositional norms. Urban juvenile courts tend to retain reoffending juveniles in the community longer than do courts serving less populous districts, since over time and with greater need the urban systems have developed more resources and institutional alternatives. Courts serving less populous jurisdictions "pull the string" quicker and send less serious delinquency cases off to state care. But everywhere, except for very serious offenses, probation is the first resort and usually the second as well.

The Probation Supervision Function. Counseling is a major stock-in-trade of the probation officer. But probation is a mixture of many things and many styles. It includes warnings, rule clarification, humanized interest and advice, a search for problem causation, advocacy, examination of a juvenile's adjustment and achievement in his various environments, connection with external individuals and agencies that might be of positive help, encouragement to undertake constructive experiences, surveillance checks, psychic probes, and more. Probation counseling is a theoretical melting pot that encompasses Freud, reality therapy, smatterings of each new therapeutic approach that has rippled through the nation (almost annually) for the past several decades, some sociological notions, simplified behavior modification, and common sense. Underneath it all is the strategy for the probation officer to gain a relationship with the youth and to serve as a model embedded in the child's mind and conscience, particularly at times of critical choices.

Relatively little family counseling is conducted by probation offi-cers except at investigation stages and at moments of crisis. Juveniles and their families are referred to external family counseling and men-tal health services. A juvenile's education is an important focus: School counselors may be encouraged to transfer a youth to other classes that are more interesting or hold out the potential for greater success. Tu-toring may be arranged. A youth may be transferred to an alternate school for youngsters experiencing difficulty with the regular curriculum.

Probation officers find jobs for youngsters, arrange summer camp opportunities, and facilitate scholarships for wilderness adventure pro-grams. Drug and alcohol recovery services—residential, educational, and counseling—have been drawn on more extensively in recent years. Educational programs may be targeted at juvenile shoplifters.

In many juvenile courts, the frequency of probation contact re-mains largely intuitive. Juveniles perceived as needing more frequent contact are seen more often than other youths. More serious, more chronic offenders fall into that category. Many probation officers begin seeing new probationers either weekly or biweekly, tapering off to fewer contacts after several months if no special problems are evident. Juvenile probation agency caseloads usually are substantially lighter than adult agency caseloads, affording greater individualization. While any number of departments average fewer than 40 youngsters on a pro-bation caseload, less well staffed departments may average at least 75 or even 100 cases per officer.

A number of probation agencies schematize frequency of contact something like the following: New probationers are seen weekly or bi-weekly for three months unless there are indications that this extent of frequency is unnecessary. After three months the frequency is reduced to a monthly basis unless there are indications that this is insufficient. The protocol provides for collateral contacts with parents, school, and other involved agencies on a declining frequency basis.

At present, there is considerable interest in a more rigorous ap-proach to classification for supervision intensity. Although different approaches are used, one that is finding favor involves an adaptation of the Wisconsin adult offender classification scheme that is predicated on a point score analysis of offender risk and offender needs. Fre-quency of direct and collateral contacts is scheduled for maximum, me-dium, and minimum supervision levels. The juvenile's assessment point total presumptively places him in one of these supervision levels, but agency policy (as with a particularly serious offense) may place the youth in the maximum supervision level even though his point score would fall into a lower supervision class. And probation officers as-sessing the youth are authorized to recommend the overriding of the presumptive level and to justify this. This overall approach provides for periodic reassessment of supervised juveniles and upward or downward movement in intensity level following approval by a staff supervisor. Well-managed departments validate their risk/needs criteria prior to initiating such an approach and periodically thereafter.

Restitution.   Restitution has become an important dimension of the probation experience. It takes two primary forms: monetary restitution and community work service restitution. The first involves paying back the victim for losses or damage suffered. Neither all victims nor all juveniles are totally honest or accurate in suggesting loss or damage costs. Some courts, with victim consent, use a trained mediator to work toward an agreement among all parties as to an acceptable restitution amount and repayment plan. This process, termed *victim–offender mediation* or *victim–offender reconciliation*, seeks also to reduce estrangement between the parties.

The actual loss amount is not always ordered. Statutes tend to provide that the actual total needs to be ameliorated by a youth's ability to earn this amount within a reasonable period of time. To help with repayment, enlightened juvenile courts have instituted job skill preparation classes to train youngsters to find jobs and hold them. Some programs have courted the private and public sectors for jobs where these youngsters can work, earn, and repay victims.

Nationally, 76 percent of ordered restitution is repaid; 56 percent of juveniles are able to repay 100 percent of the ordered amount (Schneider, 1985). Juveniles who fail to make reasonable efforts to obtain work may be returned to a court hearing for review and possible sanction. And many youngsters complete all other probation conditions satisfactorily, but their probation term is extended because they have not completed restitution payments. A small number of courts use "sole sanction restitution" as a disposition with lesser offenses. Violators do not go onto regular probation caseloads; instead the sole requirement of the court is repayment. With repayment, the case is terminated.

With community work service restitution, juveniles are ordered to perform a given number of work hours at a private nonprofit or governmental agency. Larger communities have more than 100 sites where this work may be performed. The sites typically include public libraries and parks, animal shelters, nursing homes, community centers, youth agencies, day-care centers, YMCAs, and other settings. One or two juveniles may be assigned to a particular work site supervisor. Alternatively, restitution programs provide supervised work crews, groups of juveniles that go out to a site and work under the direction of a staff member. Some courts assign larger numbers of hours than other courts. Some courts wisely have developed a matrix that is used to require more hours for more serious offenses or offense patterns than with less serious offenders, a dimension of proportionality and just deserts. Again, failure to cooperate with the work program can result in a return to court.

Research with restitution youths, using control groups, has uncovered less recidivism (Schneider, 1985), and restitution has become a prime selling point to the community as juvenile courts seek greater public acceptance for what they do. Monetary restitution and community work service restitution are becoming central components of juvenile court purpose and strategy.

INTERVENTION WITH SERIOUS AND REPETITIVE JUVENILE OFFENDERS

Retaining Juveniles in the Juvenile Justice System

Earlier, reference was made to changed legislative policies regarding serious and repetitive juvenile offenders such as the option for direct filing in criminal court used in a growing number of states and for the eased transfer from juvenile court to criminal court handling (Krisberg, Schwartz, Litsky, & Austin, 1986). Public pressures also encourage prosecutors and probation personnel in these directions, and judges take political risks in retaining these youths in the juvenile system. Research findings of criminal court handling of juveniles show that criminal court judges place many of these offenders on probation or fine them; a very substantial percentage are not jailed or imprisoned (Hamparian et al., 1982).

Within the juvenile court world, a number of intervention strategies (though not enough) have been directed toward retaining these offenders within the juvenile justice system and effectuating better controlled behavior, if not rehabilitation. These programmed approaches, directed also toward thwarting state institutionalization of juveniles, include:

> • More intensive probation supervision. Such supervision is growing in use, but the intensity varies widely. In one court intensive supervision may mean responsibility for ten juveniles, in another for twenty-five juveniles. Probation officers may be supplemented by paraprofessional aides who do much evening and weekend contacting of these juveniles in their homes or neighborhoods and may see the youths on a daily basis. More intensive supervision may take the form of intensive group counseling rather than individual counseling.

• Expansive work programs paired with other components. This may be a full-day or part-day intervention effort. The work to be done may take the form of community work service restitution or may involve the development of prevocational skills. Curfews and somewhat intensive counseling may accompany this type of program.

• Full-day programs in a special school using a low student-to-teacher ratio, group and individual counseling, and recreation.

• A full-day school and work program, the school focusing on learning disabilities and the work including paid work experiences such as helping with home remodeling.

• A full-day program where the school component is coordinated with an adventure program. School subjects, in addition to basics, may relate to marine life when the adventure component is oriented to knowledge of the sea and skills in boating.

• Tracking programs that combine a short-term secure residential experience with a phased return to family and school, a mandatory paid work requirement, and very intensive surveillance.

• Proctor or specialized foster homes that combine with an alternative school and a strong counseling component.

• Longer-term residential programs. These may be in secure settings or in open settings, seen as "staff secure," that rely on intensive internal and external program components. The settings may serve as many as fifty juveniles or as few as four.

State Institutionalization

Overall, in recent years the number of state institutional beds has neither increased nor decreased significantly. In the face of bars on status offender institutionalization, it appears, more criminal offenders have been committed to state institutions (Krisberg et al., 1986). Also there is some indication that where commitments have decreased, juveniles are retained in institutions for longer periods.

State institutions tend to be much smaller than adult prisons. A number of lawsuits aimed at improving state institutional programs have sought the establishment of a constitutional principle of the right to treatment. Decisions have gone both ways on this issue. Suits have been won in Oregon, Texas, Indiana, and other jurisdictions. Suits may also be premised on a statutory right to treatment or on the contention that deficiencies in care represent cruel and unusual punishment and therefore are unconstitutional (Volenik, 1978).

Massachusetts is best known for its accomplishments in closing down state training schools, implementing a wide range of community correctional resources, and using a relatively small number of secure beds in regional facilities, many of them operated by private nonprofit organizations (Coates, Miller, & Ohlin, 1977). Utah has moved in this direction. Other states have provided state funding for local community corrections as an incentive to turn more to local programming and reduce the extent of state institutionalization. Yet funding structures more generally provide an incentive for state commitments rather than local programs: with commitment, state funds pay for the care; to expand local programming would cost local funds. Judges have closer working relationships with local officials and, it is believed, would be more hesitant to institutionalize juveniles in state facilities if this meant using local funds to accomplish this.

IMPROVING JUVENILE JUSTICE: JUDICIAL RESPONSIBILITY

Juvenile justice achievements have derived from many sources. A broad range of individuals and groups initiated the juvenile court (Platt, 1977). Its rapid spread across the land involved spirited advocacy and activated support from a diverse constituency. Its legal procedures underwent serious challenge beginning in the late 1960s, its rehabilitative offerings have been the subject of serious questioning for twenty years now, and some critics have contended there is no longer any compelling reason to continue the juvenile court (Rubin, 1979). But it will continue, and it needs the assistance of many to make it a better instrument of justice for young people and for their communities.

Judges, particularly, have a central role to play in this venture (Rubin, 1985a). They may well be in the best position to know the strengths and shortcomings of the juvenile justice system and to interpret its needs. Also, too few others speak out in behalf of children. By interpreting the juvenile justice system to the public, the judge extends the juvenile court constituency and the number of persons who understand and might defend the juvenile justice system if the need arises. Sacrificing time during noncourt hours goes with the job, though not enough juvenile court jurists manifest interest in breakfast, luncheon, or evening meetings, committee memberships, presentations before legislatures, liaison with the media, and speech after speech both to inform and to ask assistance from the public. The position contains great clout, which reinforces the obligation of the judge to exercise these opportunities.

The more services and alternative programs a judge facilitates, the easier becomes the judicial task as hearings are less often continued and/or prolonged in search of the right program for a youngster. In their role as advocates and change agents, juvenile court judges have secured detention facilities to replace jails; expanded probation staffing capabilities; facilitated agreements with mental health agencies to serve court youngsters; helped institute private nonprofit agency youth services; steered community groups and foundations to fund medical, dental, educational, and clothing needs of youths; influenced more intelligent legislative considerations, and much more.

Inside the court exist opportunities, indeed requirements, for judges to improve court functions. They can facilitate speedy case processing. They can place demands on court and probation personnel, prosecution and defense counsel, and representatives of public and private agencies to be present at the time scheduled for a court hearing, to have their reports prepared, and to have their plans in order. When reports or plans are incomplete or vague, a judicial call for higher standards should result in better-prepared investigations and formulations the next time.

Judicial statements and attitudes are watched carefully. The words of a judge tend to carry particular weight. One juvenile court judge put it that once he went on the bench, people laughed twice as hard at his jokes. Judicial influence is an advantage, but it is a problem if the judge knows little of what he or she speaks. Judicial insights or recommendations are not necessarily more valid; the robe itself is not enough. Judicial audiences should require more from judges than good intentions or unsupported assertions.

Improving Juvenile Justice: Contributions By Others

Probation officials can make a difference. Strong departments continuously assess the quality of their efforts and search for more productive directions. They spot needs that are not being met and either reorganize their services to meet these needs or work with community agencies to have this service developed externally and available for court use. Well-executed participative management approaches bring out useful insights from line probation officers. Yet, far too many probation managers are crippled by a lack of clear direction, a timidity born of unsuccessful prior risk taking, judicial heavy-handedness, or real or imagined budgetary constraints.

Prosecutors are in a particularly strong position to make juvenile justice work better. They too are listened to intently. Their purpose is justice and not a knee-jerk "lock them up" approach. Many buy into the probation and community corrections promise but are properly not supportive of poor performance. Many are very amenable to new program directions that might avoid institutionalization or transfer to a criminal court. As an important agent for the protection of the public's safety, prosecutors have every right to insist on high-performance intervention. They are on sound ground in focusing attention on requiring juvenile restitution. They can secure improved court procedures that adhere to legal requisites and can also assist law enforcement officers in meeting the legal requirements of their tasks.

Defense counsel have a particular role in keeping the system honest. Without their presence and advocacy, procedures may be sloppy, insufficient attention may be given to individualizing juveniles, and poor quality investigations, recommendations, and service delivery may go unchallenged. Youngsters need advocates who argue their case and their best interests so that less is assumed or taken for granted. There is merit to a defense counsel's rocking the status quo boat. Defense counsel need to thwart arbitrary procedures, routinized decision making, and programmatic shortcomings.

But it is no secret that assignment to the juvenile court is often used as a training ground for a new prosecutor or defender. Representational shortcomings here, while experience is being gained, are relatively unimportant compared with errors made later as criminal court attorneys. Too frequently these lawyers overly defer to the juvenile court judge or probation official.

Others have roles in improving the juvenile justice system. Private and public rehabilitation agency staff members need to know what they can and cannot do well and need to continue finding beneficial adaptations of more traditional approaches to delinquent youngsters. Counseling services can be useful but must be in tune with family culture and the daily environment of the youths. The strengths of youngsters need to be built on. Researchers and scholars have their role. Evaluation of program impact is useful to confirm or dispel myths. Different types of programs work better with different types of youths; we should know the best fit. The scholarly examination and critique of court processes and goings-on can help us better go forth.

State legislators need to do much better. Rather than pandering to simplistic notions of crime and punishment they need to practice intelligent leadership. Legislators must better understand the merits of probation services and community programming and fund these efforts more richly. They need to better address and strengthen the juvenile justice system, the last best hope for many youngsters.

Finally, interested citizens have contributed through legislative advocacy for positive court reform directions, court watching that brings helpful reports for changes that would further court objectives, volunteering to enrich the lives of individual youngsters, membership on juvenile court citizen advisory boards that can lead to positive gains, and their provision of a wider support group that can be of assistance.

With it all, the juvenile court remains beset with a range of conflicting purposes, difficulties in integrating its service role within a legal regimen, uncertainty with what works, a difficult client group, and resource shortfalls. By definition the juvenile court landscape is not a beautiful one. Society has granted this institution an impossible assignment. Its brush strokes are sometimes faulty; its images not always clear. But it can and must fashion improved approaches and reach higher standards.

DISCUSSION QUESTIONS

1. Should juvenile court judges be specialists, serving only that court during their tenure in office? What are the implications of such a policy?
2. Should the juvenile court be replaced by a family court?
3. Should all juveniles under eighteen years of age be handled initially in a juvenile court in all states?
4. How has the U.S. Supreme Court distinguished the constitutional safeguards that protect adult offenders and those that protect juvenile offenders? What are the differing rationales?
5. If you were an indigent juvenile defendant who requested an attorney, would you prefer representation by a public defender? A private attorney appointed and paid for by the court? A private attorney donating his/her services? Why?
6. Is it better policy that probation and detention center services be administered by the judiciary or the executive? Why?
7. To what degree should the decision to detain be influenced by space availability at the detention center? The distance from the site of the offense or the police station to the detention center? A juvenile's attitude toward the offense? The severity of the offense? The parents' attitude toward their child?
8. Should all legally provable juvenile offenses be petitioned for formal hearing before a judge or referee? Explain your answer.
9. Should juveniles with the same offense and offense histories receive the same dispositions? Why or why not?
10. How does a probation officer balance an interest in restitution to a victim with a juvenile's inability to earn monies for victim repayment?
11. How can juvenile courts reduce community risks from more serious and repetitive juvenile offenders while allowing participation by such youths in community-based rehabilitation programs?

REFERENCES

American Bar Association, Commission on Standards of Judicial Administration. (1974). *Standards relating to court organization* (Approved draft) (Standards 1.10, 1.12). Chicago: American Bar Association.

Breed v. *Jones,* 421 U.S. 519 (1975).

Coates, R. B., Miller, A. D., & Ohlin, L. E. (1977). *Juvenile correctional reform in Massachusetts.* Washington, DC: U.S. Government Printing Office.

Commonwealth v. *Johnson,* 231 A.2d 9 (Pa. Super. 1967).

Cradle v. *Peyton,* 156 S.E.2d 874 (Va. 1967).

Fare v. *Michael C.,* 442 U.S. 707 (1979).

Florida Stat. Ann. § 39.04(e)4.

Hamparian, D. M., Estep, L. K., Muntean, S. M., Priestino, R. R., Swisher, R. G., Wallace, P. L., & White, J. L. (1982). *Youth in adult courts: Between two worlds.* Washington, DC: U.S. Department of Justice.

Heryford v. *Parker,* 396 F.2d 393 (10th Cir. 1968).

In re Gault, 387 U.S. 1 (1967).

In re Winship, 397 U.S. 358 (1970).

Institute of Judicial Administration–American Bar Association Juvenile Justice Standards Project. (1980a). *Standards relating to court organization* (Standard 1.1). Cambridge, MA: Ballinger.

Institute of Judicial Administration–American Bar Association Juvenile Justice Standards Project. (1980b). *Standards relating to transfer between courts* (Standard 1.1). Cambridge, MA: Ballinger.

Kent v. *United States,* 383 U.S. 541 (1966).

Knitzer, J., & Sobie, M. (1984). *Law guardians in New York State: A study of the legal representation of children.* New York: New York State Bar Association.

Krisberg, B., Schwartz, I., Litsky, P., & Austin, J. (1986, January). The watershed of juvenile justice reform. *Crime and Delinquency, 32*(1), 5–38.

Madera v. *Board of Education of the City of New York,* 386 F.2d 778 (2d Cir. 1967).

Marsden v. *Commonwealth,* 227 N.E.2d 1 (Mass. 1967).

McKeiver v. *Pennsylvania,* 403 U.S. 528 (1971).

Murray, J. P. (Ed.). (1983). *Status offenders: A sourcebook.* Boys Town, NE: Boys Town Center.

National Advisory Commission on Criminal Justice Standards and Goals (1973). *Courts* (Standard 14.1). Washington, DC: U.S. Government Printing Office.

National Advisory Committee for Juvenile Justice and Delinquency Prevention. (1980). *Standards for the administration of juvenile justice* (Standard 3.12). Washington, DC: U.S. Government Printing Office.

National Conference of Commissioners on Uniform State Laws. (1968). *Uniform juvenile court act* (Sec. 7, Comment). Chicago: Author.

Peyton v. Nord, 437 P.2d 716 (N.M. 1968).

Pima County Juvenile Court. (1985). *1984 Annual Report*. Tucson, AZ: Author.

Platt, A. (1977). *The child savers* (2d ed.). Chicago: University of Chicago Press.

Rothman, D. S. (1974). The progressive legacy: Development of American attitudes toward juvenile delinquency. In L. T. Empey (Ed.), *Juvenile justice: The progressive legacy and current reforms*. Charlottesville: University Press of Virginia, 34–68.

Rubin, H. T. (1979). Retain the juvenile court? Legislative developments, reform directions, and the call for abolition. *Crime and Delinquency, 25,* 281–298.

Rubin, H. T. (1980, July). The emerging prosecutor dominance of the juvenile court intake process. *Crime and Delinquency, 26,* 3, 299–318.

Rubin, H. T. (1981, July). Between recommendations and orders: The limbo status of juvenile court referees. *Crime and delinquency, 27,* 3, 317–335.

Rubin, H. T. (1985a). *Behind the black robes: Juvenile court judges and the court*. Beverly Hills, CA: Sage Publications.

Rubin, H. T. (1985b). *Juvenile justice: Policy, practice, and law* (2d ed.). New York: Random House.

Schall v. Martin, 104 S.Ct. 2403 (1984).

Schneider, A. L. (Ed.). (1985). *Guide to juvenile restitution*. Washington, DC: U.S. Government Printing Office.

Smith v. Daily Mail Publishing Company, 443 U.S. 97 (1979).

Sourcebook of Criminal Justice Statistics—1983. (1984). Washington, DC: U.S. Government Printing Office.

Sourcebook of Criminal Justice Statistics—1984. (1985). Washington, DC: U.S. Government Printing Office.

Swisher v. Brady, 98 S.Ct. 2699 (1978).

Volenik, A. (1978). Right to treatment: Case developments in juvenile law. *Justice System Journal, 3,* 3, 292–307.

Waalkes, W. (1964, April). Juvenile court intake: A unique and valuable tool. *Crime and Delinquency, 10,* 2, 117–123.

Chapter Eight

Preadjudicatory Detention

Charles E. Frazier

Carole Roberts '88

ABSTRACT

This chapter addresses one of the most controversial practices of American juvenile justice: the detention of youth prior to adjudication of guilt. The first two sections discuss national trends in detention rates. While these rates have decreased over the last two decades, some features of this trend are still disturbing: the number of juveniles admitted to detention has gone down substantially, but the length of time detainees are held in secure facilities has gone up. The next two sections discuss the bases for custody and legal grounds for detention. The primary aims of detention are (1) to protect the community, (2) to protect the child, and/or (3) to assure the child's appearance in subsequent scheduled court hearings. The chapter then considers the consequences of the broad legal or statutory grounds that permit officials wide discretion in making detention decisions. It is argued that detention decisions that flow from broad discretion often reflect arbitrariness and/or capriciousness on the part of the juvenile justice officials and that, to that extent, they are serious abuses of power that harm detained juveniles legally.

Another section focuses on harmful effects of standardless detention practices on juveniles. While much is made of this issue by legal scholars, there is little systematic evidence that establishes either the extent or severity of the problem. The various organizational and structural conditions of secure detention are discussed along with the undesirable effects that may result in terms of staff–inmate relations and informal practices by staff. The chapter concludes by summarizing the dangers of preadjudicatory detention and the discordant role it plays in a justice system designed to provide care, protection, and rehabilitation for troubled youths.

JUVENILE DETENTION

No study of juvenile justice and delinquency prevention is complete without consideration of preadjudicatory detention. Detention, when applied to juveniles, is defined as "temporary care in physically restrictive settings pending court adjudication, disposition, or transfer to another jurisdiction or agency" (Poulin, Levitt, Young, & Pappenfort, 1980:3).[1]

Each year nearly 500,000 youths in the United States are detained in secure preadjudicatory detention facilities ("Comments," 1983: Rubin, 1985); by some estimates another 500,000 to 750,000 are held in adult jails or lockups awaiting trial (Community Research Center,

---

[1]This definition comes from a New York report on detention, but it is a common one. See, for example, definitions established by the National Council on Crime and Delinquency in *Model Rules for Juvenile Courts.* rule 1.4 (1969), cited in Guggenheim (1977). Similar definitions are cited in Cohen (1975:11); and Sheridan (1966:23).

1980b). This practice of detaining juveniles prior to formal adjudication is highly controversial. Critics charge that (1) detention causes unnecessary and undefensible risks to juveniles' psychological and physical well-being (Lotz, Poole, & Regoli, 1985), (2) detention standards are often unclear, leading to capriciousness and arbitrariness in decision making (Cohen, 1975; McDiarmid, 1977:78), and (3) preadjudicatory detention disadvantages youths at later disposition points (Bailey, 1981; Frazier & Bishop, 1985; Tripplett, 1978).

While most states have specific statutes relating to juvenile detention, many either have no meaningful standards for detention or have legal language so unclear that any semblance of meaningful standards is lost ("Comments," 1983:95; McDiarmid, 1977:78). Many juvenile courts around the country still follow the recommendation of the National Council on Crime and Delinquency, which suggests that youths should be detained only if it "appears likely that they will commit a new offense dangerous to themselves or to the community pending disposition; when they are thought likely to run away; or must be held for adjudication in another jurisdiction (probation violations, runaways, etc.)" (National Council, 1961: 4).

TRENDS: ADMISSION RATES AND TIME IN DETENTION

The trends in detention rates have remained distressingly high despite harsh criticism of the practice and a number of efforts to implement national standards. For example, in 1958, the National Probation and Parole Association suggested standards for detention and recommended that the number of children detained in a detention facility should not be greater than 20 percent of all those offenders referred to the court. This standard was cut in half in 1961 by a recommendation from the National Council on Crime and Delinquency. By the mid-1970s, a study of thirty-eight states showed that only seven had detention rates below 20 percent and only one had a rate below 10 percent. The overall rate of detention, or the average for all thirty-eight states, was 46 percent (Poulin et al., 1980:23–25).[2] When Poulin et al. compared rates of detention by states over a ten-year period from 1966 through 1975, they found remarkable stability. For example, the states

---

[2]Still later the Institute of Judicial Administration–American Bar Association Joint Commission on Juvenile Justice Standards recommended rigorous standards for preadjudicatory detention of juveniles, reasoning that the current dangers of too much detention of juveniles outweighs the risk to society or to youth themselves of too much release. See Guggenheim (1977:1065–1067) for a discussion of these standards.

that had the highest detention rates in 1966 also had the highest rates in 1975. California, Michigan, and Florida ranked first, second, and third, respectively, for highest detention rates in four of five comparisons over the decade studied (p.49).

General declines in the at-risk youth population, even greater declines in rates of juvenile arrest nationwide, and widely publicized recommended standards have not resulted in expected patterns in the use of detention. If there are fewer youth at risk of detention and lower rates of arrest in general, there should be less need for and less actual use of detention. The patterns of detention utilization reflected in national statistics, however, show something different. As the U.S. Census Bureau's statistics on children in custody indicate, there has been a steady move in the direction of admitting fewer juveniles into detention centers since about 1974. But the statistics also show a simultaneous increase in the average length of time youths spend in detention. In effect, then, while fewer youth are exposed to the potential disadvantages of detention, those who are detained experience—or are at risk of experiencing—for a greater length of time any negative effects that might be associated with detention. Moreover, because the average length of stay has increased, at least as many youths are in detention now (based on one-day counts) as there were before drastic declines occurred in the number of detention admissions (Krisberg, Schwartz, Litsky, & Austin, 1986:21). Some sources report that a greater number of juveniles were in secure detention on any given day in 1983 than at any time in the preceding decade (Siegel & Senna, 1985:410–411).

While national figures clearly show these countertrends, they do not make clear the reasons for them. It is probably the case that decreases in detention admissions are related directly to at least two national forces. First, youth arrests have declined steadily since the mid-1970s. Because youths entering the juvenile justice system by arrest are a primary source of detention admissions, any reduction in arrests should result in declines in those admissions. From all available evidence, that has happened. Second, the national initiative to remove status offenders from the juvenile justice system in general and from secure detention in specific, which has been promoted and financed in large part by the Juvenile Justice and Delinquency Prevention (JJDP) Act of 1974, has no doubt had a major impact on rates of detention admissions (Bortner, Sunderland, & Winn, 1985; Krisberg, et al., 1986).

Explaining why the average length of stay in detention has increased and the daily population of youth in detention has remained relatively constant despite drastic reductions in the number of admissions is complex. The average length of stay in detention nationwide increased from 11.3 days in 1974 to 17.4 days in 1982 (Krisberg et al., 1986). While fewer youth are admitted to detention, keeping them for longer periods of time has the result of maintaining the same levels of utilization of space. Some observers would argue that this is a clear case of detention capacity causing detention utilization (a theme that is developed more fully in a later part of this chapter). In other words, daily population in detention centers may have remained high simply because capacity (the number of beds in facilities available at any point in time) has allowed that much utilization. The argument is compelling in explaining current trends in detention: increases in average length of stay counterbalance the effects of falling admissions.

The increases in average length of stay can be explained in two other ways: (1) As a result of the increasing severity of offenses reaching the system, there has been a move toward more formal and more harsh decisions by juvenile justice officials at all levels of processing. (2) There has been an increased tendency to use detention centers as places where adjudicated (or convicted) juvenile delinquents can be incarcerated for some period of time (Krisberg et al., 1986). Because the periods of incarceration for adjudicated delinquents are generally longer than the average stays for ordinary detainees, such cases statistically increase the average stay for all detainees. However, while both of these explanations probably play some part in current national trends in detention rates, neither is likely to preclude an effect produced by a tendency for the capacity for detention to determine its utilization.

CUSTODY AND DETENTION DECISIONS

States bring juveniles into custody, and thereby to the point where detention status becomes an issue, essentially in two ways. The first is through arrest by a police officer or an official authorized by the court (usually a probation officer), on grounds that are set forth in state statutes. The statutory grounds for arrest of juveniles include all grounds applied in adult arrests as well as, in many states, authorization to take youths into custody because (1) they are suspected of running away from home, (2) it is necessary for the protection of others, and/or (3) for the protection of the child's safety, morals, or general welfare—an arrest clause open to wide discretion (McDiarmid, 1977:77–79).

A juvenile may also be taken into custody and detained on a warrant or a signed summons issued by a judge, in most cases to remove them from situations defined as dangerous to their welfare. No clear

standards are provided in the statutes of most states as to the particular conditions that must prevail before such an order can be issued.[3] In
fact, many states use language similar to the following: "if it appears
the child is in such condition or surroundings that his welfare requires
that he be taken into custody immediately" (McDiarmid, 1977:77).

In sum, juveniles may be brought into custody initially (1) for all
the reasons adults may be taken into custody and (2) for very general
reasons relating to their own protection that do not apply to adults.
After the initial custody decision, most are released without further
detention. This release occurs two ways. First, police officers or officials charged with detention screening release juveniles to parents or
guardians, usually within a few hours of arrest or custody. Second,
juveniles may be released as a result of statutory requirements or a
judicial order mandating release after a certain amount of time (usually
twenty-four or seventy-two hours) unless a good reason for further detention is provided.

In the routine operation of the juvenile justice system, then,
preadjudicatory detention decisions are made at two stages.[4] The first
is when the decision is made to take the juvenile into custody. That
initial detention decision may be made by a police officer (or other
statutorily authorized detention screener) in cases where initial custody results from an arrest or by a judge in cases in which initial custody occurs as a result of a warrant or a summons ("Comments,"
1983:95). The second decision stage comes after the passing of some
specified amount of time. The specified time varies between jurisdictions but, as stated above, is usually between twenty-four and seventy-
two hours. Most states have some statutory provisions requiring
a detention hearing to establish whether continued detention is
warranted or mandating release unless evidence is presented showing the necessity for continuing detention ("Comments," McDiarmid,
1977:78).

---

[3]See, for example, the broad language used in the Uniform Juvenile Court Act 14
(1968 version): "A child taken into custody shall not be detained or placed in a shelter
prior to the hearing on the petition unless . . . detention or care is required to protect
the person or property of others or of the child or because the child may abscond or
be removed from the jurisdiction of the court or because . . . [there is] no parent,
guardian, or custodian or other person able to provide supervision and care."

[4]Juveniles may also be detained after adjudication and prior to disposition, and this
represents a third stage at which a decision to detain may be made. In these cases,
however, the juvenile is already an adjudicated delinquent, and detention takes on an
entirely different meaning in both legal and practical terms.

GROUNDS FOR PREADJUDICATORY DETENTION

Generally, juveniles may be held in preadjudicatory detention for three reasons: (1) to protect the child, (2) to protect society from further lawbreaking by the child, and (3) to prevent the child from absconding. The reasons given under different statutes, though phrased in various ways, all boil down to these same three considerations.

In the spirit of the highest goals of the juvenile justice system, the court envisions detention, for all of these reasons, not as incarceration or restrictive control for punishment, but rather as a way to protect juveniles from unsavory or immoral conditions or from numerous other situations that may be seen as endangering their welfare. Youths found to be away from home and in the company of "disreputable" or "dangerous" adults or juveniles are probably most likely to be detained for their own protection. Also common is detention for their own protection because there is no suitable placement available with a parent, guardian, or other adult or in a shelter or crisis facility. These "protection of the child" detention standards are much broader than any standards applied in pretrial detention of adults.

Juveniles may also be detained for the protection of the community. In juvenile justice, this consideration is not clearly separable from concern for protecting the child. If a child is prevented by detention from committing another crime, it may be interpreted under the broad mandate of the juvenile court as protection of both the community and of the child's future interests. Detention to protect the community and/or to protect juveniles themselves (either from crimes that may be committed by them while they are released awaiting appearances in juvenile court, or from harm that may come to them while their legal status awaits court determination) is understandable in the context of the juvenile justice system's underlying philosophy: the notion of *parens patriae*. When juveniles threaten society or lack mature judgment necessary to act in their own best interests, detention is justified because the state may act as surrogate father (*parens patriae*) to decide matters in the best interest of the child. Juveniles who are likely (by some set of determinations) to commit future crimes or to behave in a wayward fashion generally are acting against their own best interests. The state, under the doctrine of *parens patriae,* reserves the right to take whatever steps it defines as reasonable, just as a natural parent acting in the interest of a child.

Finally, juveniles may be detained to assure they appear at later hearings in juvenile court (i.e., to make sure they neither leave nor are taken out of the court's jurisdiction). This justification for detention has a direct counterpart in the adult criminal justice system, and both criminal and juvenile courts consider the prevention of absconding to be very important. Nevertheless, neither court nor state statutes generally have established clear standards or guidelines for determining the risk of absconding (Bock & Frazier, 1977, 1984; Goldcamp, 1983; Tripplet, 1978). The lack of precise standards and guidelines does not result from neglect or oversight. There are, in fact, no satisfactorily accurate predictors of who will abscond.

Part of the inherent unfairness in a court's inability to predict defendants' future behavior with regard to absconding is compensated for in the adult system by affording the right to bail. Bail allows the adult defendant release from detention on condition of (1) promising to reappear, (2) providing some sum of money, (3) or by securing a bail bond (Shamburek, 1978:513–514).[5]

POTENTIAL FOR ABUSE

Wide Discretion

Once the statutory and philosophical bases of preadjudicatory detention of juveniles are accepted, we are left with a major problem. How is abuse in actual application of detention to be avoided? In a justice system oriented to the care, protection, and rehabilitation of wayward youths, how many restrictive controls may be applied without resulting in abuse?

Abuse may occur if juveniles are detained when there is little evidence that detention is necessary or desirable to meet one of the generally accepted goals of detention. Abuse may also occur if the effect of detention is punitive or harmful to detainees. When juveniles are detained to assure reappearance in subsequent court hearings or to protect society from further criminal acts, one would expect some logical relationship to exist between the characteristics of juveniles, their offense histories, and whether or not they are detained. While characteristics and histories are far from full proof or even acceptable predictors of subsequent offense and/or absconding behavior, they at least are logical correlates of these behaviors. We might expect then that juvenile courts and juvenile justice officials would establish and apply criteria that logically relate to the likelihood that any given juvenile either

---

[5]While juveniles do not have the constitutional right to bail that is afforded adults, many states do allow for bail or personal recognizance of juveniles, and only a few states expressly forbid bail of juveniles (McDiarmid, 1977:78).

would fail to appear in subsequent court hearings or would commit additional offenses if not detained.

While many jurisdictions establish broad criteria to guide officials in selecting juveniles for detention, these criteria are generally so broad and so unclear in meaning that officials are left with almost entirely unguided discretion. Because of this broad discretion, in many jurisdictions almost any youth charged with a delinquent act may be detained (Frazier & Bishop, 1985; Guggenheim, 1977). Therefore, whether most state laws provide guidance or not, wide discretion is the rule. And there is always potential for abuse when this is the case. It is important to examine thoroughly the consequences of state laws allowing wide discretion in the interpretation of detention criteria. The next section addresses this issue in more detail.

Who Is Detained, and Why?

To ask who is detained requires some specification of type or place of detention. Generally speaking, juveniles may be detained in two types of facilities: secure detention facilities (including adult jails and centers exclusively used for detaining juveniles) or nonsecure or shelter facilities designed and used in cases involving hard-to-place juveniles who do not present a risk to the community. While the latter type is used infrequently, some states and local jurisdictions use temporary crisis facilities for detainment of youth; in unusual cases they may even use a private home for detention. The question of who is detained, then, actually must be answered in terms of who is detained in the various kinds of facilities. For our present purposes, we are interested in juveniles detained in any type of facility (jail, detention center, etc.) when the detention is defined as secure (i.e., when juveniles are defined as being under the state's custody and are not free to leave at will).

The situation is essentially the same when the focus is moved to the second issue at hand: *why* are youths detained? This question also must be considered carefully because we need to know why certain types of juveniles are detained in certain types of facilities. For example, there has been a fairly marked reduction in juveniles being detained in adult jails, mostly as a result of deinstitutionalizing status offenders in accordance with the Juvenile Justice and Delinquency Prevention Act of 1974. Those juveniles currently most likely to be detained in adult jails, then, are probably youths charged with more serious offenses (those that would be serious felonies if committed by adults) and who because of such charges are more likely to be transferred to criminal court jurisdiction for processing as an adult.[6] Another type of juvenile likely to be detained in an adult jail facility is one who was taken into custody in an area far from a secure juvenile facility. Generally these are rural youths.

When the importance of the detention issue is considered in relation to many others in the area of juvenile justice, research aimed at determining the underlying cause has been surprisingly sparse. That is especially true if one assumes an academic's stance and looks for research published in professional and scholarly journals rather than local studies and/or foundation or government grant reports. The latter type of research has played a critical role in bringing this whole issue to national attention to the point where major initiatives have been established to address problems relating to it. Now academic research is beginning to move us closer to a full understanding of detention issues. Research is designed to explain not only who is detained but also why particular sorts of youth are detained (Frazier & Bishop, 1985).

Among recent researchers who have applied social scientific methods and explanations in the study of detention decisions are Pawlak (1977) and Kramer and Steffensmeier (1978). Studies by these researchers found a relationship between counties' rates of detention and the availability of detention centers in those counties. Rather than being caused by the need to protect society or a particular youth population or the need to prevent absconding, these rates seem to have been caused primarily by the availability of a detention center (see also Poulin et al., 1980).

This social science theme or explanation can be tied to social theory and philosophy as far back as the turn of the century and the works of Emile Durkheim (Erikson, 1966). In brief, social scientists argued that behavioral deviation is a normal aspect of all socially organized life; societies or communities determine what its rate will be, in part by creating the capacity (in this case the availability of places to detain juveniles) to respond officially to rule violations. Contemporary

---

[6]Nonserious offenders and status offenders are still detained in adult jails in some states. Current evidence, however, suggests the rates are falling steadily. Partly because of this fact the deadline for compliance with the jail removal requirement in the 1984 reauthorization of the JJDP Act of 1974 has been extended to December 8, 1988 (Detention Reporter, November 1984). A countertrend must also be noted. Indications are strong that the direction and results of almost two decades of deinstitutionalization efforts may be reversing. Citizens, juvenile justice officials, police, and others in several states are advocating statutory power to arrest and detain status offenders in secure facilities (See Krisberg et al., 1985:9–10). We may soon see a return to the acceptance of adult jails and lockups for the detention of juveniles. (Note the language in the JJDP Act of 1974, reauthorization of 1984.)

researchers hypothesize that the greater the capacity, the greater the rate of delinquent behavior defined as requiring detention.

Critics would, of course, counter this viewpoint by saying that different regions, jurisdictions, or counties may have quite different needs, based on their particular delinquency problem. Some counties may experience more serious crime and delinquency problems, and their development of detention facilities may be seen as a *response* to both the rate and type of delinquency in the jurisdiction. Detention capacity would not be considered a *cause*, as in the argument advanced above. This counter viewpoint is, of course, as logical and as possible in empirical terms as the other one.

The studies by Pawlak (1977) and by Kramer and Steffensmeier (1978) offered no way to determine the probability of one or the other of these two views being correct. However, Lerman (1977) did reanalyze Pawlak's data, controlling for type of offense and the number of prior contacts juveniles had with the court. He found that detention rates were still associated with the availability of detention centers. Lerman's findings lend considerable support to the two studies by social scientists and to the "capacity causes utilization" theory.

Another study by social scientists examined the extent to which attitudes and philosophies of juvenile justice officials affect rates of detention. No doubt, practices vary from one jurisdiction to another regarding what officials decide about the detention status of juveniles taken into custody. Clearly, different officials hold and apply different philosophies of justice or treatment (Rubin, 1979; Farnworth, Frazier & Neuberger, 1988). Some jurisdictions involve police in the initial detention decision; others place the detention decision in the power of juvenile court probation officers. Considering just the differences between these two types of officials, Gottfredson and Gottfredson (1970) found that police officers are more likely to hold attitudes favorable to detention than are probation officers. Moreover, they found that jurisdictions that involve police officers in the detention decision have higher rates of detention than do those jurisdictions in which police are not involved.

If such findings are considered carefully, it appears likely that detention could be determined in part by the particular structure of the juvenile justice system in a jurisdiction (such as whether the structure involves police in the decision process or not) and the general philosophies of juvenile justice held by various types of justice officials (police versus probation officers). This, of course, implies that there should be wide variation in detention rates across jurisdictions, in the characteristics of juveniles selected for detention across jurisdictions, and in both rates and detainee characteristics over time.

The best and most recent research on who is detained bears out the viability of these latter hypotheses. Cohen and Kluegel (1979) studied approximately 9,000 juvenile cases processed in two metropolitan courts (Denver and Memphis) in 1972. They found that the juveniles most likely to be detained were those with a prior record of offending and those not working or attending school. They also found that orientation of the court (whether due process oriented or oriented more traditionally toward treatment and informality) and a juvenile's gender were related in complex ways to the probability of being detained. Denver, the court oriented toward due process, was more likely to detain youth charged with status offenses if they had a prior record and if they were not involved in conventional activity (work or school). These factors were not related at all to detention decisions in Memphis, the traditional court, which had the highest detention rate.

Even more interesting are the researchers' findings on the effect of gender on detention decisions. Similar to previous research findings on sex or gender bias in the juvenile justice process, several researchers found that females charged with status offenses and whose present activities did not include school or work were more likely to be detained than were males charged with the same type offenses and not involved in school or work (Bortner, 1982; Chesney-Lind, 1977; Kramer & Steffensmeier, 1978; Cohen & Kluegel, 1978).

Using national data on juveniles processed between 1975 and 1977, Black and Smith (1980) found that the two variables most related to the likelihood of detention were prior record of offenses and living arrangements. Juveniles who had prior records and those not living with their natural parents were most likely to be detained. Even more recently, Frazier and Cochran (1986) examined the initial detention cases of more than 9,000 juveniles processed in a southern state between 1977 and 1979. As did earlier researchers, they found a juvenile's prior record of offenses related to the likelihood of detention. In addition, they found a relationship between detention and other factors that may be argued as predictors of recidivism. Specifically, youths charged with serious offenses or more than one offense and those who were older were most likely to be detained. Some would argue that these factors are solid bases for predicting relative dangerousness of defendants and, therefore, are logical and reasonable grounds for holding youth in preventive detention. But the study also found a relationship between detention and factors not readily interpretable as legitimate predictors of recidivism or absconding. Specifically, black youths, rural youths, and females were generally more likely to be detained than youths who were white, urban, and male.

In effect, then, these studies show a substantial amount of variation in the specific factors related to detention in three different settings and at three different time periods. In broad terms, two types of juveniles are most likely to be detained. The first group consists of those that officials have reason to believe might pose a threat or danger to the community. Seriousness of charged offenses and the extent and type of prior record are most often found to be related to being selected for detention (see Frazier & Bishop, 1985, for an exception). Factors less commonly measured but still likely to be part of community protection considerations in many jurisdictions are school status, constructive activity, living arrangements (Cohen & Kluegel, 1979) and even the general appearance of a youth. After an initial detention decision is made in Florida, for example, care is taken to consider a youth's physical characteristics (size, strength) and any apparent indications (such as appearance) of abnormal behaviors such as sexual preference. This information is collected at admission and recorded on a form called the Room Assignment Form as a prominent part of a detainee's case file.

A second common type of detainee is a youth either defined or definable as a likely victim. These essentially are cases in which youths are detained for their own protection (from others as well as from their own tendencies). Officials believe releasing them back into the community may well result in risks greater than those occasioned by detention. The most common cases to be interpreted as probable victims are females who run away from home or who commit other status offenses for reasons relating to having already been a victim of abuse or neglect.

HARMFUL EFFECTS

Like research on who is detained and why, investigations aimed at determining the effects of preadjudicatory detention are motivated in part by the continuing controversy over the appropriateness of practices in this area of juvenile justice. Commentators and researchers have presented convincing evidence that youths risk being harmed legally, physically, and psychologically as a result of detention (Sarri, 1974; Shamburek, 1978; Wald, 1976).

To suffer harmful effects legally youths must somehow be disadvantaged in relation to dispositional outcomes of their cases. This may occur two ways:

1. A detained youth may be disadvantaged in comparison to a nondetained youth charged with the same or similar offenses. This disadvantage occurs because detainees are not as able to help in the preparation of their defense as are juvenile defendants who remain free. Detained youths cannot, for example, freely meet with and assist attorneys in the preparing of a defense. They are not as able to identify or to assist in the questioning of witnesses.

2. A detained juvenile may be disadvantaged because some officials may view detention as an indication that final dispositions must involve at least as much restrictive control as did the detention. That is, officials may perceive that detained youths are less amenable than nondetained youths to treatment or that they are somehow less good risks for dispositions involving community programs (as opposed to dispositions involving incarceration), because of an apparent need to place restrictive controls on them early in the juvenile justice process (Shamburek, 1978; Tripplet, 1978). What this implies—and there is considerable research support for this idea[7]—is that juvenile justice officials tend to be influenced by prior decisions without regard to specific circumstances of cases or traits of offenders (Bortner & Reed, 1982; Henretta, Frazier, & Bishop, 1986).

Some juveniles, therefore, may receive harsher dispositions because they cannot assist effectively in their defense and/or because being detained negatively impacts on later judgments about their suitability to less restrictive treatments.

While not a great deal of research has been aimed directly at the question of whether detention has harmful legal effects, three studies make the case clearly. Cohen's (1975) study on a sample of cases from the Denver juvenile justice system shows that to a very appreciable degree detained youth are more likely than comparable, not detained, youth to have formal petitions filed against them and in turn to receive more severe dispositions. Frazier and Cochran's (1986) study found essentially the same thing in data from eight counties in a southern state between 1977 and 1979. Detainees were found to receive more harsh intake recommendations, more severe actions from state attorneys, and both more formal and more severe court dispositions than were nondetainees, other aspects of their cases being equal.

Using statewide data for the period between 1979 and 1982 from the same southern state, a study by Frazier and Bishop (1985) found that juveniles detained continuously between initial intake and final disposition were disadvantaged with regard to whether their dispositions were formal or informal. Detainees were slightly more likely to receive the most formal dispositions (i.e., dispositions involving a for-

---

[7]Part of the evidence for this line of reasoning comes from research on adults. Studies present evidence that pretrial detention of adults affects both the likelihood of conviction and the severity of final dispositions. (See, for example, Ares, Rankin & Sturz, 1963; Foote, 1965; Frazier, Bock, & Henretta, 1983; Rankin, 1964; Thomas, 1976). Swigert & Farrell, 1977: See also Henretta et al. (1986) for a discussion of the effects of dispositions of previous cases on the outcomes of current cases.

mal court hearing) while the cases of those not detained were most likely to be handled informally (i.e., dispositions not requiring formal court appearances). Interestingly, however, this same research found no evidence that detainees receive more severe final dispositions than nondetainees when other relevant factors are held constant. This means that juveniles detained for the full time between intake and disposition were not any more likely, when other relevant factors were controlled, to receive harsh dispositions such as confinement in residential facilities (training schools).

When important legal and sociodemographic factors are controlled in sophisticated research, there is considerable evidence that being detained (either initially or continuously) impacts negatively on the likelihood that a juvenile will fare well in subsequent court decisions. While there is no basis in the research literature for suggesting malevolent intent on the part of officials when subsequent legal decisions are made, the risk of legal harm to detained juveniles is inconsistent with a system of justice aimed at care, protection, and rehabilitation.

Physical and psychological effects of detention on juveniles tend to be described emphatically in the literature. Commentators describe these effects as staggering, intolerable, brutal, and deplorable. And while no one would dispute that such effects indeed result from detention sometimes, the actual extent of them is unknown—perhaps even unknowable. Reports of sensational cases of physical abuse, sexual exploitation, or psychological torment appear regularly enough in the popular press to keep the public mindful of this problem, but there is little systematic research on the topic and no substantive base for estimating its full extent. Far more common for juvenile detainees, and because of that perhaps as serious a problem as the physical and psychological abuse that sometimes occurs in detention centers, is a detention experience characterized by inadequate care. Education, special programs, and recreation are woefully inadequate in most detention centers (Children in Custody, 1971). A typical day for a juvenile detainee may involve classroom education, some time set aside for recreation, and some time to work for the general good of the detention facility. In practice, however, the education efforts seldom get beyond faint attempts to involve a large group of youths in some elementary-level exercises that have little resemblance to what they would be doing in a public school classroom. The recreation amounts to playing cards and box games, shooting basketball, or (as often as not) watching television. Work tends to take two forms: To keep order in the detention centers, all residents are usually required to assume partial responsibility for cleaning their rooms, collecting laundry, and so on. Work also is often used for punitive and control purposes. For example, a youth may be assigned work duties such as cleaning out toilets or washing floors with toothbrushes to dramatize the power of staff over detainees and to discourage future infractions of rules (Reuterman, 1970).

Despite a growing literature identifying fairly precisely the nature and extent of the great potential for harm to juveniles in institutional settings (Bartollas, Miller & Dinitz, 1976; Feld, 1977), the issues are far from settled. Indeed, legal scholars and juvenile justice experts have grappled with the adverse effects of detention for more than two decades without much success. As recently as 1983, a treatise in the University of Pennsylvania Law Review ("Comments," 1983) described the nature and effects of juvenile detention practices as not in accord with the ideals or philosophical objectives of the juvenile justice system. The piece quotes as current several points made in the 1970s by commentators (see, for example, Guggenheim, 1977; Sarri, 1974) whose writings helped focus the national debate on the plight of juveniles in detention. The treatise also quotes an opening statement Senator Birch Bayh made in 1973 (before a subcommittee of the Senate Committee on the Judiciary) which emphasizes that some detained juveniles are "brutalized, beaten, and exposed to vicious sexual attacks" (Hearings, 1973). Others have also provided vivid descriptions of physical and psychological damage suffered by detained youth (Cottle, 1979; Fetrow & Fetrow, 1974; Fisher, 1972). These have kept the movements toward reform active.

STRUCTURE AND ORGANIZATION OF DETENTION FACILITIES

The issue of physical and psychological abuse or harm as a result of preadjudicatory detention, like many such issues, often leads to oversimplified responses. Some are content, for example, simply to contend that there was, there is now, and there will continue to be physical and psychological damage to detained youth (Lotz et al., 1985). This contention, however, also does not make clear that the risk of physical and psychological harm varies considerably depending on the type of facility in which a youth is detained, the structure and conditions in those facilities, and the training, sophistication, and resources of staff.

Juveniles might be placed as detainees in any of several kinds of facilities: adult jails and lockups, secure juvenile detention facilities (youth are locked in and are not at liberty to leave), nonsecure juvenile facilities (which often combine in the same facility youths held in preventive detention and those placed there by the court for their own protection), and shelter and/or crisis facilities (designed exclusively to serve youth on a nonsecure and voluntary basis). Each type of facility has a different organizational structure and, accordingly, a different set of conditions to which youth must respond. In addition, there is considerable variation even within the same type of facility from time to time and from place to place. The best available evidence suggests physical danger to juveniles is greatest in adult jails and lockups and least in shelter and crisis facilities, but there are glaring exceptions in both types of facilities.

Relatively little is known about varying potentialities for psychological harm although most experts would probably predict greater risks are present in facilities designed to apply higher levels of restrictive controls. This is probably a safe guess because the more secure facilities tend to house generally more dangerous persons and are less likely to have professionally trained staff. While the vast majority of physical and psychological harm experienced by detained youth probably occurs at the hands of, or as a result of contact with, other inmates, it is reasonable to expect that some of it occurs because staff sometimes abuse their position.

It is unnecessary to illustrate the ways in which the structure and conditions inside adult jails and lockups may lead to catastrophe for detained juveniles. The press has clearly dramatized youth suicides and physical and sexual assaults on them by adults. The picture is not so clear, however, in the less restrictive juvenile facilities. Unlike the conditions in adult jails, youth detained in various types of juvenile facilities are not in contact with adults, they are not locked in dingy, dank, barred cells, and they are generally not guarded by staff hardened against showing the slightest expression of human compassion. Rather, by comparison, youths detained in juvenile instead of adult facilities generally fare much better. But despite this positive comparison, their situation is still replete with potential for serious harm because (1) nearly every facility in which juveniles are detained periodically houses youths who are dangerous to themselves and to others, (2) even the most committed and professional staff weaken over time in their resolve to "make a difference," and (3) the structure designed to serve the needs of juveniles also contains detrimental elements that may cause service that is either less effective than it could be or completely ineffective.

Two illustrations using different types of juvenile facilities will help make these points more clear. Again, we do not need to describe the problems with detaining juveniles in adult jail facilities; that has been done emphatically by others (Sarri, 1974). The first illustration, therefore, is a typical secure detention facility. This type of juvenile facility is generally smaller than adult jails and has individual and/or dormitory-style rooms secured by ordinary locks on ordinary doors. The juvenile detention facility staff are more likely than adult jail staff to have some college (sometimes B.A. or M.A. degrees). They are also more likely to have programs in education and in counseling, though these are often sorely underdeveloped. Finally, juvenile detention facilities are more likely than adult jails to allow relatively free movement within the facility during a large part of the day. Like the adult jail, however, secure juvenile detention facilities tend to have published rules of conduct with prescribed sanctions (including confinement in isolation cells for more serious infractions) and a basic orientation to custody. Moreover, the general organization of the staff duties and programs in a juvenile detention facility are designed to assure safety, security, and custody (Dembo & Dertke, 1986) rather than service, aid, and treatment. Juvenile detention is, then, in almost every sense what many officials describe it to be in their vernacular: "juvie jail."

When widely varying sorts of youth are housed together in juvenile detention facilities, there are many opportunities for aggression, victimization, and general despair, despite the highly controlled conditions. Detention staff generally focus most of their energies on keeping the facility safe, orderly, and secure. These are the primary goals and the ones most likely to be emphasized in formal organizational rules. Any other program goals consistent with the rehabilitative aims of juvenile justice are usually only of secondary interest and tend not to be covered in formal rules. When, for example, a detainee attacks another youth or a staff member, there are formal policies on ways to subdue the aggressor, bring charges against either or both parties, and hand down dispositions including loss of freedom, loss of perquisites, and/or confinement in isolation (Dembo & Dertke, 1986). Specific rules cover surveillance of youth held in isolation, the conditions of isolation, the maximum length of time in isolation, and sanctions for staff who fail to assure the standards of isolation are met. Ironically, while these institutions have the authority to exercise almost total control over inmates, recent research indicates that many staff in these sorts of facilities perceive the rules as giving the greater edge for control to the inmates (Dembo & Dertke).

In the same sort of institution, rules and policies relating to service assistance and treatment are, by comparison, less developed. Staff often feel free to serve, aid, and treat when and if they want and not to do so as they wish. When they do not apply the goals of service in their routine activities the reason is often because the formal rules of custody create an atmosphere that is not conducive to service and treatment objectives.

A second illustration, one at the other end of the restrictiveness continuum of facilities, focuses on the shelter or crisis center type of facility. Shelter-type facilities have different names and somewhat different functions from one state to another, but all states probably make occasional use of these least restrictive juvenile facilities for detaining youth prior to trial. The organizational structure of shelter facilities is focused explicitly on delivery of services, shelter, and protective care to juveniles in need of such services. Custody is emphasized nowhere in the formal rules.

Juveniles who are placed in or voluntarily come to these programs are not regarded as offenders. Rather, they are considered to be victims who need the beneficent care authorized by the laws of the state. Staff are generally better educated though not necessarily better trained than those working in jails and detention centers. There also is more likely to be a strong emphasis on program services in shelter-style facilities, both because of an orientation to children as victims (neglected, abused, runaway, or disturbed) and because in most circumstances youths are not legally bound to remain at the centers. In a real sense, agencies must recruit referrals from both public agencies (police, courts, etc.) and from the community. Because of the orientation to service and the need to sell the program in recruitment, formal rules are focused on service applications and programs.

Order, also a high priority in shelter facilities, cannot be achieved in the same ways as it is in secure facilities. For the most part, programs and privileges are the tools with which staff keep order in nonsecure facilities. Youths are kept busy in program activities (education, recreation, hygiene, work preparation, group counseling, or special emphasis programs such as birth control techniques, communication skills development, or stress management strategies), and they are rewarded for orderly and productive behavior with privileges (shopping outings, movies, special desserts, etc.).

Were it the case that offenders were always and only offenders and victims were always and only victims, the shelter-type facilities and secure detention facilities would be unlikely to experience many of the problems they commonly do. Shelters would house only victims, and secure facilities would house only offenders. Such is not the case in the real world, however, and shelter facility staff know this only too well. They too must deal with youth clients who are dangerous to themselves and to others. Unlike staff in secure facilities, shelter staff do not have the options of restraining a juvenile or of using any kind of lockup as a means of dealing with an unruly or threatening youth.

Moreover, while staff obviously have the right to report actual crimes to the police, they seldom do so. Instead, what is much more likely is that shelter staff will choose among several adaptive strategies that seem to be very common among personnel in nonsecure facilities. One strategy is that staff will misrepresent their authority to youths, telling them that if they run away from the facility or cause problems, the police will arrest them and make them return to the same place.

In actual fact, police often want nothing to do with shelter facility wards. In Florida and many other states, police have no explicit authority to apprehend a youth who causes trouble in or has left a shelter facility unless that youth is under a court-ordered detention. A second tactic used in dealing exclusively with troublemakers is to invite or provoke the unruly youth to leave the facility. Nonsecure facility staff may resolve their immediate problem by encouraging the troublemaker to walk out. This informal practice goes, of course, against the primary goals and objectives of the organization at the same time that it accomplishes what staff in secure facilities cannot. It gets rid of youths who threaten order or who distract others. It allows staff to control, albeit through a subterranean means, the client population.

Every kind of juvenile institution, especially those charged with short-term preadjudicatory detention, sees a high degree of staff burnout. The clients of these programs come with many problems, and they move through and out of the programs quickly. Staff are faced constantly with the realization that little can be done with so many clients in such a short period of time. Juveniles in such facilities surely sense the lack of resolve, the despair, and frustration of staff. When this sense is combined with the physical dangers and the psychological stresses they routinely fear or experience in contacts with other youth, there is little reason to dispute the frequent claims that preadjudicatory detention harms juveniles.

SUMMARY

In this chapter we have examined one of the most persistent and perplexing issues in juvenile justice. Each year hundreds of thousands of juveniles are admitted to secure detention facilities. While there is some evidence that the numbers of youths admitted to detention are declining, a disturbing countertrend sees youths entering detention centers today being confined for longer periods of time. As a result, as many juveniles are in preadjudicatory detention on any given day in the 1980s as there were two decades ago when reform efforts on juvenile detention began.

The juvenile justice system has moved steadily in the direction of a due process orientation, but it has retained its historic philosophical slant toward *parens patriae*. That underlying philosophy, paired with the wide discretion inherent in state statutory provisions allowing the preadjudicatory detention of juveniles, has spawned and institutionalized what is perhaps the most discordant aspect of modern juvenile justice practice. Not only are there serious and compelling reasons for questioning the legitimacy of current policies and practices relating to preadjudicatory detention of juveniles, there are also substantial risks that detained juveniles actually suffer harm in the name of care and protection.

Recent research shows clear evidence that the application of statutory laws relating to preadjudicatory detention, which are exceedingly broad, and the various standards recommended by national advisory groups have done little to curb the national bent toward detention. Evidence also suggests considerable variation from time to time and from place to place in the sorts of youth who are detained. When this evidence is considered in light of the fact that the grounds for detaining youth are essentially the same nationwide, there is little reason to assume merit in the practice of detention.

Some recent evidence suggests that long-term detention decisions are made largely in a capricious and/or arbitrary manner. Notwithstanding chances that such findings may not be reproduced in studies of other places and times, the accumulated research on the effects of detention is clear enough to speak against juvenile detention in secure facilities. The fact that juveniles held in pretrial detention are disadvantaged in subsequent juvenile court decision processes (Bortner & Reed, 1982; Frazier & Bishop, 1985) should alone give great pause to advocates of wider use of pretrial detention. Yet that does not seem to be what has happened. If anything, the signals seem to predict fewer restrictions and less reserve in the use of detention.[8]

In sum, too many juveniles are held for too long a time in preadjudicatory detention. This occurs largely because there are not adequate guidelines or statutory provisions to regulate detention practices. While the frequent charges of harm to juveniles come mostly from anecdotal evidence, there is ample empirical evidence to conclude that detained juveniles definitely suffer legal disadvantages. Like their adult counterparts, juveniles held in pretrial detention are more likely to receive harsher sanctions in subsequent court dispositions than are nondetained youth with the same characteristics.

Secure preadjudicatory detention has always been and continues to be a major problem in juvenile justice. While the current standards and loose guidelines clearly could serve the goals of juvenile justice and be beneficial to some youths if they were applied judiciously, recent research shows the practices of court officials have been anything

---

[8]Both the 1980 and 1984 reauthorization of the JJDP Act of 1974 watered down the spirit of the original act. In 1980 this was done by modifying deinstitutionalization provisions to exempt habitual runaways, juveniles refusing to accept court-ordered treatment, and those who flaunt court orders. This was also done both in 1980 and in 1984 by extending deinstitutionalization compliance deadlines to allow participating states more time to achieve compliance (five years were added in 1980 and four years in 1984) (See Olson-Raymer, 1984).

but judicious. As a result, detention has created more problems for the system and for affected youth than it has solved. The best solution to current problems is to develop far more rigorous standards for detention and to have and enforce strict procedural guidelines in the actual application of detention.

DISCUSSION QUESTIONS

1. Examine the recent trends in detention admission rates and in one-day counts of the numbers of youth detained on any given day. Why are these two sets of figures distressing?

2. What are the legal grounds for placing a juvenile in secure detention?

3. Imagine yourself as an intake official in your state. How might the legal grounds for detaining a youth be misused to detain anyone you want?

4. If it were apparent that a juvenile would be at risk of harm or victimization if not detained, would you favor protective detention in a secure or nonsecure facility? Justify your answer.

5. What does most of the systematic research evidence show with regard to who is detained and why?

6. Do the factors shown in research to be related to detention logically relate to assessing a juvenile's dangerousness to the community or self or to the likelihood of absconding?

7. National data suggests that standards set by policy commissions on what proportions of juveniles should be detained have had little effect. In fact most states detain on average two or three times the recommended numbers. Give your opinion as to why these attempts to reduce detention rates have failed.

8. While physical and psychological harm is easiest to imagine when the negative potential of detention is considered, why in your opinion is there so little systematic data substantiating critics' claims?

9. At the very least, juveniles held in secure preadjudicatory detention will be deprived of their freedom, will be denied easy access to relatives and friends as well as the emotional comforts they may provide, and will find it more difficult to assist an attorney in preparing a defense. Discuss the circumstances you believe should be present before the state has the right to deny these things to a person who has not been found guilty of a crime.

10. Consider the broad goals of the American juvenile court (to provide care, protection, and rehabilitation to needy youth). Assuming that secure detention is necessary in some cases, discuss what

detention facilities should be like, what services they should provide, and how such institutions should be structured in order to assure the needs of youth are met?

11. Consider what it means to a juvenile to be held in a secure detention center. At a minimum, what provisions would you be inclined to have required by law or policy?

12. Are there any offenses with which a juvenile may be charged that you believe should never result in secure detention (assuming the juvenile has no prior offense record)?

REFERENCES

Ares, C. E., Rankin, A., & Sturz, H. (1963, January). The Manhattan bail project. *New York University Law Review, 38*, 71–92.

Bartollas, C., Miller, S. J., & Dinitz, S. (1976). *Juvenile victimization: The institutional paradox.* New York: Halsted.

Black, T. E., & Smith, C. P. (1980). *Report of the national juvenile justice assessment centers: A preliminary national assessment of juveniles processed in the juvenile justice system.* Washington, DC: U.S. Government Printing Office.

Bock, E. W., & Frazier, C E. (1977). Official standards versus actual critieria in bond dispositions. *Journal of Criminal Justice, 5*: 321-328.

Bortner, M. A. (1982). *Inside a juvenile court: The tarnished ideal of individualized justice.* New York: New York University Press.

Bortner, M. A., & Reed, W. L. (1982). The preeminence of process: An example of refocused justice research. *Social Science Quarterly,* (4), 413–425.

Bortner, M. A., Sunderland, R., & Winn, R. (1985). Race and the impact of juvenile deinstitutionalization. *Crime and Delinquency, 31*: 35–46.

Chesney-Lind, M. (1977). Judicial paternalism and the female status offender: Training women to know their place. *Crime and Delinquency, 8* (Fall): 51–59.

Children in Custody: A Report on the Juvenile Detention and Correctional Facility Census of 1975. Washington, DC: U.S. Government Printing Office.

Cohen, L., & Kluegel, J.R. (1979). The detention decision: A study of the impact of social characteristics and legal factors in two metropolitan juvenile courts. *Social Forces, 58*, 146–161.

Cohen, L. E. (1975). *Delinquency dispositions: An empirical analysis of processing decisions in three juvenile courts.* Washington, DC: U.S. Government Printing Office.

Comments, The Supreme Court and Pretrial Detention of Juveniles: A Principled Solution to a Due Process Dilemma. (1983) *University of Pennsylvania Law Review, 132*(1), 95–116.

Community Research Center. (1980a). *An assessment of the national incidence of juvenile suicide in adult jails, lockups, and juvenile detention centers.* Champaign: University of Illinois.

Community Research Center. (1980b). *Removing children from adult jails.* Champaign: University of Illinois.

Cottle, T. J. (1979). Children in jail. *Crime and Delinquency, 25 (1),* 318–334.

Dembo, R., & Dertke, M. (1986). Work environment correlates of staff stress in a youth detention facility. *Criminal Justice and Behavior, 13,* (1): 328–344.

Detention Reporter (1984) Pretrial Services Resource Center. Washington DC, Vol. VIII (November).

Durkheim, E. (1966). *The rules of sociological method* (S. A. Solovay & J. H. Mueller, Trans.; E. G. Catlin, Ed.). New York: MacMillan.

Erikson, K. T. (1966). *Wayward puritans: A study in the sociology of deviance.* New York: John Wiley & Sons.

Farnworth, M., Frazier, C. E., & Neuberger, A. (1988). *Orientation to juvenile justice: Exploratory notes from a statewide survey of juvenile justice decision makers,* forthcoming in the *Journal of Criminal Justice.*

Feld, B.C. (1977). *Neutralizing inmate violence: Juvenile offenders in institutions.* Cambridge, MA: Ballinger.

Fetrow, R. S., & Fetrow, A. (1974). How a pretrial facility can destroy the self-esteem of the juvenile. *International Journal of Offender Therapy and Comparative Criminology, 18* (1), 227–232.

Fisher, S. M. (1972). Life in a children's detention center: Strategies for survival. *American Journal of Orthopsychiatry, 42,* 368–374.

Foote, C. E. (1965). The coming constitutional crisis in bail: I. *Pennsylvania Law Review, 113:* 959–964.

Frazier, C. E., & Bishop, D. M. (1985). The pretrial detention of juveniles and its impact on case dispositions. *Journal of Criminal Law and Criminology, 76,* (4), 301–321.

Frazier, C. E., Bock, E. W., & Henretta, J. C. (1983). The role of probation officers in determining gender differences in sentencing severity. *The Sociological Quarterly 24* (Spring): 305–318.

Frazier, C. E., & Cochran, J. K. (1986, March). Detention of juveniles: Its effects on subsequent juvenile court processing decisions. *Youth and Society 17,* 286–305.

Goldkamp, J. S. (1983). Questioning the practice of pretrial detention: Some empirical evidence from Philadelphia. *Journal of Criminal Law and Criminology, 74* (4): 1556–1588.

Gottfredson, D. M., & Gottfredson, G. D. (1970, July). Decision-maker attitudes and juvenile detention. *Journal of Research in Crime and Delinquency, 6,* 177–184.

Guggenheim, M. (1977). Paternalism, prevention, and punishment: Pretrial detention of juveniles. *New York University Law Review, 52,* 1064, 1071.

Hearings before the Subcommittee of the Senate Committee on the Judiciary to Investigate Juvenile Delinquency: The Detention and Jailing of Juveniles (93rd Congress, 1st Session). 4 (1973) (opening statement of Birch Bayh, Subcommittee Chair).

Henretta, J. C., Frazier, C. E., & Bishop, D. M. The effect of prior case outcomes on juvenile justice decision making. *Social Forces, 65*: 542–562.

Kaufman, (1977). Protecting the rights of minors: On Juvenile autonomy and the limits of the law. *New York University Law Review, 52*, 1015, 1016.

Kramer, J. H., & Steffensmeier, D. J. (1978). The differential detention/jailing of juveniles: A comparison of detention and nondetention courts. *Pepperdine Law Review, 5*, (1) 795–807.

Krisberg, B., Schwartz, I., Litsky, P., & Austin, J. (1986, January). The watershed of juvenile justice reform. *Crime and Delinquency, 32*,(1), 5–38.

Lerman, P. (1977, July). Discussion of differential selection of juveniles for detention. *Journal of Research on Crime and Delinquency, 14*, 166–172.

Lotz, R. E., Poole, D., & Regoli, R. M. (1985). *Juvenile delinquency and juvenile justice.* New York: Random House.

McDiarmid, M. (1977). Juvenile pretrial detention. *NLADA Briefcase, 34*, (2), 77–81.

National Council on Crime and Delinquency. (1961). *Standards and guides for the detention of children and youth* (2d ed.). Washington, DC: U.S. Government Printing Office.

Olson-Raymer, G. (1984). National juvenile justice policy: Myth or reality? In S. H. Decker (Ed.), *Juvenile justice policy: Analyzing trends and outcomes* (pp. 19–57). Beverly Hills, CA: Sage Publications.

Pawlak, E. J. (1977, July). Differential selection of juveniles for detention. *Journal of Research in Crime and Delinquency, 14*, 152–165.

Poulin, J. E., Levitt, J. L., Young, T. M., & Pappenfort, D. M. (1980). *Juveniles in detention centers and jails: An analysis of state variations during the mid-1970s.* U.S. Department of Justice. Washington, DC: U.S. Government Printing Office.

Rankin, A. (1964). The effects of pretrial detention. New York University Law Review, *39*, (1), 641–655.

Reuterman, N. (1970). *A national study of juvenile detention facilities.* Edwardsville: Southern Illinois University.

Rubin, H. T. (1985). *Juvenile justice: Policy, practice, and law* (2d ed.). New York: Random House.

Sarri, R. (1974). *Under lock and key: Juveniles in jails and detention. National Assessment of Juvenile Corrections.* Ann Arbor: University of Michigan.

Shamburek, P. A. (1978). A due process dilemma: Pretrial detention in juvenile delinquency proceedings. *John Marshall Journal of Practice and Procedure, 11*, (2) 513–547.

Sheridan, W. H. (1966). *Standards for juvenile and family courts.* U.S. Department of Health, Education, and Welfare. Washington, DC: U.S. Government Printing Office.

Siegel, L. J., & Senna, J. (1985). *Juvenile delinquency: Theory, Practice and Law* (2d ed.) St. Paul, MN: West Publishing.

Sumner, H. (1971, April). Locking them up. *Crime and Delinquency, 17,* 168.

Swigert, V., & Farrell, R. (1977). Normal homocides and the law. *American Sociological Review, 42:* 16–32.

Thomas, W. H. (1976). *Bail reform in America.* Berkeley: University of California Press.

Tripplet, R. (1978). Pretrial detention of juvenile delinquents. *American Journal of Criminal Law, 6,* 137–165.

Wald, P. M. (1976). Pretrial detention for juveniles. In M. K. Rosenheim (Ed.), *Pursuing justice for the child.* Chicago: University of Chicago Press, pp. 119–137.

Chapter Nine

Juvenile Diversion

Arnold Binder

CAROLE ROBERTS '88

ABSTRACT

This chapter addresses the process of diversion from the juvenile justice system, providing an overview of the essential elements in the development, operation, and evaluation of diversion programs. One of the first parts of the chapter describes two early police diversion programs—one in Detroit and one in Passaic, New Jersey—developed in the 1930s. Also discussed is the influence of labeling theory, a sociological perspective based on the concept that societal reactions to deviance—condemnation and punishment—cause juveniles to be viewed as incorrigible criminals. The next section provides detailed overviews of three well-established diversion programs.

The issue of diversion has been the topic of intense debate among sociologists, social workers, and criminal justice professionals. The view of the sociologists is that most diversion programs are in fact not voluntary agencies but part of the justice system. Youths referred rather than released become stigmatized or labeled because of their contact with the diversion program. This referral of juveniles who would otherwise have been released, is referred to as "widening the net." The opposing view, held by many social workers and criminal justice professionals, is that juvenile diversion is necessary for system operation and may prevent both status offenders and delinquents from engaging in further offenses.

Moreover, it seems clear that since troubled youths often need such services as employment counseling, family counseling, academic tutoring, and substance abuse treatment and education, diversion will remain as a thriving enterprise through the end of the 1980s and into the decade of the 1990s.

THE DIVERSION CONCEPT

The process of diversion in the juvenile justice system is a function of the transition levels in that system and the array of alternatives available at each of the levels. The full set of levels in juvenile justice consists of the police, probation, prosecuting attorney, court, and custodial institution. Initial entry into the system is almost always determined at the police level, where officers may, after taking a youngster into custody, choose among such alternatives as release to parents, referral to a community service agency, and referral to probation (or court intake) either by written notice or in continuing custody. The probation officer may, in turn, release the youngster with advice but no further processing, place the youngster on a program of informal supervision, refer the youngster to the prosecuting attorney in those states where law requires initiation of court action by that office, or petition the court for a hearing to determine if judicial intervention is warranted. In states where the prosecuting attorney is required to file the court petition, that office has the option of releasing the youngster rather than initiating court action. And finally, the court itself may of course release a youth without any custodial placement.

Clearly, then, the system allows release from further processing at all possible levels—release meaning the youth is diverted from further movement in the system. That feature was evident in the law that created the first formally recognized juvenile court in the United States (Illinois Act approved April 21, 1899). It stated that the court could "commit the child to the care and guardianship of a probation officer duly appointed by the court, and . . . allow said child to remain in its own home, subject to the visitation of the probation officer."

More than allowing for diversion of youngsters at each level of the process, the wording in many state codes expresses a preference for such actions. For example, Juvenile Court Law in California (Welfare and Institutions Code, Section 202) gives as its purpose:

> to secure for each minor under the jurisdiction of the juvenile court such care and guidance, preferably in his own home, as will serve the spiritual, emotional, mental, and physical welfare of the minor and the best interests of the state; . . . to preserve and strengthen the minor's family ties whenever possible, removing him from the custody of his parents only when necessary for his welfare or for the safety and protection of the public.

And, after specifying alternative dispositions available to a police officer, that law states (Section 626): "In determining which disposition of the minor he or she will make, the officer shall prefer the alternative which least restricts the minor's freedom of movement, provided that alternative is compatible with the best interests of the minor and the community."

Hard data indicate a preference in the juvenile justice system for diversion from further processing. According to the 1985 issue of *Uniform Crime Reports* for the United States, 7,681 police agencies reported slightly more than 1 million arrests of juvenile offenders in 1984. Almost one third of those offenders were counseled and released or referred to an appropriate social service agency. When one considers further that well under 50 percent of the children with whom police come into contact in offense investigations are taken into custody (arrested), one gets a dramatic feel for the extent of diversion at the entry point of the juvenile justice system (see Black & Reiss, 1970; Strasburg, 1978; Terry, 1967; Williams & Gold, 1972).

IMPLEMENTING THE DIVERSION CONCEPT

Early Programs

The preference in the juvenile justice system for diverting youths from the path that begins with the police and ends up in an institution led to the establishment of various formal approaches aimed at regularizing and extending diversionary services. Detroit established, in the 1930s, a women's bureau that has been described by Roberts (1976, 1983) as a "prototype of police social work." The bureau's staff of police officers provided treatment and referral services for minors (under twenty-one years of age) who came to the attention of the police. While that program was oriented more toward prevention than rehabilitation, a more directly diversionary scheme, police probation, came into existence in subsequent years at many police departments. Police probation worked by means of agreements among officers, offending youths, and parents. Diversion from the path to probation (and the court) would be provided by the officers if youths and parents agreed to various behavioral and reporting conditions. These conditions might include attending school regularly, keeping out of certain areas of the city, studying a certain number of hours each day, leaving the house only with parents, and reporting to the police station once each week (Lemert, 1971:56).

As another example of an early attempt to formalize police diversion, the city of Passaic, New Jersey, established a Children's Bureau in 1937 to serve an array of troubled children, including juvenile offenders. In subsequent years, four police officers were assigned to the bureau as its Police Unit. Boone (1961:233) summarized police responsibilities: "The police personnel, under the immediate direction of the Bureau director, are obliged to turn any apprehended juvenile offender over to the Children's Bureau where his problem is analyzed and a staff member is assigned to help the child readjust." Staff at the bureau included two psychologists and a social worker. According to Boone, "Every boy or girl reported for a law violation receives an individual psychological test and counseling from the psychologist. Parents are asked to accompany their youngsters so that they may have an opportunity to discuss any referral situation with the psychologist" (pp. 234–235). And "It is the social worker's responsibility to concern herself with the child's environment—his recreational activities, home life, church affiliations, camping experiences, and extracurricular activity" (p. 255). The social worker served as the liaison when children were referred to other clinics and agencies that provided services unavailable in the bureau.

Contributions from Sociology

While those and many other programs were being established to formalize the general mandate for diversion in juvenile justice, a contemporaneous, though completely unrelated, position in theoretical sociology was being developed that would eventually have enormous impact on all of diversion. That development had early roots in 1938 with the publication of a book by the historian Tannenbaum. He used the expression "dramatization of evil" to describe the state of affairs where deviant behavior is escalated in seriousness and frequency by the very social processes established to suppress it. To illustrate, boys engage in criminal activities, but only some of these boys are arrested. A smaller group of the boys are sent to probation, to courts, and on to custodial institutions—and that may occur repeatedly. That process leads, at some point, to the boy being regarded by both the community and himself as an incorrigible criminal. The result is that the community reacts to the boy as a criminal no matter what he does and he, in turn, behaves more and more in accord with that role.

Tannenbaum's theme was elaborated and extended in 1951 by the sociologist Lemert, who distinguished between primary and secondary deviance. Primary deviance is deviant behavior caused by the usual array of genetic, social, and environmental factors that are found in social-psychological theories. But the more important secondary deviance refers to behavior that results from social reactions to the primary deviance: the process of condemnation and punishment leads to stigmatization or labeling, and that leads to reactions, associations, and behavior concordant with the label. Further elaborations of that position into what became known as labeling theory in sociology may be found in Becker (1963); Erikson (1962, 1966); Kitsuse (1962).

Labeling theory was at a high point of acceptance and influence in sociology when another social force led to the establishment of a Commission on Law Enforcement and Administration of Justice by President Johnson in 1965. That social force, dating from the early 1930s, was an insistence on an active role for the federal government in advancing the well-being of the American people. Implementation, referred to as the Positive State, was accomplished through countless programs of the New Deal and the Great Society as well as many sympathetic decisions of the U.S. Supreme Court. (A fuller explanation of the relationship between the spirit and programs of the Positive State, on the one hand, and juvenile justice on the other may, be found in Binder, 1984.) The president's commission made hundreds of recommendations for greatly increased efforts (by the federal government and other agencies) in the area of law enforcement to improve the well-being of people. As we shall see, several recommendations did lead to important federal legislation and resultant programs.

Several sociologists became staff members of and consultants to the commission and were obviously influential in its recommendations. Thus, we find in the commission's report (President's Commission, 1967:81):

The formal sanctioning system and pronouncement of delinquency should be used only as a last resort. In place of the formal system, dispositional alternatives to adjudication must be developed for dealing with juveniles, including agencies to provide and coordinate services and procedures to achieve necessary control without unnecessary stigma. Alternatives already available, such as those related to court intake, should be more fully exploited.

Two formal recommendations follow that position statement:

Communities should establish neighborhood youth-serving agencies—Youth Service Bureaus—located if possible in comprehensive neighborhood community centers and receiving juveniles (delinquent and nondelinquent) referred by the police, the juvenile court, parents, schools, and other sources.

Police forces should make full use of the central diagnosing and coordinating services of the Youth Service Bureau. Station adjustment should be limited to release and referral; it should not include hearings or the imposition of sanctions by the police. Court referral by the police should be restricted to those cases involving serious criminal conduct or repeated misconduct of a more than trivial nature. (p.83)

The Federal Contribution

Federal legislation followed, with accompanying funding authorization aimed at putting many of the commission's recommendations into effect. As early as 1968, there were the Omnibus Crime Control and Safe Streets Act (which established the Law Enforcement Assistance Administration) and the Juvenile Delinquency Prevention and Control Act. The weight of the federal government was clearly behind a major effort to prevent and control crime and delinquency, and juvenile diversion was a part of that effort. According to Palmer and Lewis (1980:7), "Within three years, hundreds of Youth Service Bureaus sprang up within the United States, and many courts increased their efforts to 'minimize penetration' into the justice system."

An attempt at unification, coordination, and expansion of federal efforts at delinquency control came with passage of the Juvenile Justice and Delinquency Prevention Act of 1974. The act contained many explicit references to diversion, including a statement in the Purpose section: "It is therefore the further declared policy of Congress to provide the necessary resources, leadership and coordination . . . to divert juveniles from the traditional juvenile justice system and to provide critically needed alternatives to institutionalization." Shortly thereafter, the following program announcement was sent to relevant agencies and people: "Pursuant to the authority of the Omnibus Crime Control and Safe Streets Act of 1968, as amended, and the Juvenile Justice and Delinquency Prevention Act of 1974, the Law Enforcement Assistance Administration is giving major priority to the diversion of youth from the juvenile justice system through use of Omnibus Crime Control discretionary funds." And a news release at the time stated that the sum of $10 million was being provided to fund diversionary efforts by public and private agencies.

Thus, the spirit of the Positive State was much in operation in this realm. And the diversion effort was thereby fully transformed from a necessary and routine part of processing juvenile offenders to the status of nearly a national passion. Hope and expectation clearly were extraordinarily high. If there were hundreds of formal programs in the first few years of initial federal attention, there were thousands in the mid-1970s. And that proliferation was accompanied in the literature by more theoretical discussions and debates, evaluations of programs, evaluative collections of program evaluations, and reviews and summaries of the state of the art. A few of those with more long-lasting interest were Altschuler and Lawrence (1981), Binder (1977), Binder and Binder (1983), Dunford, Osgood, and Weichselbaum (1982), Klapmuts (1974), Nejelski (1976), Quay and Love (1977), Rutherford and McDermott (1976), and Wright and Dixon (1977).

Examples of Diversion Programs in Operation

A More Detailed Overview of One Program   A police diversion program described in other formats (Binder & Binder, 1983; Binder, Monahan, & Newkirk, 1976; Binder & Newkirk, 1977; and Binder, Schumacher, Kurz, & Moulson, 1985) would seem a natural choice to illustrate day-to-day operations in diversion. It is surely typical of the successful and lasting programs that arose during the 1970s and has direct similarities to operational features described by Davidson et al. (1977) and Ku and Blew (1977).

The program started as a cooperative arrangement between a major university and a local police department, where referrals were handled by student interns; it expanded over subsequent years to encompass fifteen police departments and the county probation department, served by a large staff of full-time, paid employees. At the present time, referrals come at a rate of about two-thirds from police agencies and one-third from probation. Counselors have at least master's degrees in such fields as social work, counseling, or psychology and are either state licensed or being supervised for licensing.

In the broadest terms, intervention by program staff is derived from an ecological perspective in the sense that the youngster of concern is treated as an actor in interacting systems, including family, school, peers, police, and so on. The youth and family come before a counselor because his or her behavioral patterning produced a social response that led directly or indirectly to police involvement and a decision to refer. The central goal is to alter patterns of interaction between youth and community (including family) so that the friction between behavior and social response is ameliorated. In striving toward that goal, the focus may be upon a youngster's behavioral patterning and the conditions that determined its form, upon incidental community factors that magnify the social response to the behavior, or upon the interaction of those components. Family members are seen both separately and together.

Achieving the goal encompasses teaching parents effective ways of giving rewards and imposing sanctions, providing youngsters and parents with conceptual tools to evaluate the impact of possible alternative behaviors in order to select among them on the basis of a realistic estimate of probable responses to the behaviors, changing environmental conditions so that certain reactions are not evoked or so that interpersonal friction is reduced, introducing the youngsters into new settings that provide less socially irritating means of satisfying needs, teaching all family members various essentials of the effective use and interpretations of words and cues, and providing models for enlarging behavioral repertoires. The various methods in use by program staff to achieve the central goal may be classified into four broad categories: contingency control, coping skills, family communications, and environmental change. This classification scheme was adopted for purposes of description, not to inhibit counselors, who are free to adopt methods, where appropriate, that do not fit in any of the categories. Such methods include cognitive restructuring, reality testing, and anger management. Overall appropriateness of a mode of intervention is judged on the basis of its efficacy in a particular case for altering interactional patterns that seemed to produce the behavior that led to the involvement of law enforcement. Following are summaries of the four major categories of approach in counseling:

1. Contingency Control. The method starts with an analysis of the behavioral patterning of the youth and the array of effective rewards and sanctions available to the parents. These are used to write an agreement or contract that includes a listing of required behaviors (such as returning home by 10 P.M. on Saturday nights) and the consequences of conformity or failure to conform (such as denial of one day of television viewing for each five minutes of lateness in arriving home).

The principal goal in drawing up a formal agreement is to provide a basis for effective contingency management. As several investigations have shown (see, e.g., O'Leary, O'Leary, & Becker, 1967; Stuart, 1971), the parents of children who show antisocial patterns of behavior are often ineffective in communicating demands and expectations and use coercion excessively. Abusive interaction, as well as delinquent behavior, is frequently a result. The contract provides a means of starting a process of alleviating that state of affairs by substituting mutual negotiations for destructive abrasiveness and lack of control. It clarifies the respective rules and responsibilities of parents and child in day-to-day behavior and provides a basis for the establishment of relationships where reciprocity predominates.

Contingency management proceeds in the counseling context from simple contracts (set up to have a high probability of success) to more complex contracts, and then to less dependence upon the formal negotiation and more upon ad hoc decisions based upon awareness of the relationship between behavior and reinforcement, where parents see themselves as social change agents. Special emphasis is placed on teaching the parents careful observation of the behavior to be changed, careful specification of desired behavior, and the importance of prompt reward following desired behavior. Further, counselors emphasize that the value of a reward or a sanction must be determined from the perspective of the child since people (particularly of different ages) differ so markedly in what is considered reinforcing, and the value changes over time even in the case of a given individual. Where appropriate, the concept of *shaping* is taught to parents. Shaping refers to the process of eliciting a complex behavior by successive approximation. At first, similar behavior is rewarded, then only more similar behavior, and so on until only the actually desired behavior is rewarded.

The goal throughout the use of formal contracting is to develop more effective use of reward and sanction by parents. Ultimate success depends upon continuing contingency management after the termination of counseling, using the less formal array of methods found in families that do not have problem children.

2. Coping.   The concept refers to a broad understanding in developmental, situational, or motivational terms of the behavior of others and the adjustment of one's own behavior accordingly. Coping skills are equally needed by parents and children.

Let us consider the issue initially from the perspective of the parents. The emphasis is on making parents aware of the special contexts in which the behavior of children must be understood in order to respond in a manner that, at the least of the satisfactory levels, does not exacerbate a conflict situation. One scenario stands out because it occurs so frequently: A parent demands obedience from a recalcitrant child on the grounds that the rights and power of parents derive from divine decree; the slightest questioning of the divinely granted power leads to vigorous (perhaps even violent) correction.

A dictatorial parental position can only be effective if it has the support of the general social structure. But in the American social context of the late twentieth century, which encourages nonauthoritarian relationships, independence, self determination, and individuality, one cannot expect to cope with a belligerent, negativistic youngster by positions reflected in such statements as "You will do as I say because I'm your father" and "I respected and obeyed my father and you will do the same."

Coping with the developing independence of children is another area that needs attention, even in families where there is not a blatant power struggle. Obviously, children grow very gradually from the stage of infancy, where there is complete dependence upon parents, to adulthood, where there is little or no such dependence. Adjustments on the part of parents are continuously necessary, beginning perhaps with the two- or three-year-old who is given the choice of going shopping with mommy or staying home with daddy. Some parents resist the process at certain important stages or, in extreme cases, at almost all stages. They may not allow the youngster to make decisions that he or she should be making, they may demand a reporting and accounting procedure that is unrealistic, or they may not, by constant reminders of the need to perform tasks and taking care of every little need, allow the child to accept responsibility for actions. Interestingly, parents who stifle responsibility in that fashion often complain that their child is irresponsible.

The task of the counselor in these cases is to point out the existence of the difficulty and to lead the parent into beginning phases of the change from dependence to independence. Small steps are necessary, with early choice determined more on the basis of probability of success than of important progress toward independence.

Another area in which parental coping is necessary encompasses appropriate social behavior of children. It seems to many of the participants on the current cultural scene that recent times have wrought particularly vigorous social change. But even if that is not the case (humans in virtually every era think they have lived through dramatic social change), the point remains that there is a generation gap between parents and their children. What is appropriate dating behavior in the earlier generation, for example, is very likely not appropriate in the later one. The various recent changes in the social scene are obvious enough to all, and their potential effects upon parent evaluation of youthful behavior are equally obvious.

What does change in this realm have to do with the prevention of future delinquency? One relevant factor is the long-range need in effective parenting for the parent to be respected by and important to the child. Behavioral contracting is a start toward establishing parental control, but optimally it should eventually be replaced by a system where the child behaves in an accepted manner because maintenance of the attentive affection of parents is that important. Carping and nagging about behavior that is widely practiced and accepted on a communitywide basis does not encourage the development of that sort of system.

Still another consideration is the desirability of focusing, for purposes of management, upon behavior that is genuinely troublesome and potentially disruptive rather than upon behavior that is annoying because of changed value systems. Trying to control too many features of another's behavior dooms one to failure.

A final factor stems from the desirability of a relationship of honesty and trust between parents and child. While it is unreasonable to argue that children should have no secrets from parents and vice versa, there must be a limit to the extent of privacy in human relations. Beyond that bond comes evasiveness and then dishonesty. In most cases, parents can exercise little or no control over behavior that is concealed from them. Further, as distrust develops, one may find the child drifting toward more satisfying relationships in a gang or with dubious friends.

In dealing with coping problems generally, the counselor occasionally supplements directed discussion with suggested readings. And straightforward contracts are occasionally used to allow the expansion of a child's social horizons under conditions that are acceptable to parents. This might involve as simple a change as moving the curfew hour from 8 P.M. to 9 P.M. Further expansion of permitted social behavior occurs as parents understand the implications and are reinforced for earlier successes in terms of changes in other aspects of behavior.

Coping skills on the part of the children often involve adjustments to parental idiosyncracies that are beyond control mechanisms. A most obvious example occurs in the case of a heavily drinking parent who, when under the influence, is just about impossible to reason with. Coping involves understanding the hopelessness of dealing directly with an intoxicated individual and the substitution of avoidance for confrontation. Avoidance may take the form of retiring to one's room, staying with friends, or working at school on a special project.

In the broader realm of interaction, an attempt is made to teach the youngster that he or she can accomplish many desired goals in much more effective and efficient ways. The process involves agreement on method, structured trial that seems to have high probability of success, and full implementation as the behavior becomes comfortable in the overall interactional repertoire.

3. Enhancing Patterns of Communication. Several investigators (e.g., Patterson & Reid, 1970) have shown that there is faulty communication in the families of delinquents and that intervention to improve communications frequently results in diminished delinquency. The faulty patterning may include such phenomena as little information exchange by words so that decisions are based on behavioral interpretation (misinterpretation), fear of expression on the part of children because previous expressions so often led to punishment, failure to attend to the messages sent from one family member to another, frequent disparity between message intended by parent or child and message received and interpreted by child or parent, frequent discrepancy between message sent in words and message sent by accompanying gesture so that the receiver is bewildered, and the common use of negative behavior and threatened sanctions when needs and desires are expressed.

Communication patterns among family members are carefully observed by counselors in the group counseling context so that live examples may be used in attempts to increase overall information exchange, to emphasize the importance of listening and showing respect for the communications of others, to teach the importance of mutual checking so that discrepancies between message intended and message received are minimized, to clarify various levels of communication and emphasize the dangers of contradictory messages (as between a positive verbal statement accompanied by a decidedly negative set of gestures), and to teach a preference for direct expression of needs and desires in place of such coercive mechanisms as threats and tantrums.

4. Direct Environmental Action. The last of the general modes of intervention is environmental manipulation whereby counselors get out into the world of the referred youngster to negotiate changes. Occasionally the process is referred to as child advocacy (see, e.g., Davidson et al., 1977), although that expression carries political overtones that may be irrelevant to the behavioral intent. Specific intervention activities in this category include visiting a youngster's school and recommending changes in the school's approach, helping the youngster find a job, motivating another agency to provide appropriate services, and providing a "big brother" or "big sister" to interact with the youngster and act as a role model. These activities have been components of the armamentarium of social work from its earliest days.

Other Illustrative Programs. The Youth Service Center (YSC) evolved out of the Philadelphia Boys' Club in 1974 with the specific aim of diverting youths from the juvenile justice system. According to Denno (1980:348), "Program referrals to YSC comprise area youths between the ages of 10 and 18 who have been arrested and are in the process of entering the juvenile justice system, or are deemed troublesome by other agencies or their families." The treatment program emphasizes counseling by paraprofessional caseworkers who are aided as necessary by professionals such as clinical psychologists. Services of other components of the South Philadelphia Community Center, where YSC is housed, are available to the staff caseworkers as are other agencies in the area for referral of particularly difficult or troublesome cases. Treatment is terminated when (a) the treated youth so requests (participation is voluntary), (b) the youth seems uncooperative though willing to continue in treatment, or (c) the youth is judged to be rehabilitated.

In an interesting approach to evaluation of program success, Denno (1980) assessed the degree to which implementation of YSC decreased arrests in two police districts within the target area. Control for extraneous factors that could influence results was accomplished by using neighboring police districts for comparison. She stated that it was not possible to conclude from the broader picture that YSC existence alone accounted for the decline, even though there was "a 26 percent decrease in the number of arrests in its focal area" (p. 357).

In contrast to the operation of YSC, the next diversion program to be considered does not provide direct services to youths. Rather than providing those services, the Memphis-Metro Youth Diversion Project (MMYDP) acts as a brokering agency, receiving referrals from the juvenile court and then placing the referred youths with service providers. It also acts as a monitor of the services delivered by the providers and of the progress of referred youths. That broker type of operation, incidentally, is in accord with the model for juvenile diversion, the youth service bureau, originally recommended by the President's Commission on Law Enforcement and Administration of Justice (1967) and discussed in detail by Norman (1972).

Upon referral from the court, a youth and his or her parents or guardians are interviewed by an MMYDP staff member. According to Whitaker and Severy (1984:55), "This subjective yet formally structured interview was designed to generate a court intake–type needs-assessment evaluation." The assessment leads to a list of three needs in order of priority and a derived service placement recommendation based on the youth's highest-priority need. The recommendation can be for family counseling, individual counseling, drug and alcohol abuse counseling, vocational training, or "structured activities designed to provide alternative positive social experiences" (p.55). A lower-priority need was used in the determination of agency for referral when a family rejected the first choice and negotiation was necessary for agreement to participate.

In one evaluation of MMYDP reported by Whitaker and Severy (1984), more than fifty different youth-serving referral agencies were used, although 87 percent of the youths were referred to only twelve agencies. The agencies fell into one of two groups: Group A facilities were private, nonprofit agencies staffed by "bachelor's degree level staff who have had considerable experience (often in the 'case work' method) in working with youth" (p.56). Group B facilities were mental health centers staffed by counselors with master's degrees or doctorates. Whitaker and Severy found a distinct difference in mode of delivery between the youth-serving agencies (Group A) and mental health centers (Group B), possibly because mental health centers are accustomed to dealing with self-referred and highly motivated clients. Moreover, on the basis of their evaluative data they concluded: "The agencies serving youth consistently responded more quickly, provided more services, followed through with a greater percentage of the proposed service cycle, and, in general, had more success than did the mental health centers" (p.70).

In another evaluation of MMYDP, Severy and Whitaker (1984) assessed the success of the project in terms of reduction in court adjudication rates. Four years of operation of the project were compared with the four years prior to its inception, adjusted for numbers of youths arrested and referred to the court. They found a decrease in adjudications during the four years of project operations and concluded: "It is clear that the Memphis-Metro Youth Diversion Project did have a significant impact on the juvenile justice system in Memphis and Shelby County, Tennessee" (p.276).

JUVENILE DIVERSION: A CONTROVERSIAL ISSUE

We have reviewed the motivations for diversion in the juvenile justice system, provided an overview of some early attempts at diversion, summarized the contributions of sociology and the federal government in furthering the diversionary effort, and discussed the operation of representative diversion programs. That information provides a firmer anchoring for understanding a continuing controversy about diversion.

Two consequences are readily predictable when enormous hope and expectation are paired with substantial public resources and agency responses in a major social effort, as was the case in juvenile diversion: First, there will be many disappointments on the part of the people trying to advance the effort. Second, there will be people on the sidelines who, with or without evaluation data and for reasons ranging from benign doubt to status seeking, will attempt to deflate the whole enterprise.

In Carter and Klein's (1976) book on juvenile diversion, we find the following in the introduction to the first section: "We may now be dealing with something dangerously close to a *fad*. Fads are infections, bring unreasoned compliance and acceptance. In the justice and social welfare areas, we can ill afford such unreasoned patterns" (p.2). Similarly, Lundman (1976:436) stated, "Diversion may magnify rather than correct existing problems," and Bullington, Sprowls, Katkin, and Phillips (1978:70) pointed out that "a central theme of this paper is that diversionary programs currently in vogue are potentially as abusive as the programs they seek to reform. Innovations being advertised as alternatives to incarceration may prove to be merely alternative forms of incarceration."

One theme that occurs repeatedly in these and similar condemnations is that the diversionary effort all too frequently spills over into primary prevention. That is, although diversion means channeling a young offender out of a path upwards in the justice system, the police often (or too often) use the service agencies or people of the diversion network for the referral of youngsters who would have been released to parents (rather than sent to probation). The pejorative term for that result is *widening the net*. Thus, we find Austin and Krisberg (1981:171) stating: "Diversion programs also serve to strengthen the net and to create new nets by formalizing previously informal organizational practices." There were those who even argued (see, e.g., Klein, 1976; Bullington, et al., 1978) that a diversion program produces a labeling effect comparable to that produced by continued processing in the juvenile justice system. That was an interesting twist: the desirability of avoiding labeling was a prime factor in motivating the expansion of the diversion effort in the 1968–1974 era, and now some were claiming that diversion itself produces labeling.

Binder and Geis (1984) argued that more than sound empirical evidence and rational deduction are at work in many of the articles that condemn diversion. One example they give is particularly revealing of the emotional intensity in the overall posture of those who object to modern diversion:

> If diversion programs service fewer members of a protected class than population numbers would indicate as appropriate, [to those condemning diversion] it is discrimination against that class; but if the programs service more than would seem appropriate, it is discrimination to "widen the net" for that class. Diversion is clearly insidious. Thus, Blomberg points out that research has found "that diversion program clients tend to be drawn from groups that are predominately middle-class," and then concludes, "As a result, many lower-class youth who might benefit from diversion's family services are being denied these services." (Blomberg, 1980:10)

On the other hand, Alder and Polk observe the following: "Females are disproportionately involved in diversion programs in contrast to other forms of social control (i.e., arrest and court referral)" (Alder and Polk, 1982:105). Using that state of affairs together with differences between males and females in the nature of offense leading to referral, Alder and Polk see in diversion "hidden sexism." Accepting that "diversion increases stigma and increases delinquency" by the "process of secondary deviance," they conclude, astonishingly, "Therefore, by both widening the net, and by increasing the probability of later delinquency, the net result of such programs is to *significantly increase* the future number of girls who experience juvenile justice processing." (p. 106)

As Binder and Geis (1984:641) point out, "The rhetoric condemnatory of diversion arises almost entirely from persons whose professional affiliation is with the discipline of sociology." On the other hand, psychologists' and social workers' comments on diversion are almost invariably positive despite acknowledgments of operational problems in the area. There are several reasons for differences of that sort between some sociologists on one hand and psychologists and social workers on the other. Uppermost among these, as stated before, is the powerful tradition in sociology of emphasis on social arrangements rather than individual factors in the prevention and elimination of human problems. That tradition, reinforced strongly in recent years by the perspectives of radical and Marxist sociology, leads to pejorative terms like *psychologizing* when explanations of phenomena are based on such aspects of the individual as personality and intelligence.

Thus, to some sociologists, concepts like treatment, psychotherapy, counseling, behavior change, and psychological intervention have negative connotations in the context of efforts to reduce crime and delinquency. In the expression "widening the net of social control," the critics lump such phenomena as counseling and psychotherapy together with arrest, prosecution, and incarceration in places like juvenile hall. The argument is often made that the best alternative response to juvenile offenses is nothing at all (radical nonintervention in the words of Schur, 1973). One response of Binder and Geis (1984:629) to that and similar arguments is:

Many youngsters indeed might have suffered no apparent immediate consequences of their apprehension if diversion were not available. How that might have borne on their entire lives is quite problematic, as we noted earlier, despite the ready assumption by critics of diversion that the less interference the better matters will be. Presumably, any one of us can find a rebuttal to such a position by memory of some intervention into our wayward ways at some time that produced beneficial results. In addition, it seems unarguable that some youngsters might have been treated more harshly by the authorities had diversion not been available. Presumably, the tougher and more lenient aspects of the program have to be blended into some sort of evaluative amalgam before an accurate assessment of the overall merits and shortcomings of diversion can be reached.

JUVENILE DIVERSION IN THE 1980s AND BEYOND

Despite such objections, diversion seems to live on as we end the 1980s. Vitality in the realm where some predicted, and others hoped for, rapid and silent demise is well demonstrated in several recent publications. Two have been selected here to illustrate that vitality in terms of adaptations derived from earlier research findings and adjustments to changing social conditions.

Before turning to those two, however, it is worthwhile to discuss briefly the evaluation of diversion by Palmer and Lewis (1980), which contained important recommendations for diversion in the 1980s. It encompassed fifteen juvenile diversion programs that operated in California but seem representative of diversion on a national basis. Referral to the programs came overwhelmingly from law enforcement and probation; the percentage of referrals of youngsters with prior arrests varied over programs from 9 percent to 89 percent, with an overall average of 29 percent (15 percent with two or more prior arrests). The investigators were able to obtain comparison (control) groups for recidivism evaluations. The results of the study indicated:

a. Differential effectiveness over programs in the reduction of offenses. Some programs were quite effective in reducing recidivism; others were not. Overall, there was a 17.3 percent reduction in recidivism in the six-months evaluation.

b. The estimated cost savings for every 100 youths diverted rather than processed in the system was $2,900. -

c. Over all clients, individual and group counseling seemed more effective than family counseling.

d. Among the approaches used most often in the most effective programs were "expression of feelings," "expressing personal concern for acceptance of youth," and "informality—lack of social distance."

e. Among the approaches used least often in the most effective programs were "protecting, minimizing demands/pressures," "being forceful, blunt," and "familiarizing youth with authority figures."

f. Workers in the most effective programs reported the greatest positive impact coming from informality, expression of personal concern for youths, frequent contacts, and a warm, friendly atmosphere.

g. Over half (51 percent) of the clients served by the evaluated programs would have been processed further in the system if the diversion projects had not existed.

These and other results led to the following observations and conclusions by Palmer and Lewis (1980):

> Our findings and analyses suggest that diversion can serve a number of
> important goals. Included are the reduction of (1) negative labeling and
> stigmatization, (2) unnecessary social control and coercion, (3) recidi-
> vism, and (4) justice system costs; also included is (5) the provision of
> service. Achievement of one or more such objectives, even to a modest
> degree, would represent a positive contribution to individuals and/or
> society. Individually and collectively, these contributions would, and
> probably do, make diversion worthwhile. This is not to say they are
> always achieved—that every project is successful in all areas. (p. 207)

> As the 1980s get underway it will be important for individuals involved
> with diversion to build on the positive features of often divergent
> views—to incorporate their respective strengths wherever possible and
> to value basic differences as well. This linking and integrating process
> may lead to a more powerful and widely applicable system of diversion
> than is possible through any one approach alone. Thus, by bringing to-
> gether relatively different perspectives or approaches we may be better
> able to retain those values which are reflected in the underlying mission
> of diversion, while making this movement more responsive to current
> issues as well.
>   Underlying this and other tasks is the need to recognize diversion for
> what it is: a complex phenomenon that reflects both a long-term history
> and several recent, pressing concerns. This dual background has re-
> sulted in considerable strain since the early 1970s; yet conflict can be
> constructive if it promotes an eventual integration of views. To be sure,
> the integration of differing perspectives or needs is likely to make di-
> version more complex and difficult to administer than it already is. This,
> perhaps, will be the price of greater strength. (pp. 216–217)

Osgood and Weichselbaum (1984) sought to determine if "properly
implemented" diversion programs reduced such negative features of
justice system processing as stigma and coerciveness. Their data came
from nine of the eleven programs evaluated in a nationwide effort
funded by the Office of Juvenile Justice and Delinquency Prevention;
they encompassed diversion efforts over seven metropolitan areas.

The method of approach consisted of comparing the views about
the programs over four groups: diversion service providers, service
providers at justice agencies, clients of the diversion programs, and
clients at justice agencies. There were five variables of central interest
and a scale of four to eight items for each variable. The five variables
were called: coercion, social control, serving needs, clients viewed as

delinquent, and clients viewed as emotionally disturbed. To illustrate the nature of the items, "Youth[s] can choose to stop coming to this program whenever they want" was used to measure coercion, "Clients are sent to this program to pay for their crimes" was used to measure social control, and "This agency provides clients with new opportunities" was used to measure serving needs. Each item was rated on a five-point scale that ranged from "strongly agree" to "strongly disagree."

Three comparisons were central in the analysis of results: between types of service providers (diversion program versus justice system in the same community), between clients of diversion programs and clients of justice agencies, and between service providers and their clients in the diversion programs. In an attempt to assure that differing views between groups were not a function of actual differences in the characteristics of clients, statistical controls (including those for prior arrests, age, and sex) were introduced. Over the nine sites, comparison between types of service providers showed consistent differences in the direction of a more benign context among diversion programs. Thus, justice system providers characterized their programs as more coercive and more controlling and their clients as more delinquent and more emotionally disturbed. For example, over all sites the mean score on the coercion variable was 13.40 for diversion programs and 19.13 for justice programs, and the mean score on social control was 17.46 for diversion programs and 22.36 for justice programs. Both differences are statistically significant at very low probability levels.

Comparison between the views of clients of diversion programs and justice agencies was possible at only three sites. Diversion programs were seen as less coercive, less controlling, having greater emphasis on client needs, and less likely to view the clients as delinquent. Comparing service providers and clients, clients had less favorable views of the programs on coercion, social control. and serving needs, and the view of clients by service providers were more negative than clients believed.

Using these results, the investigators conclude that for clients who are diverted in place of receiving formal dispositions, diversionary services reduce coercion, control, and stigmatization. They comment, "Even if diversion programs entail some degree of coercion and social control, it is substantially less than for formal dispositions" and "diversion programs are characterized by a greater concern with servicing their clients' needs, and they reduce at least one form of stigma" (Osgood & Weichselbaum, 1984:53, 54).

Binder, et al. (1985) discussed the historical relationship between general cultural values and attitudes, on the one hand, and the methods of dealing with young offenders, on the other. They then related changes in diversionary efforts that took place from the early 1970s to mid-1980 to alterations in American values in general, and attitudes toward crime and delinquency in particular. Three such alterations stand out (1) an increased demand for accountability in the expenditure of tax monies, especially for social programs, (2) the emergence of concern for the victims of crime as a major public issue, and (3) a hardening, retributive social attitude toward serious criminal offenders, young and old, with accompanying demands for more and longer incarceration. The authors did contend, however, that compassion continues for the status offender and for the youngster who commits a first or second nonserious crime.

Given the cultural climate of the 1980s that has anchored the above and similar values and attitudes, Binder, et al. (1985) discussed the operations and evaluation of a diversionary approach that suits that climate while using the basic treatment mode discussed above (behavioral contracting, coping, communication enhancement, and environmental action). Oriented toward cost savings, it provides alternate services only for youths who have a high probability of being processed further into the (more expensive) justice system. That is accomplished by using criteria that allow acceptance into the program only for repeat and more serious offenders. Further, the approach includes restitution services for the victims of property offenses. The amount of restitution paid by offender to victim is determined at a hearing by a board of community residents on the basis of the recommendation of a restitution specialist and interviews with youth and parents. These services not only provide direct compensation for crime victims, but attempt to convey to the youngster a sense of his or her responsibility for the criminal behavior (see the relevant discussion in Shichor & Binder, 1981). Finally, the diversionary approach involves a joint effort among eleven police departments, the county probation department, and three community agencies that provide services.

Process assessment of the program showed that counseling and restitution services were provided in accordance with plans, and that the focus of attention was indeed on the more criminally oriented youngster. To summarize essential results, 68 percent of clients received counseling services, and 47 percent were seen by restitution specialists; the average amount paid by offender to victim as restitution was $177; and 71 percent of program youngsters were arrested for felonies or had prior arrests (as compared with 39 percent for a comparison group). Impact assessment compared a year of program operations with a baseline year and led to the following conclusions:

> Diversion resources seem now to be more focused on youths who would otherwise be expected to penetrate the juvenile justice system, into and beyond probation intake. Prior to implementation of the new program, 41 percent of total diversion clients were referred by noncriminal justice

sources for personal problems that are not included in the codes of the justice system. In the new programs, no clients were referred by non-criminal justice sources and 71 percent of clients had a felony-level referral offense or prior arrests.

Finally, the evaluation data support the conclusions that, in addition to direct gains for victims and young offenders, the program reduced the proportion of probation intake cases referred to the district attorney. During the baseline year, 56 percent of total cases processed by probation officers were referred to the district attorney; the figure for the new year is 39 percent. Moreover, youths served by the new program were found to have no higher recidivism rates (in terms of subsequent applications for petition) than youths of comparable severity handled during the earlier year. (Binder et al., 1985:11)

CONCLUSION

Those types of results lead to the overall conclusion that diversion remains a thriving enterprise in the 1980s—as indeed it must if one assumes that youths in trouble frequently need such services as employment counseling, family counseling, tutoring, substance abuse education, or a relationship with a "big brother or sister." A reorganization of society may eventually bring a nearly crimeless society, or continued arguments by protagonists of secondary deviance may make society considerably more tolerant and accepting of youthful deviance—though a prudent person would bet on neither. In the present and immediate future, however, we have and will have those youths who clash with society because of criminal behavior and who will benefit from services aimed at reducing future clashes.

DISCUSSION QUESTIONS

1. Explain what Tannenbaum meant by "dramatization of evil."
2. Which legislative act attempted to unify, coordinate, and expand federal efforts at delinquency control?
3. Compare and contrast the police diversion program developed by Binder and associates in California with the historical attempt in 1937 to formalize police diversion in Passaic, New Jersey.
4. Explain what is meant by the following concepts:

   Contingency management.

   Shaping.

   Coping.

   Enhancing patterns of communication.

   Direct environmental action.

5. What do the critics of diversion mean by the term *widening the net*?
6. Summarize the status of juvenile diversion in the 1980s.
7. The Memphis-Metro Youth Diversion Project in Tennessee acts as a brokering agency. With which types of agencies does it serve as a broker?

REFERENCES

Alder, C. & Polk, K. (1982). Diversion and hidden sexism. *Australian and New Zealand Journal of Criminology, 15,* 101–110.

Altschuler, D. M. & Lawrence, J.S. (1981). *A review of selected research and program evaluations on police diversion programs.* (Reports of the National Juvenile Justice Assessment Centers). Washington, DC: U.S. Department of Justice, Office of Juvenile Justice and Delinquency Prevention.

Andriessen, M. (1980). A foreigner's view of American diversion. *Crime and Delinquency, 26,* 70–82.

Austin, J. & Krisberg, B. (1981). Wider, stronger, and different nets. *Journal of Research in Crime and Delinquency, 18,* 165–196.

Baron, R., Feeney, F., & Thornton, W. (1976). Preventing delinquency through diversion. In R. M. Carter & M. W. Klein (Eds.), *Back on the street: The diversion of juvenile offenders,* Englewood Cliffs, NJ: Prentice-Hall.

Becker, H. S. (1963). *Outsiders: Studies in the sociology of deviance.* New York: Free Press.

Binder, A. (1977). Diversion and the justice system: Evaluating the results. In A. W. Cohn (Ed.), *Criminal justice planning and development.* Beverly Hills, CA: Sage Publications.

Binder, A. (1979). The juvenile justice system: Where pretense and reality clash. *American Behavioral Scientist, 22,* 621–652.

Binder, A. (1984). The juvenile court, the U.S. Constitution, and when the twain meet. *Journal of Criminal Justice, 12,* 355–366.

Binder, A. (1987). An historical and theoretical introduction. In H. C. Quay (Ed.), *Handbook of juvenile delinquency.* New York: John Wiley & Sons.

Binder, A., & Binder, V. L. (1983). Juvenile diversion. *Counseling Psychologist, 11,* 69–77.

Binder, A., & Geis, G. (1984). *Ad populum* argumentation in criminology: Juvenile diversion as rhetoric. *Crime and Delinquency, 30,* 624–647.

Binder, A., Monahan, J. & Newkirk, M. (1976). Diversion from the juvenile justice system and the prevention of delinquency. In J. Monahan (Ed.), *Community mental health and the criminal justice system.* Elmsford, NY: Pergamon Press.

Binder, A., & Newkirk, M. (1977). A program to extend police service capability. *Crime Prevention Review, 4,* 26–32.

Binder, A., Schumacher, M., Kurz, G., & Moulson, L. (1985). A diversionary approach for the 1980s. *Federal Probation, 49,* 4–12.

Black, D. J., & Reiss, A. J., Jr. (1970). Police control of juveniles. *American Sociological Review, 35,* 63–77.

Blomberg, T. G. (1977). Diversion and accelerated social control. *Journal of Criminal Law and Criminology, 68,* 274–282.

Blomberg, T. G. (1980, November). The mixed results and implications of the diversion and family intervention reform movement. Paper presented at the annual meeting of the American Society of Criminology, San Francisco.

Boone, G. C. (1961). The Passiac Children's Bureau. *Crime and Delinquency, 7,* 231–236.

Brantingham, P. J. (1979). Juvenile justice reform in California and New York in the early 1960s. In F. L. Faust & P. J. Brantingham (Eds.), *Juvenile justice philosophy: Readings, cases and comments,* (2d ed.). St. Paul, MN: West Publishing.

Bullington, B., Sprowls, J., Katkin, D., & Phillips, M. (1978). A critique of diversionary juvenile justice. *Crime and Delinquency, 24,* 59–71.

Carter, R. M. & Klein, M. W. (Eds.). (1976). *Back on the street: The diversion of juvenile offenders.* Englewood Cliffs, NJ: Prentice-Hall.

Davidson, W. S., Seidman, E., Rappaport, J., Berck, P. L., Rapp, N. A., Rhodes, W., & Herring, J. (1977). Diversion program for juvenile offenders. *Social Work Research and Abstracts, 13,* 40–49.

Davis, S. M. (1980). *Rights of juveniles: The juvenile justice system* (2d ed.). New York: Clark Boardman.

Decker, S. H. (1985). A systematic analysis of diversion: Net widening and beyond. *Journal of Criminal Justice. 13,* 207–216.

Denno, D. J. (1980). Impact of a youth service center: Does diversion work? *Criminology, 18,* 347–362.

Dunford, F. W., Osgood, D. W., & Weichselbaum, H. F. (1982). *National evaluation of diversion projects.* Washington, DC: U.S. Department of Justice, Office of Juvenile Justice and Delinquency Prevention.

Erikson, K. T. (1962). Notes on the sociology of deviance. *Social Problems. 9,* 307–315.

Erikson, K. T. (1966). *Wayward Puritans: A study in the sociology of deviance.* New York: John Wiley & Sons.

Gottheil, D. L. (1979). Pretrial diversion: A response to the critics. *Crime and Delinquency, 25,* 65–75.

Kitsuse, J. I. (1962). Societal reactions to deviant behavior: Problems of theory and method. *Social Problems, 9,* 247–257.

Klapmuts, N. (1974, March). Diversion from the justice system. *Crime and Delinquency Literature, 6,* 108–131.

Klein, M. W. (1976, October). Issues and realities in police diversion programs. *Crime and Delinquency, 22,* 421–427.

Ku, R., & Blew, C. H. (1977). *The adolescent diversion project: A university's approach to delinquency prevention: An exemplary project.* Washington, DC: U.S. Government Printing Office.

Lemert, E.M. (1951). *Social pathology.* New York: McGraw-Hill.

Lemert, E. M. (1971). *Instead of court: Diversion in juvenile justice.* Washington, DC: U.S. Government Printing Office.

Lundman, R. L. (1976). Will diversion reduce recidivism? *Crime and Delinquency, 22,* 428–437.

Mack, J. W. (1979). The juvenile court. (Original work published 1909.) In F. L. Faust & P. J. Brantingham (Eds.), *Juvenile justice philosophy: Readings, cases and comments* (2d ed.). St. Paul, MN: West Publishing.

Nejelski, P. (1976). Diversion: The promise and the danger. *Crime and Delinquency, 22,* 393–410.

Norman, S. (1972). *The youth service bureau—A key to delinquency prevention.* Paramus, NJ: National Council on Crime and Delinquency.

O'Leary, K. D., O'Leary, S. G., & Becker, W. C. (1967). Modification of a deviant sibling interaction pattern in the home. *Behavior Research and Therapy, 55,* 113–120.

Osgood, D. W. & Weichselbaum, H. F. (1984). Juvenile diversion: When practice matches theory. *Journal of Research in Crime and Delinquency, 21,* 33–56.

Palmer, T., & Lewis, R. V. (1980). *An evaluation of juvenile diversion.* Cambridge, MA: Oelgeschlager, Gunn & Hain.

Patterson, G. R. & Reid, J. B. (1970). Reciprocity and coercion: Two facts of social systems. In C. Neuringer & J. Michael (Eds.), *Behavior modification in clinical psychology.* New York: Appleton-Century-Crofts.

Pound, R., (1937). Foreword. In P. V. Young, *Social treatment in probation and delinquency: Treatise and casebook for court workers, probation officers, and other child welfare workers.* New York: McGraw-Hill.

President's Commission on Law Enforcement and Administration of Justice. (1967). *The challenge of crime in a free society.* Washington, DC: U.S. Government Printing Office.

Quay, H. C., & Love, C. T. (1977). The effect of a juvenile diversion program on rearrests. *Criminal Justice and Behavior, 4,* 377–395.

Roberts, A. R. (1976). Police social workers: A history. *Social Work, 21*(4), 294–299.

Roberts, A. R. (1983). The history and role of social work in law enforcement. In A. R. Roberts (Ed.), *Social work in juvenile and criminal justice settings.* Springfield, IL: Charles C. Thomas.

Rojek, D. G. (1982). Juvenile diversion: A study of community cooptation. In D. G. Rojek & G. F. Jensen (Eds.), *Readings in juvenile delinquency.* Lexington, MA: D. C. Heath.

Rubin, H. T. (1977). The juvenile court's search for identity and responsibility. *Crime and Delinquency, 23,* 1–13.

Rutherford, A., & McDermott, R. (1976). *Juvenile diversion.* (National Evaluation Program, Phase 1 report). Washington, DC: U.S. Department of Justice, Law Enforcement Assistance Administration.

Schultz, J. L. & Cohen, F. (1976). Isolationism in juvenile court jurisprudence. In M. K. Rosenheim (Ed.), *Pursuing justice for the child.* Chicago: University of Chicago Press.

Schur, E. M. (1973). Radical nonintervention: Rethinking the delinquency problem. Englewood Cliffs, NJ: Prentice-Hall.

Severy, L. J., & Whitaker, J. M. (1984). Juvenile diversion and system impact: Memphis-Metro Youth Diversion Project. *Child Welfare, 63,* 269–277.

Shichor, D., & Binder, A. (1981). Community restitution for juveniles: An approach and preliminary evaluation. *Criminal Justice Review, 7,* 46–50.

Strasburg, P. (1978). *Violent delinquents: Report to Ford Foundation from Vera Institute of Justice.* New York: Monarch.

Stuart, R. B. (1971). Behavioral contracting within families of delinquents. *Journal of Behavior Therapy and Experimental Psychiatry, 2,* 1–11.

Tannenbaum, F. (1938). *Crime and the community,* Boston: Ginn.

Tappan, P. W. (1950). Unofficial delinquency. *Nebraska Law Review, 29,* 547–558.

Terry, R. M. (1967). Discrimination in the handling of juvenile offenders by social-control agencies. *Journal of Research in Crime and Delinquency, 4,* 218–230.

U.S. Department of Justice (1985). *Uniform crime reports for the United States, 1984.* Washington, DC: Federal Bureau of Investigation.

Whitaker, J. M. & Severy, L. J. (1984). Service accountability and recidivism for diverted youth: A client- and service-comparison analysis. *Criminal Justice and Behavior, 11,* 47–74.

Williams, J. R., & Gold, M. (1972). From delinquent behavior to official delinquency. *Social Problems, 20,* 209–228.

Wright, W. E., & Dixon, M. C. (1977). Community prevention and treatment of juvenile delinquency. *Journal of Research in Crime and Delinquency, 14,* 35–67.

Chapter Ten

Wilderness Experiences: Camps and Outdoor Programs

Albert R. Roberts

ABSTRACT

Within the context of juvenile justice a distinction can be made between alternatives which are intended primarily to meet rehabilitation goals (i.e., structured wilderness adventure programs) and alternatives which are intended primarily to meet social control goals (i.e., juvenile training schools). The author begins with a brief statement on the origins of wilderness programs, then compares them to traditional training schools. An examination of the similarities and differences among the various established wilderness programs follows. Detailed descriptions of seven of the most widely known wilderness adventure programs are presented. Some of the more critical programmatic components are reviewed, including therapeutic camping, rock climbing, an overnight solo experience, alternative school, and family counseling. The chapter concludes by examining evaluations of the effectiveness of wilderness programs.

ORIGINS OF WILDERNESS PROGRAMS

Wilderness programs provide youths with a rigorous physical and emotional challenge unlike anything they have ever known before. In small, closely supervised groups, the juvenile offenders learn to follow instructions and to work cooperatively with other youths to accomplish a series of difficult physical challenges, thereby enhancing their own self-esteem. Most programs also strive to strengthen the youths' academic skills by incorporating aspects of learning directly related to outdoor living (e.g., map and compass skills).

The present-day wilderness programs for juvenile offenders evolved from two separate directions: forestry camps for youthful offenders and the Outward Bound model created in Wales during World War II. The earliest outdoor program for juvenile delinquents was established in the 1930s in the Forestry Department in Los Angeles County by Karl Holton. Typical work projects performed by youths (boys only) at forestry camps were "conservation, park development, road construction, safety programs, and farming; these projects [were] supplemented by individual and group counseling, recreational, educational and religious programs" (Robison, 1960:329); the usual length of stay did not exceed six months. The original purpose of Outward Bound was to train merchant seamen to succeed in accomplishing rigorous physical challenges as well as to develop group pride and a shared trust as the group worked together to achieve strenuous goals (Willman & Chun, 1973).

TRADITIONAL TRAINING SCHOOLS VERSUS WILDERNESS ADVENTURE PROGRAMS

Typically the interaction between staff and juveniles in a juvenile institution is restricted to custodial duties such as taking a head count as the youths move from one place in the institution to another; maintaining order; and carrying out professional responsibilities such as requiring the juveniles' participation in academic education, vocational education, or weekly group counseling sessions.

The ratio of juveniles to staff members varies from institution to institution, but the range is usually one counselor for 50 to 100 youths. Most of the contacts between staff and youth are superficial, and there is little opportunity for ongoing, meaningful interaction in which the staff person is perceived as a genuine role model by the youths.

In sharp contrast, it is not uncommon for a wilderness program to have a staffing ratio ranging from one adult for five youths to almost a one-on-one relationship. Youths who have become adept at conning and manipulating the institutional system quickly discover that they are not able to get away with ignoring their responsibilities or giving only half-hearted effort to a task. The wilderness model—essentially a back-to-basics approach—strips away the trappings of modern society (on which we have all come to depend) and focuses on the essential primary needs of food and shelter with the goal of fostering the development of self-confidence and socially acceptable coping mechanisms for the participants. Youths in the group are required to interact cooperatively with each other to accomplish daily tasks. For example, when the only place to sleep is a tent that the group is responsible for setting up, the entire group quickly learns that they need to work together to erect their shelter. Likewise, when the only food to eat is that which the group prepares themselves, the entire group participates. When problems arise they are dealt with immediately by the ever-present staff.

Although staff salaries for employees of privately run wilderness programs are usually well below the rate paid to institutional staff, these outdoor programs tend to attract a corps of dedicated, hardworking individuals who take a genuine interest in each youth. The fact that the adults are subjecting themselves to the same physical challenges as the juveniles makes a significant impression on the youths.

Often the small group of juveniles assigned to one adult is viewed as a substitute family unit in which the staff serve as role models who continually demonstrate mature, caring, socially acceptable behaviors. Many of the staff are hired because of their expertise in an outdoor activity such as canoeing or mountain climbing; their mastery of an adventurous skill that the youths know nothing about earns them a measure of respect at the outset. However, burnout and a high rate of staff turnover occur frequently at many of the wilderness camps because of the low salary and the round-the-clock nature of the job.

OUTDOOR PROGRAM COMPARISONS

Similarities

Although many variations occur in the structure of wilderness programs, most programs share several commonalities:

- Providing a well-organized program focusing on the mastery of difficult physical challenges.
- Creating an opportunity for heightened self-respect among youths who have a history of repeated failures in school, difficulty in social relationships, and problems with family members.
- Using the outdoors and the reality of ensuring one's own survival as the setting for teaching academic subjects.
- Learning how to work cooperatively with others to complete a task.

Most wilderness programs include the following components:

1. An *orientation phase* in which the youth is introduced to the expectations and requirements for successful completion of the program.
2. A series of increasingly difficult *physical challenges* that take into account the juvenile's desire for risk and excitement in an environment—the outdoors—that cannot be conned or manipulated. Typical challenges include rock climbing, rappelling, canoeing, backpacking, hiking, cross-country skiing, and cave exploring.
3. An *educational component* directly related to the camp experience.
4. A *"solo"* (ranging in length from one overnight to three days) in which each participant is required to survive alone in the wilderness using the skills acquired during the program.
5. A *final event*, generally a marathon run of several miles.
6. A *celebration ceremony* signifying the successful completion of the program, at which the participants may be awarded a diploma or certificate of completion.

Differences

The many areas in which camps differ are listed below:

- *Eligibility criteria.* Most programs do not accept juveniles who have committed violent offenses. Status offenders, adolescents with a history of drug abuse, youths adjudicated for property offenses, and predelinquent juveniles meet the eligibility requirements set forth by various programs. Some programs are coed; others are restricted to only boys.

- *Program auspice.* Programs are administered by private nonprofit or for-profit organizations as well as by a state office, usually a division of youth services.
- *Point of entry.* Some youths are sent directly to a program by a judge (or probation officer). Others enter the camp after serving time in a training school as a condition of prerelease. Still others are sentenced to a training school but given the option of volunteering for a wilderness experience: if successful they avoid the training school; if unsuccessful they are sent to a training school.
- *Duration of program.* The length of each program ranges from twenty-six days to twelve to eighteen months.
- *Involvement of family members.* While not a usual requirement, a few programs strongly encourage parents to attend counseling sessions with their child and/or to participate in parents' groups.
- *Type and frequency of counseling.* Some of the programs have no formal counseling component while others have group, family, and/or individual counseling one or more times per week.
- *Aftercare.* Some programs are able to provide continuity by having community-based follow-up services. Others end the relationship when the youth returns home.

MODEL PROGRAMS

Although wilderness programs exist in many states, descriptions of these programs are only rarely reported in professional journals and textbooks on delinquency and juvenile justice. For this book, information on wilderness camps was collected from many of the publicly and privately operated programs across the United States. Table 10–1 summarizes information on a number of selected wilderness programs. Seven programs that provide challenging wilderness experiences to juvenile delinquents are described in more detail in this section.

VisionQuest

Perhaps the most publicized and widely known outdoor adventure program is VisionQuest, a for-profit organization based in Tucson, Arizona. VisionQuest began in 1973 headed by Robert Burton, a contro-

TABLE 10–1 Selected Wilderness Programs: Summary of Data on Staff, Programs, and Follow-up Studies

Program and Location	Program Characteristics	Year Program Began	Number of Youths Completing Program in 1984	Number of Staff	Staff: Youth Ratio	Evaluation/ Follow-Up
Camp Woodson, North Carolina's Division of Youth Services, Fairview, North Carolina	Precamp component Trail life Solo experience 7 weeks	1976	130	19	1:7	None
Corvallis House Wilderness Program, Salem, Oregon	Groupwork that incorporates wilderness trips into the overall program Drug and alcohol education In-house school	1974	60	—	—	None
Eagle Nest Camp Experiential Reintegration Program, New Mexico	Progressive (3-stage) program designed to strengthen self-responsibility	1980	110	—	—	None

TABLE 10–1 (continued)

Program and Location	Program Characteristics	Year Program Began	Number of Youths Completing Program in 1984	Number of Staff	Staff: Youth Ratio	Evaluation/ Follow-Up
Eckerd Foundation Therapeutic Wilderness Camping Program, Florida, North Carolina, Rhode Island, and Vermont (11 different programs)	Wilderness camping Transitional classroom phase Family counseling and 18-month aftercare services 10 youths per 2 teacher-counselors	1968	579	116	1:5	None
OceanQuest (a VisionQuest program), Ft. Mifflin, Pennsylvania	Advanced program usually requiring completion of at least 2 months on VisionQuest's wagon train Instruction in water safety, oceanography, map/compass skills Group home Family involvement in support group	Reinstituted in 1984	—	11	1:1.2	None

Program / Location	Description	Year				Results
Stephen L. French Youth Wilderness (Homeward Bound) Program, Massachusetts Division of Youth Services, Brewster, Massachusetts	Wilderness experience Group counseling Community service assignments 3-day solo experience 26 days	1970	350	—	1:8	Experimental group 20.8% recidivism rate versus 42.7% recidivism rate for control group
VisionQuest, Tucson, Arizona,	Wilderness camp 6-day wilderness adventure 3-day solo experience wagon train 12–18 months	1973	—	—	1:1	43% rearrest rate (but no follow-up time frame specified)
Wilderness Camping Program, Alabama Youth Services Division	Group work Wilderness camping, stressing teamwork and mutual problem solving	1982	57	—	—	Follow-up study 9 months after completion of program: only 17% rearrested
Wolfcreek Wilderness School, Georgia Division of Youth Services, Atlanta, Georgia	Intensive and relatively short in duration (26 days) Enhances self-image by providing success experiences	1978	108	2	1:5	None

TABLE 10–1 Table 10–1 (concluded)

Program and Location	Program Characteristics	Year Program Began	Number of Youths Completing Program in 1984	Number of Staff	Staff: Youth Ratio	Evaluation/ Follow-Up
	Small staff-youth ratio of 2 instructors for each group of 10 youths					
Youth Challenge Wilderness Expedition Program, Middletown, Connecticut	Team-building approach to problem solving Bolstering self-esteem through backpacking, canoeing, and mountain climbing	1978	683	—	—	None

versial figure who has generated high praise as well as considerable criticism for his unorthodox treatment methods. VisionQuest operates several types of programs: group homes, wilderness camps, Home-Quest (a home-based family counseling program), OceanQuest, and the Wagon Train—considered the most visible of all the VQ programs.

The usual length of stay at the coed program is twelve to eighteen months, considerably longer than most other wilderness programs. Before entering the program, the youths make a commitment that includes a pledge to abstain from drugs, alcohol, and sex; to complete at least two "high-impact" programs during a one-year stay; and to remain with the program until discharge (Sweeney, 1982).

Greenwood and associates (1983) determined that the key to the program's success was the close and frequent interaction between the juvenile offender and staff members combined with the primitive conditions of the wilderness, which serve to "inspire a degree of intimacy, trust and mutual respect that goes far beyond that found in traditional institutions" (p. 86).

VisionQuest operates two wilderness camps, one in the mountains of New Mexico and the other in Franklin, Pennsylvania. Included in the wilderness experience are a "blind walk," in which the youths are blindfolded, and a "solo" that requires each participant to spend three days alone in the wilderness with only minimal food and water. There is also a six-day adventure featuring rock climbing and rappelling, culminating in a six-mile run.

VisionQuest's wagon trains, which travel fifteen to twenty miles per day, have transported youths thousands of miles cross-country in much the same way as the early settlers explored the new frontier more than 100 years ago. The adolescents must all work together to keep the wagon train on its scheduled course. Staff and youths live and work side by side in a family atmosphere. Each "family" has responsibility for its own wagon, horses, mules, and equipment. The ratio of staff to youths approaches one to one. The daily schedule was described in a VisionQuest newsletter: The youths and staff awake at 6 A.M. each day. Morning activities include watering and feeding the animals and taking down the tipis. When the wagons leave the campsite, the task of the "campjacks" is to clean up the campground and then proceed to the next location to make preparations for that night. They are responsible for setting up the tipis, digging the fire pit, and making a picket line for the animals. When the chores have been completed, the youths concentrate on the educational program.

The usual bedtime is 8 P.M. but it may be later to accommodate such activities as group or individual counseling, tutoring, or a special event. There are some breaks in the grueling schedule. One day out of every five or six is allotted for making equipment repairs, doing laundry, and having a shower. Sometimes the staff use this time to accompany the youths on a recreational outing such as a trip to a local point of interest, a sports event, a movie, or dinner in a restaurant.

A youth who wants to ride a horse or a mule must be willing to care for the animal. If an animal is not treated properly, the juvenile forfeits the privilege of riding and must walk beside the wagon train.

Parents are permitted to visit their children at various places on the wagon train's route.

Confrontations and Discipline.   Because of the close contact between staff and youths, the con games and peer pressure to be a troublemaker rarely get started. Youths are always under the watchful eye of the staff. The adolescents learn to follow the rules because they are directly related to their safety. They learn to work as a team because the activities (such as setting up tipis) require a team effort. As distinct from a reformatory, where a troublemaker gains status and approbation from his peers, youths sentenced to VQ only provoke the anger of their peers if they refuse to do or are careless in doing their share of the work (Greenwood et al., 1983).

However, misbehavior does occur, and the adolescents are held accountable for their actions. Misbehavior is dealt with by a direct confrontation between senior staff members and the youth. The controversy surrounding the VQ program has arisen mainly because of the unorthodox methods used in the confrontation process, described here:

> The staff may observe that a youth is beginning to talk back to staff, neglect duties, or provoke incidents with other youths. The senior staff decides that a confrontation is in order. It is triggered by a specific incident; perhaps the youth tries to get another youth to do his or her job, or performs a chore sloppily. The confrontation begins with loud and direct verbal confrontation, with the staff member and the youth nose to nose. Two or three more staff now gather around. The youth is continuously challenged. What is he up to? Who does he think he is? What is his problem? The youth may answer back in kind, or shrink into silence, or burst into tears, or even become physical. The staff stays on him until he works through a crisis. As things calm down, the discussion becomes more rational. Specific suggestions are made or orders given. By the time it is all over, they all go about their business as if nothing happened; the air is cleared. The staff may talk about how it went at their nightly meeting. (Greenwood et al., 1983:88)

Although the confrontational approach may be viewed as unnecessarily harsh by some persons, the youths seem to recognize its value. The following comments were made by Wayne, a sixteen-year-old participant from Pennsylvania whose mother was a prostitute. Wayne had a history of auto thefts, gang fights, burglaries, drug abuse, and running away from placements prior to being sent to VisionQuest:

> They surround you to make sure you don't hurt anyone. Then you're screaming and yelling and getting out frustrations and cussing them off the wall. Then they let you up off the ground, and you talk about things that are really bothering you. Usually things with your family. . . .
>
> I feel like I've got better control now. . . . Things that happen that pissed me off before don't anymore. I've learned to discipline myself, to sit down and talk about things with the staff. I feel as if I know them and feel comfortable around them. (Sweeney, 1982:20)

Wayne continued his comments with a comparison of VisionQuest with juvenile detention centers to which he had been sent previously:

> At detention centers I had no rights whatsoever. We just sat around and watched tv and then went to bed. If you got out of control, they'd sock it to you—choke you and grab you by your arms and legs and get you so you couldn't move. They'd grab you by your head and squeeze you. VQ is different. (p. 30)

Unacceptable actions are also handled by the youth's losing privileges or being assigned additional chores. For example, while on the wagon train a juvenile who tries to run away might be "put in the pit," which means that he is required to remain in the middle of the circle of wagons and tipis (remaining there to sleep as well) next to the firepit so that he is under continual surveillance (Greenwood et al., 1983).

OceanQuest. Programs such as VisionQuest are not without risk. One VQ component, OceanQuest, was temporarily discontinued in 1980 after a boating accident resulted in nine deaths (seven youths and two counselors) during a storm. A Coast Guard investigation of the accident found no evidence of misconduct, but the report cited several factors that contributed to the disaster: the crew's lack of experience; the extreme weather conditions; fatigue of the persons on board, who had been at sea for approximately 40 hours; and the failure of the other vessels to conduct a timely search for the missing boat (Sweeney, 1982).

Ocean voyages were reinstituted in 1984 with a 130-foot schooner called the Western Union, which had been used by the Western Union Telegraph Company for laying and repairing underwater telegraph cables until 1973, when the arrival of satellites made a cable ship unnecessary. The current headquarters for the sailing program is Ft. Mifflin in Pennsylvania. The Western Union crew is comprised of eleven staff and thirteen youths. Before juveniles are permitted to embark on an OceanQuest, they are generally required to complete the wilderness program and at least eight weeks on a wagon train. In addition, they

Case Example

The following are excerpts from a January 27, 1985, *Los Angeles Times* article written by eighteen-year-old Tawny Allen, who had successfully completed the VisionQuest program and felt that it had made a vital difference in her life. At the time the article was written she was an assistant manager of a fast-food restaurant.

Tawny mentioned that during the Quest she had tried to con the others by pretending she had hurt her ankle; the other participants carried her for eight miles. However, the staff learned of her deception and required her to undergo the Quest a second time. Her account of her experience is as follows:

> I finished Quest on my second attempt with flying colors and felt so good about myself. For once in my life I had accomplished something.
>
> After that, I went to Wagon Train. It was hard, but that's the whole idea. Doing things so hard really makes you feel good once you complete them.
>
> The Wagon Train was a very good experience for me. I got close to a lot of staff and kids. It seems the more I began to like myself, the closer I got to other people.
>
> "Residential" in Tucson was my last VisionQuest stop. There you live in houses and work on the "Direction." I needed to finish high school and go back home because I was only 16. So, I earned my way into public school and—except for a D in algebra—got all As and Bs, which was something I'd never done before.
>
> Whenever any one of the girls in my group had a problem or needed to deal with something, we'd all circle up and help her resolve it. Most of the time other people's feelings would come out too. There were things that all us kids needed to get out that we never could before. Things like being raped or abused or being put aside by our parents.
>
> One thing that was so good about the staff in VQ was that they never gave up on us. Even though we didn't give a damn about ourselves. They helped me to grow up. I faced a lot of things while I was in there and it hurt sometimes, but that's the only way you can get rid of bad feelings: Facing them and talking about them. That's what I was taught there, and it worked.
>
> When I got out, I was two years behind in school but very interested in getting my diploma. I finished it all in time to graduate the year I was supposed to—and worked at a Burger King at the same time.
>
> That was a year and a half ago. Now I'm 18, living on my own and working.
>
> My time at VisionQuest was the best time in my life. Also the hardest. VisionQuest probably saved my life, and I'm glad I was there.

need to receive the endorsement of the wagon master. Thus, youths who are given permission to enter the sailing program have worked hard and demonstrated their commitment to VisionQuest. Prior to sailing, the crew is given instruction in seamanship, swimming, and water safety as well as ocean-related education on such topics as marine ecology, oceanography, and map/compass skills.

Group Home Program. Following the successful completion of two "high-impact" programs, youths become eligible for one of the program's group homes as a way of reintegrating them into the community. Group homes are geared to meet the needs of the individual, such as offering younger youths a home that utilizes a nurturing family approach, while the emphasis in a home for older adolescents would be preparation for independent living.

Family Involvement. Family members are encouraged to attend individual counseling and support groups to discuss issues related to raising a child who has delinquent behavior. The counselors who interview the juvenile prior to entering the program also keep the family apprised of the individual's progress at VisionQuest. The counselors invite family members to visit while their child is participating in the various aspects of the overall program.

Stephen L. French Youth Wilderness Program (Homeward Bound)

The Stephen L. French Youth Wilderness Program, located in Brewster, Massachusetts, on the inner coast of Cape Cod, is under the jurisdiction of the Massachusetts Division of Youth Services (DYS). Originally the site was utilized by DYS for a youth forestry camp. Its purpose was to provide delinquent adolescents with a work-therapy program in which they were assigned such tasks as building campsites and clearing trails (Willman & Chun, 1973). In 1970 there was a reorganization, and the superintendent of the forestry camp, Alan A. Collette, developed the rigorous wilderness education program now known as Homeward Bound.

Homeward Bound is one of the few state-run outdoor experiential programs to have achieved prominence beyond its regional boundaries. The recognition it has received is due in large part to the dedication of Collette, who continues to serve as the chief administrator. The stated goal of the program is "to present its participants with the opportunity to increase self-respect through self-discipline and to experience the satisfaction of overcoming challenging physical and psychological obstacles through individual and group effort" (Collette, undated).

The courts refer approximately 350 boys (ages fourteen to seventeen) to the program annually. At the beginning of the twenty-six–day wilderness experience, the youths are placed in groups of eight, called brigades. Initially their time is spent participating in community service assignments, taking short hikes and runs, and completing obstacle courses. A counselor works with each boy individually in planning for release from the program. After the boys have been oriented to survival skills, they embark on a particular wilderness experience involving such activities as rock climbing, rappelling, canoeing, camping, cross-country skiing, and pullboating (Willman & Chun, 1973; Collette, undated). The program also provides "individual and group counseling; psychological, educational, and vocational testing; and tutoring" (Collette).

A ten-day trip across the Appalachian Trail, often through snow four feet deep, is an example of the excursions in which the youths participate. The culmination of the program (and the most difficult assignment) is a three-day solo experience in the wilderness with only "a few matches, a plastic sheet, a cooking pail and water" (Willman & Chun, 1973).

Because Homeward Bound is under the jurisdiction of the state DYS, it is not able to initiate an aftercare component that would provide much-needed continuity. Community-based follow-up activities are handled by regular DYS caseworkers (Greenwood & Zimring, 1985).

Jack and Ruth Eckerd Foundation Therapeutic Wilderness Camping Program

Through the Eckerd Foundation, wealthy Florida businessman Jack Eckerd has established a number of nonprofit therapeutic and educational camping programs to treat troubled and delinquent youths. The foundation developed its first therapeutic wilderness camping program in Brooksville, Florida, in 1968. Additional camps followed, and Eckerd currently has eleven programs: five in Florida, four in North Carolina, one in Rhode Island, and one in Vermont. These camps serve children ages nine through seventeen, with over two-thirds of the participants between the ages of thirteen and fifteen. At the Eckerd camps the emphasis is on helping children develop improved ways of dealing with their emotions and on teaching them realistic methods for solving problems.

The foundation describes its program in different terms than many of the other wilderness programs. It is referred to as a "therapeutic wilderness camping program," with considerable emphasis on the therapeutic aspect. While other programs highlight the various types of wilderness activities and mention a counseling component only in passing, the Eckerd program literature places emphasis on "an individualized, experience-based educational process aimed at developing a self-directed, self-assured learner."

In comparing the extent and rigor of the physical challenges at VisionQuest, Homeward Bound, and Eckerd, Greenwood and Zimring (1985) concluded that Eckerd's program was less "physically oriented" than the others, with more emphasis on education. They also found that many of the youths who are referred to Eckerd camps have less serious emotional and behavioral problems than youths who attend the other two programs.

The children participate in a highly structured program in which outdoor experiences are used to motivate the youths to succeed in academic education and interpersonal relationships (Greenwood & Zimring, 1985). Since 1977, the program has been accredited as an alternative school by the Southern Association of Colleges and Schools.

Although their referrals do not come solely from the court, as is the case with many other wilderness programs, a sizable percentage of campers do have a record of juvenile delinquency offenses. As of 1984, 57 percent of the participants in the program in Florida, 62 percent of those in Rhode Island, and 95 percent of those in Vermont were adjudicated as juvenile offenders. During 1984, the eleven programs served a total of 579 youths. Youths are referred to an Eckerd camp by different sources, most frequently the state division of youth services or a court order. Other referral sources include the public school system and the county mental health center (Jack and Ruth Eckerd Foundation, 1984).

The offenses committed by youths prior to referral range from runaway, incorrigible, and truant to juvenile delinquency offenses such as breaking and entering, auto theft, and burglary. The two crime categories with the greatest percentage of referrals are theft/larceny and breaking and entering.

Campers are placed in a living environment with ten children and two teacher-counselors. Each individual is dependent on the group for activities of daily living such as constructing the shelter, gathering wood for cooking, deciding upon a meal plan, and recreational activities (Jack and Ruth Eckerd Foundation, undated).

Educational Program. The education program is presented in two phases: the Experiential Program and the Transitional Classroom.

Individualized education plans are developed for each camper. In the first phase, the campers develop improved language and math skills in the course of completing a project such as developing trip and menu plans, preparing a budget, constructing the shelter, and working on the camp newspaper.

A child is ready to enter phase two when he or she has demonstrated the ability to handle a more formalized educational environment. Phase two is seen as a "bridge" between the residential program and the mainstream educational system to which the youth will return. The emphasis shifts from experiential learning to formal academic instruction.

Family Counseling.   One of the important differences between the Eckerd program and other wilderness camps is the family counseling component. In making their decisions on admission of new applicants, the Eckerd staff request that the child's family (or a family substitute) agree to participate actively in the camper's treatment. While the child is participating in the camp activities, the parent(s) attend group meetings with other parents. Periodically the camper returns home for a four-day visit. Following each home visit, the social worker meets with the family to discuss what has taken place. According to the program literature, the family worker provides follow-up services for eighteen months after the camper's graduation from the program.

Camp Woodson

Camp Woodson, located in Fairview, North Carolina, is a therapeutic, adventure-based wilderness program for adjudicated juvenile offenders. Emphasis is placed on helping youths gain self-confidence through achievement of progressively more difficult tasks. The program, which began in 1976, has 130 male and female campers per year and nineteen staff. The camp serves youths who have been sent to one of the Division of Youth Services (DYS) training schools in North Carolina. The juveniles are considered eligible for the outdoor program when they have demonstrated acceptable behavior at the training school.

The camp is typically comprised of adolescents aged thirteen to sixteen who have either revoked probation or been adjudicated for nonviolent offenses such as breaking and entering, auto theft, or shoplifting. The program has four main elements: precamp, trail life, solo experience, and therapy.

Precamp. The goal of the four-week precamp component is to initiate the group building process. During precamp, the youths participate in four activities (e.g., day hikes, ropes course, swim tests) geared to assess their physical conditioning and emotional adjustment. In addition, they attend classes on first aid, nutrition, food preparation, rope management, hygiene, clothing care, and communication tools. At the conclusion of precamp, individuals are assigned to a tent and activity group on the basis of staff observations and recommendations.

Trail Life. Campers participate in a variety of outdoor activities, including rock climbing, whitewater canoeing, hiking, backpacking, caving, and horseback riding. All physical challenges are, according to one program description, "designed in graduated levels of difficulty in order to progressively develop skill and trust levels." Each juvenile is assigned to a "tent group" of four or five youths and one staff member. Each group functions independently, living together, doing its own cooking and other housekeeping chores, and looking after its equipment. The groups spend most of their time in the wilderness, returning to the base camp periodically for more food and supplies and to repair equipment.

Solo Experience. During the last week of the program, each youth is expected to have a solo adventure camp-out, spending one night alone in the wilderness. The adolescent is told where to camp and is provided with the appropriate equipment and supplies. Camp Woodson's solos are different from those of other programs (which emphasize survival in the wilderness with minimal provisions). The purpose is to provide an experience that enables the individual to demonstrate recently acquired knowledge of the outdoors. The solo also provides the occasion for reflection and self-examination.

There is also a two-day final expedition that is more challenging than the previous expeditions. The final event stresses teamwork, decision making, and group cohesiveness. Camp ends with a graduation ceremony at which the campers are honored for their accomplishments. It is attended by family members, court counselors, and camp staff.

Therapeutic Elements. As with the other wilderness programs, staff are expected to serve as observable role models. The juveniles receive individual counseling twice a week. Sessions focus on articulating specific behavioral goals and developing methods for goal attainment.

Corvallis House

Corvallis House, located in Salem, Oregon, is a community-based group home program that incorporates wilderness trips (e.g., snow camping, skiing, rock climbing, mountaineering) as an important component of its overall treatment approach. But unlike many other wilderness models, its program is not based totally on outdoor adventures. Corvallis House began its program with a structure similar to the Outward Bound model. It has now evolved into a comprehensive program providing not only wilderness trips but also academic education, work-study, drug and alcohol treatment, and independent living programs.

The majority of the boys at Corvallis House have a history of drug and/or alcohol abuse. Residents are required to attend classes in which the facts about drugs and alcohol are taught, and treatment to help them deal with past substance abuse is provided. The facility also provides a full program of high school courses.

Wilderness Probation Program

A wilderness probation program—the Sierra II Wilderness Adventure program—was initiated in Virginia Beach, Virginia, in 1975 (Callahan, 1985). The main components of this model are group meetings for the juveniles twice a month; group sessions for parents twice a month; a wilderness excursion one weekend per month; and a twelve-day "primitive expedition" in the summer. This wilderness probation approach operates with only three paid staff and fourteen volunteers.

The program has the following goals:

1. To learn, through the group process, socially acceptable ways of handling peer pressure in the youths' own environment.
2. To learn how to survive in the wilderness.
3. To learn productive, challenging activities to occupy the youths' leisure time.

The counselors try to relate the struggle in the wilderness to the struggles with which the youths are confronted on a daily basis, such as putting more effort into resolving problems at school or at home. Callahan believes that the adolescents benefit from the weekend trips because, in addition to learning how to work successfully in a group, the excursions provide a cooling-off period during times of family dysfunction.

Included in the twelve-day summer excursion are such activities as backpacking, a canoe trip, mountain climbing, and cave exploration. The culmination is a ten- to twelve-mile run. Following the marathon run, the group discussion focuses on the individuals' accomplishments during the expedition and how the experience can improve relationships at home, school, and with peers. During the excursions, slides and videotapes are made. Shown to parents and youths during later group meetings, the slides and tapes serve to demonstrate the problem-solving skills that should be utilized by parents and children in resolving everyday problems.

PROGRAM EVALUATIONS

There have been only a handful of published follow-up studies describing the effectiveness of wilderness programs, and most of the existing data come from studies conducted a decade or more ago. While anecdotal evidence suggests that wilderness programs have had a positive effect on the youths who have participated in them, there is a need for rigorous, methodologically sound research covering various aspects of the wilderness adventure experience. Researchers should study the relationship between later success and such program aspects as length of stay, age of participants, involvement of parents in counseling, and the availability of strong aftercare.

Of the few studies conducted, one of the most widely cited was a one-year follow-up conducted by Kelly and Baer (1971). They studied 120 boys who had come in contact with the Massachusetts Division of Youth Services (DYS). The researchers developed two matched groups with 60 boys in each. The experimental group was comprised of boys who attended one of the Outward Bound schools (located in Minnesota, in Colorado, or on Hurricane Island, ten miles off the Maine coast). The boys in the comparison group had been given routine processing by DYS: some youths were sent to an institution while others were immediately paroled. The two groups were matched by "age at time of selection for the study, IQ, race, religion, offense for which committed, area of residence, and number of prior commitments to the Division of Youth Service" (p. 438).

The boys were between the ages of fifteen and seventeen, healthy, having no severe psychopathology or physical disability. They had no history of violent or sexually assaultive behavior, and all had agreed to participate in the program.

Kelly and Baer (1971:438) defined recidivism as "a return to a juvenile institution or commitment to an adult institution for a new offense within one year after parole." The one-year follow-up data showed that the experimental group had a 20 percent recidivism rate, while the comparison group had a 42 percent rate. It should be noted, however, that there were many program differences between the three Outward Bound schools studied. The Colorado and Hurricane Island programs emphasized "severe physical challenge, felt danger, and high excitement" (p. 440) and made only minimal effort to provide the participants with a verbal interpretation of the wilderness experience. Those were the schools that had the lower recidivism rates: Colorado's program had a zero percent recidivism rate; Hurricane Island's was 11 percent. Conversely, the Minnesota program, although it did stress physical challenge, was described by the researchers as having a "relatively low objective danger and excitement level" and focusing attention on interpersonal relationships and "development of a spiritual attitude" (p. 440). The recidivism rate for Minnesota's school was 42 percent.

Kelly and Baer's study produced other noteworthy findings. Their study showed that the average age of a juvenile's initial court appearance was significantly lower for those who recidivated (12.8 years) than for those who did not (14.3 years). This finding would indicate that Outward Bound may be more effective for juveniles whose first appearance in court occurred when they were somewhat older. Finally, in this study, juveniles who had been classified as "stubborn-runaways" were three times more likely to recidivate than were those arrested for other offenses.

The experimental group of juveniles in Kelly and Baer's (1971) one-year follow-up was the focus of another report five years after their Outward Bound experience. Baer, Jacobs, and Carr (1975) examined the relationship between the characteristics exhibited by youths during their twenty-six–day stay at Outward Bound and recidivism during the following five years. At the completion of the Outward Bound course, those youths who had demonstrated personal growth and completed all course requirements had been awarded a certificate. In addition to ascertaining the five-year recidivism rate for the group as a whole, Baer et al. examined the differences between the youths who had received a certificate of completion and those who had not. (A certificate had been awarded to only fifty of the sixty participants.) Of the sixty youths studied, a total of twenty-four had recidivated. The recidivism rate for those who had successfully completed the program requirements was 30 percent (fifteen out of fifty); in contrast, the recidivism rate for those who had not received a certificate was 90 percent (nine out of ten). From this study it appears that the important indicator with regard to later recidivism is not a juvenile's having been assigned to Outward Bound, but the way in which the juvenile handled the rigorous program requirements.

Behar and Stephens (1978) conducted an evaluation of a wilderness camping program for emotionally disturbed children (many of whom had also committed delinquent acts) in North Carolina. They conducted a follow-up of forty-six boys who had been released from the Carolina Boys' Camp between 1972 and 1975. A variety of post-treatment factors were examined, including school adjustment, leisure-time activities, interpersonal problems, problems at home, and delinquency. The clients showed considerable improvement in all areas with the exception of juvenile delinquency. The researchers found that the percentage of boys whose adjustment in school was considered "adequate" rose from 27 percent to 73 percent. Similarly, before attending the camp 56 percent to 71 percent of the boys were having interpersonal problems with parents, siblings and/or teachers. This figure decreased to 15 percent or lower after discharge from the camp program.

The one area in which no improvement was found was delinquency. The same percentage of parents (55 percent) reported that their child "had been arrested or in trouble with the law" before the program as after the program. Behar and Stephens did find an association between length of stay at the camp and subsequent delinquency: youths who were delinquent had been in the program only three-fourths as long as the nonlawbreaking juveniles (318 days versus 421).

The Alabama Department of Youth Services (DYS) conducted a follow-up on sixty-five boys who had participated in the Wilderness Camping Program at Oak Mountain State Park between May 1982 and September 1983. Of the forty boys for whom data was obtained, only seven (17 percent) had been rearrested during the first nine months after discharge from DYS. Most of the boys who had been assigned to the wilderness program had committed property offenses. Slightly more than half of the youths were sent to an aftercare program following the wilderness experience, while the rest of the boys were discharged. The report stated that none of the boys who participated in aftercare was rearrested. Although the rearrest rate is quite low, it should be noted that the researchers attempted to follow up sixty-five youths but obtained data on only forty of them. Although the status of the missing twenty-five boys was not known, it may well be that at least some of them did have further trouble with the law.

Greenwood et al. (1983) reported on follow-up research of VisionQuest's program that had been conducted by Behavioral Research Associates in 1979. That study found a rearrest rate of 43 percent for youths who had been released from the program for at least thirteen months prior to the study.

Willman and Chun (1973) conducted a follow-up study of the Homeward Bound program run by the Massachusetts Division of Youth Services. They found a recidivism rate (the term *recidivism* was not defined) of 20.8 percent for the Homeward Bound youths versus a 42.7 percent recidivism rate among the control group.

A major stumbling block in comparing various follow-up studies is the inconsistent way in which the term *recidivism* is defined. Some researchers equate recidivism with rearrest; others use recidivism to mean a new commitment to a correctional facility; while others speak of the recidivism rate without defining it at all. Thus, for example, the reader is cautioned that the 43 percent recidivism (i.e., rearrest) rate at VisionQuest (Greenwood et al., 1983) should not be compared to the 20 percent recidivism (i.e., recommitment) rate of Kelly and Baer's (1971) Outward Bound research, because the basis for determining recidivism in those two studies was not the same. Another factor that should also be considered is the previous history of the juveniles in the various programs. Some programs select only first-time offenders while others, such as VisionQuest, state that their programs recruit chronic juvenile delinquents.

SUMMARY

Wilderness programs have been found by several researchers to be at least as effective as institutionalization and in some studies considerably more effective. This chapter has documented the importance of wilderness programs as a preferred alternative for juvenile offenders, based on evidence demonstrating that it is much more cost-effective, humane, and replicable than institutional treatment.

Detailed descriptions were provided of the common features and programmatic differences among seven of the well-established wilderness adventure programs. Characteristic program components are therapeutic camping, canoeing, an overnight solo experience, an alternative school program, and a family counseling component.

The chapter concludes by reviewing follow-up studies on the effectiveness of wilderness programs. A major stumbling block to determining the effectiveness of these programs is the dearth of systematic longitudinal studies and the inconsistent way in which the term *recidivism* has been defined. There is a need for carefully planned longitudinal studies based on an experimental design and conducted simultaneously in several parts of the country. Only after further systematic research is completed will we be in a better position to identify and recommend for replication those programs that work best with specific offender groups.

DISCUSSION QUESTIONS

1. What was the name and purpose of the earliest outdoor wilderness program, which was established for juvenile offenders in the 1930s in Los Angeles?
2. Outline the differences between traditional training schools and wilderness adventure programs.

3. List the four common features of the established wilderness programs for juvenile offenders.

4. Discuss the objectives and major activities, staffing pattern, and average length of stay at VisionQuest or the Eckerd Foundation's Therapeutic Wilderness Camps.

5. Discuss the findings and implications of the findings from the Kelly and Baer (1971) and the Baer et al. (1975) follow-up studies of participants in the Outward Bound programs.

6. Outline the type of study design needed to conduct a methodologically sound longitudinal follow-up study of juvenile offenders.

REFERENCES

Alabama Department of Youth Services. (Unpublished). Wilderness program evaluation report: May 1982–September 1983. Mt. Meigs, AL: Division of Planning, Research and Development.

Baer, D. J., Jacobs, P. J., & Carr, F. E. (1975). Instructors' ratings of delinquents after Outward Bound survival training and their subsequent recidivism. *Psychological Reports, 36,* 547–553.

Behar, L., & Stephens, D. (1978, October). Wilderness camping: An evaluation of a residential treatment program for emotionally disturbed children. *American Journal of Orthopsychiatry, 48,* 644–653.

Callahan, R., Jr. (1985, Spring). Wilderness probation: A decade later. *Juvenile and Family Court Journal, 36,* 31–35.

Collette, A. A. (Undated). Program description, Stephen L. French Youth Wilderness Program.

Greenwood, P. W., Lipson, A. J., Abrahamse, A., & Zimring, F. E. (1983, June). *Youth crime and juvenile justice in California: A report to the legislature.* Santa Monica, CA: Rand Corporation.

Greenwood, P. W., & Zimring, F. E. (1985, May). *One more change: The pursuit of promising intervention strategies for chronic juvenile offenders.* Santa Monica, CA: Rand Corporation.

Jack and Ruth Eckerd Foundation. (1979, March 28). Program goals and objectives: Eckerd wilderness educational system camping program. Clearwater, FL: Eckerd Foundation.

Jack and Ruth Eckerd Foundation. (1984). Annual descriptive summary 1984. Clearwater, FL: Eckerd Foundation.

Jack and Ruth Eckerd Foundation. (Undated). Therapeutic wilderness camping program brochure. Clearwater, FL: Eckerd Foundation.

Kelly, F. J., & Baer, D. J. (1971, October). Physical challenge as a treatment for delinquency. *Crime and Delinquency, 17,* 437–445.

Marcus, M. J. (1984, April). Current perspectives on outdoor programming in Connecticut. In D. P. Teschner & J. J. Wolter (Eds.), *Wilderness challenge:*

Outdoor education alternatives for youth in need (pp. 134–138). Hadlyme, CT: Institute of Experiential Studies.

Robison, S. M. (1960). *Juvenile delinquency: Its nature and control.* New York: Holt, Rinehart & Winston.

Sweeney, P. (1982, February). VisionQuest's rite of passage. *Corrections Magazine,* pp. 22–32.

VisionQuest program descriptions. (Undated).

VisionQuest. (1982). Wagon Train.

VisionQuest. (Undated). *Western Union* (newsletter). Tucson, AZ: VisionQuest.

Willman, H. C., Jr., & Chun, R. Y. F. (1973, September). Homeward Bound: An alternative to the institutionalization of adjudicated juvenile offenders. *Federal Probation,* 52–58.

Chapter Eleven

Family Treatment

Albert R. Roberts

ABSTRACT

What are the objectives, focus, and content of family treatment programs for juvenile offenders and their families? This chapter provides the answers to this question. It begins by examining the research literature that documents the child's family life experiences, including extreme parental disciplinary practices, neglect, and child abuse as contributors to deviance and delinquency among youths. The next section explores several different family intervention approaches, focusing on short-term crisis intervention and behavioral contracting. Both of these approaches may utilize a family systems approach as well as education of parents on effective parenting.

Also discussed are other, related issues: at which stage of the juvenile justice process family treatment should take place; mandatory versus voluntary treatment; resistance to attending family counseling; and background and training of clinical staff. Chapter 11 concludes with a review of the studies of the effectiveness of family treatment programs. While the behaviorally oriented family systems approach seems most promising, only a few rigorous studies based on randomization and an experimental or quasi-experimental design have been completed.

THE FAMILY AND DELINQUENCY

The family is the major socializing agent to influence and help shape the child's attitudes, values, behavior, and personality. It therefore has a significant impact on the development of the child. Many sociologists, psychologists, and criminologists concur that the family often exercises the greatest amount of influence on the child's early life. Since the family has such an important socializing role on children and youth, social workers and counselors have developed family treatment programs in order to help troubled, conflict-ridden families to resolve their problems and function more adequately.

The early family life experiences of the child lay the foundation for acquired attitudes, values, and behavior patterns. The child may develop maladaptive coping behaviors such as delinquency and other behavioral disturbances as a result of intense family conflict, tension, and disruption. Several researchers have documented the influence of the above-cited variables as contributors to delinquency (Abrahamson, 1960; Andry, 1960; Biron & LeBlanc, 1977; Freeman & Savastano, 1970; Glueck & Glueck, 1968; Norland, Shover, Thornton, & James, 1979; Rodman & Grams, 1967).

Family disorganization, a lack of parental control, and parental rejection have been found to be major contributing factors to delinquent behavior. Families of delinquents frequently have the following characteristics:

Single-parent (often female-headed) households (Alfaro, 1981).

Low socioeconomic status (Jenkins, Heidemann, & Caputo, 1985; Nye, 1958; Peterson & Becker, 1965).

Small, deteriorated homes or apartments (Peterson & Becker).

Hostile, rejecting, and unaffectionate parents (Andry, 1960; Jenkins, 1985);

Multiproblem families in which parents are divorced, alcohol or substance abusers, suffering from depression or other dysfunction, and/or unemployed; in addition, siblings are often in trouble with the law (Barker & Adams, 1963).

Ineffectual parental control and a lack of consistent discipline (Coull, Geismar, & Waff, 1982; Norland et al., 1979).

Lax and Erratic Discipline

As mentioned above, a general lack of parental control has been found to be strongly correlated with delinquency. Glueck and Glueck (1968) found that parents of delinquents were inconsistent in their disciplinary practices when compared with parents of nondelinquents. For example, when a child learns that the parents are inconsistent and frequently disagree, the child learns to manipulate the parents so that one parent turns on the other. The child may not develop an adequate conscience (superego) because of the lack of discipline.

McCord, McCord, and Zola (1959) found that lax discipline (neither parent exerting much control) or erratic discipline (in which parents waver between lax and punitive discipline) were strongly associated with delinquency. In sharp contrast, parents who consistently used either love-oriented discipline (e.g., reasoning, withholding rewards, or privileges) or punitive discipline (e.g., spankings and threats of spankings) were found to have lower incidences of delinquency.

Child Abuse

A number of studies have emphasized the relationship between child abuse, maltreatment, and neglect and deviant behavior of children and youths (Alfaro, 1981; Helfer & Kempe, 1968; Kratcoski, 1982; Mouzakitis, 1981). Violence in the home encourages the use of physical aggression and abuse as a means for solving problems. It prevents youths from feeling empathy for others. It also decreases the ability of children and youths to cope with stress. Exposure to severe physical battering early in life provides a foundation and breeding ground for violent and antisocial behavior. According to Helfer and Kempe (pp. xvii–xviii):

The effects of child abuse and neglect are cumulative. Once the developmental process of a child is insulted or arrested by bizarre child rearing patterns, the scars remain. One should not be surprised then to find that the large majority of delinquent adolescents indicate that they were abused as children.

Evidence supporting the hypothesis that violence begets violence has been reported again and again. A study of violent offenders incarcerated at the California State Prison in San Quentin found that 100 percent of those violent inmates had sustained some form of extreme violence before the age of ten (Maurer, 1976). Psychologist Ralph Welsh reported that he had never examined a violent juvenile offender who was not reared in an extremely violent home. Mouzakitis (1981) found that 86 percent of incarcerated youths in Arkansas had been physically abused. In addition, research on violent murderers, assassins, and would-be assassins reveals the commonality of a violent childhood. John Wilkes Booth, James Earl Ray, Lee Harvey Oswald, Sirhan Sirhan, and Charles Manson all experienced violent upbringings (Fontana, 1976; Straus, Gelles, & Steinmetz, 1981).

Since almost all of the above-cited studies are retrospective rather than prospective longitudinal studies, they do not provide conclusive evidence that child abuse causes delinquency. In addition, the findings are often confounded by lost or incomplete records of the childhood histories of offenders. Some studies do not distinguish between different types and the intensity of abuse. Further research in this area is needed.

Nevertheless, the research has provided evidence, albeit limited, that exposure to physical violence during childhood is linked to subsequent delinquent and adult criminal offenses. Therefore, efforts to reduce juvenile delinquency should include an early intervention approach to educate and assist parents in child abuse prevention.

Delinquency Causation

This is not to suggest that faulty parenting is the only or even the predominant cause of juvenile delinquency. The etiology of this problem is extremely complex and multifaceted. After reviewing statistical associations between different conditions and their relationship to crime and delinquency, Cohen and Short (1976:66) cautioned:

> A statistical association means only that some factor occurs in connection with some phenomenon more frequently than would be expected by chance. It does not necessarily mean one causes the other. . . . No single circumstance is in itself a push in the direction of crime. Criminal events are the product of the interaction of some set of circumstances.

The classic studies on the causes of delinquency indicate that no single causative factor provides an explanation for delinquency. The research shows that many factors correlate with juvenile delinquency, including frequent and intense associations with criminals, known as "differential association" (Sutherland & Cressey, 1974); lack of bonds and attachment to parents and a lack of commitment to school (Hirschi, 1969); and involvement in a delinquent subculture (i.e., juvenile gang) that leads to delinquent behavior (Cohen, 1955).

Research has shown that some children who grow up in dysfunctional families overcome their problematic upbringing to become productive, law-abiding members of society (Pines, 1979). However, that research also shows that those youths have had the benefit of a close relationship with at least one adult role model such as a clergyman, teacher, coach, or "big brother."

Family-Focused Treatment

Based on the research studies that suggest that delinquency is the result of dysfunctional family systems, clinicians have developed family-focused treatment approaches geared to lowering delinquency rates through improved family functioning. In this chapter various family intervention methods and strategies will be examined. Although the approaches vary, all of the programs discussed treat juveniles in the context of their families rather than as persons separate and apart from the family unit.

Missouri's statewide family treatment programs for juvenile offenders attempt to treat the whole family. According to Schulte (1985), the approach of viewing delinquency as arising solely from pathology within the individual juvenile gives one "a gnawing sense that only part of the problem was being addressed." Schulte, a family therapist with the Missouri Division of Youth Services, draws an analogy between a bird returning to his cage and a delinquent youth who is sent to a training school and then returned home without any parental involvement. He views juvenile justice system efforts that do not include family involvement as similar to returning "a clean bird to a dirty cage." Within a brief time period, the bird is dirty again.

Family therapy can be utilized in a variety of ways: as a major component of a program to divert the juvenile from formal processing by the justice system; as a means of avoiding an out-of-home placement in a foster or group care home; as a supplemental service and condition of probation; as one component of a treatment program for juveniles who have been placed in a residential treatment program or training school; and as part of a prerelease or an aftercare program to help the juvenile and the family cope with exit trauma as well as to aid in the reintegrative phase of a juvenile's release from a court-ordered placement.

THE FAMILY AND THE JUVENILE JUSTICE SYSTEM

When a juvenile first comes in contact with the justice system, the family experiences turmoil. It is at this time—the entry point and first contact with the justice system—that the family may be most receptive to participating in a family-focused program.

The court serves as the referral source for many of the family counseling programs related to youths charged with committing status and juvenile delinquency offenses. In some cases the goal of the family intervention program is to divert first-time status offenders from the court system (Stratton, 1975; Wade, Morton, Lind, & Ferris, 1977). The obvious motivation for families is that by becoming involved in the counseling program they hope to avoid any further adjudication.

Early intervention enables the counselor to capitalize on the family's motivation to resolve the crisis brought on by the juvenile's arrest. Thus it is beneficial if the family counseling program begins shortly after the juvenile has been arrested. An example of such a short-term crisis intervention program was described by Stratton (1975). The program, located in San Fernando, California, generally scheduled the initial family counseling session within an hour of the juvenile's arrival at the police department. If the counselor felt that agreement was reached during the initial session, the youth was released to the parent, thereby avoiding the youth's being sent to the detention facility.

Mandatory versus Voluntary Counseling

What is the role of the court with regard to families attending a counseling program? There has been much debate as to whether family therapy programs should be mandated by the court or be made available to parents as a voluntary option. The professional literature contains numerous articles that stress the importance of treating the entire family when a juvenile is charged with a status offense or delinquent act.

Janeksela (1979) is representative of those who believe that the court should require the family to participate in family counseling and to receive careful supervision "by a specially trained crisis unit of the juvenile court" (p. 47). Court-mandated counseling is viewed as necessary because some parents attempt to shift their own responsibility for their children onto the court, even going so far as to ignore their children when they are brought to juvenile court. An inability of family members to communicate effectively is seen as a major stumbling block that has caused problems in the past and will continue to cause conflict unless there is direct intervention in the form of family counseling. Janeksela goes so far as to urge that sanctions be levied on parents who refuse to participate in counseling.

Streib's (1978) position is diametrically opposed to those who advocate court-mandated family treatment. He argues that by the time a youth is in his midteens, court-ordered counseling may actually be detrimental. Taking an extremely pessimistic view of the individual's ability to change and grow, Streib states that he does not believe that parents are capable of changing their attitudes and behaviors.

Nationwide Juvenile Court Survey.   Windell and Windell (1977) conducted a survey of juvenile courts in the mid-1970s to determine the courts' views regarding group education and training programs for parents of children brought before the court. The survey also sought to discover whether parent treatment programs were court ordered or voluntary. The researchers surveyed 476 juvenile courts in the United States and Canada and received 191 responses (a 40 percent response rate).

Of those who responded, 21 percent had some type of parent education or group therapy program for parents of delinquent youth. Those courts that did not operate their own program frequently stated that parents who needed counseling were referred to mental health programs in the community. Some courts expressed the belief that assigning parents to treatment programs is not a "judicial function." The majority of the respondents (63 percent) indicated that parents' programs were voluntary. Although only one-fifth of the responding courts had developed a parent counseling program, the researchers were encouraged by the trend toward having such programs. They noted that almost all of the programs had been developed within the three-year period prior to the survey, with 46 percent of the programs in operation for just one year or less.

Although the number of court-based family counseling programs probably has increased since the Windell and Windell survey, there have been no recent national surveys to determine the number of such programs currently in operation.

Overcoming Resistance to Family Therapy Sessions

The level of parent–youth conflict in many homes is so intense that parents sometimes demand that the police bring their son or daughter to the court or detention center for placement in a secure facility or group home. These youths are receiving the messages: "You're no good

and I want you out of the house" and "You're always getting into trouble and you've made our lives miserable." While family-focused treatment provides a means for helping the entire family to deal with its
problems, a considerable number of parents resist treatment. It is not
uncommon for parents to deny any responsibility for their adolescent's
lawbreaking behavior; they view their adolescent as the "problem," refusing to recognize that the youth's actions are a manifestation of family disturbance.

One program that attempted to offset parental resistance to counseling was the High Impact Family Treatment (HIFT) program in
St. Louis (Balmer, Kogan, Voorhees, Levin-Shaw, & Shapiro, 1979).
Whereas the typical family therapy program occurs once a week for a
one-hour session, the HIFT staff provided a concentrated two-day
treatment program. HIFT was developed on the premise that "families
of delinquents appear to be less willing to undertake long-term therapy, expecting quick and visible results" (p. 3). Furthermore, because
of travel time or difficulty in leaving work or school, it is more conve-
nient for many families to participate in an intensive two-day program
than to attend ongoing weekly sessions. Responses from families who
had completed the intensive HIFT program were highly positive. Families felt that the therapists and the court had been genuinely interested
in helping them.

As mentioned previously, active and early involvement of parents
or other key family members is vital to the success of a family counseling program. Every effort should be made to engage the youth's family
during the intake process. Information should be gathered from both
the youth's and parents' perspectives. Information from school officials
can also help the family counselor to understand the family's interaction patterns and coping strategies. A sequential listing of the exact
circumstances that led to the delinquent act can reveal the role of each
family member in the destructive cycle of behaviors; what if anything
is currently being done to resolve the problems; and the meaning of
the youth's apprehension by the police.

At the outset the treatment plan should involve recognition of both
the parents' and the youth's concerns and objectives. It is important
for the therapist to be accepting of the viewpoints and goals of all parties. The next stage should involve enlarging the family members'
views by redefining the problem in a way that can lead to constructive
change (Watzlawick, Weakland, & Fisch, 1974). Patience and realistic
expectations are important. Parents need to be encouraged to proceed
at a gradual pace in setting new rules, expectations, and punishments
(Madanes, 1981); one major problem should be approached at a time.

Parents also need to be aware that some testing and backsliding commonly occur. The effectiveness of the program can be undermined if parents expect magical cures or a quick resolution to long-standing problems.

TREATMENT STAFF

The competence level (knowledge base and practice skills) of counselors and clinical supervision of the staff are crucial to client outcomes. Yet, in numerous articles, this subject has been glossed over or omitted altogether. Frequently, the counselors at court-related family treatment programs are either recent social work graduates or graduate students who are just beginning to learn practice theories, have a limited level of knowledge and skills, and may be receiving insufficient supervision.

Stuart and Lott (1972) are among the small number of clinical researchers who have addressed this important issue by assessing the influence of the individual therapist on the success of the client. In their study, behavioral contracting was used with seventy-nine delinquent and predelinquent juveniles and their parents. The researchers found that the outcome depended more on the idiographic style of the therapist than on the characteristics of the client or the way in which the behavioral contract was formulated.

The project staff consisted of eight female and two male therapists. Of the ten staff members, five were social work students, four were professional social workers, and one was a fourth-year student in medical school. The study did not reveal the specific traits of the successful or unsuccessful therapists. Although Stuart and Lott (1972) found no significant relationship between the outcome and the counselor's status (student versus professional, gender), other researchers caution that novice therapists should not be assigned to complex cases (Patterson, Chamberlain, & Reid, 1982).

While individual personality traits may affect the therapist–client relationship, it appears that another important factor is the family's perception of the therapist as being genuinely interested in and committed to helping the family. Particularly for families who have previously experienced service delivery that was bogged down in bureaucratic red tape, a meeting with a counselor soon after the juvenile has been arrested may be welcomed (Stratton, 1975; Wade et al., 1977). In other words, if a program is established in such a way that a therapist makes contact with a family immediately after the youth has been arrested, that therapist may be regarded more highly than one who does not contact the family until a week or more has elapsed.

Flexibility in scheduling appointments is also perceived as a sign of a caring staff member. A traditional once a week for one hour therapy session can create a strain on family members if a parent is required to take time off from work and/or the youth must miss time from school. When an agency allows the flexibility of evening or weekend sessions, the family members tend to have a more positive view of the program.

Innovative Staffing Patterns

As discussed above, many family-focused treatment programs operate under the traditional model of one therapist assigned to work with each family and each therapist having a caseload of twenty or more families at a time. One-hour appointments are usually scheduled weekly. But some programs have experimented with a different type of staffing pattern.

The High Impact Family Treatment (HIFT) program, mentioned earlier, was developed in an effort to overcome families' resistance to attending ongoing weekly therapy sessions by providing an intensive, two-day treatment program. The staff felt that the targeted families would respond well to the short-term approach, which would yield visible results more quickly than traditional programs.

The HIFT program utilized a team approach of three to five therapists. The program objectives were twofold: (1) to lower the recidivism rate of youths who had committed status offenses and (2) to prevent assignment of the youths to an out-of-home placement, usually in a group home or foster home.

Although the therapists' educational level was not stated, they were required to be experienced in family dynamics and therapy. It was also essential that the therapists interact well as a team. To work on this team project the therapists needed to "accept each others' theoretical framework of family functioning. Each member must feel sufficiently self-confident to allow other team members to have different viewpoints and interpretations of family processing" (Balmer et al., 1979:5). One therapist, designated as the team leader, developed the plan for the "desired therapeutic outcome."

The HIFT program focused on four primary areas (Balmer et al., 1979:5):

1. Instilling hope in a family that feels hopeless or feels that nothing will change.

2. Having the family members recognize their dysfunctional processes within the family.

3. Possible altering of present problematic conditions toward more functional conditions.

4. Having the family begin practicing alternate processes.

The treatment process utilized by the HIFT staff is described below:

> After the treatment team has been introduced to the family, two different therapists will each meet individually for approximately a half hour with the family; the remaining therapists watch these two sessions through a one-way mirror or videotape monitor. This initial "gathering of information session" is followed by individual therapy sessions. Each family member is assigned to a therapist. . . . This forty-five minute, one-on-one session will not only provide further information about the family system (some family members feel inhibited to share information in front of the family group) but is an attempt to build alliances between a particular family member and a particular therapist.
>
> After these initial sessions, the family is asked to take a thirty to forty-five minute break; the treatment team uses that time to share information gained. . . . The team attempts to formulate some tentative hypotheses about the family's problems, processes, strengths, weaknesses, and avenues for possible change.

In the next phase of the process, the staff utilizes an "alter-ego role play" technique in which each therapist assumes the role of one family member and portrays that individual's thoughts and feelings through verbal and nonverbal means. Through this technique the therapist is able to share heretofore unexpressed aspects of the individual's beliefs.

The family members then begin to practice alternate behavior patterns with the therapists directing family members to portray how they would like the family to be. "This idealized picture typically displays closeness, flexibility, and love, providing the springboard for positive and emotional contact between family members. Such contact provides family members with a feeling of hope that change is possible" (Balmer et al., 1979:6).

On the second day of the program, family members participate in a variety of practice sessions involving, for example, the parental subunit, the sibling subunit, and the father/son relationship. Participants are encouraged to watch themselves and each other through a videotape monitor or a one-way mirror to enhance the process of improving communication among family members. At the conclusion of the second day, family members are asked to discuss their thoughts about the HIFT program. The family is then invited to return for a follow-up meeting four weeks later.

Another innovative approach to staffing is the Homebuilders program (which originated in Tacoma, Washington), in which therapists provide intensive, in-home crisis intervention services for troubled families (Kinney, Madson, Fleming, & Haapala, 1977; Kinney, 1978). The Homebuilders program has been utilized with disturbed families when traditional outpatient therapy has failed and when one or more family members are confronted with the likelihood of being removed from the home and placed in foster care, group care, or an institutional setting. For the overwhelming majority of Homebuilders' families, the problem that precipitated the crisis was an adolescent's being charged with a status offense, that is, incorrigibility, truancy, or running away from home:

Problem	Number of Families
Incorrigibility	127
Running away	81
Truancy/school disruption	97
Delinquency	19

Homebuilders' counselors are experienced in family therapy, crisis intervention, or both. Counseling staff are trained in "parent effectiveness skills, fair fight techniques, assertiveness, behavior modification, and advanced crisis intervention techniques" (Kinney et al., 1977:668). Each counselor has a caseload of approximately two families per month, or twenty families a year. Counselors spend an average of 135 hours with each family over a period of approximately eight and one-half weeks (Knitzer, 1982). When a staff member enters a home, the first action is generally to separate the family members and be certain that each person has the opportunity to talk to a counselor at length.

Although the staff prepares an individualized treatment plan for each family, some approaches to problem resolution seem to be used frequently:

"(a) helping the family to examine alternatives by modeling good communication skills, reinforcing clients as their communication skills improve, providing advocacy for clients who need support in communicating with other family members, providing community resource options that might be useful, and considering changes in environment;

(b) teaching ways to prevent crisis recurrence by using better communication skills, being assertive instead of aggressive or hostile in defining territorial boundaries, and negotiating behavioral contracts; and

(c) setting up treatment programs to maintain progress and assist in reaching future goals by presenting resources in the community, helping to make linkages in coordination with case managers, and working with case managers to support the treatment plan." (Kinney et al., 1977:669)

Program staff remain in contact with the family until Homebuilders, the family, and staff at the follow-up agency agree that there is a good prognosis for prevention of further crises. If, however, the family does encounter a crisis situation at a later time, Homebuilders staff are available to provide what they refer to as "booster shot" sessions.

Follow-up data reveal an excellent rate of success as measured by the number of clients who were able to avoid placement in an out-of-home setting. Kinney et al. (1977) reported that 134 persons from eighty families were treated. Of this number, only 13 were removed from the home while 121 were able to respond to treatment services and remain in the home.

As part of the program evaluation, the researchers tabulated the cost-effectiveness of Homebuilders' therapeutic approach versus the alternative of out-of-home care in a foster home, group care home, or psychiatric hospital. Agency personnel speculated on where each youth or parent would have been placed without Homebuilders' intervention and on the cost of those placements. They determined that it costs approximately $2,331 less per client to offer the Homebuilders' crisis intervention program than it would have cost for the individuals to be sent to an out-of-home placement. Total savings were calculated to be $312,478.00.

Another model, the Family Resource Unit, based in Springfield, Missouri, provides brief family therapy in which two therapists work with each family (Schulte, 1985). In most cases, both therapists are involved in the family therapy sessions. Initially, families agree to participate in eight therapy sessions, but the number of sessions may be increased at the request of therapist or family. A lengthier therapy program may be mandated by the juvenile office or the Division of Youth Services. In a four-year period commencing in 1981, more than 280 families participated in this therapeutic program. "The therapy offered is considered 'brief' family therapy in that the techniques or interventions are designed to quickly mobilize the family and act as a catalyst to the family's natural inclination to adjust around change" (Schulte, 1985).

The office of the Family Resource Unit contains two therapy rooms and a viewing room to enable consultants to watch the sessions, which are videotaped. The second staff person either participates in the sessions as a cotherapist or serves as a consultant by remaining in the viewing room to observe the session. Training is an integral part of the program, with one day a week allotted for that purpose.

The Family Resource Unit treats families of juveniles who are on probation as well as those who have been adjudicated for juvenile delinquency or status offenses and committed to the Division of Youth Services. The majority of the families served are single-parent families. The unit also treats various family-unit combinations (such as grandmother and grandson) and foster families.

This program uses a systems theory model for treatment, viewing the family as a system. When family members are under stress, some individuals respond in functional ways while others react in dysfunctional or symptomatic ways. According to Schulte (1985), "The family member who reacts with symptomatic behavior (i.e., the delinquent) may be seen as a sort of 'flag waver,' pointing out a need to investigate the necessity for such behavior in a particular family." Thus, Schulte views the juvenile offender as the "overt symbol" of a breakdown in the family system.

In an effort to train Division of Youth Services (DYS) workers throughout the state of Missouri in techniques of family therapy, the George Warren Brown School of Social Work at Washington University provided a specialized training program for ten DYS workers in 1981. Upon completion of the program, the youth workers were expected to introduce family therapy programs in their own region of the state.

Programs similar to the Family Resource Unit operate in four other regions of the state. During 1985, the Missouri Division of Youth Services completed a follow-up study that measured recidivism and any further delinquent behavior among 203 families completing one of the short-term family therapy programs. Follow-up data were collected at two intervals: thirty days and again six months after termination from the treatment program. Only thirty-three (16 percent) of the juveniles had committed new law violations at the six-month evaluation. Twenty (almost two-thirds) of the thirty-three failures had committed new offenses by the thirty-day follow-up (Koechig, 1985). In addition, twenty-six (12.8 percent) of the juvenile offenders' siblings had been referred to the juvenile court at the time of the six-month evaluation. However, thirty-four of the clients reported that a sibling had been referred to the juvenile court prior to family therapy. Whether we view recidivism in terms of the individual juvenile clients (16 percent) or in terms of the client and his siblings (29 percent), the success of Missouri's family treatment programs has been demonstrated. Their success is significant because they are working with troubled, ineffective, and often dysfunctional family systems. Missouri's model family treatment programs have had an important measure of success in rehabilitating juvenile offenders and their families.

TREATMENT APPROACHES

Family treatment is available in many different forms: short-term crisis intervention; a family systems approach; behavioral contracting; and education on effective parenting for the juveniles' parents, as well as various combinations of the approaches cited above. We will highlight short-term intervention and behavioral contracting, both of which may incorporate elements of a systems approach and/or parent education. Programs are generally developed to provide treatment for the family unit in whatever form the family has taken (e.g., mother/father/juvenile-in-need/sibling; mother/grandmother/juvenile; foster parents/juvenile-in-need/siblings). But, occasionally, programs are geared toward treating parents in groups separate from the youths.

Short-term Crisis Intervention

One of the important characteristics of this type of treatment is the counselor's immediate response to referrals (Stratton, 1975; Wade et al., 1977). As mentioned earlier in this chapter, the goal of this type of treatment is to initiate services as soon as possible after the juvenile's arrest, when the family may be more receptive to such intervention. Most families—particularly those who have previously experienced the delays and inefficiencies characteristic of bureaucracies—are pleased by the immediate availability of a counselor.

Wade et al. (1977) discussed the Intensive Intervention Project (IIP), which was developed in Honolulu, Hawaii, as a diversion program for first-time juvenile offenders, most of whom were referred for status offenses (49 percent were runaways and 36 percent were incorrigibles). The primary aspects of this project's treatment program were:

1. Responding immediately to referrals.

2. Providing intensive, short-term counseling services with flexible scheduling of sessions to accommodate each family's needs.

3. Emphasizing "the family as a system which is functioning maladaptively and which requires change as a unit" (p. 45).

4. Pairing counselors in male-female teams and assigning them to clients of similar ethnic backgrounds to increase the likelihood of the family relating well to the staff.

5. Using graduate student volunteers to supplement the small paid staff, which consisted of a clinical coordinator, a full-time counselor, and a half-time secretary.

6. Making referrals to community agencies to follow up on the changes begun through intensive counseling.

The crisis intervention techniques utilized by the counselors at this project were a combination of the family systems and crisis intervention techniques of Ackerman (1962), Langsley and Kaplan (1968), and Satir (1967). Those techniques are summarized briefly (Wade et al., 1977:46):

1. Intellectual understanding of causal relationships between parental and adolescent behaviors.

2. Clarification of values and demands of family members regarding critical issues.

3. Active involvement of counselors as models, with expression of feelings and thoughts to the family.

4. Training family members in expressing themselves clearly and completely.

5. Exploration of previous coping methods and their inadequacies.

6. Focusing on the present and future to facilitate active, goal-oriented problem solving.

7. Use of behavioral contracts and training in negotiating skills to foster clearly stated rules and consequences for family members' actions and compromises over disagreements.

During the first year of the project, sixty-nine families were served. The researchers conducted a one-year follow-up in which thirty-four families were contacted. The recidivism rate in those families was quite low: only 15 percent. Note, however, that the evaluation methodology in this study was weak (e.g., there was no control group, and the published report did not specify how the thirty-four families were selected). Wade et al. (1977) stated that when asked what they thought about the program, family members generally felt that it had been "quite helpful." However, families with an adolescent who had subsequent contact with the court were not as satisfied as those families that did not experience further court involvement.

Another program that provided families with short-term crisis intervention was based in San Fernando, California (Stratton, 1975). It had an experimental design in which juveniles who were picked up by the police for committing a status offense were randomly assigned to an experimental or control group, with thirty individuals assigned to each group. Those in the experimental group received short-term family crisis intervention. In most cases, the initial family counseling session was held within an hour of the juvenile's arrival at the police department. All families were expected to attend at least one follow-up meeting, and additional counseling sessions were available as needed. Families were seen an average of two and one-half times.

Many of the families were resistant to the family-focused approach, as evidenced by their missing scheduled appointments. Frequently they attempted to deny any responsibility for their adolescents' actions. According to Stratton (1975:16), "They preferred the police or counselor to talk only to the child, and wanted them to give the child specific instructions about what he could or could not do. The parents not only did not want to be present, they often wanted to abdicate any responsibility for what happened to him."

After six months, the two groups were examined with regard to rearrests, the number of days juveniles were detained in Juvenile Hall, and the program costs. The findings showed that the total number of youths rearrested was almost the same for both groups (nine from the experimental group versus ten from the control) but those in the control group had committed twice the number of total offenses (twenty-four offenses compared to twelve for the experimental group).

An examination of cost-effectiveness showed that the cost for the traditional method ($7,497) was more than double that of the family counseling program ($3,541). If the counselor felt that agreement had been reached during the initial session (held at the police station), the youth was released to the parent and avoided being sent to Juvenile Hall for detention. The greatest savings were realized from lower detention costs for the family counseling group.

A short-term family treatment program was provided for the families of forty juveniles who had been arrested for status offenses and were referred by the juvenile court in Salt Lake City to the University of Utah's Family Therapy Clinic (Parsons & Alexander, 1973). A major goal of this project was to strengthen patterns of communication in the home. In Parsons and Alexander's view, parents frequently establish too many rules and do not respond consistently when those rules are broken. This results in a lack of structure at home, which fosters a climate for acting-out behavior. The family members were given training in "solution-oriented communication patterns." In addition, the families were asked to read a behavior modification manual that described the increase/decrease of behaviors on a systems level. (The reading material was a modified version of a 1968 Patterson and Gullion manual.) The therapy sessions were conducted by graduate students in clinical psychology.

The families were divided into one experimental group, two comparison groups, and one no-treatment control group. It was found that "treatment families became less silent, talked more equally, and experienced an increase in both the frequency and duration of simultaneous speech" (Parsons & Alexander, 1973:199); the control families showed no improvement in these areas. The researchers concluded that a focus on family members per se is not sufficient to improve communication patterns. Instead, intervention should focus on specific communication processes, in particular those that enable the family to adjust to stress rather than continue patterns that contribute to its becoming dysfunctional.

Behavioral Contracting

Sometimes family treatment is provided by means of behavioral contracting. A program utilizing behavioral contracting techniques was developed in Dallas, Texas, for youthful offenders and their parents. The project was under the auspices of the Youth Services Program of the Dallas Police Department (Douds, Engelsgjesd, & Collingwood, 1977). Parents and juveniles initially participated in separate groups for fifteen hours of skills training in which parents were taught the methods and underlying principles of behaviorial contracting. Families then attended monthly meetings to assist them in incorporating contracting into their household routine.

Douds et al. (1977) determined that a common characteristic among these families was an inconsistent approach to child-rearing. The parents often vacillated "between punitiveness and permissiveness until they reach a point of helplessness where the youth is in control." Behavioral contracting dealt specifically with such issues as being consistent, clarifying one's expectations, and changing the family system from utilizing punishment to introducing rewards to improve the juvenile's behavior.

The Dallas program used the following guidelines in developing a contract (Douds et al., 1977:412):

1. Explore the existing problems and need to change.
2. Have parents and youth list what they think the responsibilities and the privileges should be.
3. Narrow the lists of responsibilities and select appropriate rewards for carrying them out.
4. Develop the written agreement.
5. Implement the agreement.
6. Review the results and repeat the steps as appropriate.

The researchers found that parental authority in the home increased and recidivism was markedly decreased. Of the juveniles who completed the program, the recidivism rate for those in the treatment group was reported to be 10.7 percent compared to 42.7 percent for those in the control group.

RECIDIVISM RATES

Have family treatment programs successfully lowered recidivism rates for juvenile offenders? A number of studies have been conducted to measure the effectiveness of family treatment. Unfortunately, only a few of them have been based on randomization and an experimental or quasi-experimental design.

Geismar and Wood (1986) reviewed and rated the methodological adequacy of thirty studies purporting to measure the effects of behavioral family treatment with juvenile delinquents. The judgment of adequacy of research design was based on a variety of generally accepted criteria of the adequacy of experimental studies:

> Whether an adequate control or comparison group was used, or in the case of single-organism designs such devices as multiple baselines; whether the assignment to experimental or control/comparison conditions was unbiased; whether change was measured before and after intervention; . . . whether or not an appropriate follow-up time period was permitted to elapse before gathering data on such indices of change relevant to delinquency as recidivism rates; whether multiple vantage points for assessing data and multiple change indices were utilized; . . . whether nonspecific treatment effects (e.g., the placebo/attention effect) were controlled for; . . . whether appropriate statistical analyses were conducted. (p. 56)

Most of the studies were found to have inadequate research designs. Geismar and Wood (1986) concluded that practitioners in the field of juvenile delinquency need "to move away from a monocular and reductionist view of delinquency to a recognition that what we are dealing with is a heterogeneous phenomenon" (p. 148). They also concluded that nonfocused family interventions—those that do not include behavioral methods and only seem to address vaguely the need to encourage better communication or an expression of feelings—are totally ineffective with juvenile delinquents.

Such researchers as Alexander and Parsons (1973), Douds et al. (1977), Johnson (1977), and Klein, Alexander, and Parsons (1977) have reported that family treatment did result in lower recidivism rates, while Druckman (1979), Gruher (1979), and others have found that this treatment approach did not lower those rates.

Johnson (1977) conducted an evaluation of a family therapy program run by the Family Intervention Unit of the Delaware County Juvenile Court in Media, Pennsylvania (a Philadelphia suburb). The juveniles, who had committed status or juvenile delinquency offenses, were all on probation at the time of the study. They were divided into an experimental and a control group, each with 190 youths. The two groups were matched on the basis of age, sex, ethnic background, parents' marital status, socioeconomic level, and type of offense (status offense, crime against person, or property crime).

All of the youths participated in the regular probation program, which provided active service to all youths; no services were withheld. For example, probation officers routinely referred the juveniles to such community services as drug rehabilitation, educational programs, vocational services, individual therapy, and guided group interaction. Thus, youths who participated in the family counseling may also have been referred to one or more of the above-cited services. The only difference between the two groups was the provision of family therapy for those in the experimental group.

Johnson examined the number of offenses recorded for both groups during the period of family counseling and for two years thereafter. Before adjudication the family treatment youths had a total of 360 petitions, and the control group had 364. During the program this number dropped dramatically for both groups, but the control group had a petition rate that was three times higher than the treatment group (eighty-nine compared to twenty-nine).

A short-term program was provided to the families of forty juveniles who had been arrested for status offenses and referred to the University of Utah's Family Therapy Clinic (discussed above). The objective was to change the interaction patterns of dysfunctional families, to help them develop patterns characteristic of "normal" or "adjusted" families as identified in earlier research (Alexander & Parsons, 1973; Parsons & Alexander, 1973).

Alexander and Parsons' (1973) study consisted of four groups: an experimental group, two comparison groups, and one control group. The experimental treatment group received behavioral contracting plus family communication skills training. The two comparison groups were a client-centered group and a psychodynamically oriented family therapy group. The control group consisted of clients on a waiting list. Measures of family conflict resolution skills (rated by independent judges) indicated that the experimental behaviorally oriented family systems treatment group did significantly better than the other three groups, with a recidivism rate of only 26 percent.

The most surprising finding of Alexander and Parsons' (1973) research was that the psychodynamic family therapy group had the worst performance, both in changing family interaction patterns and in reducing recidivism. This alternative-treatment comparison group did worse than the no-treatment control group, with a 73 percent recidivism rate versus a 50 percent rate for the control group. The implication is that some types of treatment may actually be harmful to some delinquents and their families.

Klein et al. (1977) studied the impact of family treatment on siblings of the deviant youths in the Alexander and Parsons study two and one-half to three and one-half years post-treatment. The researchers found that a family systems approach resulted in the most significant improvements in process measures and in reducing recidivism. Furthermore, the delinquency rate for siblings whose families had participated in family systems treatment was only 20 percent as compared to a 40 percent rate for the control group, and 59 percent and 63 percent for the other treatment approaches. Although the sample size was small (particularly the control group), the studies conducted by Alexander and his associates represent the best studies available in terms of the design and implementation of quasi-experimental research.

In contrast to the above positive results, a study by Gruher (1979) showed no decrease in the recidivism rate of juveniles who had family counseling. Druckman (1979) reported on a study in which family therapy was provided for female status offenders. The results showed a slightly higher rate of recidivism among families that completed the family treatment program than for those who dropped out early in the program. However, it should be noted that this was a small sample (only twenty-nine families, of which fourteen completed the program and fifteen dropped out), and the "full-time family therapists" in this study had only bachelor's degrees. There was no mention of therapy being provided by or counselors being supervised by persons with more specialized clinical credentials.

The research efforts of Alexander and Parsons (1973) and Klein et al. (1977) are viewed as classic works among family treatment studies of the 1970s. Unfortunately, those studies have not been fully replicated. Although the behaviorally oriented family systems approach seems most promising, rigorous research and empirical support of the effectiveness of family systems treatment is needed.

CONCLUSION

The family system exerts tremendous influence on the growth and development of children. The dysfunctional family often does great harm when it imparts negative attitudes and values and antisocial behavioral patterns to its children. In sharp contrast, the well-functioning family has great power to nurture and heal its children while transmitting socially acceptable attitudes, a sense of responsibility and commitment to hard work, humanitarian values, and prosocial behavior patterns. Many families, including deviant ones, have a strong desire to be supportive and caring. Through family counseling, more families can begin to learn improved methods of communication, supportiveness, and effective limit setting and discipline.

DISCUSSION QUESTIONS

1. Identify six characteristics that researchers have found to be much more common among delinquents' families than among nondelinquents' families.
2. Is child abuse an antecedent to juvenile delinquency? Support your position with research evidence.
3. Discuss the pros and cons of removing a child from an abusive family.
4. What is the nature of parental resistance to attending parent education and family treatment programs?
5. Describe the staffing pattern, intensity, and content of treatment at the Homebuilders program in Tacoma, Washington.
6. Describe the family treatment program developed by Missouri's Family Resource Unit. What was the recidivism rate for program participants six months after termination from the program?
7. Identify the seven techniques used by the counselors at the Intensive Intervention Project in Honolulu, Hawaii.
8. What did Geismar and Wood (1986) conclude after reviewing and rating the methodological adequacy of thirty studies purporting to measure the effects of behavioral family treatment with juvenile delinquents?

REFERENCES

Abrahamson, D. (1960). *The psychology of crime.* New York: Columbia University Press.

Ackerman, N. W. (1962). Adolescent problems: A symptom of family disorder. *Family process* (2), New York: Basic Books.

Ackerman, N. W. (1966). *Treating the troubled family.* New York: Basic Books.

Alexander, J. F., Barton, C., Schlavo, R. S., & Parsons, B. V. (1976). Systems-behavioral intervention with families of delinquents: Family behavior and outcome. *Journal of Consulting and Clinical Psychology, 44,* 656–664.

Alexander, J. F., & Parsons, B. V. (1973). Short-term behavioral intervention with delinquent families: Impact on family process and recidivism. *Journal of Abnormal Psychology, 81*(3), 219–225.

Alexander, J. F., & Parsons, B. V. (1982). *Functional family therapy.* Monterey, CA: Brooks/Cole Publishing.

Alfaro, J. D. (1981). Report of the relationship between child abuse and neglect and later socially deviant behavior. In J. R. Hunner & Y. E. Walker (Eds.), *Exploring the relationship between child abuse and delinquency* (pp. 175–219). Montclair, NJ: Allenheld, Osmun.

Andry, R. G. (1960). *Delinquency and parental pathology.* London: Methuen.

Andry, R. G. (1962). Parental affection and delinquency. In M. E. Wolfgang, L. Savitz, & N. Johnston (Eds.), *The sociology of crime and delinquency* (pp. 330–352). New York: John Wiley & Sons.

Balmer, J. U., Kogan, L., Voorhees, C., Levin-Shaw, W., & Shapiro, F. (1979). High Impact Family Treatment: A progress report. *Juvenile and Family Court Journal, 30,* 3–7.

Barker, G. H., & Adams, W. T. (1963, April). Glue sniffers. *Sociology and Social Research 47*(3), 298–310.

Biron, L., & LeBlanc, M. (1977). Family components and home-based delinquency. *British Journal of Criminology, 17,* 157–168.

Bogert, A. J., & French, A. P. (1978). Successful short-term family therapy with incarcerated adolescents. *Journal of Juvenile and Family Courts, 29,* 3–8.

Cobean, S. C., & Power, P. W. (1978). The role of the family in the rehabilitation of the offender. *International Journal of Offender Therapy and Comparative Criminology, 22,* 29–38.

Cohen, A. K. (1955). *Delinquent boys: The culture of the gang.* New York: Free Press.

Cohen, A. K., & Short, J. F., Jr. (1958). Research in delinquent subcultures. *Journal of Social Issues, 14,* 20–36.

Cohen, A. K., & Short, J. F., Jr. (1976). Crime and juvenile delinquency. In R. K. Merton & R. Nisbet (Eds.), *Contemporary social problems* (4th ed.) (pp. 47–100). New York: Harcourt Brace Jovanovich.

Coull, V. C., Geismar, L. L., & Waff, A. (1982). The role of the family in the resocialization of juvenile offenders. *Journal of Comparative Family Studies, 13,* 63–75.

Douds, A. F., Engelsgjesd, M., & Collingwood, T. R. (1977). Behavior contracting with youthful offenders and their parents. *Child Welfare, 56,* 409–417.

Druckman, J. (1979). A family-oriented policy and treatment program for female juvenile status offenders. *Journal of Marriage and the Family, 41,* 627–636.

Empey, L. T. (1985). The family and delinquency. *Today's Delinquent, 4,* 5–46.

Fontana, V. J. (1976). *Somewhere a child is crying.* New York: New American Library.

Fontana, V. J. (1978). The maltreated child of our times. *Villanova Law Review, 23,* 448–451.

Freeman, B., & Savastano, G. (1970, July). The affluent youthful offender. *Crime and Delinquency, 16*(3), 264–272.

Geismar, L., & Wood, K. M. (1986). *Family delinquency: Resocializing the young offender.* New York: Human Sciences Press.

Glueck, S., & Glueck, E. (1968). *Delinquents and nondelinquents in perspective.* Cambridge, MA: Harvard University Press.

Glueck, S., & Glueck, E. (1962). *Family environment and delinquency.* Boston: Houghton Mifflin.

Gruher, M. (1979). Family counseling and the status offender. *Juvenile and Family Court Journal, 30,* 23–27.

Helfer, R., & Kempe, C. H. (Eds.). (1968). *Battered child.* Chicago: University of Chicago Press.

Hirschi, T. (1969). *Causes of delinquency.* Berkeley, CA: University of California Press.

Janeksela, G. M. (1979). Mandatory parental involvement in the treatment of "delinquent youth." *Juvenile and Family Court Journal, 30,* 47–54.

Jenkins, R. L., Heidemann, P. H., & Caputo, J. A. (1985). *No single cause: Juvenile delinquency and the search for effective treatment.* College Park, MD: American Correctional Association.

Jenson, G. F. (1972). Parents, peers and delinquent action. *American Journal of Sociology, 78,* 562–575.

Johnson, T. F. (1973). Treating the juvenile offender in his family. *Juvenile Justice, 24,* 41–45.

Johnson, T. F. (1977). The results of family therapy with juvenile offenders. *Juvenile Justice, 28,* 29–33.

Kinney, J. M. (1978). Homebuilders: An in-home crisis intervention program. *Children Today,* 15–17, 35.

Kinney, J. M., Madson, B., Fleming, T., & Haapala, D. A. (1977). Homebuilders: Keeping families together. *Journal of Consulting and Clinical Psychology, 45,* 667–673.

Klein, N. C., Alexander, J. F., & Parsons, B. V. (1977). Impact of family systems intervention on recidivism and sibling delinquency: A model of primary prevention and program evaluation. *Journal of Consulting and Clinical Psychology, 45,* 469–474.

Knitzer, J. (1982). *Unclaimed children.* Washington, DC: Children's Defense Fund.

Koechig, D. (September 1985). *Questionnaire response to A. R. Roberts survey of 66 juvenile treatment programs.* Kansas City, MO: Missouri Department of Youth Services, Northeast Regional Office.

Kratcoski, P. C. (1982). Child abuse and violence against the family. *Child Welfare, 61*(7), 435–444.

Langsley, D. G., & Kaplan, D. M. (1968). *Treatment of families in crisis.* New York: Grurn & Stratton.

Madanes, C. (1981). *Strategic family therapy.* San Francisco: Jossey-Bass.

Mahoney, D. M., Fixsen, D. L., & Phillips, E. L. (1981). The teaching family model: Research and dissemination in a service program. *Children and Youth Services Review, 3,* 343–355.

McCord, W., McCord, J., & Zola, I. (1959). *Origins of crime.* New York: Columbia University Press.

McPherson, S. J., McDonald, L. E., & Ryer, C. W. (1983). Intensive counseling with families of juvenile offenders. *Juvenile and Family Court Journal, 34,* 27–33.

Mouzakitis, C. M. (1981). An inquiry into the problem of child abuse and juvenile delinquency. In J. R. Hunner & Y. E. Walker (Eds.), *Exploring the relationship between child abuse and delinquency.* Monclair, NJ: Allanheld, Osmun.

Mouzakitis, C. M. (1984). Characteristics of abused adolescents and guidelines for intervention. *Child Welfare, 63,* 149–157.

Norland, S., Shover, N., Thornton, W. E., & James, J. (1979). Intrafamily conflict and delinquency. *Pacific Sociological Review, 22,* 223–240.

Nye, F. I. (1958). *Family relationships and delinquent behavior.* New York: John Wiley & Sons.

Parsons, B., & Alexander, J. (1973). Short-term family intervention: A therapy outcome study. *Journal of Consulting and Clinical Psychology, 41,* 195–201.

Patterson, G. R., Chamberlain, P., & Reid, J. B. (1982). A comparative evaluation of a parent training program. *Behavior Therapy, 13,* 638–650.

Patterson, G. R., & Dishion, T. J. (1985). Contributions of families and peers to delinquency. *Criminology, 23,* 63–79.

Patterson, G. R., & Gullion, M. E. (1968). *Living with children: New methods for parents and teachers.* Champaign, IL: Research Press.

Patterson, G. R., & Reid, J. B. (1973). Intervention for families of aggressive boys: A replication study. *Behavior, Research, and Therapy, 11,* 383–394.

Peterson, D., & Becker, W. C. (1965). Family interaction and delinquency. In H. C. Quay (Ed.), *Juvenile Delinquency: Research & Theory.* New York: Van Nostrand Reinhold.

Pines, M. (1979). Superkids. *Psychology Today, 12,* pp. 53–63.

Rodman, H., & Grams, P. (1967). Juvenile delinquency and the family: A review and discussion. *Task force report: Juvenile delinquency and youth crime,* pp.188-221. President's Commission on Law Enforcement and Administration of Justice. Washington, DC: U. S. Government Printing Office.

Satir, V. (1967). *Conjoint family therapy.* Palo Alto, CA: Science & Behavior Books.

Savastano, F., Savastano, B., & Savastano, G. (1970). The affluent youthful offender. *Crime and Delinquency, 16,* 264–272.

Schulte, P. G. (1985). The Family Resource Unit: An alternative for treatment of juvenile offenders and their families. Unpublished paper.

Severy, L. J., & Whitaker, J. M. (1984). Memphis-Metro Youth Diversion Project: Final report. *Child Welfare, 63*(3), 269–277.

Stratton, J. G. (1975). Effects of crisis intervention counseling on predelinquent and misdemeanor juvenile offenders. *Juvenile Justice, 26,* 7–18.

Straus, M. A., Gelles, R. J., & Steinmetz, S. K. (1981). *Behind closed doors: Violence in the American family.* Garden City, NY: Anchor Press.

Streib, V. L. (1978). Juvenile courts should not mandate parental involvement in court-ordered treatment programs. *Juvenile and Family Court Journal, 29*(2), 49–56.

Stuart, R. B., Jayaratre, S., & Tripodi, T. (1976). Changing adolescent deviant behavior through reprogramming the behavior of parents and teachers: An experiment evaluation. *Canadian Journal of Behavioral Science, 8*(2), 132–144.

Stuart, R. B., & Lott, L. A., Jr. (1972). Behavioral contracting with delinquents: A cautionary note. *Journal of Behavior Therapy and Experimental Psychiatry, 3,* 161–169.

Stumphauzer, J. S. (1976). Elimination of stealing by self reinforcement of alternative behavior and family contracting. *Journal of Behavior Therapy and Experimental Psychiatry, 7,* 265–268.

Stumphauzer, J. S. (1986). *Helping delinquents change: A treatment manual of social learning approaches.* New York: Haworth Press.

Sutherland, E. H., & Cressey, D. R. (1974). *Criminology* (9th ed.). Philadelphia: J. B. Lippincott.

Thomas, R. G. (1981). The family practitioner and the criminal justice system: Challenges for the 80's. *Family Relations, 30,* 614–624.

Ulrici, D. K. (1983). The effects of behavioral and family interventions on juveniles. *Family Therapy, 10,* 25–36.

Wade, T. C., Morton, T. L., Lind, J. E., & Ferris, N. R. (1977). A family crisis intervention approach to diversion from the juvenile justice system. *Juvenile Justice, 28,*(3), 43–51.

Watzlawick, P., Weakland, J. H., & Fisch, R. (1974). *Change: Principles of problem formulation and problem resolution.* New York: W. W. Norton.

Whitaker, J. M., Severy, L. J., & Morton, D. S. (1984). A comprehensive community-based youth diversion program. *Child Welfare, 63*(2), 175–181.

Windell, J. O., & Windell, E. A. (1977). Parent group training programs in juvenile courts: A national survey. *Family Coordinator, 26,* 459–463.

Chapter Twelve

Social Work Advocacy in Juvenile Justice: Conceptual Underpinnings and Practice

Robert B. Coates

ABSTRACT

Advocacy is a long-standing intervention approach within social work, and the practice of advocacy has had considerable impact in the field of juvenile justice. The practice of advocacy within social work, however, has suffered from poor conceptualization of its scope and implementation. This chapter sets forth a conceptual framework for advocacy, identifying three types of advocacy: individual cases, community, and class. Commonalities across these advocacy types are discussed. And generic principles for advocacy practice are set forth in the context of the field of juvenile justice.

THE CONTEXT OF THE EIGHTIES

In the 1970s, advocacy became a rallying cry for many juvenile justice reformers. Advocacy efforts were part and parcel of efforts to deinstitutionalize, to develop community-based alternatives, and to make community social institutions more responsible to the needs of youth and their families. Government agencies developed "advocacy initiatives" funding public law centers, youth service coalitions whose purpose, in part, was to better educate the public regarding youth policies, and demonstration programs at the local levels.

Certainly many persons rallied behind the banner of advocacy because of the availability of funds. Too often, programs were changed in name only while the ways of doing things remained the same. Others, however, saw advocacy efforts as avenues to meaningful individual and system change.

Research for this work was originally completed in conjunction with the National Assessment Center for Alternatives to Juvenile Justice Processing, the University of Chicago, under Grant No. 79–JN–AX–0018 (S–1) from the National Institute for Juvenile Justice and Delinquency Prevention, U.S. Department of Justice. Points of view or opinions in this document are those of the author and do not necessarily represent the official position or policies of the U.S. Department of Justice or those of the assessment center.

Preparation for this work included conducting focused interviews with federal, state, and private administrators and program staff. However, to be fair, I must say that the bulk of the "supporting evidence" has come from years of observing advocates and advocacy programs, conversations with persons working in such programs, and my own efforts to work in and with advocacy programs on behalf of youth in the juvenile justice system.

I wish to thank Alden D. Miller and Lloyd E. Ohlin, who provided valuable theoretical critiques as the advocacy framework was taking shape. Appreciation is also expressed to Margaret K. Rosenheim, Frederic Reamer, Charles Shireman, Charloette Schuerman, and Betty Vos for insightful responses to earlier, unpublished drafts of this work.

By the mid-1980s, the banner of advocacy in juvenile justice had, for the most part, been furled, encased, and placed in a corner, to be used perhaps on another day. Ideological shifts by the federal administration and by significant segments of the professional juvenile justice community had led to the demise of many, if not most, of the advocacy programs funded in the 1970s. Especially devastating was the loss of privately funded interest groups who had juvenile justice as a primary focal concern.

While advocacy as a means to bring about change is still carried out by some, it has become more difficult. Severe restrictions of funding possibilities has hurt. Government is skeptical of providing funds to organizations that may turn around and question government policies. Given the hugh social service cuts by governments, foundations are hard pressed to justify funding advocacy programs when their limited funds are needed to support basic human services. And some involved in the efforts to change juvenile justice policies now find themselves in positions that make continued advocacy efforts difficult at best. For example, those involved in the community-based movement may have programs that, too often, rely solely on the state for funding. To carry out advocacy directed at policy change places them in the vulnerable position of possibly having their own program funding cut.

The strains on advocacy, however, are not limited merely to lack of funding and self-interest. Advocacy suffers from a deficit of conceptual development and from professional distrust. Advocacy is too often viewed as action carried out by the seat of the pants; yet, those experienced at advocacy follow a fairly systematic, conceptually grounded process that, when made explicit, can be learned by others.

Professional distrust takes several forms. Within a given profession such as social work, there is a strong tendency to view advocacy as the responsibility of some but not of others. Advocacy is often viewed narrowly as aimed at broad system change, making it inappropriate for the more clinically oriented practitioner. In contrast, one of the assumptions underpinning this chapter is that advocacy must be conceived broadly enough to demonstrate its place as a common thread in social-work methods, including clinical, community work, and policy analysis. Furthermore, within social work, it is instructive to recognize that advocacy is at the very historical roots of the profession; it is not some new frivolous appendage (Bruno, 1957; Fischer, 1978; Woodroofe, 1974). Additional professional distrust occurs between professions—for example, between the social worker and the lawyer. In this chapter, we take the position that important elements of advocacy can be learned from other professions without giving up one's own professional identity. And last, there exists professional distrust of advocacy efforts that include extensive involvement of laypersons. The position taken here is that such involvement is critical to the continued development of advocacy in social work in general and in juvenile justice in particular.

The purpose of this chapter, then, is to bring some conceptual clarity to what we, particularly within social work, view as advocacy and to set forth principles that can guide the practice of social work advocacy in the juvenile justice arena.

A CONCEPTUAL FRAMEWORK OF ADVOCACY

The most generic definition of advocacy in juvenile justice and in human services is "acting on behalf of clients and/or client interests." This is the kernel of the conceptual framework described here. This generic definition is stripped of most specificity. There is no reference to who does the advocating; the clients and client interests are not designated; nor are kinds of advocacy actions identified. The task here will be to fill out the specifics of a conceptual framework. The first step is to identify a number of assumptions underpinning this framework.

Underlying Assumptions

Whether one approaches advocacy from a legal, social work, psychological, or sociological framework, there are at least minimum implicit assumptions that justify and direct the practice of advocacy. Justification of advocacy work in human services and specifically in juvenile justice is embodied, in part, in the observer's assumptions, perceptions and values regarding personhood, justice, and society (Kutchins & Kutchins, 1978:14–17).

Consistent with other definitions of advocacy, our framework is developed on the assumption and value base that each *person* has certain inalienable rights: the right to essential goods to assure survival, and the right to develop skills as long as one does not infringe upon the rights of others. These rights are regarded not as earned or derived from law, but as a consequence of the person's being or existence. It is also assumed that *justice* involves each member of society having equal opportunity and access to societal resources, recognizing that individual variation will likely develop as persons use resources differently. And *society* has a responsibility to assure that these rights of persons are available to all its members. Laws are created to protect those rights (e.g., to protect the minority from the whims of the majority), and groups of common interests emerge and coalesce to push for their particular desires by participating in formal and informal political processes.

The above assumptions support or speak to the why of advocacy. Society has a responsibility to provide structures and processes that bring into reality the assumptions regarding personhood and justice. Advocacy, the participation of individuals on behalf of their own and others' interests, plays a key role in bringing about those realities.

A different order of assumptions must be considered before moving to the conceptual framework: that is, how we will think about the task of advocacy. To get at these assumptions, we will consider how others have sought to expand on the generic definition of advocacy (acting on behalf of client and/or client interests).

Advocacy is a cornerstone of the legal field. There, it is traditionally and ideally carried out in an adversarial mode. Each defendant has the right to an adequate defense. The defense attorney is not concerned with whether his client in fact committed a certain act; the client will be defended "right or wrong." The lawyer's responsibility is to advocate on behalf of the client, just as the prosecutor's is to advocate on behalf of the state. It is the responsibility of a judge/jury to decide the outcome of the case (Berman & Greiner, 1972:386–399).

While social work advocates can work with lawyers in individual cases and class action suits, the legal model has several flaws as a foundation for developing an advocacy model for social work or the human services. First, in a strictly adversarial stance it is often difficult to assume the presence of an impartial judge. Second, defending the client "right or wrong" contradicts ethical codes of some human-service workers and their professional associations. In social work, for example, representing the client's interests is of fundamental importance. But what if those interests clash with those of other clients (i.e., child versus parent)? For the social worker the advocacy posture may be more often one of a proactive negotiator than one of a pure adversary.

Social workers offer their own definitions of advocacy: acting on behalf of the "disadvantaged" (Brager, 1958), "championing the cause of the client" (Briar, 1967), "champion of social victims" (Ad Hoc Committee on Advocacy, 1969), or actions of a third party to change a decision of an individual or group where there is a power imbalance (Sosin & Caulum, 1983:13). While these definitions may focus on the primary mission of social work, they limit our thinking about advocacy in two ways. First, they fail to underscore the important role of clients as self-advocates and as advocates for others. Second, although certainly not intended, there is sentiment of apology: that is, becoming involved in political struggles is dirty, yet we must become involved because of social injustice. The view of this author is that advocacy is ingrained in the fabric of a free society. Advocacy as a strategy is used to champion the causes of many groups, not simply the disadvantaged. Advocacy strategies are carried out by proponents of a strong defense, by the National Rifle Association, by industries, and by a multitude of other national and local groups concerned about issues important to them. There need be no apology, implied or otherwise, for working with the "disadvantaged" in insisting that their voices are heard, understood, and responded to.

Another assumption underpinning the conceptual framework is that advocacy is the task of direct service providers as well as of community workers and policy analysts. A number of professional squabbles have emerged about whether or not advocacy is a legitimate function of direct service (Scurfield, 1980:613). The view here is that it is and has been historically. The roots of advocacy in social work are not only traced to Addams, Abbott, and Lathrop; these roots can also be traced to the casework traditions of Richmond, Reynolds, and Towle. For example, the writings of Richmond and Towle are as apt today as they were sixty and thirty years ago:

> Absence in any given community of the social resources and expert services of many kinds which have so enriched case work becomes a double challenge to that community's case workers—a challenge to their ingenuity in developing possible substitutes for needed resources and a challenge to their public spirit, which should push hard to secure the community agencies still lacking. (Richmond, 1922)

> Granted the existence of basic biological drives and variation in constitutional endowment, the social worker operates on the assumption that the individual is fashioned largely by the circumstances and interpersonal relationships of his environment and, in turn, fashions them. The social worker's primary focus is on environment, broadly conceived, as a means to development and on environment as treatment when development is obstructed. (Towle, 1954)

The last assumption has to do with the conceptual beginning point for developing an advocacy framework. Often advocacy efforts are described in terms of the doers of advocacy: consumer advocacy, legal advocacy, social work advocacy, and so on. Focusing on the doers puts more emphasis on the differences between the advocates than on some of the common strategies employed whether one is a social worker, a lawyer, or a consumer advocate. Because we are ultimately interested in the practice of advocacy, regardless of who does it, the framework presented here is constructed on the nature of the person or persons who are supposed to benefit from the advocacy.

The assumptions underlying the advocacy framework may be summarized as follows:

1. Each person has certain inalienable rights: the right to essential goods to assure survival and the right to develop skills as long as one does not infringe upon the rights of others.

2. Each member of society should have equal opportunity and access to societal resources, recognizing that individual variation will likely develop as persons use resources differently.

3. Society has a responsibility to assure that these rights of persons are available to all its members.

4. Advocacy should be conceived in ways allowing for the development of self-advocates on equal footing with "professional advocates."

5. Advocacy should be defined broadly enough to encompass the range of groups that carry out such activities.

6. Direct service providers do and must continue to advocate on behalf of their clients.

7. The conceptualization of advocacy should be constructed around the nature of person or persons benefiting from advocacy efforts rather than around the doers of advocacy.

The Three Part Advocacy Framework

The succeeding paragraphs will set forth a framework for advocacy, based upon a three part typology. The typology is derived by keeping the above assumptions in mind and by answering the following four questions:

1. What type of client is the advocacy addressing?
2. In what arena does the advocacy occur?
3. What kinds of activity shape the advocacy effort?
4. At what general goal is advocacy directed?

We will address these questions by framing answers in model types (summarized in Table 12–1). The advantage of the typological approach, here, is that it is a method that yields distinctions and clarity in what is usually viewed as entangled complexity. A disadvantage is that what actually underlies what we are treating as modal categories of the three advocacy types, typology, is a series of continua; thus there are more nuances within and overlaps between the model types than may seem apparent.

Beginning with the first question, clients are viewed as being in one of three modal categories. The first, corresponding to individual-case advocacy, is the individual client. Although the word *individual* usually implies single, its meaning is extended here to include family, such as in instances of family counseling where the unit of focus is not one individual but members of a family. Analogously this category includes small groups: for example, a church youth group where the focus is on the small group whose members are known to one another. The second category of client, corresponding to community advocacy, is a composite of individuals in a community who have similar problems or needs but may not be known to each other: for example, youngsters in the sixteen–nineteen age range in a local community who must contend with the lack of organized recreational opportunities. The third category, corresponding to class advocacy, is a class of individuals across larger jurisdictional boundaries—city, county, state, nation—who have similar problems or needs. For example, the plight of juveniles incarcerated in jails for adults would represent a class of clients on whose behalf advocates could act.

The modal arena for each type of advocacy is probably clear. For case advocacy it is dyads, triads, and small groups, particularly as they intersect with natural helping networks and with public and private social service and social control agencies. For community advocacy, the locus of action is in the local community, focusing on local interest groups and local agencies. The arena may very well expand around specific issues, but the base of operations and intended impact is at the local community level. In class advocacy the arena can be quite expan-

TABLE 12–1 Advocacy Framework

Advocacy Type	Client	Arena	Activity	Goals
Individual case	Individual, small group	Dyads, triads, small groups, community agencies and services	Casework, brokering services	Linking client to resources, generating resources, changing processes
Community	Composite of individuals in local community with similar problems or needs	Local community	Community/ interest group organizing	Generating resources, changing processes, linking clients to resources
Class	Class of individuals across larger jurisdictional boundaries with similar problems or needs	City, state, nation, international	Coalition/ interest group organizing	Changing processes, generating resources

sive, including the nation; in fact, it can be international, as with involvement in the International Year of the Child.

The modal type of activity associated with case advocacy is casework, direct and indirect. Direct casework involves extensive contact with the client while indirect does not (brokering services would be an example of the latter). The modal form of activity in community advocacy is community organizing—mobilizing and working with local interest groups. The modal activity for class advocacy is coalition building and working with interest groups but generally on a larger scale than that which will occur with community advocacy. A second major model activity associated with class advocacy—class action suits in the legal system (*Morales* v. *Turman*, 1974)—will be dealt with only in a tangential fashion here.

The goals of each type of advocacy generally overlap although there are different priorities for each type. Those general goals are (1) linking clients to existing resources, broadly defined to include education, skill training, jobs, money, health care, housing, and relationship support; (2) generating resources where they are needed but lacking; and (3) changing processes that impinge on access to resources and on the manner by which clients are handled by public and private social service and social control agencies. Such processes incorporate both policies and procedures. For example, one may want to influence the policies of a state youth corrections agency regarding the allocation of funds across institutional and community-based programs and also influence the procedures used to determine which type of youngster is eligible for which type of program.

Case advocacy will usually focus on linking clients to resources, with a second priority on generating resources and a tertiary focus on changing processes. Community advocacy comes the closest to placing equal weight on each goal, depending on the needs of particular groups, but linking clients to resources generally plays a somewhat secondary role. Class advocacy typically focuses most directly on changing processes, with generating resources a close second. Class advocacy is much less likely than the other types of advocacy to focus directly on linking individual clients to resources.

A significant difference between this conceptual framework of advocacy and other attempts is that advocacy related to policy goals is seen as cutting across (in varying degrees) the advocacy types. Policy is not of interest only to the class advocate. The individual case advocate may seek an exception to school suspension policy for a client. In a small community, if the suspension policy is seen as negatively affecting other, similar youths, the advocate may become involved in

community advocacy efforts to change the policy and resulting procedures. If the school is part of a metropolitan jurisdiction, the advocate
may choose to become involved in a coalition cutting across local community boundaries, seeking suspension policy change on behalf of a
class of affected youth.

Commonalities across the Advocacy Types

Construction of modal types emphasizes distinctions and differences between the types of advocacy. However, the commonalities that
cut across those types allow us to include each under the rubric of
advocacy.

The most obvious commonality is contained in the generic definition of advocacy "acting on behalf of client and client interests."
Whether one is working on the individual, community, or class level,
goals and actions should be clearly linked to client interest. This
sounds simpler and easier than it actually is. An individual client may
have conflicting self-interests, members of a client family may disagree, and broader groups or classes of clients may oppose each other's
interests. Some client interests may be unrealistic, requiring that those
interests and desires be at least somewhat tempered in the face of the
constraining realities of the situation. Nonetheless, even tempering
client interests ought to be done with utmost emphasis on those interests rather than on the efficiency of the system, the strains on decision
makers, or the vested interest of professionals. Those "clients" will
have their advocates too!

Client participation—self-advocacy—is a second commonality. The
participation of clients in advocacy is important for three reasons.
First, their input at each advocacy level can often provide clearest direction. Their experiences, their descriptions of actual situations, their
articulation of need will ground advocacy activities in concrete realities. Second, their participation can serve as an antidote to the self-
aggrandizing professional; they can serve to keep the professional advocate honest. Third, with proper support and training, they are in
many instances their own best advocates. Fourth, client participation
empowers the client in modilizing resources, and this experience can
be drawn upon in future situations.

The third commonality is the common vehicle for advocacy across
the three types, namely relationship. Whether individual, community,
or class, advocacy functions through an interpersonal enterprise. This
is probably clearest at the individual and community levels, where advocates work closely with clients, families, teachers, and leaders in the
local community. But it is equally the case on the class level. Relationships are built not only within interest groups but across interest

groups and with key people in power who are in position to decide upon proposed changes. Communication, transfer of ideas, identification of need, and comparing and contrasting of strengths and weaknesses of policy are brought about through relationships. Relationship is not the sum total of advocacy, but it is the vehicle.

Two essential ingredients of relationship have particular import for advocacy. The first is being able to place one's self in the role of the other. Trying to view the problem and/or situation from the vantage point of other actors not only provides the possibility for leverage, but may in fact facilitate the relationship. This may be referred to as empathic rather than sympathetic understanding. One does not have to accept the other's position, but one can try to grasp it. Second, in order to get people to alter their behavior they must have some stake in the advocate's position. What they are likely to gain from changing their ways of doing things? Will there be less stress? Can the advocate offer more than intangible support for knowing that they are doing the "right thing."

The fourth commonality speaks to part of the advocacy process. While relationship is seen as a necessary vehicle for advocacy, it is also difficult to imagine those activities occurring without some degree of tension, (e.g., tension between advocates and decision makers who generate and implement policy). At times, in human services, we seem to believe that tension or conflict ought to be rooted out in the interests of coordination and efficiency. In our quest for consensus we often overlook the constructive, creative possibilities that can emerge out of tension among participants (Coser, 1956).

Advocacy takes place in a political context whether one is trying to encourage a teacher to use a different disciplinary approach with a student, attempting to win community acceptance for a group home, or laboring to convince legislators that more monies ought to be made available for purchase of services from the private sector. People will have opposing points of views; some will not want to change the way they have been doing things. Tension or conflict is inevitable if we are trying to change anything of particular significance.

Having raised the issue of tension and conflict as a commonality across the types of advocacy does not mean we are promoting the idea that open warfare is needed to alter systems. Advocates need to learn how to manage tension and conflict in a political context. In fact, what one can achieve will be greatly influenced by the ability to know when conflict is realistic and when it is unrealistic. Furthermore, successful advocacy will depend upon advocates learning how to use conflict and tension in such ways as to move forward, allowing opponents and neutrals to save face by offering reasonable opportunities for them to support the positions being advocated.

VIGNETTES OF ADVOCACY TYPES

Individual Case Advocacy: John in the Vise of Peers and Family

Ellen is a school social worker who works in a middle school. John's case was referred to her by his English teacher. The teacher believed that John had been displaying an increasing amount of acting out behavior in the classroom and often appeared to be preoccupied and bothered. She was particularly concerned that John, whom she perceived as a "good kid," was becoming too involved with youths who were delinquent or otherwise getting into trouble. The following information was gathered by Ellen as she talked with John and his family members.

John is a fourteen-year-old seventh grader. An average student with above-average potential, he was held back in the third grade because of reading deficiency. While gains have been made in reading ability, John is at best ambivalent about school. John, a handsome youth, is tall for his age, about 5 feet, 11 inches. He is an active participant in town football. His number one passion is engines. He has demonstrated considerable ability in dismantling and putting together car parts. He is also an excellent artist. These two skills have prompted him to consider such future vocations as draftsman, architect, and engineer. John also has an excellent sense of humor.

John's family is a blended family. His parents divorced when John was six years old. Both parents have since remarried. A twelve-year-old brother lives in John's household; the seventeen-year-old brother lives with John's father and stepmother in a distant state. A five-year-old half-brother by his father and stepmother has a very "special relationship" with John. Of the four brothers, they share the same features and hair coloring and have been very close.

The relationship among the four parents of this family set is generally quite supportive with very good communication channels. They have demonstrated abilities to deal with difficult crises and make difficult decisions. This was best illustrated when at the age of fourteen John's older brother reached an impasse in his relationship with his mother and a joint decision was made for the brother to live with his father. That arrangement has worked out quite well for all concerned.

John's current relationship with his mother and stepfather is strained and ambivalent. Tension has arisen principally in two areas. First, John has had a difficult year in school, with grades falling. There has been sporadic intervention on the part of his mother to set down a structure for doing homework and studying. Second, John has been hanging out with a group of youths regarded as troublemakers. Increasingly, John has been getting into trouble at school, on the school bus, and in various local community businesses. Money has been missing from the home. When confronted by his mother and stepfather, John claimed not to know how the money was taken. His responses to being grounded and other punitive intervention have been "I don't care" and "So what," responses that led his mother and stepfather to an impasse.

Prior to John's trip to be with his father and stepmother for a week, his mother and stepfather called seeking advice and assistance and encouraging the father to take the opportunity to find out what was happening. John has had fairly close relationships with his father and stepmother. Both are professional human-service workers. John generally spends a week at Christmas, a spring-break week, and six–eight weeks in the summer with his father and stepmother. They also communicate weekly by phone. This provides an opportunity for John's mother and father to confer about what is happening in the two families.

During his stay with his father and stepmother, John entered into very forthright conversations about his difficulties; many of these conversations were initiated by John. Clearly, John has issues involving trust and authority. He does not believe that his parents should select his friends. Yet admits that he is at risk with some of his friends. He has participated in minor acts of vandalism. Some of his friends have committed shoplifting, breaking and entering, and theft; many use drugs. John is not into drugs and alcohol although one of his associates is a dealer. John is quite conflicted over what he should and can do. He wants to dissociate from this network of friends. But is not clear that he can do this or that he can do it without the potential for danger—he may know too much. He has noted that he perhaps "should get out of the neighborhood before he gets into serious trouble." He also indicated that he knows that he has done some things that he is not "proud of" and that he knows his father would not be proud of. And he really does not want to continue in that way.

John's father and stepmother made it clear that he was welcome to move in with them. They reiterated that he was loved by four parents and that they saw he was a "good kid" in a very difficult situation. Ways of developing alternative opportunities for friends and fun were thoroughly discussed.

John's father and stepmother are fearful of what could happen if John does not successfully disengage from the delinquent peer group, and they believe that the best solution is probably for him to come to live with them. They are taking steps to attempt to shore up John and his mother while at the same time holding out the option of John's moving. They believe it is important for John to participate in making such a decision but worry about how much time can elapse before such a decision has to be made.

Based on her assessment of the above information, Ellen is taking several steps to deal with John's situation. While there is considerable stress and strain upon John and his family, she believes that the family system as a whole offers considerable strengths.

Ellen is initially playing the role of advocate for John in his immediate family situation. She is working with his mother and stepfather to provide more rewards for positive behavior, including dissociation from the delinquent peer network. When punishments are required she is trying to see that they are realistic in magnitude and duration. And, wherever possible, she encourages them to involve John in helping establish rewards and punishments for specific behaviors.

Ellen is trying to convince the parents that one possible positive hook for John is his interest in engines. John complains of boredom and wants a car to work on. His mother will not consider this as an option because John is too young. The social worker is pointing out that the issue is not driving but rather constructive use of spare time. She is also trying to deal with John's interest in getting a job. His mother resists this notion because it would require "one of the parents to drive him to and from work." Ellen is working on alternative transportation—bicycle or moped. (The latter would also build upon John's mechanical interests.)

Ellen is also working with the English teacher and the school's vocational counselor to provide an informal support network for John: to provide him with encouragement, realistic opportunities for immediate jobs, and long-term career options. Additionally, and perhaps most difficult, she is trying to sort out ways for John to establish friendships with a different set of youngsters. She is exploring the possibility of setting up through the school a group of youths who are interested in cars. Possibilities include afterschool training in engine repair, motorbike repair, and track. Such a group would have adult supervision but would be much looser than the typical school classroom experience. From her experience she knows that there are youths other than John who could benefit from this afterschool experience. However, it cannot be just another school experience; it must provide an opportunity for fun and hands-on experience.

While Ellen is taking these steps to shore up John's current situation, she is also trying to monitor carefully the extent of John's continuing involvement with the delinquent peer group and the extent of danger to John. She is working with John and his mother to clarify and consider the possible move of John to his father as a viable, constructive alternative—particularly if the above efforts fail to ameliorate the situation.

Community Advocacy: Responding to Youth Needs in Yorktown—Setting Up a Group Home

A group of youth workers in the predominately middle-class, urban community of Yorktown were concerned about youth crime and ways in which the community could respond to it. The group gathered data on community delinquency rates and school dropout percentages and mapped out the general and youth-specific services available for delinquent youth in the community. Based on their analysis of these data and their belief that communities should provide some middle-range alternatives between probation and sending youth away to training schools, the group decided that the community and the youth would be better served by a group home available locally.

At the outset, the goal in establishing the community-based group home was not only to neutralize community resistance to the home but also to garner enough community support so that community resources could be drawn upon to meet the needs of the group home residents. Given that the objective included continuing working relationships with significant segments of the community, the level of conflict during the initial stage of gaining acceptance could not be so great as to alienate persons controlling community resources reserved for serving the youth. This factor had significant implications for how inevitable conflicts could be managed and how images of the program, staff, and future residents would be constructed for the local citizenry.

The group, familiar with the community, had in mind a tentative site for the group home. The facility which had adequate space and safety features was located in an area accessible to other service resources but not too near institutions such as elementary schools, which would feed the fears of local residents. The group was aware of and sensitive to the fact that many community members did not share their views about or concern for the youths who were getting into trouble; in fact some community residents were fearful that a group home nearby would lower property values and pose an unwanted and unnecessary risk to the neighborhood.

Although the planning group had done their homework and developed a high-quality program plan, there was no guarantee that the local residents would accept the idea of establishing a group home in their midst. In addition to documentation of a community problem and development of a proposed solution, the planning group clearly would have to focus on the political arena in which implementation would take place. So they began to identify persons and organizations that would likely be for or against the group home proposal. The group thus sought to engage segments of the community, especially those they thought were likely to play a pivotal role in their chances for success.

As the group worked to develop a strategy for engaging the community, they examined the community's experiences and history with similar issues and community services. They asked a number of questions: Does the community or segments of it have a history of organizing in order to block these kinds of service programs? If so, does it rely primarily on its political leaders to carry forth the struggle, or does it also have strong grassroots interest groups? In other words, how do the community and its various segments view the kinds of concerns shared by the planning group? Does the community have a history and capacity for organizing to support or to block such efforts?

To obtain answers to these questions, the group paid careful attention to the local newspapers and newsletters to determine what had been happening in the area around these kinds of issues during the past year. The group also contacted some key informants who were helpful in relating the history of the community. From these data the group was able to make judgments about how they and others could influence and glavanize local residents through persuasion and through informal ties among members of the planning group, potential neighbors, and the community leadership.

Another salient area of concern was the formal power structure and procedures for establishing the group home. The advocates discovered that an appearance before a zoning board would be necessary. They therefore sought answers to such questions as: Who chairs the meeting? What will the board be most concerned about? How sympathetic are its members to residential facilities? How do the members perceive youth in trouble and the role of the community in dealing with youth crime?

The group identified potential supporting and opposing interest groups within the community. A local chapter of the League of Women Voters and a number of church leaders were identified as potentially supportive; community officials, police, and school officials were identified as potentially hostile. Some of the neighbors were identified as persons who had previously expressed a desire for administrators to take stronger, more punitive actions against acting-out youths in the local schools. This issue and response had been expressed at local PTA meetings on several occasions. Thus, the strength of potential negative response by some neighbors and their position in the local community network gave the group much concern. They had clearly identified a segment of the local neighborhood that would have to be handled very carefully.

Of particular interest were the adjacent neighbors. As the planning group attempted to view the plans through the eyes of their neighbors, they anticipated some opposition based on fear—fear of potential danger that residents of the proposed home may present to the surrounding families and their children and fear that property values may drop because of the home's presence. The group realized that whether or not the fears were well grounded they must be taken seriously and dealt with straightforwardly. It was hoped that by exposing neighbors to the staff and the nature of the program and by talking about the kinds of youngsters who would reside in the home some of the neighbors' stereotypical images about the youths could be altered, they would better understand the safeguards to be implemented by program staff to reduce undue risks, and they would come to understand that they and program staff shared similar values about property. It was further hoped that discussions with neighbors would lead to a realization that program staff and neighbors shared some common understanding of home life and that program staff were, in part, attempting to replicate that kind of quality living and living space for their charges.

After analyzing all of the information gathered, the planning group remained committed to establishing the group home. They turned to deciding on a strategy for achieving that goal. The group decided they had three choices: attempt to sneak in, direct their attention to community officials, or adopt a two-pronged strategy whereby they would attempt to influence the neighbors as well as deal with the formal political structure of the community. Because they knew the community had a capacity and a history of organizing at the grassroots level, the last strategy was selected.

A number of actions and events occurred simultaneously during this action phase of garnering support and neutralizing resistance to the group home. Because of space considerations, we will focus here only on actions directed at the neighbors. Staff were able to arrange a meeting with three of the neighbors over coffee on their turf—at the home of one of these neighbors.

The neighbors cited the danger that the group home would be forcing on their own children. They did not mention property values although staff assumed that this concern simply was not voiced. The neighbors clearly viewed the group representatives as "do-gooder social work types." The group felt that they had little choice but to be open with these neighbors, for at least their passive acceptance would be important for any ongoing operation of a community-based group home. These group representatives sought to alter the neighbors' perception of them as do-gooders by acknowledging the realistic risks involved. They shared their plans for setting up safeguards that would offer protection for both the youth participants and the community. They described the staffing capability and nature of the program. And the group attempted to give the neighbors some ownership of the program by indicating that they wanted to operate a truly community-based program, which in part meant they desired neighbor participation on the Community Policy Board. The outcome of this exchange was that two neighbors agreed not to oppose the group's plans but would take a "wait and see" stance. The third neighbor was willing to help the group think through strategies for gathering support. This neighbor volunteered to speak on the group's behalf at the zoning hearing.

The group's simultaneous interactions with other community interest groups had mixed results. The group was able to neutralize police and school officials. Some political officials remained opposed, others supportive, and still others waited to see which way the political winds would blow.

The group's efforts were moving forward steadily with a fair chance of being successful. At this point, attention shifted to preparation for the zoning hearing. Clearly the group was engaged in an interactive process. Through their efforts and those of others the list of potentially supportive and opposing interest groups had changed, and the relative power balance among interest groups—including the group itself—had changed.

This particular group was successful in establishing their group home with adequate community support and participation to provide a community-based program for its clients. In dealing with the community field, the initiating group demonstrated the importance of identifying opposing and supporting forces, ferreting out vested interest, taking the role of the other, and taking reflective action.

Class Advocacy: Deinstitutionalization in Utah Youth Corrections

The state of Utah had been known in the 1950s and 1960s for operating a rehabilitation-oriented juvenile justice system. Juvenile court judges were active nationally in promoting this direction, and youths requiring institutional care were handled within the Department of Social Services. The state operated one training school for delinquents, at Ogden; it was known variously as the Industrial School for Boys and the Youth Development Center (YDC).

During the early and mid-1970s, the training school came under increasing criticism from within and outside the system. Some staff and some judges were beginning to question the nature of the program and the overall experience of youth at the school. These concerns along with those of outside interest groups culminated in a 1975 lawsuit brought against the school by the American Civil Liberties Union. Issues raised in the lawsuit included (1) inappropriate use of the school's secure unit; (2) censoring the mail; (3) alleged abuse; (4) right to treatment, or the inadequacy of existing treatment programs; and (5) the mixing of a host of status offenders with delinquent youth. At that time the training school housed about 350 youths. Over half of these were either status offenders or youths handled for the Bureau of Indian Affairs.

While the lawsuit was by no means the only condition leading to reform in Utah, it did serve as a catalyst and a focal point requiring administrators to take action. Administrators took the position that they wanted to respond in a responsible, rational manner to best serve the youth and the state of Utah. The situation would require direct action regarding the training school, but more broadly, it was an opportunity to reconsider and if necessary to reshape the scope of juvenile corrections.

Individuals in the private and the public sector began seeking information on what was happening nationally in the area of juvenile justice. Considerable attention was given to the Massachusetts experience with deinstitutionalization. Utahans traveled to Massachusetts, and reformers and observers of that experience were invited to present findings and share their experience in Utah.

In the late 1970s, as a result of the CATY Commission, several community-based alternatives were funded on an experimental basis. These programs were used in part to dramatically reduce the population at the YDC, allowing staff there to focus their efforts more directly on the delinquent youth. And Governor Scott Matheson, a strong proponent for youth- and community-based services, appointed a blue-ribbon commission to consider the philosophy and direction of youth corrections. Representatives from across the juvenile justice system, the public, and the legislature made up this commission. After much consideration and deliberation this commission supported a philosophy of reintegration, accountability of youth to the state through a range of community-based services including small, program-oriented secure units, and the gradual phasing out of the YDC.

The legislature in 1980 created a separate Division of Youth Corrections within the Department of Social Services. Its first director had been the governor's staff assistant to the blue-ribbon commission. He provided much of the philosophical and overall direction to the planning of the deinstitutionalization effort. This director resigned in late spring 1980. He was replaced by another person with close ties to the governor.

Under that person's direction, another task force comprising a cross section of juvenile justice people worked out a master plan for implementation. Again there was a consensus commitment to alternatives; this task force focused on strategic questions and served to rein-force a commitment to the phaseout of the YDC. The work of this group drew heavily from studies done by groups within and from out-side the state. Key strategic steps included (1) creation of three admin-istrative regions, making it easier to work with youth and community services in a regionalized manner; (2) construction of two secure units housing up to thirty youths each—youths to be divided among two living pods; (3) contracting with the private sector to provide a diverse continuum of programmatic resources ranging from nonresidential services (including intensive tracking) to foster care, to group homes, to secure units; and (4) the YDC would not be closed until the secure units were in place and functional.

During 1983 the director was asked to take over the crisis-plagued Department of Corrections. His replacement was a person with long-standing involvement in both the private and public sector response to delinquents. Having been involved in the private sector before joining the staff of his predecessor, he provided a natural link as the system attempted to increase that sector's capacity for responding to delin-quent youth.

By January 1984, the two secure units were functional and much of the desired community-based continuum was in place. Without much fanfare, the YDC was closed.

The actual process of deinstitutionalization in Utah was much more complex and in much more jeopardy than the above account sug-gests. Space is too short to describe many of the internal and external actions. The process clearly took place in a political context. Strongest resistance to the effort came from residents and influentials in Ogden who were fearful of loss of jobs and the resulting effects on the local economy. Plans were undertaken to put the old training school grounds to public use. Some concern was expressed about public safety, but these concerns were blunted by pointing out that the new secure units would provide more community protection then the train-ing school, which had had a deplorable record for escapes. One might wonder if administrators might have almost overstudied and over-planned, but enough charismatic leadership was provided to keep the interest and commitment levels high. Perhaps the most remarkable feat politically is that many disparate individuals and groups including judges, legislators, administrators, and private individuals, when inter-viewed, point to their pivotal roles in bringing about the reforms. This suggests a significant stake in the direction of the division.

In many ways the major class advocacy efforts never end. In spring 1985, the director resigned to take another position. The new director, who was a key administrator within the division for some time, re-mains committed to the division's direction. But the process continues.

There is renewed concern about the accountability of the new community-based system. Given Utah's high birth rate there is continued concern about the adequacy of the number of secure beds. Programming for female delinquents remains an issue. And occasionally there is even a fond nostalgic recollection by a few voices for the good old YDC days. As in other states, for Utah's gains to be maintained, attention must continue to focus on providing creative programming options that provide hope for youths and responsible protection for the community as well as keeping a keen eye focused on the political arena and the every-shifting political winds of support and resistance.

THE GENERIC STEPS OF ADVOCACY

Space does not permit a detailed description of practice steps and issues related to each type of advocacy. There are, however, generic steps of advocacy that apply across types (see Table 12–2). These will naturally vary by advocacy type and by the specifics of each situation. Just because a specific strategy worked in one situation does not mean that it will be appropriate in another. The need to develop and weigh alternative strategies and their consequences is present in each situation.

1. Identifying and Justifying a Need.

The initial step in advocacy is to document and justify a particular need. With an individual client this may include listening to the person's story, developing a chart of the person's social network, and testing. At the community level documentation may include a community

TABLE 12–2   Generic Steps of Advocacy

1. Identifying and justifying a need.
2. Identification of desired change.
3. Identifying the targets for change.
4. Assessing the available resources.
5. Assessing the political scene.
6. Developing and implementing advocacy strategies:
   a. Leverage.
   b. Negotiating stance.
   c. Use of power.
   d. Timing.
   e. Selection of tactics and strategies.
7. Follow-up.

survey of a particular population such as youth, a survey of social service programs and the kinds of clients they serve, and listening to specific interest groups as they talk about their issues and concerns. At
the class level, documentation and justification may include analyzing
the impact of policy across communities or interviewing a sample of
service providers across a state. For example, to what extent are youth
held on detention status in local jails.

2. Identification of Desired Change.

With the client or representatives of the client population, advocates need to specify what change they desire to bring about. This will
likely require partializing and setting priorities. An advocacy group
can be so diffuse in its desired ends that little if anything can be accomplished. For instance, the client advocate working with a client
with postrelease depression needs to be more specific than simply
trying to make the client feel better. What will it take for the client to
feel better about himself/herself: establishing supportive relationships
with significant others, obtaining meaningful employment, and/or re-
learning basic life skills for a changed society?

3. Identifying the Targets for Change.

Once a desired change has been identified, the advocate will want
to identify the targets for change: whatever needs to be altered in order
to ameliorate the situation. When working with a youth who is having
disciplinary problems at school, one may discover specific behaviors of
the youth, family members, and teachers that become the targets for
change, thereby creating a set of relationships where the youth is able
to handle frustration and disappointment in less disruptive ways. At
the community level, a survey of youth may have identified police harassment as a primary issue of concern. An advocate will want to determine to what extent police harassment is the consequence of a few
individual police officers, of leadership, or of policy. This determination will provide a picture of the target that needs to be changed and
will be invaluable at the stage of strategy development.

4. Assessing the Available Resources.

In order to formulate action strategies, the advocate will want to
assess the resources that can be brought to bear on the client's situation, the community problem, or the policy issue in question. Resources and strengths of the client will need to be determined. How
committed is the youngster to resolving the problem? What skills and

insights does the client possess that will be useful in bringing about change? At the community or class level what strengths does the impacted client group have to offer? How can members of the group be involved in a meaningful way? The more the client or client group is involved, the greater their stake and sense of ownership of any resolution. Client involvement will also mean that the problem-solving skills and relationships developed in this particular situation can be drawn upon to prevent or deal with other problems that inevitably will occur in the future.

In addition to assessing client or client group resources, the advocate will want to look at the resources of the client's social network or the group's relationship with other potentially supportive groups and actors. It there a significant adult whom the youth trusts and respects? Are there other groups in the community or in the state experiencing similar problems? Are there natural allies due to geographic or community identification?

5. Assessing the Political Scene.

Just as it is important to know the environment in terms of resources and to clearly identify targets for change, it is equally vital to know the environment politically. Who is likely to support what position? Who is likely to oppose it? Here we are looking not only at individuals but also at interest groups. Who has a stake in maintaining things as they are, and who has a stake in making changes? What do people have to win or lose? Are there swing groups? These will typically be individuals and groups in formal decision-making roles who have little interest in the issue per se but will have a considerable stake in how programs are administered or monies distributed (Miller, Ohlin & Coates, 1977).

Have local citizens organized in the past to defeat similar proposals? How did they fight politically? These questions need to be addressed before one selects advocacy strategies. Answers will provide indicators of the political climate, forces, and type of oppositional maneuvering that one will likely encounter.

Most of this information can be obtained by carefully analyzing a community's local newspapers for the past six months or a year. More detail can be gained by talking with key people within the infrastructure of the community. Members of each advocacy group will have experiences and perceptions to draw upon. However, it is typically not wise to rest solely upon an individual's or group's preconceived judgments, because they will likely be colored by the importance of a particular issue. A study identifying factors related to successfully setting up group homes showed that agencies having long experience with a community were as likely to fail as agencies that did not have such experience (Coates & Miller, 1973). This failure was explained in part by agencies being overly confident that they had support and knew their communities well. They may have known pieces of the community very well, but their vision was so narrow that they had neither anticipated nor prepared to do the kind of community mobilization work required to set up a new program.

Will new or emerging groups have a stake in the planned change? A classic example of emergent group involvement in class advocacy can be found in the Massachusetts deinstitutionalization effort. The restructured system relied extensively on private providers for services previously provided by state employees. Some of the private agencies had existed for years, many were newly established, and most were new to the delinquency field. Within a brief period the private sector became a major force for maintaining the restructured system, preventing a significant shift back to the training schools. It had been given an opportunity to develop a stake in the new system. This stake was not only developed around economics although that was obviously important; it was formulated on a philosophy of and commitment to how best to intervene in the lives of the delinquents.

In Vermont, the governor and many legislatures developed stakes in a deinstitutionalization effort, in part because of what they believed could be done with the old training school. Plans had been set in motion to implement a Job Corps training program at that location as soon as the Department of Corrections could remove its clients. The campaign theme for the governor and for others had been "Jobs for Vermonters."

6. Developing and Implementing Advocacy Strategies.

Having gathered useful information regarding the problem or issue, the client or client group, and the political environment, the advocate must develop a range of alternative advocacy strategies. Advocates will want to be particularly aware of leverage, negotiating stance, use of power, timing, and selection.

Leverage entails getting the attention of the key decision makers at whom advocacy efforts are directed. In part, it informs them as to how we justify our involvement in the case. It also suggests trying to find something that may have been overlooked in the client's general situation that could be helpful in getting the decision maker to act or alter a prior decision. For example, a probation officer's background check on a youngster may not have been thorough enough to turn up the fact that an uncle living two blocks away from the youth's home is willing to see that the youth attends school and is willing to intercede on his behalf within the school setting. Or it may be that a neighbor is willing to hire the youngster part-time so that he/she can earn money for restitution purposes. It may be that the advocate's presence and case are justified by the regulations governing the agency whose actions are under question. For example, a client has been detained in isolation for forty-eight hours. Or a client who is in the Department of Corrections has been denied family visits for three months. These kinds of actions are likely to run counter to the formal regulations governing the agency, thereby justifying the involvement of an outside advocate.

Leverage also involves relationships. If individual advocates have relationships with key persons in schools, the business world, and the juvenile justice system, they will be able to use those relationships as legitimate entries to the systems involved. The extent to which this can be done depends on the level of trust and respect developed over time. Boards of directors of advocacy programs can also foster leverage and legitimacy. If an advocacy program has the president of the local PTA on its board, access to the school may be easier and perceived as more legitimate. The same could be said of local businessmen, police, and other juvenile justice officials. An important caveat here is not to overload boards with juvenile justice personnel to the point that the advocacy program becomes too close to the official system. It is important to build bridges, but advocacy efforts can be co-opted easily if those ties are too binding.

Bringing resources to bear on the client, getting a teacher to respond somewhat differently to a youngster, having the parent implement a different set of techniques of punishing and rewarding the client will involve negotiations—often delicate negotiation. In cases that are not clear-cut violation of laws or regulations, bringing about change will essentially mean changing the view and behavior of the responsible decision maker, be it teacher, parent, or judge. Advocates are seldom in a position of possessing enough overt power to dramatically alter the situation. They will most likely be in a position to try to influence, entice, and cajole. Change will come about if they can change points of view and provide enough stake in the proposed change so the decision maker may have something to gain or at least have little to lose. In other words, advocates must be keenly aware of the politics of the situation and how the suggested change impinges upon those politics.

These comments suggest that often the advocate must be something other than the stereotype one who rails against the system, who defends the client right or wrong, who sees things in absolutes and in clear-cut rights and wrongs. The advocate must be a prodder and a catalyst but need not view all who disagree as adversaries. Perlman (1979:194) describes this aspect of the advocacy role quite aptly:

> If he (significant other) is openly resistive, we need to take care to act in full awareness that being our client's advocate does not mean we are thereby the other's adversary. Rather, our task is to draw him into a shared, partway advocate position. This means, then, that such annoyance or counterhostility that his behavior may rouse in us be put on ice until later, and that our attitude must be one that expresses, "I can see how you feel, even though . . . "

One of the most important strategies for negotiating is to "take the role of the other," looking at the situation from the other's point of view. How will the proposed change affect that person's world? What will cause problems for him? For example, what are the likely consequences perceived by a school administrator when group home staff try to convince him/her to accept three of its charges in the public school? It is not simply a matter that these young people have a right to a public education. The administrator may very well respond that the potential acting-out behavior of the youths prohibits the other students from exercising their rights to an education. While it is important to debate ethical issues, mere intellectual or ideological debate is unlikely to move the issue very far. What is needed is to get down to the pragmatics of the situation. What can be done to assure that group home staff will work with the school to prevent such acting-out behavior or to intervene in ways that will be accepted by the school system as supportive and timely? If there is a major incident will staff be available immediately to school personnel? Will staff be willing to sit down with the concerned teacher to discuss the youngster's home environment to determine how the school fits into the youngster's overall situation? Will staff be able to augment the teacher's efforts by providing individual education attention to the youths after school? Is there empathy on the part of advocates and staff for the teacher whose task of teaching thirty pupils may be made even more difficult by adding students who have already had less than satisfactory school experiences.

Power should be used efficiently in each advocacy type. In this business there is no need for overkill. Conditions and issues change; persons who are opponents on an issue one month may be the best of allies on a different issue the next month. If the same job can be done by applying some general pressure without publicly embarrassing an individual, why choose the latter course? One of the facts often overlooked by advocacy groups is that many issues have considerable room for honest differences of opinion. Reflecting on these differences should not necessarily be equated with personal betrayal.

Similarly, the act of compromise, a much maligned art, has a place in advocacy. It is often said, "Why settle for half a loaf?" The question is "Would you settle for three quarters?" And even half a loaf may be far better than a crumb. To a youngster who wants to make some money, a job with a fast-food chain may not be as good as a job that would launch a career, but it is better than none. This does not mean that we should discontinue working with other kinds of employment opportunities; it means that we take what we can get and then try for more.

The best-laid plans and strategies can go awry because of poor timing. One cannot overstate the importance of knowing the appropriate time to move. In order to know when to take a given action, one must have adequate information about the politics of the environment in which change is being sought. Has the father or mother taken on a new, demanding job making it more difficult to find the time to get involved in the youngster's situation? Does the relationship between husband and wife need shoring up before they can advocate effectively for their child? Is the decision maker embroiled in other administrative matters such as budgets? How strong politically is the decision maker? Could he/she use the support of anyone, including a juvenile justice child advocate? In other words, how does the desired change fit into the ongoing tugs and pulls of the system, be it family, school, or court? Who may possibly lose and gain from the change, and are these losses or gains related to timing of action? In some cases timing of action is obvious. One would not normally try to enroll a child who has been away from school for some time in public school in the month of May. One would most likely look for a summer program and seek enrollment for the fall.

When considering timing for community and class advocacy efforts, close attention must be given to the needs of the internal interest group coalition as well as to the conditions of the external environment.

To act before the interest group coalition is prepared or ready can be suicidal. Individuals and subgroups can be separated and played off against each other by an astute outsider. However, moving too slowly can be equally destructive. Group members will need to see a result, even if it only consists of movement or action. Some of these results may only increase immediate tension or conflict with outside groups yet have a solidifying effect for the interest group coalition. The group can obviously benefit from such results only for so long without jeopardizing the achievement of its primary advocacy goals. The advocate must remember that all members of the coalition are not committed equally to the task at hand. Strategies that take too long to unfold or that yield minimal results will become tedious and boring for the membership. And tedium can lead to self-destruction of the coalition.

These concerns with internal interest group relationships must, of course, be considered in the context of the external environment. A series of escapes from the local detention will no doubt prompt concern for public safety. Advocates can take the opportunity to link public safety with the need to look at the quality of life in the center, to argue for improvement of its program, or to press the issue of decentralizing the detaining of youngsters to counter conditions of overcrowding.

Timing should involve a review of all the data at hand including the case that has been documented to support the advocacy coalition's position, its political strengths and vulnerabilities, sources of opposition and their strengths and weaknesses, and the chances of successfully carrying out the advocacy strategies. Upon review, the best decision may be to decide to withdraw and fight another day. Particularly at the level of the local community, to move against insurmountable odds may be more ruinous for the causes of advocacy than not to act at all. The dilemma for the local advocacy group is constant; to bring about change yet to be in a position to continue monitoring and impacting the system.

Advocacy strategies must be selected in the context of specific issues and political situations reflecting the depth and experience of the advocacy group. Specific strategies should be appropriate to the issue, the audience, and the skills of the advocates. What kinds of information are likely to sway the decision makers? For the administrator, it may be information that will make life easier; conversely, it may be information that clearly shows the advocacy group is capable of making life much more difficult if changes are not brought about. For the legislator, the information may have to be tied to cost-efficiency arguments or to votes. Some administrators and some legislators will be persuaded by the merits of the arguments in terms of what is best for young people; these persons still need supporting information to be supplied in a clear and precise manner so they can use the information to influence others.

Reasonable expectations about the strategies and tactics to be used by a particular advocacy group are important. Some groups will not be comfortable with direct-confrontation politics but will prefer to sift though disparate data concerning an issue, weighing the pros and cons and issuing white papers to be distributed to influentials. Others will prefer to attack an issue by supporting class action suits. Still others will engage the political machinery ranging from boardroom politics to politics of the streets. The advocate organizer runs considerable risks by expecting the group to operate outside of its own skills and experience (Alinsky, 1971). An underlying assumption here is that a range of strategies and tactics is appropriate and each strategy may actually derive some benefit from the other.

A major pitfall even for experienced advocates is using the same tactics and strategies over and over again. Two obvious results are that (1) opposition forces can easily predict what is likely to occur and will thereby be in a better position to defend, (2) members of advocacy groups will become bored with the same routines. Perhaps less obvious is that strategies and tactics used in one place and one time period may be quite inappropriate in a new location and time. Professional groups that were opposed to deinstitutionalization efforts in one state may be neutral or favorable in another. For example, the social work community was skeptical and at times oppositional to the deinstitutionalization effort in youth services in Massachusetts, while in Utah many of the key reform advocates were social workers. If the advocate assumes, based on past experience, that a group will be opposed a potential support base will have been ignored if not alienated to the extent that it will line up in the opposition's camp (Dear & Patti, 1981:282).

Once strategies have been selected and begun, it will still be necessary to continue being flexible, to continually assess the results of the efforts, and to be prepared to modify entirely or discard specific strategies. One of the worst things that can happen to an advocate or an advocacy group is to become convinced that a particular strategy or tactic is "right".

7. Follow-Up.

Probably the most frequently overlooked step of advocacy is follow-up. Have the desired results actually occurred? When an employer has been convinced to give a youth a chance at a job, is the advocacy task over? No! The case advocate must be available for the youngster or the employer to call if difficulties arise. It is crucial to check back in a couple of days and then weeks to see how things are going. If nothing else, the employer, the teacher who takes a risk, the parent who is struggling to change, and the youth who is trying to be more than a ping-pong ball deserve a pat on the back; quite likely they will need even more. Regardless, most rewards in this field are intrinsic. The teacher will not get paid extra to teach a child who lives in a group home. Providing simple praise and recognition where deserved not only is the decent thing to do, it can go a long way toward creating opportunities for other youth.

Too often, when checking back, one will discover that good intention has been lost in the paperwork or has been overwhelmed by the pressures of meeting the needs of a lot of other people. One may very well have to apply additional gentle pressure, devise new strategies for the situation, or involve other persons. The case that "ended" may have just begun.

Follow-up is equally significant with community and class advocacy. Hard-won changes can evaporate quickly if there is no continued attention to or awareness of the situation. At the community level, it may be useful to have members of the advocacy group involved in committees established to monitor the planned change. This may mean representatives working on committees within the school or on review boards with the police department. This kind of supportive activity can also build the kinds of relationships needed to be in a better-informed and respected position to continue doing advocacy in the future.

Class advocacy is also a continuous process. Simply having a particular policy reflected in legislative packages is not enough. If one is successful with an authorization bill, one must then be concerned that monies are actually designated for that purpose in the appropriations bill. If successful at that point, one still must follow up to be certain that the executive agency's expenditure of monies is consistent with the intent of the legislation (Sosin, 1979:265).

And what about reform efforts? If there is any truism about reform it is "nothing is written in stone"—as it properly should not be. Today's *reform* may very well be the target of tomorrow's *reform*. The issue of deinstitutionalization provides an excellent example of the need for follow-up. Deinstitutionalization is largely an "anti" movement (anti-institution and anti–medical model). However, getting youths out of institutions is not the sole purpose of this particular youth policy. As discovered in Massachusetts, Vermont, and Utah, concerned advocates must turn their attention to the new system. Is it providing a more humane set of experiences than the former? Is the new system really community based? How is the new system being circumvented? How can the new system be monitored? How can it be improved (Coates, Miller, & Ohlin, 1978: Massachusetts Advocacy Center, 1980)? Reform efforts do not come to a neat conclusion. They are embroiled within political and professional conflicts bringing about a fairly constant ebb and flow of reform and retrenchment. Thus, the class advocacy task is seldom if ever finished.

SUMMARY AND CONCLUSION

The continuing place of advocacy in juvenile justice remains somewhat precarious due in part to confusion about its intent and its method of practice. In an attempt to provide some clarity to the conceiving and doing of advocacy, a conceptual framework is presented to explain types of advocacy and to set forth principles and steps for advocacy practice.

In my view, advocacy has always had a place in juvenile justice. Its salience has ebbed and flowed with the times. The 1970s were a decade when advocacy, at least in name if not always in practice, emerged formally and was explicitly acknowledged by professions in the field and by funding agencies. The 1980s thus far have witnessed a retrenchment. However, acting on behalf of clients and client interests is a theme historically embedded in social work and other helping professions generally and in juvenile justice specifically. Sharpening our understanding of advocacy in terms of its justification, forms, and practice should provide a stronger, more legitimate foundation for advocacy within juvenile justice. This will no doubt be an ongoing process.

The three types of advocacy described above differ with regard to client populations served, arenas, activities, and goals. They share, however, much in common. The steps of the advocacy process for all three types are quite parallel. These generic steps include (1) defining and justifying the problem or issue, (2) identifying the desired change, (3) identifying change targets, (4) assessing resources, (5) assessing the political environment, (6) developing and implementing strategies, and (7) following up advocacy efforts to assure that outcomes continue.

Qualitative aspects of advocacy practice are equally important to each type of advocacy. These include (1) involvement of client(s) as advocates, (2) viewing the process and obstacles from other persons' perspectives, (3) providing supporters and opponents with a stake in the proposed changes, and (4) engaging in realistic conflict when necessary while avoiding unrealistic or symbolic conflict.

The direction of policy and practice in juvenile justice during the coming decades can be influenced significantly by social workers and others engaged in advocacy. These advocates can play meaningful roles in defining issues, facilitating change, and assuring that quality services are indeed delivered to youths in trouble. The risks associated with doing advocacy are real; not becoming engaged seriously in advocacy would pose even greater risks for our youth and our society.

DISCUSSION QUESTIONS

1. Define and illustrate the three types of advocacy.
2. Describe how "taking the role of the other" can facilitate advocacy efforts.
3. Discuss and illustrate the importance of timing for each of the three advocacy types.

4. You have been assigned the task of establishing a group home in your local community. Describe the advocacy steps you would take to enhance the probability of the group home's acceptance.

5. You are a clinical worker in a diversion program. You have been assigned the case of a thirteen-year-old boy who is experiencing difficulties in school, especially reading problems. He has also come to the attention of police for curfew violations. The police describe him as hanging out with delinquent youths. What kinds of additional information would you need in order to develop an individual case advocacy plan? How would you obtain that information?

6. Indicate how the need for class advocacy could be made by working with social workers involved in individual-case advocacy efforts.

REFERENCES

Ad Hoc Committee on Advocacy. (1969). The social worker as advocate: Champion of social victims, *Social Work, 14,* 6–22.

Alinsky, S., (1971). *Rules for radicals.* New York: Random House.

Berman, H. T., & Greiner, W. R. (1972). *The nature and functions of law.* Mineola, NY: Foundation Press.

Brager, G. A. (1958). Advocacy and political behavior. *Social Work, 13.* 5–16.

Briar, S. (1967). The current crisis in social casework. In *Social work practice* (pp. 19–33). Selected papers from the 94th Annual Forum of the National Conference of Social Welfare. New York: Columbia University Press.

Bruno, F. T. (1957). *Trends in social work, 1874–1956.* New York: Columbia University Press.

Coates, R. B., & Miller, A. D. (1973). Neutralization of community resistence to group homes. In Y. Bakal, *Closing correctional institutions* (pp. 67–84). Lexington, MA: Lexington Books.

Coates, R. B., Miller, A.D., & Ohlin, L. E. (1978). *Diversity in a youth correctional system: Handling delinquents in Massachusetts.* Cambridge, MA: Ballinger.

Coser, L. (1956). *Functions of social conflict.* New York: Free Press.

Dear, R. B. & Patti, R. J. (1981). Legislative advocacy: Seven effective tactics. *Social Work, 26,* 289–295.

Fischer, J. (1978). *Effective casework practice: An eclectic approach.* New York: McGraw-Hill.

Kutchins, H. & Kutchins, S. (1978). Advocacy and social work. In G. H. Weber & G. J. McCall, (Eds.), *Social scientists as advocates.* Beverly Hills, CA: Sage Publications.

Massachusetts Advocacy Center. (1980). *Delinquent justice: Juvenile detention practice in Massachusetts.* Boston: Massachusetts Advocacy Center.

Miller, A. D., Ohlin, L. E., & Coates, R. B., (1977). *A theory of social reform: Correctional change processes in two states.* Cambridge, MA: Ballinger.

Morales v. *Turman,* 383 Federal Supplement 53 (1974).

Perlman, H. H. (1979). *Relationship: The heart of helping people.* Chicago: University of Chicago Press.

Richmond, M. (1922). *What is social casework?* New York: Russell Sage Foundation.

Scurfield, R. M. (1980). An integrated approach to case services and social reform. *Social Casework, 61,* 610–618.

Sosin, M. (1979). Social work advocacy and the implementation of legal mandates, *Social Casework, 60,* 265–273.

Sosin, M., & Caulum, S. (1983). Advocacy: A conceptualization for social work practice. *Social Work, 28,* 12–17.

Towle, C. (1954). *The learner in education for the professions: As seen in education for social work.* Chicago: University of Chicago Press.

Woodroofe, K. (1974). *From charity to social work in England and the United States.* Toronto: University of Toronto Press.

Epilogue

Chapter Thirteen

The Future of Corrections in Juvenile Justice

Robert B. Coates

ABSTRACT

This chapter sets forth six issue areas that will continue to shape the future of juvenile corrections. The issues are set forth in terms of polarities that so often characterize related policy debates. The issues are (1) institutions versus community-based programs, (2) rehabilitation versus punishment, (3) rehabilitation: a meaningful goal or an albatross, (4) determinate versus indeterminate release, (5) victim versus offender, and (6) private versus public sector administration of programs. We contend here, that once one looks beyond the rhetoric there is more compatibility among these polarities than is usually envisioned. How we deal with these apparent polarities will have a profound influence on the shape of juvenile correctional policies in the future.

INTRODUCTION

Trying to detect the future of corrections in juvenile justice is a task similar to trying to detect a clear image in a mirror that has splintered into a thousand thin lines. This piece is designed to address some of the issues and nuances that will shape that future rather than to attempt to predict it.

The issues that will shape the future of corrections in juvenile justice can be identified partially by reflecting upon recent history. In the past two and one-half decades we have experienced the push for diversion, deinstitutionalization, and community-based corrections. We have also seen moves toward passage of violent-offenders bills, set length of institutional stays to replace indeterminate release, and the questioning of rehabilitation as a meaningful goal of corrections.

These apparent contradictions in desired policy are not as contradictory as they might seem on the surface. The environment that would allow them to coexist and strengthen each other, however, is one of a delicate balance. This environment and consequent balance is seldom achieved, in part, because as a field we continue to emphasize rhetoric, polarities, and unrealistic expectations.

This Epilogue is divided into six parts. Each discusses a polarized issue that is likely to continue to shape the future of juvenile corrections. The polarities are (1) institutions versus community-based programs, (2) rehabilitation versus punishment, (3) rehabilitation: a meaningful goal or an albatross, (4) determinate versus indeterminate release, (5) victim versus offender, and (6) private versus public sector administration of programs. The debate and resolution of these issues has had and will continue to have a profound impact on the practice of social work.

In its beginnings, the profession of social work was closely related with corrections. As social work developed through the years, social work training and social work leadership tended to shy away from corrections. Yet many social work graduates continue to practice their profession within the corrections arena. The polarized issues listed above strike frequently at the ethos of social work. Many of the critiques underlying the debates are sound and are suggestive of changes needed within social work practice and education. Some critiques go to the core of the social work mission and need to be addressed responsibly within the arena of social work.

INSTITUTIONS VERSUS COMMUNITY-BASED PROGRAMS

Debates continue to rage regarding the relative merits of institutions and community-based programs (Klein, 1979; Sarri, 1981), as if one must support one approach over the other as a policy. Depending upon the case, either approach is described as unworthy of further investment of scarce resources. But the question is one of needs within a given state. It is important to determine how many youths from a treatment and social control perspective should be worked with while in a secure setting, a semi-restrictive setting, an open group home setting, a foster care setting, or their own homes.

Massachusetts, Pennsylvania, Vermont, and Utah are among those states that have gone the furthest under the banner of deinstitutionalization (Coates, Miller, & Ohlin, 1978; Schwartz, 1984). In each of those states, secure care remains a viable option for some youths. The institution may be small in size and located closer to the youth's home than the old training schools, but these newer facilities are none-the-less institutions. They are small, secure, and typically packed with programmatic options (Kelner, 1985).

In these states, the debate regarding institutions is framed around questions of for whom and for what purpose. Secure care facilities are reserved for youth who have committed violent offenses or who have a long history with other program alternatives within the correctional system. Most of the youth in secure care, even those who have committed serious offenses, have been worked with first in less restrictive programs. A fundamental purpose of these secure facilities is community protection. However, short-term community protection is not obtained without regard for long-term community protection; that is, these facilities incorporate extensive program options (Kelner, 1985).

The key to making secure facilities work without overwhelming the system is the range and richness of other program settings. To the extent that group homes, foster care, wilderness programs, tracking programs, and other nonresidential programs exist, the pressure on secure care is reduced. Where such a range of program alternatives does not exist, secure care becomes a matter of first choice rather than last.

Despite the relatively positive influence of deinstitutionalization efforts in several states, during the late 1970s and early 1980s, the number of youths incarcerated in detention centers and training schools nationally actually increased:

> With a few notable exceptions, there continues to be a heavy reliance on the use of detention centers and training schools. Despite a declining youth population, declining serious juvenile crime rates, and the relatively high costs and limited benefits of institutional care, the number of juveniles incarcerated on a given day in detention centers and training schools is increasing. Also, juveniles are being confined in such facilities for longer periods of time. There is no solid evidence that these policies of increased juvenile incapacitation are positively affecting public safety. Incarceration policies are largely unrelated to rates of serious youth crime. (Krisberg, Schwartz, Litsky, & Austin, 1986)

In part, the debate about institutions and community-based programs occurs because of little attention to and little agreement about what is meant conceptually when we use the term *community-based corrections* (Doeren & Hageman, 1982; Felton & Shinn, 1981). Community-based corrections is not new. It has a long history, dating at least back to the beginnings of probation and parole. In the late 1960s and 1970s, however, community corrections began to incorporate much more extensive use of residential programs: group homes and halfway houses. By the early 1970s, most states could boast of their model community-based programs for juvenile offenders, and many states were experimenting with such programs for adult offenders (Vinter, Downs, & Hall, 1975). Yet there remained little consensus on what was meant by "community-based."

With only probation and parole as community based, it was fairly easy, on the surface, to distinguish between community-based and institution-based corrections. As group homes and halfway houses developed, it remained common to describe them as community based, with little interest in whether any empirical differences actually existed between these small residential settings and the larger residential settings of training schools. Many observers, however, began to question the easy acceptance of such differences. Even though they were smaller and perhaps less remote geographically, we soon discovered that the small group homes and halfway houses could be just as institutional as the large training schools.

Only recently have we begun to focus on what constitutes community linkage—a notion implied in the term *community-based*. Two perspectives on community linkage provide us with initial steps toward differentiating community-based and institution-based programs. The first focuses on organizational linkages with the community. For example, how many local persons are on the program's board? How many resources are derived from the local community rather than from state or federal sources? How many local residents participate in the program as volunteers? What is the nature of the program catchment area (Spergel, Korbelik, Reamer, Lynch, & Alexander, 1979)? The second perspective focuses on the experiences of the client. To what extent are clients linked with community resources? What is the nature of interaction between program clients and community residents or community organizations? This perspective sets forth the position that

> a key set of variables that provides a basis for differentiating among programs is the extent and quality of relationships between program staff, clients and the community in which the program is located. (If clients come from outside the program community itself, relationships need to be considered with the community in which the program is located and the community from which the client comes or to which the client will return.) The nature of these client and staff relationships with the community provides the underpinning for a continuum of services ranging from the least to the most community based. Generally, as frequency, duration, and quality of community-relationships increase, the program becomes more community based. (Coates, et al., 1978:7)

This framework for looking at the "community-based" concept was combined with social climate concerns (client relationships with staff and with other clients) to provide the structure for a "normalization–institutionalization" continuum allowing for assessment of over a hundred programs. Great differentiation was found among program types. For example, some group homes were as institution-like as some of the secure care facilities (Coates, et al., 1978). Group homes that scored well on the continuum generally were small in size (no more than eight to ten youths), had youths in program components outside the home (for example, school, recreation, and vocational training), had staff who were not only caring, but also willing and able to advocate for their program's youths in the community, and typically emphasized youth participation in decisions affecting the youths and the home.

We anticipate that the two perspectives on community linkage—the organizational perspective and the client perspective—may be empirically related. That is, does increased participation of local community residents serve to increase client linkage? Some preliminary research directed at the compatibility of these two perspectives suggests that they are positively related (Altschuler, 1983).

Without clear conceptual ideas about that which we debate, any ensuing discussion quickly dissipates to an exchange of ideology. Furthermore and perhaps much more important, without clear conceptualization there is little that can be used to guide policy decision making. There is little basis for guiding program development, contracting with private agencies, or maintaining quality control.

REHABILITATION VERSUS PUNISHMENT

Rehabilitation is a horse badly beaten, but not yet dead and very unlikely to die. The rehabilitative ideal is attacked by some who perceive it as coddling offenders without providing punishment (Van den Haag, 1975). Others attack the notion of rehabilitation because they perceive it as incorporating insidious elements of social control and punishment (Greenberg, 1972). And, of course, many denigrate rehabilitation efforts because "nothing works" regardless of the presence or absence of punitive elements (Lipton, Martinson, & Wilks, 1975). This latter issue will be addressed later. Here let us focus on rehabilitation and punishment.

My position, perhaps unpopular with some social workers, is that rehabilitation in theory and in practice is closely tied to and contains aspects of social control and is frequently regarded as punitive by clients who experience it. To me the question is not whether rehabilitation and punishment are opposites (they are not) but rather what is the nature and extent of the punishing experience within any rehabilitative effort? Furthermore, as human service providers are we aware of the power and the extent of social control that we wield? Social control is part and parcel of the socialization process; if exercised appropriately, it can be a necessary and positive influence. In the hands of the well meaning, but unaware, the social control and punitive element of rehabilitation can be counterproductive and potentially damaging.

In the hands of the aware and ill intentioned, it can lead to devastation and abuse of human life and social relationships. It is this powerful potential of rehabilitation efforts for rebirth and for destruction that make them potentially both good and evil.

The debate, rehabilitation versus punishment, is often misdirected by focusing on the extremes to support ideological positions. Perhaps we would move further by directing our attention to what are appropriate societal responses to particular offenses or offenders, incorporating the need to punish and hold persons accountable for their acts while at the same time offering some long-term hope for restoration of the offender to the community.

In this context, one might better be able to consider a range of alternative responses. For example, suppose an individual has been convicted for a second burglary. We may decide that the individual is best punished and held accountable by sending him to a minimum-security institution with an excellent job training program. Or we may decide that because such an institution does not exist in our state, restoration and rehabilitation are important, but we do not want the offender to lose sight of making right his wrong. In this instance, we may sentence the offender to a nonresidential job training program, to 350 hours of community service, and to a victim–offender mediation program where personal restitution may be considered for the victim.

Punishment can be fitted not only to meet the crime but to meet the needs of the community and the offender (in terms of restoration) in the context of what is available in a particular jurisdiction. In judicial systems where such discretion is allowed, it is common practice to weigh sentencing alternatives. In recent years the private sector has actively engaged in working with defense attorneys and public defenders to draw up alternative sentencing plans containing strong punitive sanctions but reducing the necessity for extended jail time. The National Center for Institutional Alternatives has probably done the most to popularize this notion and carry out this work on a national level (Ranii, 1981).

An example of alternative sentencing can be seen in a case originating in Indiana. A seventeen-year-old youth was charged along with two codefendants (one juvenile and one adult) on three counts of burglary (Class B felonies). The youth had had only one former conviction, that of theft. This particular case was waived to the adult court, but the juvenile court retained jurisdiction for dispositional purposes. As an adult, the defendant was faced with a maximum sentence of 20 years.

The youth had a good part-time mechanic's job and was within three months of graduation from high school. He had very good work references as well as good references from his shop teacher. During the time between his guilty pleas and the dispositional hearing, the defendant voluntarily participated in victim–offender mediation meetings where he agreed to provide restitution to each of the victims. The alternative sentencing plan that was submitted and accepted contained (1) a suspended sentence with 30 days of local jail time to be served during consecutive weekends after graduation from high school, (2) successful restitution to the victims, (3) 180 hours of unpaid community service (an appropriate site and supervision was worked out by the persons putting together the plan), and (4) adult probation for a period of four years. The plan was presented as "an alternative set of punishments" that offered more benefit to society, the victims, and the offender than did traditional incarceration.

To deny the place of punishment within rehabilitation is as absurd as assuming that the best response to all offenders is jail. I suspect that many of us involved in rehabilitation efforts inside and outside of the corrections arena acknowledge the punitive elements of rehabilitation in our guts—but we do not like to admit it professionally. Somehow it does not sound professional. Social workers in corrections receive a poor reputation within the profession because such work is tainted by the explicit punitive characteristics of corrections. Some wonder why social work as a profession even bothers to teach about social work in corrections. Clearly the punitive element of rehabilitation is more explicit within corrections, but is it nonexistent in other settings (including private practice, where treatment is supposedly more purely voluntary in nature)? What about the couple who seek assistance with a child's behavior problems and with whom the therapist works to set up a reasonable, humane set of clear expectations and sanctions? Punishment is a bad word. We prefer to talk about behavior controls, environmental constraints, milieu therapy, ego strengthening, negative reinforcements, or withholding positive reinforcements. Yet it would appear that each of these phrases captures at least in part the intent of modifying behavior through a combination of positive supports and the threat of negative consequences and/or withdrawal of positive supports: that is, punitive actions.

REHABILITATION: A MEANINGFUL GOAL OR AN ALBATROSS?

Rehabilitation has become a much maligned goal of corrections. In debate it has given way to the litany that "nothing works" (Lipton et al., 1975) and to the idea of selective incapacitation. Yet, in practice, rehabilitative goals remain much in force. The "nothing works" argument, supposedly based upon empirical research results, has probably had more far-ranging impact within academic and funding circles. Within academia there has been much discussion about the death of rehabilitation (Allen, 1981; Wilson, 1975). But voices of disagreement can be found even there. Some argue for rehabilitation approaches from a philosophical and theoretical stance (Cullen & Gilbert, 1982). The nature of personhood, the responsibility of society for its members, and the nature of personal and social change are raised. Others take strong issue with the empirical base for the nothing-works contention (Gottfredson, 1979). Is the nothing-works position based upon a strange mixture of apples, oranges, and lemons? Is it reasonable for social programs to have strengths and weaknesses? Is it possible to use research to strengthen intervention approaches? And is it possible that researchers still need to refine their questions and their measurements?

The debate has had its impact upon practice, forcing practitioners to be even more thoughtful in developing intervention strategies. There is more awareness of the importance of informed evaluation and research. And lowered expectations of rehabilitation have taken some of the pressure off the practitioner. The most negative impact has been the erosion of resources for rehabilitation. But it is not clear whether this erosion is due largely to questions about the efficacy of rehabilitation or to the general economic times.

The debate about the value of rehabilitation has had considerable positive effects on rehabilitation efforts. More attention is being directed at how caseworkers and others can have positive impact on the client and on the client's social network (Hawkins & Fraser, 1983). Research has demonstrated that short-run gains in residential programs can be quickly eroded as the youngster moves back to his community setting (Coates et al., 1978; Klein, 1979; Miller & Ohlin, 1985; Whittaker, 1979).

Practitioners in many states are devoting more thought and resources to the transition period, when youths move back to their home environments. The Georgia youth corrections system is restructuring in a way that will give the case manager control of an individual case as the youth moves through community-based and institutional programs (M. Young, personal communication, 1984). The Utah youth corrections system is now developing new programs and approaches to this critical transition phase (Utah Division of Youth Corrections, 1986). There is a growing recognition that professional workers cannot do the job alone; that systemic changes are as important as changes in insight; and that systemic change will occur only when professionals work in concert with others in the youth's network. For example, families traditionally have been viewed as a primary source of the delinquency problem, and significant lasting change often requires focusing intervention strategies on the family system. (A detailed review of family treatment approaches and intervention techniques is provided in Chapter 11.) In short, the scope of rehabilitation has been enlarged beyond the individual client.

For practitioners and many state policymakers, rehabilitation remains a goal worth pursuing. These groups may be more realistic in their expectations than in the past, but they remain no less committed to the hope of being able to improve the lives and life circumstances of the young people with whom they work. For these persons, the "albatross" would be dismissing the challenge and giving up the hope that persons can and do change.

DETERMINATE VERSUS INDETERMINATE RELEASE

During the late 1970s and early 1980s, juvenile justice has experienced some significant shifts away from the original purposes of the juvenile court and juvenile corrections. An experiment taking place in various ways in a fair number of states is that of determinate sentencing. Numerous states have by statute adopted determinate sentencing policies for serious or violent offenders, and several states have now either adopted determinate sentence statutes or created administrative release guidelines that establish explicit times or ranges of time to be served by delinquents who have committed an act that would be a crime if committed by an adult (Forst, Fisher, & Coates, 1985).

These policies contradict some of the basic assumptions of the original juvenile court: that juvenile offenders should be handled quite differently from adult offenders, that the juvenile court and youth corrections are designed to operate in the best interest of the child, that the objective of the juvenile justice system is rehabilitation of the youth and not applying fixed time of punishment, and that rehabilitation is an open-ended process requiring treatment of each youth as an individual, thus "time served," as it were, is indeterminate depending on the successful rehabilitation of the youth.

Determinate sentencing has received support from at least three rather disparate groups. First, there are those who believe that youth must be held more accountable and punished for their delinquent acts, particularly acts of a violent nature or acts against the person. We have heard expressed the desire to "get tough," to block the revolving door of our correctional facilities, to stem the "wave" of juvenile crime; these are the code words of some who push for determinate sentencing policies for juveniles. A second group, traditionally in opposition to the get-tough group, consists of persons who are very skeptical about the juvenile justice system's ability to fulfill its original mandate to rehabilitate. Because these skeptics question the justice system's ability to rehabilitate, they cannot justify holding a youth in an institution solely for treatment purposes. They desire set sentences in order to place parameters on how long treatment personnel can hold onto a youth. And they support determinate sentences that do not exceed the amount of time an adult would receive for committing the same offense. Still a third group has pushed for determinate sentencing from a legal rights perspective. These persons are interested in promoting equal justice. That is, youths who commit serious crimes should be institutionalized for longer periods of time than those who commit relatively minor crimes. Clearly, individuals from these three groups may not share a common language nor common goals, but one result of their collective positions is a focus on determinate sentencing. None of these positions has by any means won the day; they continue to be debated even in those states that have adopted such policies. And they are heatedly disputed in those states that fear their adoption.

A recent five-year study of indeterminate and determinate release procedures in selected states suggests that determinate release policies are not necessarily as divergent from the traditional objectives of the juvenile courts and corrections as might be expected (Coates, Fisher, & Forst, 1985). While treatment personnel were initially fearful of the consequences of set time for rehabilitation objectives, the time parameters constraining interventions have led to creative program development. Treatment programs are now more likely to be designed in modules and tailored to the individual youth. Staff indicate that much of the pressure of trying to convince a parole board of a youth's progress is now relieved. And because release dates are set early, upon a youth's admission to the program, planning for release and aftercare has become a priority.

When comparing determinate and indeterminate systems, length of time served was more proportional with the crime committed in the former. And more explicit, formal safeguards such as hearings were present in the determinate states.

The debate about indeterminacy and determinacy has had subtle effects on many indeterminate states. Efforts are being made to implement more safeguards in these states. Still, many staff in the traditional indeterminate states remain firmly convinced that progress toward goals rather than time served should determine release (Coates et al., 1985).

Determinate policies must be closely monitored and reviewed. If they are not implemented very carefully, one consequence is overcrowding. Appropriate lengths of stay must take into consideration available resources. Length of stay in some instances will include both residential and nonresidential settings. Thus, in terms of program and security levels, the mix of programs is closely related to the successful implementation of these policies.

VICTIM VERSUS OFFENDER

The classic dichotomy in justice is that of victim versus offender. The victim is the wronged; the offender is the wrongdoer. Traditionally, we are so fearful of direct contact between victim and offender that the state becomes the symbolic victim, virtually removing individual victims from the criminal and juvenile justice process.

In recent years we have witnessed the surge of the victims' movement. While no total consensus exists regarding direction, the movement has had many consequences, some quite visible. Included among the latter would have to be Mothers Against Drunk Drivers (MADD), which has been a key catalyst behind legislation generating stiffer and frequently mandatory penalties for drunk drivers. Others in the victims' movement have focused on increased accountability of offender to victim, increased victim participation in the justice process, adequate services for victims in crisis, and direct compensation from the state for losses due to crime (Hudson, 1984). In the field of juvenile justice, two program paradigms have been particularly sensitive to victim needs as well as to those of offenders: (1) restitution programs and (2) victim–offender mediation programs.

Restitution programs operate on the principle that youth are to be held personally accountable for their law-violating behavior (Schneider, 1985). A bond has been broken with the community, and repayment or restitution in some form must be made in order to restore the broken bond. Thus restitution is a means for providing assistance to victims (Barnett, 1977). In some instances restitution, in terms of monies or personal service, is made directly to the victim. On other occasions restitution, in terms of community service, is made to local community groups such as city/county parks, churches, senior citizen groups, and so on. This latter form of restitution is generally referred to as "symbolic restitution." In other words, the restitution is not made directly to the victim but to some segment of the community, underscoring that the community as a whole has also been victimized.

Recent research (Schneider, 1986) on restitution programs at several sites across the country has documented that these programs not only have positive results for victims and community agencies in the form of repayment for losses but also have at least modest positive impact on the youths. Youths participating in restitution programs tended to have lower rates of recidivism than youths in control groups (pp. 549–550).

The second program paradigm, victim–offender mediation, brings the victim and offender together in a face-to-face meeting, with a trained mediator to negotiate possible restitution to the victim (Umbreit, 1985). The meeting provides the victim with the opportunity to share feelings about being victimized and to obtain answers about why the crime occurred. The offender has an opportunity to share feelings and to understand the impact of the law-violating behavior. In addition to personalizing the victim–offender relationship, most meetings result in a restitution contract worked out between the two parties.

Most victim–offender mediation programs work with property offenders and their victims. Some, however, focus on more serious crimes. In Genesee County, New York, for example, through its Sheriff's Department, a victim–offender mediation program works with offenders committing crimes such as negligent homicide, attempted homicide, and rape (Umbreit, 1985:21).

Exploratory research indicates that over 60 percent of the victims who have the opportunity to participate in mediation programs do so. They participate because of their desire to recover loss, to help the offender stay out of trouble, and to be meaningfully involved in the justice process (Coates & Gehm, 1985). Victims were highly satisfied with the resulting contracts. All but one indicated that they would participate again, and 75 percent of the victims believed that the offender had been adequately punished. Four fifths of the victims and offenders felt that justice had been served in their cases. Offenders expressed fear about meeting the victims but generally felt good about the process, indicating that it had provided them an opportunity to "make things right."

These two program paradigms illustrate that correctional responses can take into consideration the needs of both victims and offenders. Crime is a human problem. It has significant impact upon victims and their families and upon offenders and their families. And it has a collective impact upon the communities in which we live. To ignore the needs of victims or to see the victims movement as a threat to the corrections establishment would be a gross misjudgment. To view all victims as seeking revenge would be a serious misreading of victim motivation and would lead us to further the victim –offender polarity as well as to adopt reactionary correctional policies needlessly.

PRIVATE VERSUS PUBLIC SECTOR ADMINISTRATION OF PROGRAMS

Since the late 1960s, there has been a fairly steady growth of provision of services to juvenile offenders from agencies based in the private sector. This growth is in part attributed to dissatisfaction with public services, inflexibility of public services, and movement toward deinstitutionalization and community-based corrections. The private sector was thought to provide a rich potential for diversified programming without becoming permanently committed to a particular program approach.

Recently, two divergent trends have occurred with considerable implications for private sector programming. First, many more for-profit private agency groups are now moving beyond the emphasis on community corrections. Some of these groups are contracting to run entire institutions, and in one state a private group is seeking to administer the whole adult corrections system. A partial response to this developing growth is the second trend, that is, public sector reconsideration of the desirability of contracting for any private services.

The movement away from purchase of private services is fueled by a number of concerns: (1) dissatisfaction with the quality of service, (2) inability to monitor and contract adequately for specific services, (3) entrenchment of the private sector with specific program ideas, therefore not providing the kind of creative laboratories originally envisioned, (4) discomfort with the for-profit movement, and (5) fear that the private sector is encroaching to a point where the state agencies will be left only to administer rather than provide service.

While neither of these two trends is full blown or widespread at the moment, each bodes ill for private sector service as it was originally envisioned. The for-profit trend has grave implications for the economic survival of small, grassroots-oriented, not-for-profit agencies. Sizable profit corporations with statewide or national bases can compete economically in ways not available to the smaller groups. For example, when moving into a new market a widespread corporation can "borrow" from its profit elsewhere to offer services below actual costs. And of course, right or wrong the for-profit question raises the issue of the "morality" of making money through social service at the expense of the less fortunate. While emotionally charged, with proper monitoring and controls this issue is probably a true red herring. All who are paid to work in social service—private-not-for-profits, private-for-profits, and public sector employees—are *paid* to serve the "less fortunate." And none of those groups can exist long if they continue to operate at a loss.

The public sector's questioning of contracting for private services is obviously threatening to the private sector's survival. In many places, private and public sector relations are quite positive. Where these relationships are in disarray both sectors probably bear some responsibility. If flexibility, diversity, and innovation were part of the justification for purchasing from the private sector, then states have a responsibility to continually assess the needs of the client population and the appropriateness of their program mix, private and public. Funding decisions should be based on this match. Private sector agencies should not be lulled into believing that because they received monies in the past they will continue to do so in the future. Needs of clients change. It is reasonable to expect that programs will need to change if they are to continue to compete.

This type of systematic matching of client needs with program options requires evaluation. Evaluation of contracted programs should be a top priority for state correctional agencies. Even though private sector programs can provide a richer, more diversified, and more flexible array of program options than a state might otherwise have, the state remains responsible for the quality of service provided to its charges for the protection of its citizens.

The task of evaluating private sector programs often proves to be a knotty problem engulfed in tension and the political arena. State decision makers worry about what is happening in the programs. Private providers often complain about what they believe to be excessive paper documentation requirements. And sometimes a political contest for power and influence takes place when a state agency decides not to renew a contract with a private provider. In practice, evaluation too often receives such a low priority and is done so haphazardly that little useful information is yielded to guide policy or programmatic decision making or, with the exception of gross abuse, to stand up under the political heat brought to bear by a disgruntled private provider.

The state and the private sector do not have to see each other as natural enemies. Inevitably there will be some tension, but there are many commonly shared goals. For example, the good private programs frequently welcome systematic evaluation because it is not in their interest, ideologically or practically, for badly managed, abusive programs to exist. And many private providers are attempting to be better at what they do. Some carry out fairly extensive evaluations of their own programs in order to determine what is working well and what is not.

While evaluation of private sector programs is a fundamental responsibility of a state agency, evaluation can provide a service to all involved. Evaluation efforts must be lodged clearly within the overall mission of the agency. Evaluation criteria must be identified clearly within program contracts. And evaluation should be conceived of as an ongoing process involving all persons who come into contact with a given program. Systematic evaluation can be used to strengthen programs and the system as a whole through technical assistance and training.

CONCLUSION

Youth corrections is buffeted continuously by winds of change. The pressures for change generate a state of paralysis for some and generate opportunities for growth for others. Much of the stir in recent years, and probably in the past too, has been fueled by political concerns, by differing views of personhood and the role of society, and by competition for resources. The debates in the field, frequently arising from conscientious thought and reasoned empirical investigation, have too often reached the heights of symbolic conflict sparked by simplistic rhetoric, false polarities, and unrealistic expectations.

Rhetoric is a useful device for inspiring supporters and for getting movements off the ground. But at some point rhetoric can become a stumbling block to implementation of reform-oriented policy. Dealing with polarities can be useful in winning debate points and identifying conflicting elements within a personality or within a family system. But the goal of these approaches is to build off the strengths of the polarities toward a stronger integration. And unrealistic expectations can undermine the most laudable and desirable policy.

We need to dream in order to stretch our imaginations—to move beyond the status quo. But we must remain in touch with reality in order to bring about lasting change. The future of juvenile corrections will depend in large part on how we as professionals and as citizens are able to engage the real philosophical and practical issues that we face.

DISCUSSION QUESTIONS

1. Discuss the premise that juvenile corrections policy is often shaped by rhetoric, polarities, and unrealistic expectations?
2. How can our understanding of the term *community-based* shape the debate regarding use of scarce correctional resources?
3. What is the place of punishment in juvenile corrections? Can the social worker adhere to the goal of rehabilitation in a punitive context?
4. What are some of the positive gains forthcoming from the attack upon rehabilitation as a reasonable corrections goal?
5. What are some of the consequences of determinate release policies for correctional programming?
6. Can one begin to balance victim and offender needs in the corrections context? If so, how?
7. Discuss the critical roles of public administrators in a system that contracts extensively for services with the private sector.

REFERENCES

Allen, F. A. (1981). *The decline of the rehabilitative ideal.* New Haven, CT: Yale University Press.

Altschuler, D. (1983). *Examining community-based linkages: An exploratory com-*

parative analysis. Unpublished doctoral dissertation, University of Chicago, Chicago.

Barnett, R. E. (1977). Restitution: A new paradigm of criminal justice. *Ethics: An International Journal of Social, Political, and Legal Philosophy, 87,* 279–301.

Coates, R. B. (1981). Community-based services for juvenile delinquents: Concept and implications for practice. *Social Issues, 37,* 87–101.

Coates, R. B., Fisher, B., & Forst, M. (1985). *Institutional commitment and release decision making for juvenile delinquents: An assessment of determinate and indeterminate approaches—A cross-state analysis.* San Francisco: URSA Institute.

Coates, R. B., & Gehm, J. (1985). *Victim meets offender: An evaluation of victim offender mediation programs.* Valparaiso, IN: PACT Institute of Justice.

Coates, R. B., Miller, A., & Ohlin, L. (1978). *Diversity in a youth correctional system: Handling delinquents in Massachusetts.* Cambridge, MA: Ballinger.

Cullin, F. T., & Gilbert, K. E. (1982). *Reaffirming rehabilitation.* Cincinnati, OH: Anderson.

Doeren, S., & Hageman, M. (1982). *Community corrections.* Cincinnati, OH: Anderson.

Felton, B. J., & Shinn, M. (1981). Ideology and practice of deinstitutionalization. *Social Issues, 37,* 158–172.

Forst, M., Fisher, B., & Coates, R. (1985). Indeterminate and determinate sentencing of juvenile delinquents: A national survey of approaches to commitment and release decision-making. *Juvenile and Family Court Journal, 36,* 1–11.

Gottfredson, M. (1979). Treatment destruction techniques. *Journal of Research in Crime and Delinquency, 16,* 39–54.

Greenberg, D. (1972). Rehabilitation is still punishment. *Humanist, 32,* 28–32.

Hawkins, J., & Fraser, M. (1983). Social support networks in delinquency prevention and treatment. In J. Whittaker & J. Garbariano (Eds.), *Social support networks: Informal helping in the human services* (pp. 333–352). Hawthorne, NY: Aldine Publishing.

Hudson, P. S. (1984). The criminal victim and the criminal justice system: Time for a change. *Pepperdine Law Journal, 11,* 23–61.

Kelner, G. (1985). *Staff and resident perceptions of new youth corrections facility environments and programs.* Unpublished doctoral dissertation, University of Utah, Salt Lake City.

Klein, M. (1979). Deinstitutionalization and diversion of juvenile offenders: A litany of impediments. In N. Morris and M. Tonrey (Eds.), *Crime and justice: An annual review of research* (pp. 145–201). Chicago: University of Chicago Press.

Krisberg, B., Schwartz, I. M., Litsky, P., & Austin, J. (1986). The watershed of juvenile justice reform. *Crime and Delinquency, 32,* 5–38.

Lipton, D., Martinson, R., & Wilks, J. (1975). *The effectiveness of correctional treatment: A survey of treatment and social control.* New York: Praeger Publishers.

Miller, A., & Ohlin, L. (1985). *Delinquency and community.* Beverly Hills, CA: Sage Publications.

Ranii, D. (1981). Helping attorneys empty the jails. *National Law Journal, 4,* 1–3.

Sarri, R. (1981). The effectiveness paradox: Institutional versus community placement of offenders. *Social Issues, 37,* 34–50.

Schneider, A. L. (Ed.), (1985). *Guide to juvenile restitution programs.* Washington, D.C.: National Criminal Justice Reference Service.

Schneider, A. L. (1986). Restitution and recidivism rates of juvenile offenders: Results from four experimental studies. *Criminology, 24,* 533–552.

Schwartz, I. (1984). New moves in juvenile justice. *Public Welfare, 42,* 28–31.

Spergel, I., Korbelik, J., Reamer, F., Lynch, J., & Alexander, J. (1979). *Evaluation of the Illinois status offender services project.* Chicago: University of Chicago, School of Social Service Administration.

Umbreit, M. (1985). *Victim offender mediation: Conflict resolution and restitution.* Washington D.C.: National Institute of Corrections.

Utah Division of Youth Corrections. (1986). *Task force report on issues in community programming and supervision.* Salt Lake City: Utah Division of Youth Corrections.

Van den Haag, E. (1975). *Punishing criminals: Concerning a very old and painful question.* New York: Basic Books.

Vinter, R., Downs, G., & Hall, J. (1975). *Juvenile corrections in the states' residential programs and deinstitutionalization.* Ann Arbor: University of Michigan, National Assessment of Juvenile Corrections.

Whittaker, J. K. (1979). *Caring for troubled children: Residential treatment in a community context.* San Francisco: Jossey-Bass.

Wilson, J. Q. (1975). *Thinking about crime.* New York: Basic Books.

National Survey and Assessment of Sixty-six Treatment Programs for Juvenile Offenders: Model Programs and Pseudomodels

Albert R. Roberts

ABSTRACT

Changing the antisocial and deviant behavior patterns of juvenile offenders is one of the major problems confronting society today. Enormous amounts of financial and staff resources have been invested in juvenile offender treatment programs. This article reports on a national survey of sixty-six juvenile justice programs. It includes data on the average annual cost of eleven different types of programs, the total number of youths completing each program, the programs' duration, and the reasons given by juvenile justice administrators for viewing their respective programs as worthy of replication by other agencies. Unfortunately, as documented within this article, only five of the sixty-six respondents had conducted evaluative research on the effectiveness of their programs. Nevertheless, this survey found several programs that seem promising because of their relatively low cost and their capacity to treat large numbers of juvenile offenders in relatively short periods of time (approximately three to four months). The author concludes with suggestions for planning and implementing both quasi-experimental and longitudinal research.

This survey sought to identify innovative treatment programs nationwide that have been effective in rehabilitating juvenile offenders. Media attention has traditionally tended to focus on the negative aspects of juvenile correctional programs while the innovative programs go unnoticed. Professional literature on juvenile correctional programs abounds, but it has only limited usefulness to decision makers because it is primarily descriptive and anecdotal in nature, rather than being based on valid and rigorous research.

Adapted from a paper presented at the Annual Conference of the Academy of Criminal Justice Sciences (ACJS), Orlando, Florida, March 17, 1986. Reprinted with permission from the *Juvenile & Family Court Journal*, 38, No. 3, pp. 39–45.

A review of the literature on juvenile correctional programs revealed a scarcity of data on their effectiveness as well as a lack of information on the types of programs to which juvenile correctional administrators are giving high priority. Not since 1976 has there been a national survey on the trends and effectiveness of juvenile correctional programs.

Ten years ago, there was a national survey of forty-two correctional programs (Vinter, 1976). It focused on policy and program alternatives and "the extent to which program conditions and practices conform or depart from" the standards set forth by the National Advisory Commission on Criminal Justice Standards and Goals. The comparative survey also focused on the characteristics of the youths in the programs surveyed; the types of offenses they committed; characteristics of program staff; and techniques used to control, treat, and educate the juveniles. Three basic types of programs were examined: institutional facilities, group homes, and day treatment programs. The major findings of the 1976 survey were as follows:

1. Youths who had committed serious property or personal crimes comprised over 30 percent of the population in the less restrictive alternatives to incarceration such as group homes and day treatment. Conversely, a sizable number of youths (close to one third) had been arrested for nonviolent offenses (e.g., status offenders) but were housed in the same closed institutions to which repeat violent offenders had been sent.

2. There was wide heterogeneity and diversity among youths committed to institutions. In some settings, juveniles were predominantly white; in others, the population was mainly nonwhite. Overall, there were a disproportionately large number of black youths at the institutions.

3. Looking at the race and gender of those in staff positions, the researchers found that blacks and women were underrepresented in administrative positions.

4. Female status offenders were disproportionately represented in the juvenile facilities.

The 1985 survey discussed here was undertaken to fill the knowledge gap and provide juvenile correctional planners and administrators with comprehensive evaluations and a state-of-the-art report on innovative programs. The three major objectives of this study were:

1. To identify programs that administrators consider most worthy of replication by other correctional agencies.
2. To identify the standards and rationale for selecting a program as most worthy of replication.
3. To synthesize material on both common and unique components of juvenile correctional programs in the United States.

In this regard the survey investigated:

- Types of programs.
- Administrator's rationale and criteria for selecting the model program.

- The most promising feature of the program.
- The annual cost per youth.
- Effectiveness, positive outcomes, and/or follow-up measures.

Methodology

In mid-July 1985, I developed and mailed a two-page questionnaire to juvenile correctional departments or their counterparts in all fifty states and the District of Columbia. This constituted a sample of 151 agencies. A follow-up letter, with another copy of the questionnaire, was sent to the non-respondents in mid-September. By December 1985, responses had been received from sixty-six programs.

The goal of this study was to obtain information on model juvenile correctional programs worthy of replication by other states. Program administrators were asked to provide the following information: their rationale for selecting the program, program objectives, the number of juveniles completing the program each year (for the past three years), the overall annual cost, and evaluation results. In addition, respondents were asked to send a written description of their program and a copy of any evaluation reports.

A multiple classification system was developed in order to rate each program on the basis of internal and external validity. The plan called for first examining each study to determine whether it included the race, sex, and age of the juvenile offenders. If none or only one of these was given, the study was rated as having low external validity. Second, each program that had completed an evaluation was rated for internal validity on the basis of the following scale:

No information on experimental group size—low internal validity.

No information on control group size—low internal validity.

Information on the use of matching—moderate internal validity.

Random assignment and statistical analysis used—high internal validity.

Outcome measure(s)—the more outcome measures that were used, the higher the internal validity.

Follow-up—the longer the period of time between completion of the program and the point in time when the follow-up measures were taken, the higher the internal validity (follow-up one year or longer after posttreatment completion indicates moderate validity).

Treatment program description—subjective criteria were established for a systematic and comprehensive program, based on the degree to which treatment components were described. Programs were given a high rating if they provided the following details: source of clients, number of clients served, type and duration of individual and group counseling, and use of performance contracts, contingency point systems, treatment plans, or other behavior modification principles.

Limitations.   The sampling procedure used resulted in responses from a sample of sixty-six programs representative of all regions in all sections of the United States. However, the generalizability and universality of the findings cannot be inferred, because only five of the sixty-six respondents had completed evaluative research on the effectiveness of their programs.

The survey findings are based on self-report data obtained from juvenile correctional administrators who were willing to cooperate and complete the mailed questionnaire. Thus, the reliability of the information provided is limited. Perhaps only the better organized and effective programs responded. It is also conceivable that the administrators with the least successful programs (e.g., those that are the most costly or serve the smallest number of juveniles) constitute the nonrespondents to this study. Many of the nonrespondents may feel that they have no model program on which to report, or they may believe that research surveys are a waste of their time and effort.

Another limitation relates to the researcher's goal of identifying model programs that had included rigorous methodology such as an experimental design or a design that would include postprogram outcome measures. The strength of the data analysis is limited because only five programs had completed evaluation research studies.

Finally, several programs responded to the questionnaire but neglected to provide all the information requested, such as the annual cost of their program. While a national survey that utilizes a mail questionnaire allows the researcher to obtain a full range of information in a cost-effective and expedient manner, it results in sacrificing the depth that an interview study of one program would provide. The survey approach also limits the researcher from obtaining certain types of data (e.g., first-hand psychological measures and direct observations of juvenile participants in each program).

Advantages.   Having discussed the limitations of survey research, it is also important to note the major advantages of this approach. It provides the researcher with a method for obtaining a considerable amount of information on a large number of programs located at great distances from one another. The survey research approach also provides a relatively inexpensive method of collecting a large body of information and gaining significant knowledge about the philosophy, objectives, content, and effectiveness of juvenile correctional programs. It therefore provides a basis for gathering comparative information from agency administrators, a vehicle for disseminating information on innovations and model programs to program planners, and a basis for facilitating policy development on new programs in juvenile justice.

Findings

The sixty-six responses came from every region of the United States. Table A–1 lists the types of programs identified and their frequency. The two types of model programs most frequently identified by the respondents were:

- Specialized secure treatment programs for violent juvenile and sex offenders (nine respondents).
- Wilderness programs (seven respondents).

The two types of model programs selected least frequently were:

- Family treatment (four respondents).
- Academic educational programs (four respondents).

It is important to note the recent development of specialized secure treatment programs for juvenile sex offenders and violent offenders. This group poses a difficult challenge for administrators and social workers because these juveniles have a high recidivism rate and they are perceived as a threat to the safety of the community. Eight of the nine model programs for violent juvenile offenders identified in this survey began between 1980 and 1984. The program in operation the longest is the Colorado intensive treatment program for violent juvenile offenders, which began in 1972. Surprisingly, only one of the nine programs—the Colorado program—has conducted an evaluation of its effectiveness. It found a recidivism rate of 33 percent for the violent juveniles who completed the program in the years 1975 thru 1977 and a recidivism rate of only 8.33 percent for the new sex offender program, which began in 1981. This was one of the few model programs that had high validity in terms of its follow-up study and the degree to which the characteristics of program participants and the treatment components were specified.

TABLE A–1   Model Juvenile Offender Programs

Type of Program	Frequency
1. Secure treatment programs for violent juvenile offenders	9
2. Wilderness programs	7
3. Vocational/career education	6
4. Behavior modification and differential treatment	6
5. Juvenile restitution programs	5
6. Community-based treatment programs	5
7. Positive peer culture	5
8. Prerelease and aftercare programs	5
9. Small residential treatment programs	5
10. Academic education programs	4
11. Family treatment programs	4
12. Miscellaneous	5

Generally, the program administrator's selection of a model program was not based on a scientifically derived hypothesis. The questionnaire asked administrators to describe their rationale for selecting the particular program as a model worthy of replication by other states. Most respondents gave a nonscientific rationale for selecting their model program. Typical responses included:

- "Innovative and focuses on a select group of juvenile offenders" (treatment program for sex offenders).
- "Provides an alternative design where traditional methods have not been effective" (secure treatment for violent juveniles).
- "Youths are quickly made aware of inappropriate behaviors" (behavior modification program).
- "Cost effective and easy to replicate" (regional, nonsecure detention service).
- "Places assaultive and aggressive students in one area, which is more advantageous to operation than having them spread out through facility" (positive peer culture).
- "Healthy treatment that appears to be effective" (positive peer culture).

Most of the model programs did not include a rigorous and scientifically sound evaluation or follow-up study. This lack of evaluative research on the effectiveness of juvenile correctional programs leads to the conclusion that with only a few exceptions the scientific assessment of juvenile corrections is at a primitive level. Only five of the sixty-six respondents indicated that a six-month (or longer) postrelease follow-up study had been conducted to determine the program's effectiveness in reducing recidivism. The programs that had done an evaluation were:

1. Denver's secure treatment program for violent adolescents.
2. The District of Columbia's Community Services Program (a restitution program).
3. The California Youth Authority's Planned Reentry Program.
4. Missouri's statewide family therapy program for troubled youths.
5. Springfield, Missouri's Family Resource Unit.

Several other programs stated that evaluations had been done in the form of monitoring by the state agency's headquarters office staff. They said they had been told that theirs was a "good" program. But those respondents did not send any documentation to substantiate their statement.

The four types of programs that are the least expensive to operate are family treatment, community-based (day) treatment, wilderness programs, and prerelease and aftercare programs. Analysis of information on program costs and the number of juveniles served yielded the following calculations:

Family treatment: three family treatment programs served a total of 436 youths and their families at an average annual cost of $589 per family in 1984.

Community-based treatment: four programs served a total of 362 youths in 1984 at an average annual cost of $1,450.

Wilderness programs: five programs served 1,085 youths at an average annual cost of $1,739 per youth.

Prerelease and aftercare: three programs served a total of 448 juveniles at an average cost of $3,086 per juvenile.

Juvenile restitution programs appear to be the most inexpensive of all the programs. Only two of the restitution programs that responded to the questionnaire sent information on their annual budget. They indicated that they served a total of 7,250 youths in 1984 at an average cost of only $82 per youth. Unfortunately, the programs did not specify whether and to what extent juvenile probation staff were responsible for monitoring restitution orders. If probation staff do regularly monitor restitution orders, the cost of their work needs to be included in the budget figure. Even though the $82 figure is probably an underrepresentation, it still indicates that restitution programs are extremely cost effective.

In contrast to the relatively inexpensive programs just discussed, the following three program categories were found to be the most expensive:

Program Type	Average annual cost per juvenile
Secure treatment for violent juveniles	$26,712
Positive peer culture	16,323
Behavior modification and differential treatment	15,916

The majority of the model programs were relatively short in duration when compared to traditional training school commitments for juvenile offenders. Programs typically ranged in length from one month to six months: The average length of time to complete a wilderness program ranged from one month at Connecticut's Youth Challenge Program to three months at New Mexico's Eagle Nest Camp. Family therapy in Missouri averaged 120 days, with families attending an average of seven sessions each. Time spent in prerelease and aftercare programs varied from four and one-half months in the California Youth Authority's Planned Reentry Program to seven months in the Florida program; the New York City Juvenile Aftercare program lasts one year.

There was great variation in the amount of time juveniles spent in small residential treatment programs. In a Missouri group home program that provided a wilderness experience, juveniles stayed for four weeks, while in Georgia's Fort Yargo group home the youths stayed for twelve months. Likewise, the amount of time spent in community-based day treatment programs varied widely from two months of short-term foster-type care at

Georgia's Attention Homes to two years of counseling and academic instruction at the Ashland Day Treatment program in Kentucky.

The average length of stay for juveniles adjudicated to a behavior modification and differential treatment facility was under six months. For example, the length of stay at Alabama's Intensive Treatment Unit ranges from four to six months, while the average stay at Miami, Florida's Better Outlook program is six months.

Conclusion

In view of the millions of dollars expended each year to protect society and care for and rehabilitate juvenile offenders, it is astonishing that so few systematic research and follow-up studies have been conducted by juvenile justice agencies. We need basic information on the effectiveness of the programs that have been selected as model programs. Legislators, administrators, and correctional planners need to know which types of programs work best with which types of offenders.

In my view, a program that is selected as a model program should have demonstrated its effectiveness in reducing recidivism rates for juvenile offenders over time. The effectiveness of a program should be based on the results of a comprehensive evaluation or follow-up study. These program evaluations and research studies should meet generally accepted scientific standards with regard to sample construction, research design, statistical methods, and ethics of research.

Future research needs to be planned to assure that both quasi-experimental and longitudinal research is carried out. These studies should plan to include the following:

1. A clearly delineated selection criteria for the sample before randomization according to demographic descriptors, psychiatric history, prior juvenile offenses and commitments, family structure, school problems (suspensions, failed courses, and grades repeated), and current offense.

2. Random assignment of juveniles to experimental and comparison groups.

3. Detailed delineation of experimental treatment and quasi-control procedures.

4. Delineation and specification of outcome measures (including school performance, psychosocial status, and future offenses) by using carefully validated instruments and criteria.

5. A time frame for the follow-up intervals that extends to at least one year posttreatment. It should include follow-up measures at six months, one year, eighteen months, two years, and three years posttreatment to better determine whether success has a lasting effect over time.

6. A large enough number of youths in the experimental and comparison groups for adequate statistical analysis (including the assess-

ment of the significance of differences in outcome between comparison and experimental groups.

It is hoped that with increased knowledge correctional administrators will be in a better position to commit resources and staff to programs that are effective in managing both violent and self-destructive juveniles as well as in reducing recidivism.

REFERENCE

Vinter, R. D. (Ed.). (1976, June). *Time out: A national study of juvenile correctional programs.* Ann Arbor: University of Michigan.

The Privatization of Corrections: Methodological Issues and Dilemmas Involved in Evaluative Research*

Albert R. Roberts
Gerald T. Powers

The Move toward Privatization

During the past three years there has been a rapid growth of private sector involvement in all aspects of corrections. Privatization refers to private sector contracts to (1) operate correctional facilities or (2) provide various social services and educational and medical programming on behalf of juvenile detention and correctional facilities. In order to reduce prison overcrowding and improve living conditions in jails and prisons, several states have recently passed legislation requiring their respective state departments of correction and county jail boards to offer contracts to private entrepreneurs to build and operate juvenile and adult detention facilities, prison health-care centers, halfway houses, group homes, and other community-based facilities.

The private corrections vendors have been politically astute at influencing legislators and key administrators of correctional bureaucracies. The proponents of privatization believe that, in most cases, the private sector is better equipped to build and operate correctional facilities in a cost-effective manner than its public counterparts. A variety of companies and organizations are designing and managing correctional facilities for a fee. Among the best known of these newly emerging companies is the Correctional Cor-

*Reprinted with permission from *The Prison Journal*, vol. LXV, pp. 95–107. Albert Roberts is an Associate Professor and Gerald Powers is a Professor, School of Social Work, Indiana University, Indianapolis. Dr. Roberts is the editor of *Social Work in Juvenile and Criminal Justice Settings* (Springfield, IL: Charles C Thomas), 1983. Dr. Powers is the senior author of *Practice-Focused Research* (Englewood Cliffs, N.J.: Prentice-Hall), 1985. Dr. Roberts would like to acknowledge the cooperation of Samuel Streit, Superintendent of the Eckerd Youth Development Center, during Dr. Robert's visit to the Okeechobee, Florida, facility in December, 1984.

poration of America (CCA), headquartered in Nashville, Tennessee. It manages the Tall Trees community-based residential facility for the juvenile court of Memphis and Shelby County, Tennessee. It also manages Silverdale, the 250-bed Hamilton County penal farm in Chattanooga, Tennessee. In Houston, CCA recently opened an alien detention center which it manages with its own personnel under contract with the Federal Bureau of Prisons.

In addition to the CCA, other large private sector firms include Control Data Corporation, Eclectic Communications, Inc. (ECI), the Salvation Army, the Eckerd Foundation, the Magdala Foundation, and Volunteers of America.

Control Data Corporation (CDC), headquartered in Minneapolis, has entered into over 60 contractual programs to provide education and training to inmates in correctional institutions in 23 states. Control Data is a private sector vendor developing customized high-tech education packages for inmates and correctional staff. Several of their early programs (developed between 1979 and 1981) include a prerelease program, a PLATO computer-based inmate education program, and a vocational training program to train inmates as electronic and computer technicians, word processor operators, and computer programmers. In January 1984, CDC created a Corrections System Division, which has the objective of developing and marketing high-tech education and training programs.

The Salvation Army of Florida employs over 200 counselors and provides almost all of the programming for individuals convicted of misdemeanor offenses. It has expanded its Florida program to New York, Mississippi, and Tennessee. The Jack and Ruth Eckerd Foundation, which is known for operating wilderness camps for juveniles in the Southwest, is operating the Eckerd Youth Center (previously called the Florida School for Boys at Okeechobee).

As a cost-saving measure, legislation has been passed in the states of California, Florida, Massachusetts, and Texas requiring state agencies and municipalities to contract with private providers for the provision of correctional services. This type of legislation had led to the rapid growth of small group homes, halfway houses, and other community-based facilities.

The Need for Evaluation: A Recent Exemplar

With this proliferation of private initiatives in what has traditionally been a public monopoly, there emerges the obvious need for evaluative research to assess the relative effectiveness of these two ideologically different approaches to the delivery of correctional services. Unfortunately, there is very little empirical evidence to help inform the debate which surrounds the whole privatization movement. Conflicting claims abound regarding the presumed effectiveness and efficiency of the various private correctional models that are currently in operation. The claims are largely anecdotal in nature and virtually devoid of any creditable supporting evidence. This has only served to heighten the political and emotional tone of the debate, which at the moment appears to be largely tied to issues of turf and thus highly suspect given the vested interests of the contending parties involved.

The implementation of effective program evaluation is a complex and difficult undertaking under the best of circumstances. But the problems are compounded substantially by the various legal, ethical, and practical constraints involved in any attempt to use correctional inmates in evaluative research. It has been suggested that "the demand for program and system evaluation has exceeded the research capabilities of corrections as well as the state of evaluative art" (Nelson, Ohmart, & Harlow, 1978). This has resulted in a plethora of studies of questionable value, which has further eroded the confidence of correctional administrators in the capacity of researchers to produce results that are of any practical or even theoretical value.

A recent example of this will serve to illustrate the point. In August 1982, in response to a legislative mandate, the Florida Department of Health and Rehabilitative Services transferred from public to private sector operation an existing secure facility for juvenile delinquents. A contract to manage the Florida State School for Boys at Okeechobee was awarded to the Jack and Ruth Eckerd Foundation. According to its mission statement, the Eckerd Foundation was prepared to "expand current programs and seek out other avenues of youth care programs within the limits of manpower and finances" (American Correctional Association, 1984:3). This was interpreted as meaning that the Florida Department of Health and Rehabilitative Services (HRS) would realize cost savings under the new management structure, which in turn would be expected to deliver a program that was qualitatively equal or superior to that provided by the state (American Correctional Association).

A year after the Eckerd Foundation assumed operational responsibility for the school, the National Institute of Corrections awarded a grant to the American Correctional Association (ACA) to conduct an evaluation of this precedent-setting transfer of a state-operated secure juvenile facility from public to private sector management. The evaluation was fraught with methodological difficulties from the onset, many of which are chronicled in the various working drafts and response documents prepared by the ACA, the Eckerd Foundation, and HRS.

Without going into needless detail, one important aspect of the evaluation illustrates the problem. According to the ACA evaluation team, there was insufficient baseline documentation available to utilize a "before and after" comparison design which would have enabled the Okeechobee school to serve as its own control. Therefore, it was decided that an alternative design would be employed in which the performance of the privately operated school at Okeechobee would be compared with a similar state-run facility in Marianna, Florida—the Arthur G. Dozier School for Boys. It was assumed that the Dozier school could be substituted for comparison/baseline purposes despite the presence of several significant differences between the two schools, including the distribution of residents according to sentencing categories as well as race.

To be more specific, a comparison of the overall distributions at the two schools revealed that the Okeechobee facility had a higher percentage of residents incarcerated for more serious offenses and a greater proportion of black students. According to the records, 50.5 percent of the Okeechobee students, as compared with only 12.2 percent of the Dozier students, had a record of two or more prior placements in a training school for theft of a firearm. The clear majority of Dozier students were confined for either misdemeanor offenses, victimless crimes, or felonies involving crimes against property. In addition, the Okeechobee population had a higher percentage of black offenders (58.7 percent) than did the Dozier population (44.1 percent).

To handle this problem of nonequivalency between the two facilities, the ACA team utilized a delinquency rating mechanism developed by Herbert Quay (Quay, 1964b). In effect, through the use of a personality inventory, a behavior checklist, and a social history rating form, a typology of delinquent behavior was used to classify the students into one of four subtypes: immature-dependent, neurotic-anxious, agressive-psychopathic, and subcultural delinquent. Using Quay's classification system, the evaluation team found no statistically significant differences between the Okeechobee and Dozier students with respect to the four subtypes. It was assumed, therefore, that any differences discovered between the two schools relative to selective outcome measures, such as institutional adjustment and/or program participation, could be attributed to factors related to the inherent advantages or disadvantages of the privatization variable.[1]

What appears to have occurred was the methodological equivalent of a "shell game." By instrumental sleight of hand, what was clearly a significant difference with respect to the seriousness of offenses among residents appeared not to be a difference at all once the Quay typology was superimposed on the respective distributions. In other words, ordinal differences of the type which most correctional experts would agree could profoundly influence institutional functioning, were cleverly dismissed in favor of a nominal classification scheme that created the illusion of equivalency. There was also little recognition of the fact that the Okeechobee experiment was still very much in its formative stages as compared to the well-established Dozier

---

[1]All juvenile offenders will not respond in the same way to a specific treatment program. Quay's differential typology, which was developed in the mid-1960s, was used extensively at the Robert F. Kennedy Federal Youth Center in Morgantown, West Virginia, starting in 1969. The basic assumption underlying differential treatment was that different behavioral types of delinquents require different types of treatment. The purpose of the Quay typology was to assign delinquents to treatment groups and to the four separate cottages at the Kennedy Youth Center on the basis of their behavioral characteristics and psychological orientation (Roberts, 1971). Although this approach has its faults, it was recognized as a systematic effort at developing a differential classification system. However, it was developed approximately 20 years ago; a new type of offender has emerged since that time. Compared to the offender of the 1960s, the offender of the 1980s is significantly more violent, is more likely to have a history of drug abuse, and has a higher probability of being violent while under the influence of drugs. In addition, training schools have considerably more racial conflict and racial violence than there was 20 years ago (Irwin, 1980: Palenski, 1983), at the time the Quay typology was developed.

program. It was no small wonder, therefore, that the Okeechobee program was found to be wanting in a number of critical programmatic areas.

This is but one of a number of serious methodological liabilities in the evaluation of the Okeechobee experiment. But it illustrates well the type of problems that plague programmatic evaluation, especially as it relates to the field of corrections. If we hope to make informed decisions about the efficacy of programmatic innovations such as the privatization of correctional services, then we need to rigorously adhere to the basic tenets of science which we know are critical to the development of valid and reliable knowledge. These tenets are described extensively elsewhere (Babbie, 1983; Bloom & Fischer, 1982; Holzner & Marx, 1979; Miller, 1983), but there are a number of factors that seem to us to be fundamental prerequisites of any informed approach to correctional evaluation.

Evaluating from a Dual Perspective

We start with the assumption that any effort to evaluate program effectiveness must deal with issues related to both outcome and process. *Outcome* addresses the question of what happens as a result of client exposure to program requisites, while *process* addresses the question of what actually goes on in the program itself. When we turn our attention to the former, we are concerned primarily with *effects,* or more specifically, dependent variables. When we examine the latter, we are concerned with *causes* or independent variables. We mention this distinction simply to emphasize the point that, in our judgment, any assessment of one of these dimensions in the absence of the other inevitably represents an incomplete model of evaluation.

Studies that look solely at outcome are designed to determine whether a program seems to be working, that is, whether, according to some predetermined measure of success—such as *recidivism*—an expected or desired result has in fact occurred (Powers, Meenaghan, & Toomey, 1985). No attention is paid to what happens to the clients during their exposure to the program. In the jargon of the field, such "blind" endeavors are known as "black box" studies because they typically reveal little with respect to what goes on during the course of the program itself. Therefore, there is no way of knowing what aspects of a particular program are functionally related to the observed outcomes.

Studies that look solely at process, on the other hand, may learn a great deal about what is taking place within the program itself, but have little basis upon which to conclude that these events bear any relationship to outcome. Process studies have as their goal an understanding of what is happening in a particular program, why it is happening, and whether it is happening the way it was intended to happen. As such, these studies focus on *means* rather than *ends.*

There are wide variations with respect to what actually happens to juvenile offenders during the course of their correctional experience. This is true not only when one compares different programs, such as Okeechobee and Dozier, but also when one considers the functioning within any particular program. It is not surprising, therefore, that most of the research concerning the efficacy of various correctional intervention strategies tends to be equivocal (Blackmore, 1981). When we fail to pay attention to the differential effects a given intervention has on clients, there is the very real possibility that any positive and negative results may tend to neutralize one another, thus erroneously suggesting that no significant effects have occurred at all.

The ultimate form of evaluation enables us to discover causal links—that is, to know what components of a program produce what kinds of effects, with what types of clients, under what kinds of conditions. This would provide us with the kind of information we need in order to make informed judgments concerning the relative merits of competing programmatic strategies. Thus, the basic question is not one of whether privately run correctional programs are more or less effective and/or efficient than their public counterparts in some monolithic or global sense, but rather in what specific ways and in relation to what particular types of problems or client populations might one approach be superior to another.

To answer these questions, two distinct but interdependent models of research are called for—one is referred to as intensive or idiographic research, and the other is called extensive or nomothetic research (Chassan, 1967). *Intensive design research methods* attempt to draw conclusions about the effectiveness of particular intervention strategies when used in relation to individual cases. The prototype of this form of research is the time series design in which repeated measures of one or more target behaviors are recorded, initially during a preintervention baseline period and thereafter during a programmed intervention phase (Herson & Barlow, 1976).

By means of this approach, direct comparisons can be made with respect to client functioning between the baseline and intervention periods, thus providing a method for determining the characteristics of, and variations in, the change process as it relates to individual offenders. The basic purpose of these repeated measures is to rule out competing explanations of any observed changes in the offender's target behavior. To put it another way, successive observations enable the evaluator to determine whether the planned intervention, or some other independent variable, is responsible for the observed changes in a particular resident's behavior.

There are a number of variations on the basic intensive design model, each of which contains certain characteristic limitations that need to be understood before they are employed. These cautions are discussed extensively elsewhere and will not be repeated here (Glass, Willson, & Goffman, 1973; Jayaratne & Levy, 1979). It is important to keep in mind, however, that while the various intensive designs provide a set of very useful tools for evaluating the impact of direct programmatic intervention on individual offenders, the findings they produce cannot of themselves be generalized to any given population. In an aggregate sense, however, they do provide a systematic means by which to identify individual response patterns and changes among program participants. This, in turn, enables us to refine our theories and generate more viable hypotheses for further study within the context of the extensive design models.

Extensive design research methods are concerned primarily with the testing of research hypotheses involving groups of subjects rather than the intensive study of individual cases. The purpose for conducting such investigations is to explore general classes of events as a basis for arriving at scientific generalizations. Typically, this involves the random assignment of subjects to one of two equivalent groups—with one group being exposed to an experimental condition (intervention), and the other group serving as a control (Campbell & Stanley, 1966). Similar to the intensive design models referred to earlier, preintervention or baseline measures are taken for both groups, followed by one or more postintervention measures of the same behaviors. Since only the experimental group receives the planned intervention (i.e., the independent variable), it is assumed that any observed differences between the two groups with respect to the expected outcome (i.e., the dependent variable) are attributable to programmatic factors. Through the use of various statistical tests of significance, qualified inferences can be formulated concerning the populations from which the sample subjects were initially drawn.

We have suggested that the development of program-relevant knowledge occurs along two major axes that are at once both distinct and interdependent. This dual perspective is graphically depicted in Figure B–1, which captures the complementary and reciprocal nature of the relationship between these two important knowledge-building strategies.

Both the intensive and extensive research models are essentially problem-solving processes in that they involve the identification, analysis, reso-

FIGURE B–1 The Relationship between the Intensive and Extensive Designs of Research in Program Evaluation

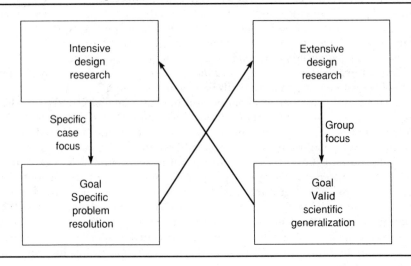

lution, and verification of some sort of problem—either practical or theoretical. But they also differ substantially with respect to purpose or goal. The purpose of the extensive research models is generally to conduct orderly inquiries into some facet of the empirical world toward the goal of arriving at valid scientific generalizations. The intensive research models, on the other hand, attempt to apply the known generalizations developed through the extensive models to specific practice situations for the purpose of arriving at well-founded, highly probable conclusions concerning the relevance of that knowledge to specific problem situations.

Defining Success through Multiple Evaluation Measures

The overriding concern of the evaluation specialist is determining *what works*. The starting point is defining success, goal attainment, or precisely what one means by "program effectiveness."

The major objective of juvenile rehabilitation programs is usually the modification of behavior. Measuring changes in human behavior is extremely complex and rarely definitive. All too often, what evaluators strive to measure is "program effectiveness" or "recidivism," rather than the idiosyncratic needs and changes in behavior among individual offenders. Thus, the authors are recommending that we start at the individual level and then proceed to the group level. First, let us determine the needs, abilities, and attitudes of a small group of individuals. Second, place them in one or more programs. Third, measure each individual's changes in posttreatment behavior and attitudes (based on pre- and postmeasures). And finally, look at the patterns of responses and changes of program participants in comparison to a control group.

Need for Behavioral Objectives.   Vital to any evaluation effort is the specification of individual and program objectives, and outcome measures for ascertaining the effectiveness of programs. All too frequently, juvenile correctional facilities and rehabilitation programs have neglected to delineate specific behavioral objectives. These types of programs indicate that their objectives are to punish, rehabilitate, humanize, minimize suffering, and/or correct juvenile lawbreakers. General objectives such as these are not quantifiable. They must be restated in behavioral terms in order to be measurable.

Monitoring.   Program evaluations can be used as a crucial tool for monitoring the progress of a project. This is accomplished by checking each component of the project for its success in furthering the overall and specific objectives of the project. Program evaluations provide a mechanism for identifying problems, determining their scope, and formulating alternative solutions to them before they have become so exacerbated that they endanger the success of the project. By determining the success level—at specified phases, including the beginning, interim, and completion phases of the project—the evaluation can determine the degree to which the project objective(s) is being met. Assumption: Project will provide vocational training to 25 juvenile offenders so they can obtain marketable job skills.

Performance Measures. Some measures determine the overall progress of a project toward meeting its objective. Other measures track the success of several components of a project as a means of providing interim indicators of a project's progress.

Overall Measure—Rearrest Rate among Participants. If a project participant is successfully rehabilitated upon release from the project, he will not reenter the juvenile justice system; that is, he will not be rearrested for any offense, assuming a project goal of 80 percent success. Rearrests among participants ought to remain below 20 percent six months after release.

Interim Measure—Number of Participants. If a project goal is to provide social-work skills to 200 juvenile offenders within one year, at the end of three months of project operation 50 initial participants should complete the social skills program.

Overall Measure—Job Permanency. The degree to which project participants secure gainful employment upon release and remain employed for at least one full year after release. For example, it would have been useful if the Okeechobee evaluation study had included the following measures: the number of students completing the vocational training program in baking; the number and percentage of those students who were placed in jobs as bakers upon release and who remained employed for at least one year.

Interim Measure—Participant's Attitude. A positive attitude among project participants is necessary for project success; that is, belief in the potential of the program, belief in oneself, determination, and commitment to change. Therefore, periodic surveys will be made of the clients' opinions of the project's success, with emphasis on their sense of hope. The evaluator could use an instrument such as the Community Adjustment Scale or develop an instrument which includes open-ended questions such as the following:

a. How do you feel about the project so far?

b. What sort of problems have you been having?

c. Do you feel the project is helping you to feel good about your progress toward obtaining a marketable job skill?

Outcome Measures.

1. Reduction in the number of suspensions/expulsions from school among project participants (six months postrelease).

2. Reduction in subsequent arrests (after completion of x number of months in juvenile offender vocational project).

3. Number of youth working part-time in service jobs six months after release.

4. Number of youths working full-time in trade for which they completed vocational training certificate in the institution (six months postrelease).

Conclusion

This article began with a review of the recent growth in the privatization of corrections. Several methodological issues related to the conduct of evaluative research in correctional settings were examined, and a strategy for assessing both the process and outcome of programmatic interventions was suggested. An exemplar was provided of the first federally funded (by the National Institute of Corrections) evaluation of a privately operated juvenile institution. Through this illustration, we examined the type of methodological problems that may be encountered by other researchers who evaluate the effectiveness of privately operated correctional facilities. However, the methodological problems are no different from those that have plagued the correctional field in the past. We are simply more aware of them at present because of the political pressures for accountability that occur in the wake of any new approach to corrections which changes the status quo. If future comparative assessments of two correctional facilities are to yield valid findings—ultimately leading to improved correctional programs—then they should utilize experimental or quasi-experimental designs.

In the final analysis, if we are serious about our desire to answer the many questions concerning the relative effectiveness and utility of privately run correctional facilities, then there will need to be a commitment on the part of key decision makers to allocate the funds necessary for appropriate research initiatives.

BIBLIOGRAPHY

American Correctional Association. (1984.) *Private sector operation of a correctional institution.* (Study of the Eckerd Youth Development Center, Okeechobee, Florida). College Park, MD: Author.

Babbie, E. (1983). *The practice of social research* (3d ed.). Belmont, CA: Wadsworth.

Blackmore, J. (1981, October). Does community corrections work? From the experts, a resounding "Maybe." *Corrections Magazine,* 15–27.

Bloom, M., & Fischer, J. (1982). *Evaluating practice: Guidelines for the accountable professional.* Englewood Cliffs, N.J.: Prentice-Hall.

Campbell, D. T. (1969, April). Reforms as experiments. *American Psychologist,* 24, 409–429.

Campbell, D. T., & Stanley, J. C. (1963). *Experimental and quasi-experimental design for research.* Skokie, IL: Rand McNally.

Chassan, J. B. (1967). *Research design in clinical psychology and psychiatry.* New York: Appleton-Century-Crofts.

Empey, L. T., & Lubeck, S. G. (1971). *Explaining delinquency: Construction, test, and reformation of a sociological theory.* Lexington, MA: Heath Lexington.

Glass, G. V., Willson, V. K., & Goffman, J. M. (1973). *The design and analysis of time-series experiments.* Boulder, CO: Laboratory of Educational Research Press.

Herson, M., & Barlow, D. H. (1984). *Single case experimental designs* (2d ed.). Elmsford, NY: Pergamon Press.

Holzner, B., & Marx, J. H. (1979). *Knowledge application: The knowledge system in society.* Boston: Allyn & Bacon.

Irwin, J. (1980). *Prisons in turmoil.* Boston: Little, Brown.

Jayaratne, S., & Levy, R. R. (1970). *Empirical clinical practice.* New York: Columbia University Press.

Miller, D. C. (Ed.). (1983). *Handbook of research design and social measurement* (4th ed.). New York: David McKay.

Nelson, K., Ohmart, H., & Harlow, N. (1978). *Promising strategies in probation and parole.* Washington, DC: U.S. Department of Justice; National Institute of Law Enforcement and Criminal Justice, Law Enforcement Assistance Administration.

Palenski, J. E. (1983). Race relationships in prison: A critical social work concern. In A. R. Roberts, *Social Work in Juvenile and Criminal Justice Settings* (pp. 363–372). Springfield, IL: Charles C Thomas.

Powers, G. T., Meenaghan, T. M., & Toomey, B. (1985). *Practice focused research: Integrating human service practice and research.* Englewood Cliffs, NJ: Prentice-Hall.

Quay, H. C. (1964a). Dimensions of personality in delinquent boys as inferred from the factor analysis of case history data. *Child Development, 35,* 479–484.

Quay, H. C., (1946b). Personality dimensions in delinquent males as inferred from the factor analysis of behavior ratings. *Journal of Research in Crime and Delinquency, 1,* 33–37.

Roberts, A. R., (1971). *Sourcebook on prison education: Past, present and future.* Springfield, IL: Charles C Thomas.

Rossi, P. H., & Freeman, H. E. (1985). *Evaluation: A systematic approach* (3rd ed.). Beverly Hills, CA: Sage Publications.

Schmidt, P., & Witte, A. D. (1980). Evaluating correctional programs: Models of criminal recidivism and an illustration of their use. *Evaluation Review, 4,* 585–600.

Juvenile Justice: Reform, Retain, and Reaffirm*

Diane C. Dwyer
Roger B. McNally

Introduction

The juvenile justice system, and particularly the juvenile court, continues its demise. Parens patriae, its philosophical cornerstone, has slowly been eroded and replaced with the adversarial model of justice. This demise has escalated to the point where many delinquents are now considered adults and held fully culpable for their aberrant behavior. In fact, the Federal posture as promulgated by the Office of Juvenile Justice and Delinquency Prevention (hereafter OJJDP) clearly states that " . . . there is no reason that society should be more lenient with the 16 year old first time offender than a 30 year old first offender" (Regnery, 1985:4). Furthermore, many states have supported this notion by enacting codes (legislatively) to process (certification, waiver, etc.) juvenile offenders in the adult criminal court.

This trend, although not surprising, is reshaping the juvenile justice system to the extent that many believe it to be on the verge of extinction. To some, this is a most desirable outcome; however, to others, it signifies a major failure for social justice, especially for adolescents.

This paper is the fourth in a series of research papers ("The Child Savers—Child Advocates and the Juvenile Justice System," "Juvenile Court: An Endangered Species," and "The Juvenile Justice System: A Legacy of Failure?") which have chronicled the birth and transformation of the juvenile justice system. Consequently, this effort is the result of an evolutionary

*Reprinted with permission from the *Federal Probation Quarterly* (September 1987), pp.47–51. This article is based on a paper prepared for the 1986 Annual Meeting of the American Society of Criminology, Atlanta, Georgia, October 1986. Part of this article previously appeared in the November 17, 1986 issue of *Juvenile Justice Digest* (vol. 14, no. 22) under the title, "A Compromise Is Needed in Juvenile Justice Reform."

Dr. Dwyer is Assistant Professor, Social Work Department, and Dr. McNally is Associate Professor, Criminal Justice Department, at the State University of New York at Brockport.

process detailing the present course of events and the consequences should these trends go unabated. The focus of the article will be to critique the OJJDP position on juvenile reform and recommend a more moderate compromise. The authors will call attention to significant new research and the policy reform recommendations of other influential interest groups, namely the National Council of Juvenile and Family Court Judges and the United Nations General Assembly on Criminal Justice.

The authors espouse the position that it is incumbent upon researchers and reformers to identify those elements of the system that are rational and those which need to be replaced. Close attention must be paid to the direction in which the juvenile justice system is heading in order not "to throw out the baby with the bath water."

Historical Perspective

In order to appreciate the present dilemmas, controversies, and conflicts in juvenile justice, it is important to view it from an historical perspective. The longstanding tradition involving state intrusion into the parent-child relationship is rooted in English common law. Implicit in this is the power of the state to intervene in families and to remove children in order to protect the interests of the larger community. Simply stated, this is the court operating on a parens patriae basis, the philosophical spirit of juvenile justice since its inception. This rationale is clearly expressed by the Illinois Supreme Court in 1882:

> It is the unquestioned right and imperative duty of every enlightened government, in its character of parens patriae, to protect and provide for the comfort and well-being of such of its citizens as, by reason of infancy, defective understanding, or other misfortune or infirmity, are unable to take care of themselves. The performance of this duty is justly regarded as one of the most important of governmental functions, and all constitutional limitations must be so understood and construed so as not to interfere with its proper and legitimate exercise.

Hence, with the guiding philosophy of parens patriae, juvenile justice was formally born in 1899. For the next 60 years, this system of justice went relatively unchallenged and unchanged until a flurry of litigation (*Kent, Gault, Winship*) attacked the very spirit of juvenile justice.

From this new perspective the failure of parens patriae to serve the best interest of youth while forgoing the protection of society has evolved to the inevitable; that is neither the restoration of youth nor the protection of the community from his criminal behavior transition.

Transition

With the foundation of the system in serious jeopardy, a series of trends continued to emasculate its integrity. These include the cynicism about rehabilitation; the perceived escalation of violent juvenile behavior; the application of proceduralism to court proceedings; the creation of chronic (violent) offender codes; the general belief in the courts' inabilities to effectively punish or to treat youth; and a changing public and political atmosphere concerned with a punitive approach to crime and criminals.

Research findings and public policy have supported the notion that the juvenile justice system is too tolerant of juvenile offenders. Two of the most incriminating reports resulting in the reshaping of policy, have been Wolfgang et al., *Delinquency in a Birth Cohort,* and Martinson's "Nothing Works" studies. The data and implications of these studies have resulted in policy formulation indicating that the juvenile justice system is antiquated, serving *neither* the youth, the victim, nor society.

The response has been a reduction in treatment/therapeutic efforts and a shift to control and incarceration of juveniles. Implicit here is punishment at the exclusion of any other effort since the underlying tone has been that "nothing works" in an appreciable manner to affect recidivism rates.

Juvenile Justice: The Federal Perspective

The Federal government's direction toward juvenile justice for the past 10 years, vis-à-vis OJJDP, has been classically "reactionary." Consistent with public and political trends toward conservatism—and the portrayal, by the media, of juvenile crime escalating out of control and becoming increasingly violent—the response has been that the traditional system of juvenile justice at best is outdated and at worst is a total failure.

With this perception and the public's general attitude toward crime and criminals, the Federal posture has been to alter the juvenile system with "get tough" reform measures. These measures were expressed in policy, the policy of grants, and legislative mandates (i.e., selective incapacitation, preventative detention, certification, etc.) aimed at controlling and punishing those who profile this perception. Assumed here is that the perception is accurate. Some, including the authors, challenge the assumption that juvenile crime has been spiraling out of control. Rather, it is our belief that it is largely mediahyped and grossly overstated (Gilber, 1981).

Nonetheless, a policy review statement (Fall 1985) by Alfred Regnery, chief administrator of OJJDP ("Getting Away with Murder: Why the Juvenile Justice System Needs an Overhaul"), clearly reflects the classical school response to criminal behavior and the corresponding Federal initiatives; namely, punishment is a first priority.

Enlightenment or Futility

Consequently, in an effort to deal with juveniles, pragmatism has slowly been shaping policy predicated on the notion that criminal behavior is largely a matter of choice (Regnery, 1985:3). This rationale has resulted in certifying more delinquents to adult courts; tracking chronic offenders in an effort to get them off the streets quicker; maximizing their incarceration; and fostering the position that deterrence and punishment should be the model of justice for juveniles who commit crimes.

Ironically, this response assumes that the traditional efforts to deal with juvenile crime have in fact been a failure and that the "new" findings are clearly valid and therefore rational for the development of contemporary policy. These authors suggest a note of caution.

Wolfgang's Philadelphia studies indicate, among other things, that a small number of chronic delinquents are responsible for a disproportionate amount of serious crime, i.e., "seven percent (7%) of the youths studied were chronically delinquent but accounted for 75% of all serious crimes" (*Juvenile Justice Digest*, 85:1). One can readily see why, proportionally, selective incapacitation and preventive detention have become the logical conclusion.

This type of reaction reinforces conclusions that criminal behavior is largely an outcome of rationality. This classical school reasoning totally negates factors that should be considered. The concept of maturation is ignored when OJJDP suggests that there is no reason that society should be more lenient with a 16-year-old first-time offender than a 30-year-old and that to maintain a distinction between youth and adults is counterproductive.

Moreover, policies that foster predictive efforts to forecast criminal behavior are not only questionable in terms of validity, but they continue to reinforce stereotyping. Selective incapacitation efforts tend to fall disproportionately on minorities and are entirely retrospective. The implications of this cannot be taken lightly. Targeted individuals are known high-rate offenders based on past criminal behavior. Consequently, tracking efforts result in the identification of the offender only *after* he has committed a crime rather than being prospective.

Folly of Rehabilitation

The hallmark of the juvenile justice system has been the restoration of youth through interventions whose premise are oriented toward rehabilitation. Since Martinson's work of the late sixties suggesting that "with few and isolated exceptions, the rehabilitative efforts that have been reported had no appreciable effect on recidivism" (Martinson, 1947:36), subsequent policies embrace deterrence through punishment, e.g., certifying more delinquents to adult court. Aside from exacerbating an already overloaded court docket and overcrowded prison population, this implies the futility of rehabilitation and the desirability of punishment.

Furthermore, the distinct absence of Federal initiatives (grants) to fund programs that are aimed at the restoration of youth through proactive models is a further sign that the Federal government's (OJJDP) priorities are primarily focused on the narrow group of chronic offenders. The freezing of OJJDP's funds for fiscal 1986 and the proposed dismantling of this agency is another clear sign as to the future of juvenile justice in America!

Implications and Current Research

Present attitudes, policy, legislation, etc. toward crime and criminals strongly suggests that crime, regardless of who commits it, is the product of choice and rational decisionmaking. Correspondingly, the response to this line of reasoning is a just deserts model; let the punishment be commensurate with the crime. This classical school thinking, although over two centuries old, has come full cycle, thereby relegating the spirit and intent of juvenile justice to the annals of history.

The tide has turned, and one can see the expression of this earlier thinking when scrutinizing the Federal posture. What concerns these authors is the belief that crime is a matter of choice, irrespective of maturational levels or other factors (i.e., psychological problems, etc.) and that the *best* response is the certainty of punishment. This trend totally neglects any of the controversy surrounding deterrence theory.

Research to Consider

The image of rampant, spiraling youth crime has resulted in an intolerance toward selected adolescents. To those few that become labeled the "serious habitual offender," "chronic violent offender," "multiple delinquent offender," etc., the system has widened the net to ensure that deterrence will be a product of swift and certain justice. By waiving those violent delinquents to the adult system, implicit is the belief that this is the most rational response. Moreover, the serious habitual offender label begins to take on multiple meanings. Some states (Minnesota) are waiving to adult court youth who commit two felonies that may be property crimes. Consequently, as more delinquents become labeled serious offenders, the traditional delinquency category diminishes.

Recent research on very violent youth, those who commit murder, produces some intriguing findings that should caution us to this deterrence response and suggest other alternatives to be examined for the violent few.

Dorothy Otnow Lewis (M.D.) et al. have been conducting research on children who commit murder ("Biopsychosocial Characteristics of Children Who Later Murder: A Prospective Study") and on youth who are considered very violent ("Violent Juvenile Delinquents"). Their findings are rather timely and suggest an alternative response as compared to conclusions drawn from the Wolfgang studies.

In their study on children who later murder, the researchers document the childhood neuropsychiatric and family characteristics *prior* to the commission of the act. The profile of these children included psychotic symptoms, major neurological impairment, a psychotic first-degree relative, violent acts during childhood, and severe physical abuse (Lewis et al., 1985:1161). Significant findings included documentation of a history of extreme violence *before* committing murder, the spontaneity, impulsiveness, and the unpredictability of the behavior. When they compared the data of the murderers with that of ordinary delinquents, it was the presence of all five variables (psychotic symptoms, neurological impairment, etc.) that distinguished the murderers from the control group.

Many conclusions were drawn that ". . . suggest violence alone is not as good a predictor of future aggression . . . " (Lewis et al., 1985:1166). Hence, studies that are focused on tracking chronic antisocial behavior (*after* the commission of criminal acts), such as the Wolfgang studies, may be neglecting some very useful data that may not only assist in explaining violent behavior but point us in an alternative direction to incarceration. More specifically, the researchers suggest that ". . . violent juveniles are likely to be dismissed merely as incorrigible sociopaths and simply incarcerated . . . and that enlightened psychological, educational and medical programs can and should be derived to meet the needs of these multiple damaged children" (Lewis et al., 1981:318).

Summary and Implications

What does the data suggest? Should we continue on the present course or do these findings necessitate a re-examination of the present trends? Have we been simply overacting to juvenile crime, or is it time to get tough and accept the erosion of the juvenile justice system as inevitable? Perhaps there is room for change based on sound analysis of past and present trends to embrace a spirit of progressive reform.

These authors believe that the roots, i.e., parens patriae, of juvenile justice were in response to good and needed reforms. The rationale for a separate system of justice is no different today than in the late 1800s; if anything, advocacy is imperative in view of concepts and programs predicated on forecasting future behavior. Furthermore, to ignore the need for a benevolent institutional structure for treating juveniles does and will continue to ignore the fact that adolescents are *not* simply short adults. The punitive response appears to symbolize frustrations with crime and criminals and the need to provide a "quick fix" to a most complex problem.

Transferring youth to criminal court does not appear to be solving any problems other than implying a lack of confidence in the concept of juvenile justice. The consequence has been to broaden the definition of behaviors that qualify one for certification. Additionally, the desired outcome of more arrests, convictions, and lengthier sentences has not been fruitful. A study funded by OJJDP in the early '80s concluded that the apparent reason for transferring/waiving juveniles to adult courts, that they will receive stiffer sentences, does *not* appear to be substantial. (Hamporian et al., 1982). Nonetheless, states continue to redefine traditional delinquent behavior for the expressed purpose of "getting tough" even when it has been demonstrated that the disposition will be no, or minor, imprisonment.

In view of recent research studies, Federal efforts have been aimed at early identification, tracking, and, ultimately, incarcerating the chronic violent offender. In order to identify and react to the few who commit a very large, disproportionate amount of crime, these Federal initiatives end up reinforcing the perception that minorities (blacks and Hispanics) are largely responsible for all the violent crimes. This retrospective approach also neglects ethical considerations, as well as ignores empirical problems in prediction efforts (Cohen, 1983). Again, it is difficult not to conclude that many programs, policy decisions, legislative mandates, etc. are born out of frustration rather than logic.

Recommendations

This article is predicated upon the belief of these authors, supported by current research, that juvenile crime is neither rampant nor becoming increasingly violent. Furthermore, the authors believe that the policy trends of the past 10 years have been primarily reactionary and frequently promulgated from frustration, an intolerance to the violent few, the need to develop "quick fix" responses, i.e., swift and certain punishment, and the belief that youth have been coddled too long in the name of parens patriae.

What follows are recommendations that these authors believe are essential to reforming and restoring the juvenile justice system to a viable, credible social institution, one predicated on *presumptive innocence of those it serves*. *The authors strongly argue for the retention* of a separate system of justice with its primary goal to safeguard the well-being of the young to assure that they have the right to mature and become responsible adults.

Consequently, the authors *endorse* both the United Nations model code on juvenile justice promulgated August 1985 and the 38 recommendations approved by the National Council of Juvenile and Family Court Judges (NCJFCJ) in July 1984. Embodied in these organizations' policy statements are critical recommendations for the retention of and process for juvenile justice. In general, both organizations struggled with controversial issues relating to philosophy, confidentiality, transfer, research, treatment, disposition, accountability, discretion, etc.

Although these authors support the general policy statements of these organizations, we will highlight some of their recommendations given the data presented in this article. Therefore, the authors recommend:

1. The continued *individualized treatment* approach as the primary goal of juvenile justice. To include the development of medical, psychiatric, and educational programs that range from least to most restrictive, according to individual need.

2. That the *chronic, serious juvenile offender*, while being held accountable, be retained within the jurisdiction of the juvenile court. As a resource, specialized programs and facilities to be developed focused on restorations rather than punishment.

3. That the *disposition* of juvenile court have a flexible range for restricting freedom with the primary goal focused on the restoration to full liberty rather than let the punishment fit the crime.

   a. That in no case dispositions be of a mandatory nature but left to the "discretion of the judge" based on dispositional guidelines.

   b. That in no case should a juvenile (under 18 years) be subject to capital punishment.

4. That in situations where the juvenile court judge believes that the juvenile under consideration is non-amenable to the services of the court *and* based on the youth's present charges, past record in court, his or her age and mental status, may *waive jurisdiction*.

    a. That in *all* juvenile cases the court of original jurisdiction be that of the juvenile court, and

    b. The discretion to waive or not to be left to the juvenile court judge.

    c. Hence, proportionality would be appropriate with these cases. However, these high risk offenders should be treated in small but secure facilities.

5. That policy-makers, reformers, and researchers continue to strive for a greater understanding as to the causes and most desired response to juvenile crime. *Research* should be broad-based rather than limited to management, control, and punishment strategies.

Lastly, these authors call for the appropriation of public money for the support of programs with the expressed *purpose* of serving as a clearing-house, funding mechanism for traditional and experimental programs, training juvenile justice personnel, and serving the interest of juvenile justice as a significant priority by continuing and stimulating debate.

BIBLIOGRAPHY

Bender, Lauretta, M.D. "Children and Adolescents Who Have Killed." *American Journal of Psychiatry.* Vol. 116, 1959.

Castellano, Thomas C., and Theresa Delorto. "The Justice Model in the Juvenile Justice System: Washington State's Experience." Paper presented at 1986 Academy of Criminal Justice Sciences Annual Meeting, Orlando, FL, March 1986 (unpublished).

Chaiken, Marcia R. and Jan M. Chaiken. "Offender Types and Policy." *Crime and Delinquency.* Vol. 30, No. 2, April 1984.

Fischer, Craig (Ed.), "Judges Urge Guidelines for Disposition of Serious Cases." *Criminal Justice Newsletter.* Vol. 15, No. 2, Nov. 15, 1984.

_____. "New Evidence Found of Chronic Delinquency." *Criminal Justice Newsletter.* Vol. 16, No. 24, Dec. 16, 1985.

_____. "OJJDP Works with Police to Get Tough with Repeat Offenders." *Criminal Justice Newsletter.* Vol. 15, No. 24, Dec. 24, 1984.

_____. "United Nations Congress Adopts Liberal Juvenile Justice Code." *Criminal Justice Newsletter.* Vol. 16, No. 18, Sept. 17, 1985.

Gilber Seymour. "Treating Juvenile Crime." *New York Times,* Dec. 12, 1981.

Laughlin, Jerry N. (Ed.), *The Juvenile Court and Serious Offenders: 38 Recommendations.* Reno: National Council of Juvenile and Family Court Judges, 1986.

Lewis, Dorothy, et al. "Biopsychosocial Characteristics of Children Who Later Murder: A Prospective Study." *American Journal of Psychiatry.* Vol. 142, No. 10, Oct 1985.

_____, "Violent Juvenile Delinquents: Psychiatric, Neurological, Psychological and Abuse Factors." *Vulnerabilities to delinquency.* New Haven: Spectrum, 1981.

Martinson, Robert. "What Works? Questions and Answers About Prison Reform." *The Public Interest.* Vol. 35, Spring 1974.

McNally, Roger. "The Juvenile Justice System: A Legacy of Failure?" *Federal Probation.* Vol. 48, No. 4, Dec. 1984.

Metropolitan Court Judges Committee. *Deprived Children: A Judicial Response.* Reno: National Council of Juvenile and Family Court Judges, 1986.

Regnery, Alfred S. "Getting Away with Murder: Why The Juvenile Justice System Needs An Overhaul." *Policy Review.* Vol. 34, Fall 1985.

Von Hirsch, Andrew. "The Ethics of Selective Incapacitation: Observations on the Contemporary Debate." *Crime and Delinquency.* Vol. 30, No. 2, April 1984.

Wolfgang, Marvin E., et al. (1972). *Delinquency in a Birth Cohort.* Chicago: University of Chicago Press.

Biennial Report and Program Description of the California Youth Authority*

The CYA: What Is Its Role?

The Youth Authority's mission is to protect the public from the consequences of criminal activity. It provides for the department to (1) make available a range of differential services for youthful offenders committed by the courts; (2) help local justice system agencies with their efforts to combat crime and delinquency; and (3) encourage the development of state and local crime and delinquency prevention programs.

The department was created by law in 1941 to provide institutional training and parole supervision for juvenile and young adult offenders. It is the largest youthful offender agency in the nation with roughly 7,700 young men and women in institutions and camps, and another 5,200 on parole. As part of the state criminal justice system, the Youth Authority works closely with law enforcement, the courts, district attorneys, probation, and a wide spectrum of public and private agencies concerned with the problems of youth.

The Youth Authority is a unit of the Youth and Adult Correctional Agency, whose secretary reports directly to the governor. The department carries out its responsibilities through four branches—Institutions and Camps; Parole Services; Prevention and Community Corrections; and Administrative Services. The latter provides training, budgeting, facilities planning, and other functions for the entire department as well as relevant research studies.

The department receives most of its youthful offender population from court commitments—from both the juvenile and criminal courts. About one fifth of the incarcerated offenders are young adults sentenced to the Department of Corrections whom the courts order housed by the Youth Authority. At most, they remain with the Youth Authority only until their 25th birthday. Those with additional time to serve are then transferred to state prisons.

---

*Reprinted with the permission of the California Youth Authority. The largest juvenile and youthful offender agency in the United States. It is comprised of eleven institutions, six conservation camps, and aftercare programs.

Unlike these adult prison cases, those committed directly to the Youth Authority do not receive determinate sentences. Their parole release is determined by the Youthful Offender Parole Board, a body that is administratively separate from the Department of the Youth Authority. In practice, the period of incarceration is determined by the severity of the commitment offense and the offender's progress toward parole readiness. The incarceration time may not exceed the limits of determinate sentences for adults committing the same crime. In addition, the Youth Authority's jurisdiction for most serious felony offenders, both juveniles and young adults, ends on their 25th birthday.

Positive Programs for Offenders

Institutions and Camps. The department's offender population is housed in 11 institutions, six conservation camps, and one prerelease center. Two institutions are used primarily as reception center-clinics, where new commitments are screened and tested before being assigned to a permanent program to meet their training needs. Female offenders are housed either at the coeducational Ventura School or the all-female El Centro Training Center.

Two additional conservation camps are located inside institutions—the El Paso de Robles School and DeWitt Nelson Training Center. The Preston School and Youth Training School have training programs for young men to be assigned to the camps. Offenders, in most cases, are expected to spend a part of their incarceration time in camp programs where they gain valuable work experience fighting fires, and doing conservation work and other public service projects.

Youth Authority institutions vary in size and programs offered. The largest is the 1,590-bed Youth Training School where an extensive vocational program is stressed. Several institutions provide primarily remedial and academic education through the community college level, while others emphasize vocational programs. Evening education programs are being increasingly provided for those who hold daytime jobs.

The department reinforces the offender's accountability for his past criminal behavior through programs of public service, victim assistance, and restitution. The department works intensively with private industry to develop jobs for offenders. Several firms have established Free Venture job programs within the institutions.

Specialized programs also are available for offenders with special needs, such as alcohol, drug abuse, and psychiatric treatment. All incarcerated offenders are involved in individual and/or group counseling.

Community Corrections: A Cooperative Effort to Prevent Crime. The Youth Authority works closely with public and private agencies throughout California to gain support for community corrections and juvenile justice programs, and to encourage programs designed to reduce youth crime and delinquency. This work is carried out through the Prevention and Community Corrections branch, which assigns consultants in three regions statewide to provide training, technical assistance, and consultation to local government and private agencies concerned with the problems of crime and delinquency. The department also works with a state Juvenile Justice, Crime and Delinquency Prevention Commission to improve communication with the county commissions, law enforcement agencies, probation departments, and private agencies that seek to reduce crime and delinquency. Funding is administered for youth service bureaus and delinquency prevention projects statewide.

Parole Services.   The Youth Authority provides parole supervision for offenders released to the community. Parole staff work from 40 parole offices and suboffices in four administrative regions. Parole agents help parolees with their initial readjustment to the community, including residence placement, family counseling, jobs development and placement, and school enrollment. To enhance public protection, intensive counseling and surveillance are provided for specialized caseloads of sex offenders, gang-involved wards, those who have problems with drugs and alcohol, and parolees who experience severe emotional and behavioral problems. Parole staff work closely with law enforcement, and also with the Youthful Offender Parole Board when conditions of parole are violated.

The Youth Authority and its Programs

The Organization.   The Department of the Youth Authority is the largest youthful offender agency in the nation. Its mission is to protect society by providing training and treatment to juvenile and young adult offenders in 11 institutions and six conservation camps, with aftercare services and supervision during parole. The department also works closely with all elements of the criminal justice system. It strongly supports delinquency prevention programs conducted in communities statewide, and it cooperates fully with law enforcement and the courts on issues of mutual concern.

During 1984 and 1985, while the incarcerated offender population increased sharply, the department launched new statewide programs which seek to break the cycle of delinquent and criminal behavior.

The effort includes many new approaches as well as renewed emphasis on programs already in progress. The aim is to increase public participation and expand involvement with the business sector, to make maximum use of existing facilities, to make young offenders accountable for their behavior through public service, victim restitution, and other approaches, and to realistically update training and education programs to provide the maximum opportunity for success when offenders return to the community.

Organizationally, the Youth Authority is a part of the Youth and Adult Correctional Agency, a cabinet-level administrative body whose secretary reports directly to the governor. The department has a close working relationship with the Youthful Offender Parole Board, whose seven members, all appointed by the governor, are responsible for determining parole release, parole revocation, and other decisions involving Youth Authority wards.

Administratively, the department is organized into four branches. Institutions and Camps is responsible for young offenders while they are incarcerated. Parole Services supervises the offenders after they are returned to the community. Prevention and Community Corrections carries out an expanding program of crime and delinquency prevention, training, consultation, technical assistance, and coordination with local justice agencies and community members. Administrative Services provides major support services, including budgeting, accounting, research, food management, and staff training.

Highlights of the activities of each branch during 1984 and 1985 are found later in this biennial report.

Legislative and Policy Trends.   During the past two years, the department moved strongly to increase public protection with new programs to require offender accountability for their law violations, to improve their chances for obtaining and keeping jobs when they return to the community, to require restitution for victims, and to establish special supervision programs on parole for sex offenders. A bill requiring registration of juvenile sex offenders was passed into law in 1985 as a part of the governor's public safety program.

The Youth Authority also has established partnerships with private industry to help provide jobs for young offenders while they are incarcerated, and afterward, on parole. Several firms have established Free Venture–Private Industry partnerships within Youth Authority institutions, including a reservations annex operated by Trans World Airlines at the Ventura School. These programs provide vital jobs and training for offenders, with wages comparable to those paid in the community, from which a portion is deducted for victim restitution and costs of housing and food. Major improvements also have been made in institutional education programs.

Other important steps taken during 1984 and 1985 include:

- *Public involvement:* The department substantially strengthened its ties with citizens statewide to obtain their support and participation in ongoing programs. Thousands of men and women serve the department's institution, camp, and parole programs as volunteers. They serve as tutors and companions in institution programs, as counselors for young men and women on parole, and as consultants for ongoing and planned studies and activities. A Citizens Participation Task Force, with representation from the private sector as well as from all branches of the department, was organized through the director's office to strengthen community participation in the Youth Authority's programs.

- *A Minority Ward Steering Committee,* which included community representatives as well as Youth Authority staff members, addressed issues involving the overrepresentation of ethnic minorities among offenders in institutions. The department has moved to require all staff to be especially sensitive to the needs of minority wards and to ensure nondiscriminatory practices in the treatment of staff and wards. In addition, a group of community leaders has been organized to provide leadership in dealing with the problems of the disproportionately high numbers of minorities in the criminal justice system.

• *Amenability studies:* By policy change, the department has decided to place more emphasis than in the past on the circumstances of the offense in determining whether or not an offender is amenable to treatment in Youth Authority programs. State law requires the courts, before they sentence an offender who has been found unfit for juvenile court and remanded to adult court, to order a study by the Youth Authority to determine whether the individual is amenable to treatment and training in Youth Authority programs. Additional law changes to clarify the amenability process, which has been a point of contention in the criminal justice system, are being studied.

• *Public Service:* Incarcerated young offenders are also required to participate in programs of public service. This gives them an opportunity to demonstrate a measure of accountability for past behavior while gaining valuable work experience. During 1985, every institution and camp, as well as several parole units, had public service programs in operation, with young offenders performing cleanup, maintenance and other tasks for public and nonprofit agencies in the community.

• *Accountability:* In general, youthful offenders are required, before parole is granted, to demonstrate accountability for their commitment offense and to show they are prepared to contribute to society in a positive manner. The department has implemented institutional grooming and dress code policies which encourage offenders to look their best before they return to the community on parole, thereby increasing prospects for employment. As a result of legislation passed in 1984, the department has established a policy to hold its youthful offender population accountable for paying for intentional damage to state property.

Institutions and Camps. During 1984, the ward population in the Youth Authority's ten institutions and six conservation camps increased from 5,825 to 6,324. In 1985, the population continued its upward trend, surpassing 7,000 by the end of the year. The department also added an 11th institution when the El Centro Training Center, a facility for 60 female offenders, opened late in the year.

By the end of 1985, the number of incarcerated offenders in Youth Authority institutions was the highest in the department's 43-year history. The increase during the last two years was due to a number of factors, including longer lengths of stay and a higher number of parole revocations, but primarily to a new law that went into effect on January 1, 1984, pertaining to young adult offenders sentenced to the Department of Corrections. The law, Senate Bill 821, gave an option to judges who sentence offenders aged 16 to 20 to state prison to order them housed in the Youth Authority until their 25th birthday or expiration of their sentence, whichever is first.

During 1984, 662 of these young adults were sent to the Youth Authority. In 1985, commitment of these "M" cases, as these offenders are identified, accelerated, bringing the total for the two-year period to more than 2,000.

To accommodate this population increase, a number of steps were taken during 1984 and 1985:

- The 11th institution became reality as part of an agreement with Imperial County, from which the El Centro Training Center was leased. By the end of 1985, it began filling up toward its capacity of 60 female offenders, most with serious drug or alcohol problems. The program seeks to help them overcome these problems by teaching new skills and habits.

- Three hundred rooms at the Youth Training School were double-bunked, increasing the institution's capacity from 1,200 to 1,500.

- An 80-bed living unit was opened as an addition to the Oak Glen Youth Conservation Camp, increasing the facility's capacity from 50 to 130.

- At the Ventura School, a unit used by male offenders was converted to occupancy by females, and 68 rooms were double-bunked.

- Additional beds were placed in open dormitories in both institutions and camps.

- Arrangements were made with several Northern California counties to place a small number of juvenile offenders in their juvenile halls.

- The Social, Personal and Community Experience project (SPACE), formerly a parole program in a central Los Angeles location, was reassigned to the Institutions and Camps Branch where it is a residence center for 45 offenders who are due to be paroled in the near future. It has been renamed the Silverlake Pre-Parole Center.

- Programs are being carried out to extend education classes to evening hours and weekends to make maximum use of institutional facilities.

The department's population planning was carried out in 1984 and 1985 in accordance with an agreement with the U.S. Office of Juvenile Justice and Delinquency Prevention for separating juveniles and adults. The agreement, fully implemented by February 1984, provides for the department's offender population to be classified into three categories: Juvenile (juvenile court minors under 18); "Swing" (juvenile court commitments who have passed their 18th birthday and criminal court commitments who are under 18); and Adult (criminal court adults, age 18 and over). With a number of exceptions involving special programs, the agreement requires that juvenile court minors not be in contact with criminal court adults in the same institution. The swing group, however, can mingle with all categories of offenders in the same institution.

Program Activities.   The department's program emphasis in 1984 and 1985 sought to strengthen offender accountability for their behavior and to enhance their opportunities for employment during and after parole. Public service programs for offenders, both in institutions and parole, were substantially expanded. Following is a description of new and significant programs carried out in institutions and camps:

• *Employment preparation:* In 1983, a department evaluation found that more than half of all parolees were unemployed, and that most had minimal job skills along with a poor work attitude. As a result, a Ward Employment Committee was established in 1984 to coordinate efforts for employment program improvements. A new and extensive program was started, including expanded vocational testing, employability skills instruction in all institutions and camps, jobs training and placement services. These included agreements with the Employment Development Department and with the administration of the Job Training Partnership Act. One institution, the Nelles School, began an employability program to help prepare all of its wards for the job market from the day they first arrive at the facility. This program is based on a premise that employability is the key to a ward's eventual success or failure on parole.

• *Free venture:* As part of the department's emphasis on jobs for offenders, private industry is encouraged to establish enterprises within institutions which would offer "real-world" employment for offenders. During 1985, two small industrial plants were established at the Youth Training School and Preston School. As the year ended, plans were completed for Trans World Airlines to open a reservations center in January 1986 at the Ventura School. A second operation, by Olga Corp. of Van Nuys to establish a power sewing operation at the same institution, also is planned for early in 1986. Ventura will thus have an aggregate of about 50 wards employed. They will earn prevailing wages from which a portion will be withheld for restitution of crime victims and to defray the cost of their room and board. At the Youth Training School, plans have been completed to open a microfilm processing business early in 1986. This will provide jobs for 75 young offenders.

• *Education programs:* Education programs in institutions and camps were an important part of the emphasis on jobs development for wards. During 1984, 600 high school diplomas, 250 GED certificates, and 35 associate in arts degrees were awarded to incarcerated offenders. In 1985, the totals were 750 high school diplomas, 260 GED certificates and 40 associate in arts degrees. Increasing use was made of computers as instructional tools. Competency Based Education, an approach which seeks to ensure that offenders, when they leave the system, have the basic competencies necessary to reenter the community successfully, started in 1984. Further development is continuing, with full implementation expected by 1987. Other major progress in educational programs during 1984 and 1985 included the expansion of speech and language therapy, an experimental instrumental enrichment program, an expansion of library services to make them survival and employment resource centers, intensive vocational guidance and counseling programs, and modernization of the department's vocational shops and programs. The need for expanded programs for developmentally disabled and non-English speaking wards is also being investigated. One especially unusual event held in 1984 was a jobs "fair" for incarcerated women at the Ventura School, believed to be the first of its kind held anywhere in the nation. The fair provided female young offenders with employment opportunities in the construction industry and other fields in which women traditionally have not worked. A similar event is scheduled for early 1986.

• *Public service:* During the past two years, all institutions and camps established public service programs in which ward work crews provided needed services upon request to other governmental and non-profit organizations. The program has three basic goals—to give offenders an opportunity to provide some restitution for past illegal behavior, to give them a sense of responsibility toward their community, and to provide them with opportunities for personal growth. For the two years of 1984 and 1985, camp crews spent a total of 212,539 man-hours fighting fires, equaling $744,000 in services at minimum wage. In addition, camp and institution wards completed 426,192 hours of public service, the equivalent of $1,491,700 in services. Late in 1985, the department completed training and activated a team of young offenders at the Karl Holton School who will be available for search and rescue missions in the mountains.

• *Emergency preparedness:* A comprehensive program to control ward-disturbance emergencies, prepared in conjunction with the Department of Corrections under the direction of the Youth and Adult Correctional Agency, was approved in mid-1984 by the governor's office. The plan includes extensive staff training, an operational plan at each institution, establishment of an emergency operations center, and mutual aid agreements with local law enforcement, fire departments, hospitals, and other local resources. In 1985, the plan was further refined and standardized for all institutions and camps.

• *Day labor/ward labor program:* Use of ward labor for repair projects and new minor construction was expanded during 1984 and 1985. In 1983, legislation was passed which increased to $200,000 the maximum cost of individual construction projects in which they could work. During mid-1983 through mid-1985, $2 million in construction work was completed by ward labor, providing a broad range of on-the-job construction work training.

Parole Services.   In contrast to institutions, the number of parolees supervised by the Youth Authority declined substantially in 1984 and 1985, from 6,871 to 5,736 during the two-year period. As a result, one of the department's 28 parole offices—the Foothill office in northern Sacramento County—was closed and its caseload area was assumed by the neighboring Sacramento and Chico units.

The department's parole staff have a dual role. They help wards in their reintegration to the community by arranging for educational, job-training, housing, and counseling services. They also work closely with law enforcement and the Youthful Offender Parole Board to provide public protection. Parole staff may either take preventive action before a possible law violation occurs, or take corrective action in case of violations of the law and conditions of parole. During the past two years, the department has increased its emphasis on working with local law enforcement to apprehend missing parolees or escapees from institutions.

Public Protection. A number of programs were undertaken or expanded in 1984 and 1985 to strengthen public protection in the supervision of parolees. These included:

• *A pilot apprehension unit* was established in 1984 in the Los Angeles area to work closely with law enforcement in locating and apprehending missing parolees and institution escapees. During its first 12 months of operation, there was a 29.1 percent increase in apprehensions in Los Angeles County, compared to an initial objective of a 10 percent increase.

• *Gang Information Network:* A Gang Information Services Unit has been placed under the administration of Parole Services. It is responsible for developing, coordinating, and sharing information with law enforcement and other justice system components concerning wards within the department who are significantly involved with gangs. This unit, along with other designated staff from each parole region, institution, and camp, participate in a departmental gang information network which provides for regular group and individual information-sharing about wards and gang activities. It is estimated that more than half of the department's current population has been involved with street gangs.

• *Specialized caseloads* of parolees are supervised by staff with expertise in specific areas, such as substance abuse, placement problems, psychiatric treatment, and special employment needs. A study completed in August 1984 recommended an increase in specialized caseloads, including one for sex offenders. As a result, a pilot sex offender caseload was established in San Francisco. Preliminary results of the new unit appear encouraging, and establishment of similar units elsewhere in the state is being considered. The study also recommended continuation of a special parole reentry program in Central Los Angeles, one of the highest crime areas in the state. In this unit, new parolees receive more intensive supervision during their first 90 days in the community. Also being considered is a plan to establish caseloads which focus on wards with significant gang involvement.

• *Firearms policy:* A Youth Authority policy permitting field parole agents to carry firearms continued in 1984 and 1985, with the completion of initial training and the issuance of weapons to 165 parole agents who completed the program. During the two years, there were no significant incidents involving the use of firearms.

• *Increased parole revocations:* The rate of parole revocations increased to 217 per 1,000 in 1984 and 242 in 1985, compared with 168 per 1,000 five years earlier. This trend is largely the result of discretionary action by the Youthful Offender Parole Board in areas of technical violations, property offenses, and drug involvement. Such actions are in line with board and department policy to protect society by enforcing accountability for law violations in the community.

Special Programs. One special parole unit, the Social, Personal and Community Experience Project (SPACE) in the city of Los Angeles, was transferred to the Institutions and Camps Branch. Parole Services continued to operate these other special projects, in addition to the regular parole offices, in 1984 and 1985:

• *Transitional Residential Program* includes two residence centers in Los Angeles and Orange Counties for up to 37 parolees. The program provides 24-hour supervision, and wards have access to the community only for such specific purposes as jobs and services from a local support agency.

• *NETWORK Program* provides intensive support for difficult-to-place parolees who are supervised in four residential facilities in San Diego County. NETWORK staff work closely with law enforcement and community organizations to provide job survival training, work experience, and education to help parolees become self-sufficient. The program has a residential capacity of 25 parolees, including up to five females, and provides follow-up parole services to approximately 75 more.

• *Gang Violence Reduction Project* uses gang leaders as consultants in East Los Angeles to direct gangs toward peaceful interaction and positive behavior. During 1984 and 1985, the 10 gangs in the target area were increasingly directed toward public service programs, such as removal of graffiti, and have begun meeting together in handball and other sports competitions. Relative peace has been maintained among gangs in the target area, although a continuing need remains for conflict resolution.

• *Interstate Services Unit* is a specialized operation based in Sacramento that is responsible for administration of interstate compacts on juveniles and adults. These compacts provide for prior notification of probation and parole releases among the various states, investigations of plans and mutual agreements for supervision, caseload supervision of Youth Authority parolees placed in other states, and for the return of parole violators. The unit also coordinates the return of runaway juveniles to their home state.

There was an increased emphasis on public service and education programs for Youth Authority parolees in 1984 and 1985. Some examples:

• A program to provide individualized academic instruction at San Jose State University's School of Education served approximately 41 parolees from the Santa Clara Valley Parole Office. The program is known as Remedial Education and Academic Development for Survival (READS).

• In the Fresno Parole Office, a program to encourage parolees to complete their high school education was started in 1984 in conjunction with the Fresno Unified School District, which provides a certified teacher. In two years, five graduated from high school.

Volunteer Services.   Although not as extensively used as in institutions and camps, volunteers are employed in Parole Services in a number of programs. These include:

• *Vista Volunteers:* Conducted under the auspices of ACTION, a federal agency, the project provides 10 volunteers recruited by local parole staff to recruit other volunteers and service providers to help parolees with employment preparation, substance abuse education, and literacy services.

• *Volunteers in Parole:* Under contract with the California State Bar Association, this project provides volunteer attorneys who sponsor and help parolees as they return to the community. Projects are located in Sacramento, San Francisco, Alameda, Santa Clara, Los Angeles, Orange, and San Diego Counties, with more than 200 matches provided.

Prevention and Community Corrections.   In addition to its responsibilities for youthful offenders committed by the courts, the Youth Authority provides statewide leadership in such areas as juvenile justice, community corrections, and crime and delinquency prevention. Regional offices for the Prevention and Community Corrections Branch are maintained in Sacramento, San Leandro, and Glendale, with suboffices in Tustin and Fresno. Consultants are responsible for the mandated inspection and monitoring of local facilities in which juveniles are detained. Staff work closely with state and local agencies and private organizations to provide technical assistance, consultation, funding assistance, and training.

Public Protection.   A basic commitment for Prevention and Community Corrections is to work with other elements of the criminal justice system to protect the public from the damaging effects of crime. Major 1984 and 1985 activities in this area include:

• Appointment of a statewide coordinator of victim services to provide special consultant services to local communities as well as to the Youth Authority.

• Establishment of a sex offender task force, which held public hearings throughout the state to gather information from victims and criminal justice experts in order to develop new programs and seek possible future legislation.

- Several training seminars on victim services, culminating in the Annual Governor's Conference on Victim Rights in April 1985.
- Workshops on the Clergy and Victims of Violence.
- Staff services to a number of organizations concerned with victim services.

Training. Forty-two training courses were conducted annually for law enforcement and probation staff to meet basic core and annual training requirements of the Board of Corrections and Peace Officers Standards and Training. In addition, 10 to 12 specially requested outreach courses were provided each year. All told, approximately 3,000 training hours were presented for approximately 2,050 students, with 74 cities and 37 counties represented among the trainees. In addition, in 1984 eight training seminars were conducted on juvenile court fitness hearings procedures in cooperation with the California District Attorneys Association and the Chief Probation Officers of California.

Institutions. Inspections were conducted at 47 juvenile halls, 24 jails, and 53 county camps to determine their suitability for the detention of minors in 1984; and 47 juvenile halls, 24 jails, and 55 county camps were inspected in 1985. The department continued to work cooperatively with country officials to assure compliance with minimum state standards. Staff provided assistance to local jurisdictions regarding compliance with the Juvenile Justice and Delinquency Prevention Act of 1974 to reduce by 75 percent the number of status offenders or nonoffenders held in secure facilities.

In 1984, Assembly Bill 3306 authorized $1 million to fund a pilot program of one or more regional youth educational facilities. The San Bernardino County Probation Department was awarded the grant to operate a 40-bed facility for two years to receive wards from San Bernardino and Riverside Counties.

Crime and Delinquency Prevention. The Youth Authority has a statutory mandate to exercise statewide leadership in crime and delinquency prevention. A major communications vehicle for this program is a citizens commission which advises the director of the Youth Authority. In 1984, legislation was approved to increase the commission's size from eight to 16 members in order to provide a fuller statewide span of representation. The legislation also assigned a new name to the commission, designating it as the State Commission on Juvenile Justice, Crime and Delinquency Prevention. Four regional advisory committees also were established to improve communication to all parts of California.

Other major activities involving delinquency prevention:

- Twenty Transfer of Knowledge workshops were held, bringing together experts from various parts of the criminal justice system to present programs dealing with specific problem areas. The workshops covered these subjects: Wilderness Intervention, Correlations between

Delinquency and Abuse, Interagency Strategies, Violence in the Community, Juvenile Restitution/Community Service, Early Gang Intervention, Crime and Violence among Asian/Pacific Islander Youth, School Safety and Academic Excellence, Alcohol, Drugs and the Teenage Driver, Community Schools, Delinquency Prevention, Youth Violence and Senior Citizens as Victims, Classification of Youthful Gang Members in Local Detention Facilities, Group Home Training, Runaway and Homeless Youth, Model Juvenile Bureau/Unit, Parenting and Neighborhood Strategies against Youth Gang Violence, and Black and Hispanic Involvement in the Criminal Justice System. Several more are planned for 1986.

• Funding was provided for 16 youth service bureaus—four of them added during 1984. In addition, nine local delinquency prevention programs were funded in 1984 and eight in 1985. Funds shared totaled $1,395,260 for the youth service bureaus and $202,400 for the delinquency prevention programs in 1985.

• An additional $4.2 million in both 1984 and 1985 in federal funds allocated by the Governor's Office of Criminal Justice Planning was given to local programs for diversion, restitution, intervention, and prevention.

• Ongoing staff services were provided to local law enforcement, whose work with juveniles is an essential part of the criminal justice system's efforts to protect society. Regional law enforcement advisory committees have been established to set priorities for services to law enforcement. Members are from local law enforcement agencies.

In addition:

• A Northern California Gang Investigators Association was established.

• The 40-hour Basic Juvenile Law Enforcement Officers Training Course was substantially revised to include new subject areas in which juvenile officers must have expertise.

State Planning. Ongoing services were provided to the California Corrections Executives Council, composed of correctional administrators representing the Youth and Adult Correctional Agency, including the Youth Authority, Department of Corrections, Board of Prison Terms, Youthful Offender Parole Board, and the Board of Corrections, as well as the Chief Probation Officers of California and the California State Sheriffs Association.

The council works cooperatively on major state and local correctional issues.

Administrative Services. The Administrative Services Branch furnishes staff, management, and support services for the entire department. The branch, composed of six divisions—Financial Management, Information

Management, Personnel Management, Program Research and Review, Program Support, and Training—participated in many of the activities described elsewhere in this report.

Following are highlights of branch activities during 1984 and 1985:

• A Research Advisory Committee, including prominent academicians, researchers, and practitioners from outside the Youth Authority as well as department staff, was organized to provide guidance on issues needing research-based information. The committee gave priority to these issues: crowding, classification, and the increased usability of the management information system.

• Research efforts under way during the two-year period included the impact of crowding on staff and wards, factors which influence ward risk, an examination of the criminal careers of former Youth Authority wards over a 10-year period, analysis of violent incidents by parolees, and a study of juvenile probation camps. A study of youth service bureaus, completed at the request of the legislature, concluded that the bureaus provide services to the intended target populations of predelinquent and less seriously delinquent youth.

• Expanded use of wards in day labor projects resulted in considerable cost savings to the department in addition to giving the young offenders valuable on-the-job experience in roofing, carpentry, concrete, sheet metal, welding, plumbing, electrical, masonry, and tile setting.

• Food service menus were standardized in all institutions and camps, providing a uniform balanced diet to wards and eliminating costly waste. As part of the program, a food service training manual was developed and training was provided for 113 food service personnel.

• A three-year information systems plan was adopted in 1984. During 1985, obsolete data processing equipment was replaced and word processing capability was increased in several facilities in order to increase productivity.

• A new performance appraisal system for managers was developed and implemented. A pilot program to offer monetary bonuses to managers who demonstrate superior accomplishment was initiated in 1985.

• Six mandated training programs, including use of restraints, CPR, and management of assaultive behavior, were standardized statewide.

• Parole staff were trained in comprehensive skills development to handle parole violators.

• Community college accreditation was obtained for training center courses.

• The basic academy program for new peace officers was strengthened with new field experience exercises and a comprehensive physical conditioning component.

• A management development program was started under the leadership of a steering committee of top departmental managers working with outside members from private industry, other public jurisdictions, and academia. The advisory group is the first of its kind in state government.

• Validation was completed of a departmental physical ability testing program, which requires that group supervisor and youth counselor candidates demonstrate the physical ability to perform their duties. The tests are administered in place of a previous employment restriction based on age.

• A preemployment screening unit was established to investigate the employment suitability of candidates for entry-level peace officer classes. Through 1985, approximately 1,300 such background investigations were completed.

• An intensive recruitment program for entry-level peace officer positions began in 1985. Staff participated in numerous jobs expositions and conferences.

• With a departmental budget of more than $280 million in 1985–86, a major effort was initiated to improve budget administration. An accounting system was implemented to recover court-ordered restitution payments from young offenders committed to the Youth Authority.

Statistical Highlights

First Commitments.[1]   After two declining years, new admissions increased in 1984 by 11 percent from 1983. This upward trend continued in 1985, recording a 17 percent increase over 1984. These increases are the result of the placement in Youth Authority facilities of cases sentenced to the California Department of Corrections (CDC cases). This placement effective January 1, 1984, was authorized by Section 1731.5(c) of the Welfare and Institutions Code. Direct commitments to the Youth Authority actually decreased 12 percent from 1983 to 1984 and 1 percent from 1984 to 1985. Juvenile court commitments declined by 5 percent in 1984 from 1983 but increased 4 percent in 1985. Criminal court commitments, which dropped 36 percent in 1984 from 1983, continued declining in 1985 with a 28 percent decrease from 1984.

Area of First Commitments.   In 1984, 58 percent of all first commitments to the Youth Authority were from Southern California; 45 percent were from Los Angeles County. In 1985, 60 percent were from Southern California with 39 percent from Los Angeles County.

Court of First Commitments.   Commitments to the Youth Authority can come from either the juvenile or the criminal courts. In 1984, the distri-

---

[1]First commitment includes CDC cases committed under Welfare and Institutions Code Section 1731.5(c) unless otherwise specified. CDC cases may have had prior Youth Authority commitment. However, for the purposes of this report, they are treated as first commitments.

bution for direct Youth Authority commitments was 83 percent from the juvenile courts and 17 percent from the criminal courts. In 1985, this proportion was 88 and 12 percent, respectively. In 1984, when the CDC cases are included, the ratio becomes 66 percent juvenile court and 34 percent criminal court; in 1985, it was 60 percent, and 40 percent, respectively.

Age of First Commitments. The average age for all first commitments to the Youth Authority in 1984, including CDC cases, was 17.7 years, an increase of 0.3 years over 1983. This average age increased another 0.3 years in 1985 to 18.0 years. However, the average age for direct Youth Authority commitments was only 17.2 years in 1984, a decrease of 0.2 years from 1983. This age decreased to 17.1 years in 1985.

First Commitment Offenses. The most common commitment offense for all first commitments in 1984 and 1985 was burglary followed by robbery and assault and battery. Commitments for violent offenses (homicide, robbery, assault and battery, forcible rape, and kidnapping) made up 41 percent in 1984 and 40 percent in 1985.

Length of Stay. Institutional length of stay for Youth Authority wards paroled in 1984 was up to 16.1 months from 1983's 15.0 months. This further increased to 17.1 months in 1985. The institutional length of stay for wards paroled in 1985 is the longest in Youth Authority history. It reflects changes in commitment offense patterns, laws, and the Youthful Offender Parole Board time-setting policy.

Long-Term Trends. Youth Authority institution population at the close of 1984 was 6,350, an 8 percent increase over 1983. This increase continued in 1985, ending the year with a 13 percent increase over 1984 at 7,116. The parole population decreased 6 percent during 1984 to 6,488 and decreased 12 percent during 1985 to 5,736. However, the Youth Authority is adding 2,900 beds as a result of new prison construction from 1988 to 1991.

Profiles of First Commitments[2]

California Youth Authority Males. *Home Environment.*

- Fifty percent came from neighborhoods considered below average economically, 44 percent came from average neighborhoods and 6 percent were from above-average neighborhoods.
- Forty percent lived in neighborhoods with a high level of delinquency, and 34 percent lived in moderately delinquent neighborhoods. Only 7 percent were from neighborhoods considered nondelinquent.

---

[2]Does not include CDC cases committed under Welfare and Institutions Code Section 1731.5(c).

- Thirty-two percent came from homes where public assistance funds comprised all or most of the family income.

Family.

- Seventy-two percent came from broken homes. However, at least one natural parent was present in 92 percent of the homes.
- Fifty-two percent had at least one parent, brother, or sister with a delinquent or criminal record.
- Less than 1 percent were married at the time of commitment, and 5 percent had children.

Delinquent Behavior.

- Eighty-six percent had at least one conviction or sustained petition prior to commitment to the Youth Authority, while 23 percent had five or more convictions or sustained petitions prior to commitment. Sixty-eight percent had a previous commitment to a local facility.

Employment/Schooling.

- Of those in the labor force, only 7 percent were employed full time while 73 percent were unemployed.
- Fifty-five percent were last enrolled in the tenth grade or below. Thirteen percent had reached the 12th grade or had graduated from high school at the time of commitment.

California Youth Authority Females.   *Home Environment.*

- Forty percent came from neighborhoods considered below average economically, 49 percent came from average neighborhoods, and 11 percent were from above-average neighborhoods.
- Thirty-four percent lived in neighborhoods with a high level of delinquency, and 30 percent lived in moderately delinquent neighborhoods. Only 8 percent were from neighborhoods considered nondelinquent.
- Thirty-six percent came from homes where public assistance funds comprised all or most of the family income.

Family.

- Seventy-five percent came from broken homes. However, at least one natural parent was present in 88 percent of the homes.
- Fifty-seven percent had at least one parent, brother, or sister with a delinquent or criminal record.
- Less than 1 percent were married at the time of commitment, and 18 percent had children.

Delinquent Behavior.

- Eighty-two percent had at least one conviction or sustained petition prior to commitment to the Youth Authority, while 15 percent had five or more convictions or sustained petitions prior to commitment. Forty-two percent had a previous commitment to a local facility.

Employment/Schooling.

- Of those in the labor force, 82 percent were unemployed and 3 percent were employed full time.
- Sixty-six percent were last enrolled in the tenth grade or below. Ten percent had reached the 12th grade or had graduated from high school at the time of commitment.

Age.   A breakdown by the age at admission of 1984 and 1985 first commitments is displayed in Table D–1. A composite of the average age of commitments since 1974 is provided in Table D–2. Until 1982, the average admission age was relatively stable. Changes in departmental policy and commitment laws in the early 1980s virtually barred the majority of criminal court cases—who are traditionally older than juvenile court cases—from commitment to the Youth Authority. The rise in the average admission age from 1984 and 1985 commitments is commensurate with the inclusion of CDC cases placed in Youth Authority facilities as first commitments. The average age of Youth Authority cases actually continued the decline begun in 1982.

Commitment Offense.   The offenses which resulted in commitment to the Youth Authority or to the Department of Corrections (for those CDC cases housed in the Youth Authority) are shown in Table D–3. The most common offenses for both Youth Authority and CDC cases were burglary, robbery, and assault and battery.

Average Daily Population

An overview of the Youth Authority's average daily population since 1974 is presented in Table D–4. From 1983 to 1985, the average daily population in Youth Authority facilities increased 14 percent to a total of 6,616, rising well above the design capacity of the department's facilities.

Institutional Population

A summary of the Youth Authority's ending populations on December 31, 1984 and 1985 is detailed in Table D–5. The total Youth Authority population in 1985 increased approximately 12 percent from 1984, with the admission of CDC cases representing the largest proportion of the increase.

TABLE D-1 Age at Admission of First Commitments to the Youth Authority, 1984 and 1985

Age at Admission	Total		Total CYA		CYA Juvenile Court		CYA Criminal Court		CDC W&I 1731.5(c)*	
	Number	Percent	Number	Percent	Number	Percent	Number	Percent	Number	Percent
1984										
Total admissions	3,216	100.0%	2,554	100.0%	2,128	100.0%	426	100.0%	662	100.0%
11 years	2	0.1	2	0.1	2	0.1	—	—	—	—
12	—	—	—	—	—	—	—	—	—	—
13	23	0.7	23	0.9	23	1.1	—	—	—	—
14	111	3.5	111	4.3	111	5.2	—	—	—	—
15	315	9.8	315	12.3	315	14.8	—	—	—	—
16	593	18.4	588	23.0	576	27.1	12	2.8	5	0.8
17	942	29.3	992	36.2	842	39.5	80	18.8	20	3.0
18	580	18.0	397	15.5	241	11.3	156	36.6	183	27.6
19	393	12.2	120	4.7	16	0.8	104	24.4	273	41.2
20	196	6.1	51	2.0	2	0.1	49	11.5	145	21.9
21 and older	61	1.9	25	1.0	—	—	25	5.9	36	5.5
Mean age	17.7 years		17.2 years		16.9 years		18.9 years		19.5 years	

1985

	Total admissions									
	3,756	100.0%	2,521	100.0%	2,213	100.0%	308	100.0%	1,235	100.0%
11 years	1	0.0	1	0.0	1	0.0	—	—	—	—
12	9	0.2	9	0.4	9	0.4	—	—	—	—
13	17	0.5	17	0.7	17	0.8	—	—	—	—
14	106	2.8	106	4.2	106	4.8	—	—	—	—
15	320	8.5	320	12.7	320	14.5	—	—	—	—
16	618	16.5	615	24.4	603	27.2	12	3.9	3	0.3
17	934	24.9	897	35.6	839	37.9	58	18.8	37	3.0
18	679	18.1	397	15.7	289	13.1	108	35.1	282	22.8
19	599	15.9	102	4.0	29	1.3	73	23.7	497	40.2
20	366	9.7	48	1.9	—	—	48	15.6	318	25.8
21 and older	107	2.9	9	0.4	—	—	9	2.9	98	7.9
Mean age	18.0 years		17.1 years		16.9 years		18.9 years		19.6 years	

*Committed under Welfare and Institutions Code Section 1731.5(c); may have had previous CYA commitment.

TABLE D-2   Mean Age at Admission of First Commitments to the Youth Authority, 1974–1985 (by sex and committing court, in years)

| | Males | | | Females | | | Juvenile and |
Year	Total	Juvenile Courts	Criminal Courts	Total	Juvenile Courts	Criminal Courts	Criminal Courts
1974	18.1	16.6	19.6	18.2	16.6	19.6	17.1
1975	18.0	16.7	19.5	18.0	16.7	19.5	17.4
1976	18.2	16.8	19.5	18.2	16.8	19.5	17.6
1977	18.0	16.8	19.5	18.0	16.8	19.5	17.5
1978	17.9	16.8	19.4	17.9	16.8	19.4	17.5
1979	18.0	16.8	19.5	18.0	16.8	19.5	17.6
1980	18.0	16.8	19.4	18.0	16.8	19.4	17.4
1981	18.0	16.7	19.3	18.0	16.8	19.3	17.6
1982	17.6	16.8	19.1	17.6	16.9	19.1	17.0
1983	17.4	16.9	19.0	17.4	16.9	19.0	17.0
1984 Total	17.7	16.9	19.3	17.7	16.9	19.3	17.3
CYA	17.2	16.9	18.9	17.3	16.9	18.9	17.0
CDC*	19.5	—	19.5	19.5	—	19.5	19.5
1985 Total	18.0	16.9	19.5	17.3	16.7	19.5	18.0
CYA	17.1	16.9	18.9	16.9	16.7	19.0	17.1
CDC*	19.6	—	19.6	19.7	—	19.7	19.6

*Committed under Welfare and Institutions Code Section 1731.5(c); may have had previous CYA commitment.

Length of Institutional Stay

The average amount of time Youth Authority cases spent institutionalized is depicted in Table D-6. Increasing steadily from a low of 10.9 months in 1977, the 1985 length of stay of 17.1 months is the longest average in Youth Authority history.

This significant increase is primarily the result of changes in commitment offense patterns, laws, and the time-setting policy of the Youthful Offender Parole Board.

YOUTH AUTHORITY UPDATE

A Report on Current Programs in the Department for 1986–87

Offender Population, Program Activity at Record Levels

At the beginning of 1987, the Youth Authority had an offender population of 8,200 in its institutions and camps, and was providing for them with an unprecedented level of new, innovative, and promising programs. There were public service programs in every institution and camp, along with extensive evening education classes augmenting regular daytime school programs. By stepping up program services, the department was advancing its mission of protecting society through the expansion of training and education opportunities for offenders who will return to the community.

Some of the major program directions being undertaken are as follows:

Public Service.   During the first nine months of 1986, incarcerated offenders spent 700,000 person-hours working on public service projects, not including the time spent by camp crews on firelines. These activities not only provide valuable work experience; in addition, they give the young men and women an opportunity to help the community to which they previously had been a problem.

Victim Restitution.   A portion of funds earned by young offenders in camp programs and in such other work programs as Free Venture—a partnership with private industry to create jobs within institutions—is earmarked for victims of crime. In this way, offenders may become more accountable for their past and future behavior. In December 1986, a check for $29,000 was presented to the California Crime Victims program—the first payment made from the earnings of Youth Authority wards who worked in Free Venture programs.

Employment Preparation.   A partnership with private industry is developing vocational testing, employability skills instruction, training and placement services to strengthen the ability of offenders to obtain and keep jobs. It has been well established that young offenders who can compete successfully in the workplace are most likely to leave criminal careers behind them.

Day Labor/Ward Labor.   Construction costs have been substantially reduced and young offenders have been given vital job training under professional supervision. These work crews have performed numerous special repair and maintenance improvement projects at Youth Authority facilities.

Substance Abuse Programs.   With an estimated 85 percent of the department's offender population believed to have a background of substance abuse, all institutions and camps have established formal programs to deal with this problem.

Sex Offender Programs.   A 60-bed specialized counseling program was opened in 1986 at the Nelles School to provide specifically for sex offenders. Specialized parole units with caseloads of sex offenders were established statewide during the year after a successful experience with a one-year pilot project in San Francisco.

Competency-Based Education.   The department is emphasizing a new educational approach that gives all offenders, no matter what their capabilities, the basic competency needed to reenter the community successfully. In

TABLE D-3 Commitment Offense of First Commitments to the Youth Authority, 1984 and 1985 (by court)

Age at Admission	Total		Total CYA		CYA Juvenile Court		CYA Criminal Court		CDC W&I 1731.5(c)*	
	Number	Percent	Number	Percent	Number	Percent	Number	Percent	Number	Percent
1984										
Total, all offenses	3,216	100.0%	2,554	100.0%	2,128	100.0%	426	100.0%	662	100.0%
Offenses against persons	1,324	41.2	1,061	41.5	849	39.9	212	49.8	263	39.7
Homicide	116	3.6	94	3.7	57	2.7	37	8.7	22	3.3
Robbery	627	19.5	480	18.8	405	19.0	75	17.6	147	22.2
Assault and battery	457	14.2	397	15.5	331	15.6	66	15.5	60	9.0
Forcible rape	99	3.1	70	2.7	42	2.0	28	6.6	29	4.4
Kidnapping	25	0.8	20	0.8	14	0.6	6	1.4	5	0.8
Offenses against property	1,497	46.5	1,147	44.9	982	46.1	165	38.7	350	52.9
Burglary	972	30.2	687	26.9	602	28.3	85	20.0	285	43.0
Theft (except auto)	274	8.5	241	9.4	188	8.8	53	12.3	33	5.0
Auto theft	191	5.9	174	6.8	158	7.4	16	3.8	17	2.6
Forgery and checks	35	1.1	32	1.3	21	1.0	11	2.6	3	0.5
Arson	25	0.8	13	0.5	13	0.6	—	—	12	1.8
Narcotics and Drugs	180	5.6	165	65	144	6.8	21	4.9	15	2.3
All other offenses	215	6.7	181	7.1	153	7.2	28	6.6	34	5.1

1985

Total, all offenses	3,756	100.0	2,521	100.0	2,213	100.0	308	100.0	1,235	100.0
Offenses against persons	1,493	39.8	969	38.4	829	37.5	140	45.4	524	42.4
Homicide	180	4.8	109	4.3	81	3.7	28	9.1	71	5.7
Robbery	699	18.6	411	16.3	359	16.2	52	16.9	288	23.3
Assault and battery	471	12.6	364	14.4	321	14.5	43	13.9	107	8.7
Forcible rape	101	2.7	54	2.2	42	1.9	12	3.9	47	3.8
Kidnapping	42	1.1	31	1.2	26	1.2	5	1.6	11	0.9
Offenses against property	1,778	47.3	1,174	46.6	1,052	47.5	122	39.6	604	48.9
Burglary	1,183	31.5	700	27.8	652	29.4	48	15.6	483	39.1
Theft (except auto)	308	8.2	242	9.6	197	8.9	45	14.6	66	5.4
Auto theft	223	5.9	183	7.2	159	7.2	24	7.8	40	3.2
Forgery and checks	31	0.8	22	0.9	18	0.8	4	1.3	9	0.7
Arson	33	0.9	27	1.1	26	1.2	1	0.3	6	0.5
Narcotics and drugs	263	7.0	215	8.5	188	8.5	27	8.8	48	3.9
All other offenses	222	5.9	163	6.5	144	6.5	19	6.2	59	4.8

*Committed under Welfare and Institutions Code Section 1731.5(c); may have had previous CYA commitment.

TABLE D-4 Average Daily Population of Youth Authority Wards in Institutions, 1974–1985

Institution	1974	1975	1976	1977	1978	1979	1980	1981	1982	1983	1984*	1985*
Total population	4,537	4,602	4,432	4,003	4,405	4,924	5,179	5,669	5,810	5,869	6,081	6,638
CYA reception centers												
NRCC—males	662	699	654	679	700	688	677	771	756	777	749	802
NRCC—females	226	247	235	244	248	258	275	333	323	344	340	381
SRCC—males	337	351	300	306	324	324	340	392	386	383	405	421
SRCC—females	43	37	24	23	22	11	1	—	—	—	—	1
VRCC—males	19	24	21	23	26	33	13	—	—	—	—	—
VRCC—females	37	40	41	37	35	17	6	—	—	—	4	—
YTSC—males	—	—	33	46	45	45	43	47	47	49	—	—
CYA schools—males	3,260	3,362	3,290	2,908	3,200	3,669	3,900	4,227	4,311	4,309	4,485	4,917
Fred C. Nelles	388	386	349	321	374	428	450	512	538	549	552	588
O. H. Close	343	347	340	344	354	368	369	397	395	398	397	426
El Paso de Robles	138	352	387	333	409	423	449	461	462	460	467	497
Karl Holton	385	386	379	335	366	399	399	417	436	436	436	448
DeWitt Nelson	378	378	355	291	326	339	344	382	403	404	406	437
Preston	421	399	386	357	380	471	514	559	563	569	615	658
Youth Training School	976	892	886	726	967	783	1,044	1,124	1,145	1,127	1,266	1,481
Ventura	194	198	189	183	189	282	309	352	346	347	327	356
South Community Drug Center	21	5	—	—	—	—	—	—	—	—	—	—

SPACE/Silverlake†	16	19	19	18	19	22	22	23	23	19	19	26
CYA camps—males	367	348	328	305	341	355	405	454	460	486	553	609
Ben Lomond	74	69	68	61	70	73	70	76	77	83	85	90
Mt. Bullion	75	69	65	62	69	70	71	75	75	81	88	94
Pine Grove	71	69	68	65	70	67	75	76	75	82	84	93
Washington Ridge	71	70	64	59	66	67	67	76	75	80	83	91
Oak Glen	76	71	63	58	66	74	68	59	51	53	103	129
Fenner Canyon	—	—	—	—	—	4	54	92	107	107	110	112
CYA schools—females	202	165	144	101	129	160	186	210	226	234	255	288
Ventura	200	163	142	100	128	159	185	209	225	233	254	285
SPACE†	2	2	2	1	1	1	1	1	1	1	1	—
El Centro‡	—	—	—	—	—	—	—	—	—	—	—	4
Department of Corrections	46	28	16	10	35	22	11	29	23	38	21	21
Federal institutions	—	—	—	—	—	—	—	9	34	25	18	1

*Includes cases committed under Welfare and Institutions Code Section 1731.5(c).
†Coed SPACE program discontinued June 30, 1985. Superceded by Silverlake program for males only July 1, 1985.
‡Program started November 1985 for females only.

TABLE D-5 Institutional Population of December 31, 1984 and 1985 (by institution)

Institution	December 31, 1984			December 31, 1985			Percent Change		
	Total*	CYA	CDC W&I 1731.5(c)†	Total*	CYA	CDC W&I 1731.5(c)†	Total*	CYA	CDC W&I 1731.5(c)†
Total population	6,350	5,760	590	7,148	5,867	1,281	+12.6	+1.9	+117.1
CYA reception centers	761	634	127	881	636	245	+15.8	+0.3	+92.9
NRCC—males	347	283	64	434	295	139	+25.1	+4.2	+117.2
NRCC—females	1	1	—	1	1	—	—	—	—
SRCC—males	413	350	63	446	340	106	+8.0	−2.9	+68.3
CYA schools—males	4,704	4,369	335	5,314	4,515	799	+13.0	+3.3	+138.5
Fred C. Nelles	560	560	—	687	687	—	+22.7	+22.7	—
O. H. Close	404	404	—	456	456	—	+12.9	+12.9	—
El Paso de Robles	469	469	1	549	548	1	+17.1	+16.8	+100.0
Karl Holton	437	436	93	480	474	6	+9.8	+8.7	+500.0
DeWitt Nelson	413	320	81	489	253	236	+18.4	−20.9	+153.8
Preston	638	557	160	689	498	191	+8.0	−10.6	+135.8
Youth Training School	1,423	1,263	—	1,493	1,135	358	+4.9	−10.1	+123.8
Ventura	339	339	—	442	436	6	+30.4	+28.6	+600.0
SPACE/Silverlake†	21	21	—	29	28	1	+38.1	+33.3	+100.0

CYA camps—males	596	479	117	608	399	209	+2.0	−16.7	+78.6
Ben Lomond	82	82	—	94	93	1	+14.6	+13.4	+100.0
Mt. Bullion	98	91	7	96	57	39	−2.0	−37.4	+457.1
Pine Grove	86	49	37	97	48	49	+12.8	−2.0	+32.4
Washington Ridge	85	41	44	89	35	54	+4.7	−14.6	+22.7
Oak Glen	133	133	—	121	121	—	−9.0	−9.0	—
Fenner Canyon	112	83	29	111	45	66	−0.9	−45.8	+127.6
CYA school—females	263	252	11	313	287	26	+19.0	+13.9	+136.4
Ventura	263	252	11	266	240	26	+1.1	−4.8	+136.4
SPACE‡	—	—	—	—	—	—	—	—	—
El Centro§	21	21	—	47	47	—	—	—	—
Department of Corrections		21	—	27	25	2	+28.6	+19.0	+200.0
Federal institutions	5	5	—	5	5	—	—	—	—

*Includes diagnostic, parole temporary detention and other guests.
†Committed under Welfare and Institutions Code Section 1731.5(c).
‡Coed SPACE program discontinued June 30, 1985. Superceded by Silverlake program for males only July 1, 1985.
§Program started November 1985 for females only.

TABLE D-6 Mean Length of Stay in Institutionalized Wards Prior to Release on Parole, 1974–1985 (by institution of release, in months)

Institution of Release*	1974	1975	1976	1977	1978	1979	1980	1981	1982	1983	1984†	1985†
Total‡ mean length	12.3	12.7	12.0	10.9	11.3	12.0	12.9	13.1	14.2	15.0	16.1	17.1
Males	12.4	12.7	12.0	10.9	11.3	12.0	13.0	13.1	14.3	15.1	16.1	17.1
Females	11.6	11.2	11.2	10.8	11.8	12.1	12.5	12.1	13.9	13.1	16.2	17.1
CYA institutions‡												
Schools and Camps (males)	12.4	12.7	12.0	10.9	11.2	12.0	12.9	13.1	14.2	15.0	16.1	17.0
Fred C. Nelles	10.3	10.8	10.4	11.1	11.9	12.5	14.0	13.2	15.0	15.9	16.8	17.8
O. H. Close	10.9	10.1	10.3	8.7	9.9	10.5	11.6	11.2	12.9	12.9	14.4	14.5
El Paso de Robles	11.4	12.5	11.0	11.0	11.4	12.7	13.2	14.6	15.3	15.2	16.0	17.6
Karl Holton	12.4	11.2	11.3	10.3	10.5	11.1	10.3	11.2	11.9	12.2	12.9	11.3
DeWitt Nelson	12.9	13.3	11.2	10.2	11.3	12.7	12.7	14.0	13.7	14.5	14.6	18.2
Preston	18.0	18.1	16.0	15.3	14.9	16.4	16.8	16.8	17.2	17.8	19.7	18.9
Youth Training Schools	15.1	15.2	14.1	11.7	11.6	12.1	13.7	13.7	15.5	17.0	17.6	19.9
Ventura	11.9	13.5	13.1	11.5	12.1	11.3	12.0	12.3	13.9	15.2	15.7	17.7
Camps	8.6	9.1	9.0	8.4	8.6	9.1	10.9	10.3	11.6	12.9	15.2	15.9
Schools (females)	11.4	11.9	11.0	10.4	11.2	12.0	12.5	11.9	13.7	12.4	16.2	17.2
Ventura	11.4	11.9	11.0	10.4	11.2	12.0	12.5	11.9	13.7	12.4	16.2	17.2
CDC and federal institutions	13.1	11.6	19.4	18.8	20.7	14.4	14.2	20.7	17.7	19.7	20.9	27.1

*Includes time in reception center clinic.
†Excludes those committed under Welfare and Institution Code Section 1731.5(c).
‡Includes all institutions operating during periods shown.

the past five years, the number of credentialed, full-time teachers in institutions and camps has been increased from 292 to 390. In 1986, legislation was approved to provide State Lottery funds for Youth Authority educational programs—an estimated $500,000.

Public Protection. A Gang Services project was started in the Los Angeles area in 1986 to combat the serious gang problem in the inner city. It is designed to provide intensive supervision and service to 150 of the most active hard-core gang members in the target area. The project includes a close working relationship with other justice system agencies, including law enforcement and community groups. An Apprehension unit, also in the Los Angeles area, continued operation in 1986, with a total of 145 escapees and missing parolees apprehended during 1985–86. Unit staff also helped law enforcement clear many unsolved criminal cases. In general, these efforts are strengthening cooperation between the Youth Authority, law enforcement, and other justice system agencies.

A Blueprint for the Future: New Construction, Programs

With the department's population of incarcerated offenders projected to climb over 9,000 by the end of the decade, new construction and program strategies are planned.

These plans include two 600-bed institutions, plus additions to the Ventura, Preston, El Paso de Robles, and Nelles Schools. There also will be a major reconstruction of the Fenner Canyon camp.

Other program approaches also are being developed to help reduce population pressures, including increased use of temporary detention for parolees, the use of electronic surveillance devices as an alternative for detaining parole violators, and increased use of community resources. This includes the strengthening of local programs to prevent delinquency and divert young people from the criminal justice system.

A New Agenda: Education, Employment and Training, Substance Abuse Counseling*

DYS: A New Agenda

In recent years, the Massachusetts Department of Youth Services has been the focus of much attention, both nationally and internationally, as a result of its success in establishing and maintaining a community-based system of juvenile corrections.

On almost a weekly basis, the department welcomes a variety of visitors, be they journalists assessing how "The Massachusetts Experiment" of the 1970s is surviving in the 1980s, or juvenile justice administrators from other states and around the world seeking alternative ways to treat juvenile offenders. Why is it more efficient, more effective, less costly?

The Department of Youth Services has not always enjoyed its current reputation. When Massachusetts closed its training schools in the early 1970s and for several years thereafter, the commonwealth's Juvenile Correctional System was questioned by professionals both within the state and elsewhere. But while that period was one of turmoil and instability, it was also one of creativity and innovation. And while the evolution is not complete, DYS today is an effective and predictable agency, staffed with professionals and committed to its dual mandate: to protect the public and to appropriately treat juvenile delinquents.

The strength of this system lies in the diverse range of programs that have been developed to meet the complex needs of our population.

The recent completion of a five-year capital outlay plan has enabled DYS to expand its secure capacity to an adequate level. Presently, 10 percent of the department's population resides in small secure programs for specified periods of time. These programs are self-contained, with complete educational and clinical components, and feature a staff-to-client ratio of three to one.

---

*Annual Report of the Massachusetts Department of Youth Services, the state juvenile correctional agency with the largest number of community-based educational and treatment programs in the nation. Reprinted with the permission of Edward J. Loughran, Commissioner, Massachusetts Department of Youth Services.

The heart of the DYS system is its broad range of open community-based programs designed to provide varying degrees of structure and supervision to DYS clients, while allowing them to remain in the community.

With this system in place, the department has been able to devote more of its efforts to preparing DYS clients for discharge. In this regard, the department is striving to improve its educational offerings, to provide effective counseling in the area of substance abuse, and to equip clients with the skills necessary to find meaningful employment and take their place as productive, law-abiding members of society. These efforts comprise a new and ambitious agenda for DYS in its attempts to combat the many problems associated with juvenile delinquency.

As the department enters its 17th year, DYS can view its recent past with pride in what has been accomplished, and look to the future, confident in its ability to successfully meet the challenges that lie ahead.

Education

Upgrading the quality of education in DYS residential programs is a department priority. Although most youths enter DYS with a very low grade level, many are able to attain their high school equivalency while committed to DYS. Some even receive college credit. DYS teachers employ innovative teaching methods, and computer sciences have been integrated into many curriculums. The department has recently completed an educational needs assessment study and is seeking to upgrade teachers' salaries in order to attract and retain quality teachers.

DYS youths attend school on site, five days a week, 12 months a year. Classes are usually limited to four to six students. In some DYS residential programs, youths attend regular high schools in their community. Their attendance and progress are carefully monitored by the staff. Many residential programs have added computer science to their educational programs.

Employment and Training

The department is putting more emphasis on preparing DYS clients to be productive members of the community when they are discharged. No longer satisfied with placing clients in part-time jobs, DYS now strives to provide its youth with the vocational skills and opportunities necessary to embark upon fulfilling careers.

DYS recently entered into the development of a supported work model for training clients which may be the first of its kind in the nation. Eight DYS youths will undergo extensive training at the Worcester Marriott Hotel. The program will result in a permanent, unsubsidized job and a possible career in the hotel industry. In recent years, DYS has upgraded and professionalized the food services in all residential programs. This has provided the department with a resource that is the basis for a first-rate culinary arts program. Vocational education is a big part of a DYS client's treatment program. Every effort is made to equip clients with skills that will enhance their chances for employment when they are discharged.

Drug and Alcohol Abuse

Although relatively few youths are committed to DYS on drug or alcohol charges, 85 percent of the department's clients are drug and/or alcohol abusers, and DYS is committed to combating this problem. Most DYS residential programs now hold voluntary Alcoholics Anonymous and Narcotics Anonymous meetings on a regular basis. Drug and alcohol awareness is also taught in the classroom. Counseling is available for those clients not residing in a DYS program.

A course on identifying drug and alcohol abuse and how to deal with it in an effective way is part of the basic training offered at the DYS Training Academy. This training is mandatory for all DYS employees.

The Kids Care Program at Northeastern Family Institute's Shelter Care Program in Middleton is a unique and effective way to combat drug and

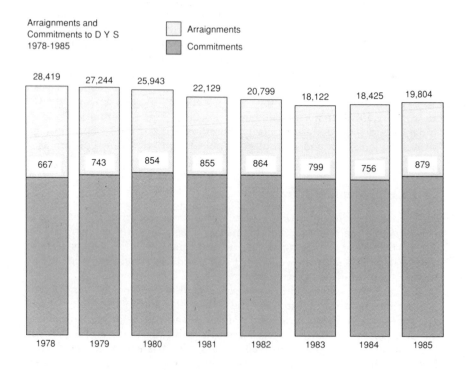

Arraignments and
Commitments to D Y S
1978-1985

☐ Arraignments
▨ Commitments

Year	1978	1979	1980	1981	1982	1983	1984	1985
Arraignments	28,419	27,244	25,943	22,129	20,799	18,122	18,425	19,804
Commitments	667	743	854	855	864	799	756	879

alcohol abuse among youth. Under Kids Care, DYS clients, who have turned around on drugs and alcohol, go out to speak at elementary and high schools throughout the state. Recently, the Kids Care Program has joined with the Governor's Alliance against Drugs.

1985 New Commitments to DYS

In 1985 new commitments to DYS rose by 16 percent. This dramatic increase was not anticipated but may be explained in part by a 7.5 percent increase in juvenile arraignments between 1984 and 1985. Almost 50 percent of the 1985 new commitments to DYS come from 10 of the 74 courts handling juvenile cases in the commonwealth. For the second straight year, the Metropolitan Boston Region handled the most new commitments.

Commitments by Court

Court	1985	1984	1983	1982
Boston Juvenile	77	54	34	49
Springfield Juvenile	60	56	54	61
Dorchester	51	44	47	53
Worcester Juvenile	48	49	30	55
Lowell	41	33	19	34
Holyoke	37	17	37	28
Lawrence	35	41	19	29
Cambridge	26	23	16	21
New Bedford	26	21	27	22
Lynn	24	20	27	21

Commitments by Region

Region	1985	1984	1983	1982
Metro Boston	196	163	153	170
Northeast	188	149	155	171
Western	184	137	192	175
Central	179	159	140	168
Southeast	132	148	169	180

The "typical" new commitment to DYS in 1985 was a white male, aged 15 years and seven months, committed to DYS on burglary charges. His family income was $10,000, and his parents were divorced or separated. He was a chronic truant or dropout who had not gone past the eighth grade. He had no job skills and frequently used drugs or alcohol.

Offenses

	1985	1984	1983	1982
Murder	3	5	4	1
Manslaughter	4	1	3	4
Armed assault	80	74	59	60
Unarmed assault	79	54	63	58
Armed robbery	23	16	17	23
Unarmed robbery	28	23	28	32
Sexual assault	43	31	24	17
Kidnapping	2	0	1	1
Threats	9	9	5	8
Other	0	0	3	1
Arson	13	9	14	13
Burglary	205	193	225	286
Larceny	160	145	128	150
Receiving stolen property	27	27	29	29
Damage to property	46	39	46	35
Sex offenses	9	11	8	6
Motor vehicle	59	41	47	52
Public order	55	49	48	32
Controlled substance	32	23	23	24
Fraud	2	3	0	8
Unspecified delinquency	0	3	24	24

Age, Gender, Ethnicity, and Family Income

	1985	1984	1983	1982
Age				
9–12.5	14	13	12	13
12.6–13.5	42	20	36	25
13.6–14.5	101	83	106	130
14.6–15.5	260	199	188	202
15.6–16.5	288	251	262	293
16.6+	174	180	195	200
Gender				
Male	785	648	705	761
Female	94	108	94	103
Ethnicity				
White	571	541	555	615
Black	192	128	138	158
Hispanic	108	76	93	85
Other	8	11	13	6

Age, Gender, Ethnicity, and Family Income   (*continued*)

	1985	*1984*	*1983*	*1982*
*Family Income**				
0–5,328	**122**	101	123	149
5,329–7,130	**57**	67	94	131
7,131–10,188	**85**	87	109	160
10,189–17,316	**109**	130	133	149
17,317+	**137**	120	141	142

*Incomplete information. Not available for all youths at the time of intake.

A large majority of 1985 new commitments had completed only the eighth grade or less.

Education*

Last Grade Completed	Total Number of Clients
4th	2
5th	17
6th	107
7th	171
8th	296
9th	179
10th	57
11th	7
12th	1

*Incomplete information. Not available for all youths at the time of intake.

Only 20 percent of the 1985 new commitments came from families where parents were married and living together at the time of commitment.

Parent's Marital Status*

Married and living together	144
Divorced or separated	371
Never married	109
Either or both deceased	57
Other	24

*Incomplete information. Not available for all youths at the time of intake.

Client Flowchart: Options Available to DYS and the Courts after a Juvenile Commits a Delinquent Offense

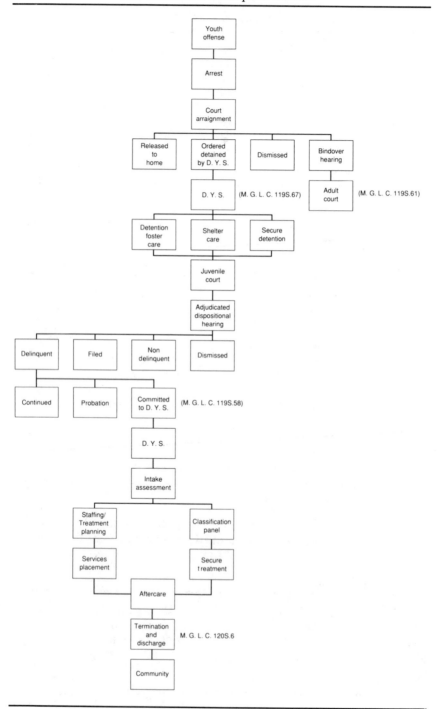

The DYS Budget

	July 1, 1984–June 30, 1985	July 1, 1985–June 30, 1986	Fiscal Year 1986
Central administration	$ 2,695,597	$ 2,832,000	6.5%
Purchase of services	19,749,305	23,259,291	54.5
Stephen L. French Youth Forestry Camp	816,107	830,517	2.0
Field services	4,660,717	5,113,572	12.0
Consolidated secure facilities	8,640,959	10,678,399	25
Boston Offender Project	511,277	*	*
Total	$37,073,959	$42,713,779	100%

*Absorbed in other accounts.

The DYS Budget FY82–FY86

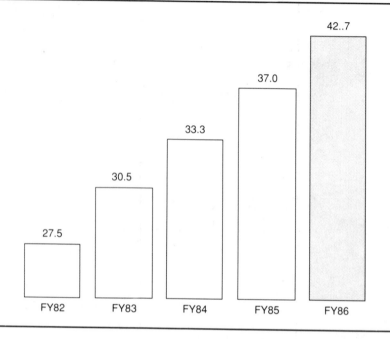

Author Index

Subject Index

About the Author

Albert R. Roberts is an Associate Professor and Chairperson of the Planning and Management Curriculum at the Indiana University School of Social Work in Indianapolis. He received his doctorate in social welfare (with a split minor in criminal justice and social research) from the University of Maryland. His extensive experience includes ten years as a social work educator and researcher and twelve years as a criminal justice educator, corrections researcher, and director of several federally funded research projects. Professor Roberts recently completed the national organizational survey of the structure and function of 184 victim assistance programs.

Professor Roberts is a prolific writer with over sixty publications in social work, criminal justice, corrections, and public health journals. *Juvenile Justice* is his tenth book. His other recent books include: *Battered Women and Their Families; Runaways and Nonrunaways;* and *Social Work in Juvenile and Criminal Justice Settings.* In addition, Professor Roberts is the founding editor of the Springer Publishing Company's fifteen volume Series on Social Work.

Professor Roberts is a Fellow of the American Orthopsychiatric Association. He has been a consultant to such agencies as the National Council on Crime and Delinquency, the Maryland Division of Correctional Services, the U.S. Office of Education, and Research for Better Schools, Inc., in Philadelphia.

ABOUT THE CONTRIBUTORS

Arnold Binder is a Professor in the Program in Social Ecology at the University of California at Irvine. In 1972, Dr. Binder founded, and for 15 years served as the director of the Community Service Programs of Orange County. Some of the most notable programs of this agency are the victim services and prevention program, the police crisis assistance program, the youth services program, the youth shelter program, and the child abuse prevention program. Dr. Binder has written numerous articles in the areas of juvenile diversion and child abuse prevention. His newest book (co-authored by Gilbert Geis) is entitled *Juvenile Delinquency*. For many years he has served as an associate editor of the *Journal of Criminal Justice: An International Journal*.

Robert B. Coates is a Professor at the Graduate School of Social Work, University of Utah in Salt Lake City. He received his doctorate in sociology from the University of Maryland. Prior to joining the University of Utah faculty, Dr. Coates was the research director at the PACT Institute of Justice in Valparaiso, Indiana. Dr. Coates also served as a research associate and the Associate Director of Research at the Center for Criminal Justice, Harvard Law School. Dr. Coates has published widely in the area of deinstitutionalization of juvenile offenders and victim-offender mediation. He was the co-author (with Lloyd Ohlin and Alden Miller) of two books on the Massachusetts deinstitutionalization project entitled: *Diversity in a Youth Correctional System: Handling Delinquents in Massachusetts* and *A Theory of Social Reform: Correctional Change Processes in Two States*.

Charles E. Frazier is a Professor of Sociology and Associate Director of the Research Center for Studies in Criminology and Law at the University of Florida at Gainesville. Dr. Frazier is the author of many articles and final reports on preadjudicatory screening and juvenile detention practices. He has also directed several major research projects on differential detention and jailing of juveniles. These projects have been federally funded by the Office of Juvenile Justice and Delinquency Prevention (OJJDP) and the Florida Division of Youth Services.

Roslyn Muraskin is an Assistant Professor and Chair, Department of Criminal Justice and Security Administration at Long Island University, C.W. Post Campus, Brookville, N.Y. She is a Ph.D. candidate working on her doctoral dissertation at the John Jay College of Criminal Justice of the City University of New York. Professor Muraskin has extensive experience working for several criminal justice agencies in New York City including supervisor of the Pre-trial Release Program at the New York City Department of Probation, and assistant supervisor, Vera Institute of Justice. She has also served as a research and management consultant to the Suffolk County Police Department.

H. Ted Rubin is the Senior Associate for Juvenile and Criminal Justice at the Institute for Court Management of the National Center for State Courts in Denver, Colorado. He has been with the Institute for Court Management for over twelve years, serving in various positions including assistant executive director and senior staff attorney. Early in his career, he worked as a caseworker and a psychiatric social worker. He was also a judge for six years for the Denver Juvenile Court. Mr. Rubin has over forty publications in the area of the law and the juvenile court. His most recent books are: *The Courts: Fulcrum of the Justice System* and *Behind the Black Robes: Juvenile Court Judges and the Court.*

A Note on the Type

The text of this book was set in 10/12 Palatino using a film version of the face designed by Hermann Zapf that was first released in 1950 by Germany's Stempel Foundry. The face is named after Giovanni Battista Palatino, a famous penman of the sixteenth century. In its calligraphic quality, Palatino is reminiscent of the Italian Renaissance type designs, yet with its wide, open letters and unique proportions it still retains a modern feel. Palatino is considered one of the most important faces from one of the Europe's most influential type designers.

Composed by Weimer Typesetting Co., Inc., Indianapolis, Indiana